Cultural Theory and Late Modernity

University of the
West of England

BOLLAND
LIBRARY

**Please ensure that this book is returned by the end of
the loan period for which it is issued.**

For Hillevi

Cultural Theory
and Late Modernity

Johan Fornäs

SAGE Publications
London•Thousand Oaks•New Delhi

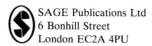 SAGE Publications Ltd
6 Bonhill Street
London EC2A 4PU

SAGE Publications Inc
2455 Teller Road
Thousand Oaks, California 91320

SAGE Publications India Pvt Ltd
32, M-Block Market
Greater Kailash - I
New Delhi 110 048

British Library Cataloguing in Publication data

A catalogue record for this book is
available from the British Library

ISBN 0 8039 8900 8
ISBN 0 8039 8901 6 (pbk)

Library of Congress catalog card number 95-70166

Typset by Photoprint, Torquay, S. Devon
Printed in Great Britain by The Cromwell Press Ltd,
Broughton Gifford, Melksham, Wiltshire

Contents

Prelude

This book is the concentrated product of many years of research and discussions. It has been born out of an interdisciplinary dialogue within the partly overlapping fields of studies of youth culture, media and communication, popular culture and popular music. I have for a long time been extremely lucky in finding fruitful spheres for intersubjective dialogues. Since its inception in 1987, the seventy network members of the research programme for youth culture in Sweden (FUS) have offered me much inspiration and pleasure, particularly Professor Ulf Boëthius, Michael Forsman, Hillevi Ganetz and Bo Reimer, who helped me organize and develop it and have been helpful discussants in my work on the first, rudimentary versions in Swedish of the chapters in this volume. The Swedish Council for Research in the Humanities and Social Sciences (HSFR) made all this possible through generous funding of both the research programme and a six-year position and youth cultural researcher from 1986 to 1992. Brutus Östling and his publishing firm Symposion have also been of great help in this work. Another important forum has been the programme for youth culture at Stockholm University (USU), in which I have also had rewarding dialogues and cooperation with too many highly competent colleagues to mention them all here. Professor Kjell Nowak, Cecilia von Feilitzen, Peter Dahlgren and all other dear multidisciplinary colleagues of the Department of Journalism, Media and Communication (JMK) at Stockholm University have provided me with a creative environment, since I arrived there from the likewise open-minded Gothenburg University Department of Musicology in 1986, then led by the inspiring Professor Jan Ling. I owe a lot to my earlier co-researchers Ulf Lindberg and Ove Sernhede, with their backgrounds in literature–pedagogics–education and sociology–psychoanalysis–social work, and who have shared so many ideas and experiences with me. My interest in cultural theory got its first post-school push through an involvement in various radical leftist organizations and alternative music movements during the 1970s, in which I was encouraged to pursue intellectual studies and organize collective discussions of the power of culture to move people within the contradictions of capitalist society. From the beginning, it must have been the strong belief that my parents Marianne and Evert instilled in me that made all of this possible. Without the competent and enthusiastic support from my editors at Sage Publications, Stephen Barr, Louise Murray, and Nicola Harris, publicity manager, Janey Walker, and freelance editor, Justin

Dyer, this book would never have been realized. Some of its final pieces were put together during a visiting professorship at the Department of Communication Science of the Catholic University of Leuven in Belgium, invited by Professor Keith Roe and his hospitable colleagues. Professor Simon Frith in Glasgow has helped with some details and been a good and supportive friend with whom I have had many fascinating discussions of musical taste. Peter Dahlgren and Ulf Lindberg have given me invaluable feedback on a version of the manuscript, for which I am deeply grateful. The book is dedicated to the popular culture researcher illevi Ganetz, who since our paths were united in 1983 has always generously shared her rich ideas and life with me. Thank you all!

Johan Fornäs
Stockholm, May 1995

1

Opening

Culture is a web of flows, multiplying, converging and crossing. Some of the interconnecting whirls of culture are clearly visible on the surface, others are hidden deep below. Some are strong and irresistible, others local and temporary. They flow in various directions and intersect at different levels. Above all, they are polyphonic, resulting from complex intersubjective processes of communication rather than directly from objective external nature or from within a singular subject. Cultural processes are communicative practices. We do not passively submit to pre-existing frames, rules and codes, but reshape and recreate ourselves, each other, our worlds and our symbolic forms in an at least potentially open, active and creative process. All this has always been true, but recent developments of late modernity have made it unusually clear.

Culture is everywhere in human life and society. We are human by understanding and interpreting what we perceive, that is, by constructing symbols where something stands for something else. Symbols make it possible to think of what is not present, and thus to reflect upon the past and plan the future, to explore the other(s) and speculate about the unknown. By collectively shaping such symbolic patterns we construct a world and give ourselves specific positions in it.

No one descends twice into exactly the same cultural river: culture is not a static structure but an everchanging flux. No one escapes being moved by it: subjects are not fixed entities but evolving constructions. No one emerges from this flow without leaving some small trace of his or her movements: human actions have effects. The river of culture is also a mixed, communal bath: cultural phenomena are shared with others, being means of intersubjective intercourse and communicative action.

The same is true of cultural theory. It moves, is heterogeneous and dialogic, and has now become a focal point in many different discourses. Late modernity is saturated by communication media, which increasingly put culture in focus, in a double process of mediatization of culture and culturalization of the media.[1] Mediatization and culturalization have enabled new ways of theorizing the modern processes, social spheres and

---

[1] 'Mediatization' refers to the process whereby media increasingly come to saturate society, culture, identities and everyday life. John B. Thompson (1990) uses the somewhat awkward term 'mediazation' in much the same sense.

subjective identities which are both their conditions and their results. Like culture in practice, culture in theory is necessarily the result of communicative processes, which have to cross traditional disciplinary borders.

This book proposes a polydimensional theory of culture as communication, itself constructed through communication with a vast range of other theories. It is not primarily an introduction or a critical evaluation of these other theories as such, but a new voice which uses their echoes to offer a set of models for understanding various aspects of how culture works. Its aim is not to present theories of culture (even though it may partly also be used as an introduction to some of these), but to offer a cultural theory in and for the specific late modern phase in which it has been made possible through the interdisciplinary dialogues that have recently emerged, and in which it aims to take part. This constructive rather than faithfully reproductive approach will inevitably at some points fail to do full justice to many of the important points of conflict and difference that exist between the different theories which are used as elements in my project. A fully satisfactory presentation of both all these other theories and my own answers would have exploded the frames of this book. The thinking reader will hopefully get many impulses to continue this communicative dialogue by thinking further and better, in counterpoint to this text and the texts it refers to.

The text will work through making distinctions and connections, to delineate dimensions and reconstruct interfaces. There will be several long passages that sum up important arguments from theoretical discussions in various fields, but these are meant to lead to the proposal of fresh models discerning and linking crucial aspects of culture and communication in better ways. Sometimes small empirical illustrations will be used for exemplification, at other points discussions of the historical and present meanings of central concepts will become tools to reconstruct useful theoretical models. The purpose is to offer a rich and complex way to understand culture, a set of conceptual tools and models which have proved to be practicable in specific late modern cultural analyses. Its late modern perspective on culture as communication is also a communicative perspective on culture in late modernity.

Four tendencies and dimensions of culture

This presentation of the general contours of the dynamics of culture will make an odyssey through four stages, related to the main dimensions of culture and communication. They have been brought into focus by four recent developments in cultural theory, which also appear in everyday thinking as well as in many different academic disciplines (cf. Habermas 1985, pp. 132ff or 1988/1992, pp. 6f and 33ff).

First, late modernity is also a super-modernity, where modernization processes have been extremely rapid and profound, affecting people's relation towards history. In many research areas as well, *modernization and historicization* have become focal and shared themes, inviting inter-disciplinary co-operation. The accelerating modernization process, dis-cussed in the next chapter, has demanded new, unorthodox and unusual forms of understanding, to deal with emergent social, cultural and psychological forms. The concept of late modernity has begun to gain wide acceptance among scholars, offering a temporal perspective on the present historical dynamics of cultural phenomena. The need to search for roots and develop existing routines is balanced by an increasing emphasis on the search for new routes in life as well as in research, in response to super-modernized conditions. Like all other concepts and theories, the ones proposed here are not eternally valid, but bound to processes of the present. As forming a late modern understanding of culture in general, they are particularly relevant to the understanding of late modern culture itself, and are becoming increasingly aware of their historically specific constructedness.

In the next three chapters, some other important dimensions of culture and communication will be mapped out – levels and aspects that call for polydimensional theoretical models. Culture involves communicative encounters between interacting subjects and symbolic texts within contex-tual frames. Different theories specialize in analysing each of these mutually interdependent constituents. Therefore, cultural theorization has to let theories of social spheres and communities, of aesthetic forms and genres, and of identity and subjectivity meet and interact. Another way to formulate this is to underline that cultural phenomena are pointing in several directions archaeologically as well as teleologically.[2] On one hand, they have causes and determinants in various dimensions. Their *roots* can stretch towards objective material forces, objectivized institutional frames, truly social groups and norms, subjective competences, interests, needs and desires, or (reflexively) towards the rules and codes of another (or the same) cultural genre. On the other hand, they have effects and meanings on different levels. Their *routes* might point toward thematizing and changing nature and technology, institutions, social relations and interac-tions, individual subjectivities or generic forms and fields. The interpret-ation and explanation of such phenomena can choose to emphasize either of these directions and dimensions, assisted by different theoretical tool-boxes, but it is important to notice that no such single interpretation suffices alone. There are always both roots and routes of cultural phenomena: they are determined by something and they in their turn formulate something that affects something. Roots as well as routes also go in many directions simultaneously: there is no single root that explains such a phenomenon fully, and no single route that sums up its total meaning and effect.

[2] The pair archaeology/teleology is inspired by Ricoeur (1965/1970). The pair roots/routes derives from the debate of ethnicity and cultural identity; cf. Gilroy (1993c).

After the temporal dimension follows a discussion of the objective or external factors and spheres related to nature, materiality, technology, social institutions or economic and political systems. They are formed by and for social relations, but present themselves as rigid and external frames around the cultural forms of acting individuals and communities. A discussion of power and resistance then frames a presentation of various ways of conceptualizing social relations and communities, that is, the social interaction aspect of the intersubjectively shared world in and by which people live. Processes of *differentiation and heterogenization* have accelerated, among social groups, subcultures and identities as well as in conceptual models. Pluralizations similar to those which have accentuated the need for multicultural communication and openness towards otherness have also made interdisciplinary co-operation and non-reductionist paradigms necessary, in order to cope with processes, societies, cultures, lifeworlds and individuals characterized by several interconnected yet separate dimensions. Like the first, historicizing trend which contextualizes abstract models of spheres, symbols and subjects temporally, this second one re-embeds all such concepts in specific social contexts or institutional embodiments. This localizing and differentiating tendency underlies the whole emphasis on separations and interconnections which runs through this presentation of cultural theory as multidimensional, and it will be explicitly thematized in Chapter 3.

A third tendency is that *culturalization and mediatization* have problematized the meanings of symbols, texts and discourses in everyday communication, thereby making them more focused. This has provoked a linguistic, cultural, communicative or pragmatic turn within philosophical, social, behavioural and historical sciences.[3] The prefix 'cultural' has come to denote a growing subfield within academic fields like history, sociology, anthropology and psychology, and the interpretive paradigm of the humanities and aesthetic disciplines has generally acquired a much more legitimate status within hard-core social or even natural sciences. One result is that cultural theory has finally been accepted and even moved towards the centre of an increasing number of fields, as Chapter 4, on symbols, is at the centre of this book. The intersubjective and cultural dimension has broken the formerly rigid (Cartesian) dualisms of subject and object, spirit and body, individual and society, which in its turn has opened up new options for interdisciplinary contacts.[4] Not only have objectivist realism and positivism been seriously disturbed by this rise of

---

[3] 'In recent years, however, the very models of explanation that contributed most significantly to the rise of social history have been undergoing a major shift in emphasis as Marxists and Annalistes alike have become increasingly interested in the history of culture', writes Hunt (1988, p. 4). She thinks that 'women's history and gender studies have been at the forefront of the new cultural history' (p. 18) and that the connection of linguistic–cultural aspects with gender identities is particularly important.

[4] Bernstein (1983) argues that this cultural turn has moved beyond the old struggle between objectivism and relativism.

new discourse and communication paradigms, but so has the old philosophy of the subject or of consciousness. Instead of constructing theories on the basis of how singular, individual subjects confront the objects of the external world (whether society or nature) in terms of goal-oriented and strategic action, it has become common to start with the third pole: the intersubjective, symbolic modes and texts that bind subjectivity and objectivity together.

My own research specialities are mass-mediated popular culture, popular music and youth culture. The examples chosen will often thematize the interplay between them. Media and popular culture, music and youth are all important to the understanding in our time of each other, our languages, our selves and our world. They offer clues to an understanding of future tendencies and challenges to some established theories of society, communication, symbols and subjectivity. This bias towards media, music and youth is therefore not only a matter of personal taste, but can be motivated more by principle, as can the focal position of Chapter 4 and the very theme of the book itself, *cultural theory*.

The central part of the book, Chapter 4, thus scrutinizes the specificities of the cultural level in its own right: creativity and taste, symbols and texts, styles and genres, meaning and interpretation. The ways in which cultural phenomena relate to the cultural dimension again have to do both with roots (causes, determinants) and with routes (meaning, effects). After discussing the relation between music, image and word in the partly hierarchical interplay of various media and forms of expression, this chapter leads to a consideration of aesthetics and mediatization.

A fourth cultural tendency is increasing *reflexivity and self-referentiality* both in everyday life and in research. It appears in the self-mirroring styles of cultural texts which will be discussed at the end of Chapter 4. But it also affects individual subjectivities, and Chapter 5 will use a cluster of spotlights to thematize how culture both produces and is produced by acting subjects, through symbolic practices of socialization and subject formation.

The trend towards reflexivity affects not only symbols and subjects, but also theoretical work, making it more self-aware and self-problematizing. The progress of modern scientific knowledge is no longer any simple and unidimensional affair, and much new theorization concerns the ambivalent effects of science itself. Ulrich Beck (1986/1992) thinks of the most recent modern period as one of reflexive modernity, where modern processes and institutions such as science have turned against modernity itself.[5] In earlier stages, modernizing demystification mainly attacked older, pre-modern prejudices and obstacles. Nowadays, the deconstruction of myths and prejudices and the reflection on social and cultural problems are more

---

[5] 'Reflexivity is a criterion for an attempt at least to identify thresholds between what we call premodern and modern. I know that's an uneasy topic, but nobody helps us; we find ourselves in the modern condition' (Habermas 1992a, p. 474). Cf. also Giddens (1990 and 1991) and Ziehe (1993).

often directed against the destructive effects of modern devices themselves. Modernity has thus become more self-conscious and aware of its
own troubles, as 'progress' has become a problem as much as a goal. This
reflexivity is to be found in art and science as well as in the relations of
everyday life. It implies a denaturalization and demystification of
traditions. Both the pre-modern ones and those that belong to modernity
itself are more often understood as what they always are: contingent
intersubjective and 'historical constructions.

It may be tempting to lean back towards the established routines of one's
discipline, accepting a researcher's role, theories and methods as given.
This is now harder than ever, however, and theorists are instead forced to
see the position and function of their own social sphere, that is, how
research relates to systems and lifeworld areas, to power hierarchies and
social relations, to textual genres and subject formations.

The demand for reflexivity might seem to necessitate the formulation of
all ideas in a strictly personal voice, explicitly stressing the fact that all
'truths' are contextually anchored. I do not think this is always justified.
This book will mainly be expressed in a rather general and abstract tone.
Its genre and mode of writing could well have been but are not autobio-
graphical. Even so, it will still be obvious that it is the voice of a subjective
temperament, by the choice of metaphors, style, form and content. It is not
always fruitful to emphasize the localized identity of the author, in order to
relativize what is written. One can instead argue that this text is to some
extent not my own personal expression, but the result of a certain
interpretive community or field in which I have worked. The dominant
form of reflexivity will not point towards the personal subjectivity or
autobiography of its author, but towards the dialogic elements of the
theoretical text itself, in reflections on how theory is constructed and how
the models offered relate to what they refer to.

This route order is fairly arbitrary. There is no necessary priority of any
of these levels. Starting with objective and objectivized spheres does not
mean they are primordial or fundamental – they are shaped by subjects in
social interaction aided by symbolic forms, rather than given in advance by
nature. Ending with subjectivity is not meant to imply that subjects are
only the result of social and symbolic structures – one could as well argue
that subjects are necessary for such structures to arise. Choosing a certain
order of presentation is made necessary by the linear logic of the written
and printed word, and it has been aided by didactic motives. Some order is
needed, and there were pragmatic reasons why I chose to follow this
precise route. Besides this initial warning, I cannot find any way to avoid
the meta-assumptions that might be implied by my (or any other) specific
order. A materialist would perhaps be happy if the objective basis and
institutional frames were designated as the most fundamental level. An
interactionist would prefer the social aspects to come first. A textually
oriented discourse theorist might want the symbolic order to be the
primary one. From the perspective of psychologism, it might feel awkward

to have to wait until the end of the tour to find a treatment of inner subjectivity. To me, it is easy to see that the order could have been changed almost arbitrarily, without disturbing the fundamental assumptions of my model. Why not try reading Chapters 3, 4 and 5, on spheres, symbols and subjects respectively, in any other order to see what new ideas are then produced?

Overlappings and repetitions cannot be avoided in a text like this. Certain key concepts are used long before they have been clearly defined. Already when discussing modernity and spheres in Chapters 2 and 3, I have to take for granted a certain understanding of concepts like symbols or subjects that will not be argued for until later. This might be yet another reason to sometimes read the text in other directions than the linear one.

Communicative theorization

A long route will thus be navigated through time and space, mapping the flows of culture by separating and interrelating dimensions of modernity, spheres, symbols and subjects. Navigation is necessary in waters as complex as these, but the end result is only a provisional and approximate construction, a rough map or a set of tools for thinking, to be used in further studies of culture.

Theories are instruments to 'look' with: glasses to look through and maps to look at. Their concepts and models are used for a mental 'viewing' of complex phenomena which are otherwise not so easily discerned or understood. The visual metaphors often used when describing theoretical work – including the etymology of the word 'theory' as 'seeing' or 'making visible' – stress its aspects of distance and control, favouring the image of a single thinking subject confronting an external world of objects.[6] But theoretical work is as much an intersubjective process built on dialogic discourses which contain both community and conflict.

The abstract models of useful theories are certainly constructions, but they are not only formal 'thought abstractions' freely invented by imagination. They are made possible by abstractions working for real, 'real abstractions' or socio-historical processes which in practice reduce complexity.[7] The development of differentiated and abstract forms of social

[6] Gilligan et al. (1990, pp. 314–29) have suggested an alternative terminology for social and psychological phenomena, where themes, rhythms, sounds and the interplay of polyphonic voices are used as metaphors, inspired by aurality, orality and music rather than vision. While it is hard to do without visual metaphors, it is certainly useful to reflect upon them and sometimes try terms with other connotations.

[7] This idea was elaborated by Marx (1858/1986 and 1867/1976), arguing that concepts like 'human labour' or 'commodity value' cannot be thought until social practices have started to compare all kinds of work and reduce them to a unifying measure (time). The most abstract categories attain a validity across all hitherto existing historical periods, but are still products of historical processes and remain most relevant in those societal contexts where they emerge. The term was coined by Sohn-Rethel (1970/1978), and has been used by several critical theorists, including Habermas (1981/1988, pp. 332ff and 374ff).

interaction makes it possible to think of culture and communication, spheres, symbols or subjects, as both differentiated and general concepts, because certain social practices, on one hand, discriminate between them while, on the other hand, tending to equate various specific activities or phenomena. Well-grounded theoretical models reconstruct abstract patterns which have emerged in social and cultural life. Their concepts are contextually anchored, though they may also shed light on their own embryonic roots back in earlier historical phases. There is thus a 'prefiguration' of concepts in reality, making wise mental constructs conditioned reconstructions rather than free inventions. The fact that theories often compete and contradict each other does not necessarily imply that they are all (or most of them) pure fictions, but rather that the human reality they aim to reconstruct is itself full of mutually contradictory sub-aspects and ambivalent tendencies. Different interpretive communities simply develop different sides of it. In regarding theories as contextually anchored reconstructions of historically produced patterns of abstractions and differentiations, this intersubjective paradigm for knowledge is simultaneously constructivist and realist.[8]

Each theory starts with a primary distancing step which breaks with the usual, immediate pre-understanding of a phenomenon by introducing a surprising angle or concept which opens up unforeseen differentiations or connects what was first seen as separate. This step is a reduction, making an incisive cut in the complex web of reality and reducing the inexhaustible complexity of culture, in order to formulate models for orientation in a chaotic world. Every researcher has to construct his or her own network of perspectives, choosing some theories and rejecting others.

To understand meaningful phenomena, one has to make interpretive guesses and then check their validity by various explanatory techniques which produce a certain distance from the phenomenon in question. The hermeneutic philosopher Paul Ricoeur has developed a model starting with a first, non-reflected understanding, then passing through more or less systematic processes of explanation, leading to a deeper understanding which includes meanings that were first hidden.[9] If all meanings were

---

[8] It thus moves beyond the dilemma of relativism and objectivism; cf. Bernstein (1983).

[9] E.g., Ricoeur (1969/1974 or 1976). This inspires John B. Thompson (1990, pp. 22 and 281ff) to see 'social–historical analysis', 'formal or discursive analysis' and 'interpretation/re-interpretation' as three methodological 'phases of the depth-hermeneutical approach'. The three levels mentioned by Phil Cohen (1972/1980, p. 83) – historical, structural/semiotic and phenomenological analysis – might seem to be completely different. But when they are reconstructed in reverse order by Willis (1978, pp. 189ff) – as indexical, homological and integral analysis – a related hermeneutic process is implied. In fact, both Hegel and Marx used a dialectical methodological movement from an immediate impression of pseudo-concrete manifestations and appearances through the reconstruction of a series of abstract concepts reaching down to essential grounds of reality and then back again to a rich and structured understanding of concrete totality (cf. Marx 1858/1986; Kosík 1963/1976; and Taylor 1975). Cf. also the discussion of meaning-making in Chapter 4 below.

already known to those who used them, no interpretive efforts would be needed, still less any systematic theoretical work.

Different explanatory moves then compete with one another in dialogic 'struggles of interpretation', through which understanding is enriched and deepened. Increasing late modern reflexivity makes it easier to recognize these processes, to understand both culture and theory as communicative. If it is understood that interpretations may vary and have to collide in order to be improved, then it is no longer possible to trust in one direction of explanation as the only possible one. Even though each explanation has to make simplifying or reductive moves, any resulting model should keep the possibility open for other perspectives to arise, other voices to emerge. Even though we cannot do everything at once, we can accept and acknowledge the principal need for a bricolage of theories in order to catch something of the polydimensionality of culture. No theoretical perspective alone can offer a unitary and all-encompassing model of cultural phenomena. Reductions need not lead to reductionism, as long as one understands that all theorizing is part of a continuous, intersubjective and communicative dialogue. All reductions are only provisional, and others might always turn up as equally legitimate. These interpretive dialogues tend to be fierce struggles, but even though one has to engage critically in them, it should be possible to accept this interpretive struggle as such as valuable, just as consensus need not be reached on each issue in order to estimate everyday communication as indispensable and fruitful.

Theory not only reduces complexity but should also increase it, by showing that real phenomena are not as simple as is generally assumed. Therefore, this book not only makes reductions by focusing on certain chosen themes and proposing simplifying models, it also deconstructs other reductions by pointing at complications and differentiating dimensions in need of being kept apart. Clarifying *distinctions or separations* and interdisciplinary *connections or combinations* presuppose each other. Differentiation and unification interplay on many levels – not only in the mutual, physical, social or cultural practices and discourses of gender and other identity orders, but also in research itself, under headings like analysis and synthesis. Discourses let differing voices run apart and make the analytical and dialogic separations necessary for a fruitful synthesizing or juxtapositioning combination of elements, with meaningful symbols as the basic unifying tool.

This book outlines a polydimensional and heterological approach to culture in late modernity. It works the way symbols function in discourses: bringing together signs and meanings into voices which run in various directions, simultaneously combining and separating ideas. While carefully distinguishing aspects that are too often confused, it will join lines of thought which have too often been separated into isolated ponds: cultural studies, social theory, hermeneutics, psychoanalysis, theories of identity and subjectivity, media studies . . . The aim is to build bridges by identifying distinctions, or to find the delimiting doors in order to open them.

> Because the human being is the connecting creature who must always separate and cannot connect without separating – that is why we must first conceive intellectually of the merely indifferent existence of two river banks as something separated in order to connect them by means of a bridge. And the human being is likewise the bordering creature who has no border. The enclosure of his or her domestic being by the door means, to be sure, that they have separated out a piece from the uninterrupted unity of natural being. But just as the formless limitation takes on a shape, its limitedness finds it significance and dignity only in that which the mobility of the door illustrates: in the possibility at any moment of stepping out of this limitation into freedom. (Simmel 1909/1994, p. 10)

There are different ways to respond to the challenges inherent in the human existence, formulated in culture and intensified in the historical phase of late modernity. The dynamic openness can be embraced as a potential for fertile hybrid crossings, free play and resistance towards power structures, but it can also be feared and resisted by a search for fixed values and safe closures. Within cultural theory too, some react to the wild interchange of thoughts by building solid castles with walls to keep others away. This book answers otherwise, as part of an open dialogue between differing and often conflicting voices. Its enemy is monocular and mono-logical reductionism – the fundamentalism of theoretical work.

New ideas develop in dialogues across borders, in creative meetings between different voices and traditions. The growing late modern potential for inter-theoretical communication is, however, restricted by the persistent closures of some dominant gatekeepers in the field who systematically misread, neglect or scapegoat certain useful theories. Unorthodox juxtapositions are needed to dissolve such impasses and aporias. Critical theory, hermeneutics and psychoanalysis have all been revitalized by the sharp provocations from poststructuralism and other deconstructionisms, necessitating reformulations to counteract earlier tendencies towards essentialism, ethnocentricity and élitism. Rather than discard them, they ought to be updated in an ongoing, communicative theoretical work.

Some theorists want to relate the levels of culture hierarchically to each other. Economist explanations declare the economic forces of capitalist commodity production to be the basis that historically drives technical, political, psychic, social and cultural modernization forward, and logically overdetermines their synchronous functioning. Opposing cultural sociologists may instead argue that social strategies to accumulate status and power are more fundamental. This is again contradicted by some psychoanalytical theorists who find certain unconscious drives or subject structures at the bottom of everything. Some text-oriented postmodernists then say that all is basically a game of signifying discourses, switching the causal and systematic determinations once again.

Instead of such totalizing modes of thought, it should be possible to construct lines of determination that do not exclude others, even in opposite directions, so that no level is singled out as the most fundamental or primary one. There are several possible ways of understanding culture, and studies of culture should have a capacity for holding different alternatives open in a public discussion. Cultural phenomena are never 'nothing-but' economic relations, sociocultural status markings, psychodynamic flows of desire or stylistic symbol games. Each such set of concepts works only as a spotlight, directing attention to certain more or less important aspects of cultural processes. Even those who choose to concentrate upon one single conceptual field should acknowledge the existence of others and reflexively relativize their own models. A sociological analysis of taste hierarchies can, for example, be quite useful without a priori rejecting the knowledge coming from interaction analysis, style interpretation or psychoanalysis.

In opposition towards reductionist, monocular, monolithic 'nothing-but' explanations one may adopt a constructivist and polydimensional spotlight model of understanding. Dimensions have to be separated and traditions connected, in pendulating movements of distance from and closeness towards what is studied, where each theoretical model is like a spotlight that sheds light on one important aspect of it. And many will actively want to work in a less pure and more hybrid manner, which necessitates a meta-understanding that opens spaces for the theories to be combined, in order that they do not contradict or 'destroy' each other.[10] Since everything cannot be seen from one single position, it is useful to move and shift perspective, in cultural studies as well as in everyday social life.

Openness towards other theories is related to the multidimensionality of one's own models. It is because culture is many-sided that different aspects are always possible. Many theories are monistic in striving to reduce culture to one single logic; others develop dualistic schemes where two main sides are contrasted and interrelated. The model proposed here tries to incorporate some of these but is generally more closely akin to Ricoeur's communicatively polydimensional hermeneutics.

Theories develop through dialogues that are both communicative and conflictual. The ways in which some streams have opposed and criticized others will be used to improve rather than to dismiss those other traditions. There is always a dream of starting anew, of clearing the house and inventing a new and pure beginning where all the ideological illusions of old models will be definitively transcended. Such purist–fundamentalist–reductionist strokes may be very inspiring, but are as often regressive, by inducing a repressive unlearning. I will here instead try the hybrid, communicative and dialogic form of theorizing. It might not be as simple or as elegantly rounded off, but is instead more rich and open.

All communication is a meeting around common understandings, but it is also always a conversation between voices which are necessarily different. This also applies for theoretical construction work, which

---

[10] Donald (1991, p. 8) uses the metaphor of the threshold for the boundary and interchange point between theoretical traditions like psychoanalysis and cultural theory.

demands an opening of dimensions that let other thoughts in. New thoughts arise through theoretical bricolage, where theories communicate not only on the basis of what unites them, but also and importantly through their differences. A polydimensional understanding of culture and communication is needed to let various theoretical models and traditions interact, to produce new theories by hybrid bricolage work developing through dialogues and communication between traditions whose differences are to be retained, rather than either through reductionist closures or through non-problematizing additive identification of crucially conflicting theories. This is an effort towards such a communicative production of theoretical models.

Studies of culture and communication therefore demand multi- and interdisciplinarity, on many levels. It is crucial to develop new forms of co-operation and exchange capable of preserving the competence of individual parts while creating platforms for collective work. Institutionalized power structures and strategical systemic demands from state and market are to be counteracted by new spaces for communication and webs of interaction, where different methods, materials and models are combined. The result will sometimes just be a multidisciplinary addition of complementary traditions and competences, but more intense encounters will also produce truly interdisciplinary transgressive hybrid theories, which will in their turn offer new insights for others to use in new theoretical bricolages.[11]

Such interdisciplinary bricolage is no simple eclectic addition of incompatible models. A creative effort is needed to make such syntheses productive. But this discovery of the combinatory potentials of explanatory traditions is the way new thoughts in general arise. Marx, Freud, Kristeva, Ricoeur, Bourdieu or Habermas would all have been secondary figures today if they had only been faithful disciples of, for instance, Hegel, Charcot, Lacan, Gadamer, Lévi-Strauss or Adorno. To elaborate the contradictory relations between different theoretical systems can be a very creative work, resulting in new concepts and new meanings, just as stylistic bricolage produces new artefacts and new meanings out of an inventive montage of old ones. This is particularly important within studies of culture, which do not form any unitary science, but are crucially an open field where a plurality of traditions meet in interpretive struggles.

This polydimensional model also applies to research itself, as a cultural process in its own right. First, it involves an 'objective' framework of institutional forms which have to be favourable to those interdisciplinary connections that are to be developed. Second, there is a social dimension of interactive forms and social relations in groups which have to function if co-operation is to be productive. Third, the styles of writing, taste for theories and the symbolic genres of the theories themselves have to work well together, as a sort of cultural aspect to interdisciplinarity. Finally, a subjective context concerns how people like to interact and how their mentalities and desires can be fruitfully combined.

Several other distinctions need also to be upheld better in the discussion. The dichotomy between quantitative and qualitative methods, for instance, is often too simply connected to a difference between natural and human sciences or between social science and the humanities, to the struggle between positivism and hermeneutics, between explanatory and interpretive traditions or between theoretical and empirical research. All these distinctions are actually separate, but ideological debates sometimes tend to mix them in confusing ways. All of these positions consist of highly diverging tendencies. Let me just mention a few examples.

Even if quantitative research dominates many social sciences, and qualitative methods are often preferred in aesthetic studies, there is no total fit between these two dichotomies. There are sociologists who are fully as qualitative and hermeneutic as any literary researcher, and musicologists also collect statistical data. The fact that aesthetic disciplines explicitly focus on meaningful texts make them tend towards the interpretive and qualitative side, but structuralist semiotics is only one example of how rather strict explanatory models may be used in qualitative studies too. There are even branches of hermeneutics where quantitative methods are used – even the great anti-positivist Adorno did so in studies of the authoritarian personality (cf. Adorno et al. 1950/1969). And far from all quantitative social scientists share any 'positivist' paradigm.

As for the polarity between theoretically and empirically oriented research, it does not at all coincide with any of the others, in spite of what is sometimes presupposed. Literary works or musical sounds are as much empirical data as are survey figures, interview transcripts or observational protocols. How they can be used is another matter. Some statisticians attack qualitative methods for their loss of contact with the hard facts of true data, while many qualitative sociologists accuse their quantitative colleagues with similar arguments. Opposite accusations of a naïve lack of theory also cross in both directions. Such charges are used to construct oneself as either in direct contact with the 'real' reality (whether hard figures or soft ethnography) or as equipped with advanced reflexive conceptual tools. In some cases such criticisms fit some of their targets, but if the whole field is taken into account, they are as often quite misleading. These different polarities can never be reduced into one single dichotomy of two camps.

So as not to run aground on the seas where culture is reconstructed in theory, one has to keep the points of the compass apart, to locate and separate aspects and dimensions in order to understand how they interrelate. Reductive models do not catch the complexity of cultural research, their criticisms do not hit their targets, and the strategies they assign are barren. All types of research contain (or should contain) moments of subjectivity and intersubjectivity, theoretical work and encounters with unforeseen empirical material, induction and deduction. They only look different depending on what is studied by whom from what perspective.

This also means that the models proposed in this book are provisional. They are intended to form not a final and total theory, but rather a working tool-box which has to enter the stream of new studies and new theorizing to prove its worth. It is necessary to accept such a contingency of knowledge in the modern world: researchers as well as all human beings have to learn to live without final guarantees. In my own cultural studies, I have repeatedly found certain ways of thinking problematic, others useful, and it is these experiences of cultural analysis that I want to sum up here, not in the form of a gigantic collection of empirical studies of culture in praxis, but as a condensed model of culture in theory.

Critical understanding

Late modern demands on dialogic self-reflection not only underpin a new non-reductionist interdisciplinarity in cultural studies, but also transform the relation between cultural interpretation and critical thinking. To understand meaningful phenomena, no simple collection and measuring of facts will suffice, as Habermas has argued on behalf of an interpretive and critical sociology:

> Sociology must seek a *verstehenden*, or interpretive, access to its object domain, because it already finds there processes of reaching understanding through which and in which the object domain is antecedently constituted (that is, before any theoretical grasp of it). The social scientist encounters *symbolically prestructured objects*; they embody structures of the pretheoretical knowledge with the help of which speaking and acting subjects produced these objects. . . .
>
> Understanding [*Verstehen*] a symbolic expression fundamentally requires participation in a process of reaching understanding [*Verständigung*]. Meanings – whether embodied in actions, institutions, products of labour, words, networks of co-operation, or documents – can be made accessible only *from the inside*. Symbolically prestructured reality forms a universe that is hermetically sealed to the view of observers incapable of communicating. The lifeworld is open only to subjects who make use of their competence to speak and act. They gain access to it by participating, at least virtually, in the communications of members and thus becoming at least potential members themselves.
>
> In so proceeding, the social scientist has to draw on a competence and a knowledge that he has intuitively at his disposal as layman. So long, however, as he does not identify and thoroughly analyse this pretheoretical knowledge, he cannot control the extent to which, and the consequences with which, he also *influences* as a participant – and thereby alters – the process of communication into which he *entered* only to understand. . . .
>
> In thematizing what the participants merely presuppose and assuming a reflective attitude to the interpretandum, one does not place oneself *outside* the communication context under investigation; one deepens and radicalizes it in a way that is in principle open to *all* participants. In natural contexts this path from communicative action to discourse is often blocked; but is always ingrained in the very structure of action oriented to reaching understanding. . . .
>
> To understand a symbolic expression means to know under what conditions its validity claim would have to be accepted; but it does *not* mean assenting to its validity claim without regard to context. (1981/1984, pp. 107, 112, 130 and 135f)

An intense intersubjective engagement and interpretive work are thus needed in social and cultural studies, not least since their objects are already imbued with conceptual structures of meaning, which also include the researcher him/herself, and are not totally separated from the theory used to explain them. The recent ethnographic and interpretive paradigms in media and communication studies have argued similarly.[12]

However, a deep understanding of cultural phenomena can only be reached through a distancing theoretical critique. Critical theory judges the strength and weakness of a society and distinguishes emancipatory from authoritarian tendencies. It creates a distance, separating the critic from the criticized, whether it is a problematic reality or competing thoughts about it.[13] Cultural theory should be critical in both these senses: against lacks and deficits of late modern culture, and against misleading conceptions in contemporaneous ideologies which emerge out of these problematic cultural conditions. Its critique is 'immanent' – it recovers contradictions in its targets and finds it important to show how modernity as an unfinished project nourishes needs and ideals which it then hitherto has in practice denied. The measure of criticism is extracted from that which is analysed, rather than imposed from without. There is no pure and innocent sphere outside of late modern culture from where it can be criticized. One has instead to come to grips with the questioned phenomenon to deeply understand its ambivalent foundations, in an ongoing dialectics of closeness and distanciation, empathy and analysis, understanding and critique.

Theorizing starts from a pain and a want: an experienced pain which propels it forward, and a lack of knowing which wants to be filled. Culture, society, subjectivity and nature all produce plenty of suffering in human life. A lack of happiness or meaning may find relief in the magic construction of models that open up new worlds of imagination where existence is recharged with fascinating significance: fantasizing about what exists also creates visions of what does not yet exist, pointing at what hitherto prevents it from becoming and thus starting a movement towards it. The lack of community forces people to invent their own imagined worlds by practices of writing, and these are no mere illusions but function as means of communication with others in interpretive communities; in theory you can develop being alone into meetings with others at a distance. A lack of freedom or justice provokes the study of mechanisms of oppression and iniquity, a study that becomes a vehicle for attaining emancipatory agency and autonomy. All these motives for thinking have their dark sides, just as modern culture has. Theory can tend to get lost in its imagined worlds, academic communities are often isolated from other strata, and the power of knowledge may transform knowledge into

---

[12] See, e.g., Radway (1988), or Silverstone et al. (1991).

[13] 'Critique', 'criticism' and 'crisis' share roots back to the Greek *krīnein*: judging, deciding or separating.

dangerous power and control over others. This is yet a reason for critique to continue, not only of culture and society, but also of other theories and ideologies.

As has been underlined by Ricoeur (1969/1974 and 1981), understanding is not the opposite but rather the condition of a successful critique. It is only when one has managed to understand a text, a subculture or a discourse by entering into its symbolic webs of meaning that one can develop any effective criticisms of them. If some interpretive studies seem uncritical, it is because they understand too little rather than too much.

This perspective moves beyond an opposition between critical and interpretive studies. Now and then it is believed that studies interpreting how various communities shape meanings out of texts are necessarily non-critical, or that critical research can never really understand what it criticizes. But critique and understanding need to support each other, in polyvocal conflicts of interpretation. Critique without understanding is deaf, understanding without critique is mute, or: 'Hermeneutics without a project of liberation is blind, but a project of emancipation without historical experience is empty' (Ricoeur 1986, p. 237).

Empathic understanding and distancing critique are not as opposed as often believed. The hermeneutics of suspicion continually interacts with the hermeneutics of understanding.[14] The necessity of accepting difference and plurality does not exclude an intensified critique of multiple power structures or an active interest in emancipation. To understand something does not necessarily imply accepting or liking it. Critique has to understand and interpret in order to hit its target, and a critical theory that does not accept otherness becomes totalitarian dogmaticism.

A critical illumination of old thought-forms is an important tool for reflexivity in conflicts of interpretation, but it is never possible to jump out of this 'metaphysical' history into any pure sphere of new and real insights. Old concepts (from science or from everyday life) should be confronted, reinterpreted and developed rather than abandoned. Instead of forgetting and cutting off the always inadequate ideas of the past, there is no way other than to start with them, reflect upon them and use them better. It is time to leave scientist illusions of a total break between absolute theoretical truth and common lifeworld ideology behind, while not resigning into a complete relativism that denies the specificity of systematic and concentrated theoretical reflections and always feels obliged to substitute 'emic' reproductions of everyday experiences as such for well-grounded intellectual constructions.[15]

---

[14] Ricoeur (1969/1974); cf. how Ernst Bloch (1959/1986) discusses the interplay of a 'warm' (utopian) and a 'cold' (critical) stream within Marxism.

[15] This is a critique both of 'élitist' Althusserian dogmatism and of the 'populism' inherent in some anthropological ideologies. Pike (1967) contrasts 'emic' concepts of the observed with the 'etic' ones of the ethnographer. Williams (1976/1988) takes etymology seriously in cultural studies, Laplanche and Pontalis (1967/1988) and Bettelheim (1983/1991) in psychoanalysis.

It is this general hermeneutic mode of thinking which motivates the etymological interrogation of a series of key terms and concepts in this text. Instead of turning away from the meanings inherited from traditional uses of these terms and simply stipulating fresh definitions, important insights are gained by reflexively interpreting them. Purists who once and for all try radically to cut loose from this historical–metaphysical ballast of conceptual associations are in the end again caught up by historically deposited connotations which continue to work unconsciously if they are not brought up to consciousness by explicit reflections. One can never step out of the polysemic heritage which is built into the words used to understand, whether in everyday life or in the most abstract theoretical work. This conceptual care as part of an awareness of how language functions is focal in the linguistic–communicative turn and should be self-evident to a historicizing and interpretive theory of culture.

While all cultural theory and knowledge contains power dimensions, no theory should therefore be reduced to only an instrument of manipulation. Research that sees only power and no resistance in society, culture or science is half-blind. The enlightenment of modernity has to be enlightened about itself, but the critique of its totalizing instrumental rationality should not itself become totalitarian (Habermas 1985, pp. 134f). It is important to remember the communicative rationality which modernization develops further, and which is the motor behind this increased self-critical reflexivity. The following study of culture in theory will therefore develop both a communicative and a critical perspective on the processes of understanding and explanation which underpin both research and everyday life – a hermeneutics which is at once dialogic and reflexive.

2

Modernity

Time is a fundamental dimension of life and culture. It may be represented in space, through written words and graphic models, but its very temporality can never fully be reduced to spatiality. Reflection and theorizing have in themselves a spatializing trait. Thinking in models, forms and structures implies a certain spatialization of even the most thoroughly temporal experiences. Every distinction between levels and dimensions, aspects and differences, rests upon a certain freezing of time-flows into visualizable shapes, but it has to be remembered that such translations of time to space are only approximating metaphorical constructions. The tendency to conceptualize social, cultural and psychological phenomena primarily as spaces is problematic, in that it runs the risk of missing the processual qualities and principally unfinished openness of history. A renewed theoretical fantasy is needed to find concepts that catch the tendencies of becoming, the fluidity of human praxis and the breaks and continuities of time.

At present, history is inseparably associated with modernization. For at least the last two hundred years, modernity has been a constantly modern concept – an unusually stable tradition! Ideas of modernization thematize in specific ways the dialectics between time and space, process and structure, change and continuity. Culture moves in and through time and modernity – they are the modes of movement itself, propelling the symbolic streams which carry human subjects across interconnected spheres. This chapter will propose a set of dimensions for the moves of and in modernity – its continuous and recent changes as well as various orientations within and towards it. It will start by characterizing the modern project through a set of concepts which together sum up its main traits. In a second step, three important dimensions of the modern will be outlined, in order to facilitate the more fruitful interaction of different theories of modernity.

Characteristics of the modern

The concept of modernity traces a developmental logic underlying or rather within some of the historical processes particular to our epoch. As has been argued by Jürgen Habermas, this perspective reflects and reconstructs a historical project, anchored in human praxis and institutions, formulated by philosophers, scholars and artists. This project resides in the processes of intersubjective interaction, and while being based on empirical tendencies, it also opens up a normative, critical and utopian potential. The modern project is a task which can be accomplished in more or less desirable ways. Its promises have not yet been fulfilled, and it has therefore not lost its impetus.

The history of modernity is a complex one, constructed out of many indices into an identifiable narrative.[1] Modernization is associated with a series of historical processes on various levels, from economy and politics to culture. Capitalist development, industrialization, urbanization, democratization, secularization and civilization are but few of their labels, invented by a series of thinkers from Kant and Hegel through Weber, Marx and Nietzsche to Foucault, Elias and Habermas. Different theories take different sides of a comprehensive and complex historical process as their starting-point, uncovering different foundations, motors and characteristics of our age. Theories of modernization are the most general and polydimensional of them all.

Modernity connotes a range of different associative fields, each of which offers something valid but also contains some problematic implications. Discussions of modernity may, for example, focus upon *recent times*, the very present period, in contrast to the more distant past, which is studied by historians. This fits well with the origins of the concept. The late Latin word *modernus* has to do with 'the present', that which is 'for the day'. It originates from the Latin *modo*, meaning 'right now', but through the figure 'moderately remote' (related to *modus*, which means 'measure' or 'manner'). That which is close to us in time implies an interest in the specificity of our own epoch, in contrast to purely historical studies of the distinctive character of the distant past. This answer to what modernity is contains a grain of truth, but is not sufficient. There is plenty of research into the present that cannot be said to be oriented towards modernity. An interest in the present as contrasted with the past further implies an interest in the past's relation to the present: the theme of modernity includes a historical dimension. Modernity, finally, is not completely new – it has its own, and by now pretty long, history. Studies of modernity may scrutinize the topicalities of recent times, but not as unrooted in the past.

Another shade appears when studies of modernity take an interest in the phenomenology of *the evasive present moment* in its transient immediacy, regardless of whether it is the present of yesterday or of today. Here, the phenomenological experience of a passing unique moment is in focus, in contrast to objectified structures. An intensified present is an important aspect of modern life. But then again, theories of modernity are full of structural concepts. An intensification of the experience of the present

---

[1] Ricoeur (1983–5/1984–8) explores the dense mutual relations of time and narrative, and shows how time needs narrative to become human.

belongs to modernity, but it can also take place in other contexts, and is not the whole truth about the modern.

Thirdly, discussions of modernity engage in *the new*, in trying to historicize different concepts and look for what is changing in society and culture – changes of the present and in its recent history, phenomenologically and structurally. Theories of modernity are in this view the opposite of theories of the reproduction of traditions, archetypes and other stable structures in human or social life. What historical changes have made our epoch different? The modern present is more acutely aware of fast and deep changes than was the pre-modern one. This intense feeling of the transient unicity and contingency of the present moment and of recent times permeates everyday life as well as reflective theorizing.

This trait of modern life and modern thinking implies a necessary and radical *historicization* of all social, cultural and psychological theories – an emphasis on historical perspectives and transformations. Institutional, interactive, symbolic and subjective forms change through time, sometimes continuously, sometimes in leaps. Against all naturalization of such patterns, it is important to point to their fundamentally dynamic character.[2] All the ideas and concepts that are presented in this text itself must be understood as situated in the present phase of modernity, although some may seem universal or at least have a very long pre-history. However, not all changes and new things are immediate signs of the modern. Modernity theory is about certain more long-term transformation processes, with a set of specific traits.

The processes of change which combine to form modernization have three things in common: they tend towards an *irreversible dynamization*, an *ambivalent rationalization* and a *differentiating universalization*. This means that they are intense and cannot easily be reversed, even if they might take different forms; they promote a two-sided rationality with both positive (creative and emancipatory) and negative (destructive and oppressional) potentials; and they are increasingly general and global in their capacity to create new pluralities by separating social and individual life-spheres.

Irreversible dynamization

The restlessly *dynamic* character of modernity has already been mentioned.

> Constant revolutionising of production, uninterrupted disturbance of all social conditions, everlasting uncertainty and agitation distinguish the bourgeois epoch from all earlier ones. All fixed, fast-frozen relations, with their train of ancient and venerable prejudices and opinions, are swept away, all new-formed ones become antiquated before they can ossify. All that is solid melts into air, all that is holy is profaned, and man is at last compelled to face with sober senses, his

---

[2] This is emphasized by a long Marxist tradition of thought, including Fredric Jameson (1981, 1988a and b, 1991), who consistently argues for the necessity always to historicize.

real conditions of life, and his relation with his kind. (Marx and Engels 1848/
1965, pp. 34f.)[3]

This dynamism is closely related to the increasing urge to historicize
concepts of societies, cultures and subjectivities. It is not only the
structures of life that change, but also the means by which we reflect upon
them. Modern understanding cannot avoid reflecting upon the time-
boundedness of its own categories.

Reinhart Koselleck (1979/1985) depicts the modern view of history
through three theses. First, history appears to be 'generally at the
disposition of men; that is, conceived as makeable', as a result of the
emergence of history as an independent, general and singular key concept
out of the pre-modern plurality of specific histories – a semantic process
indicating 'a new space of experience and a new horizon of expectation'
(p. 201). Secondly, the modern understanding of history separates
people's plans temporally from their realizations: history is experienced as
incomplete and therefore with an open future (p. 208). Thirdly, there is a
widening gap between expectations and experiences, between hopes for
the future and lessons from the past (p. 276). The intensified communicative processes of modernity have connected various temporal processes into
one complex stream, while at the same time opening them up towards the
future. We now live in different intersecting 'chronotypes' whose increasing interconnections force us to thematize change itself as a general
phenomenon in all fields of life and society.[4]

This implies that the reproduction of intersubjective patterns has been
problematized, that increasingly many traditions have been denaturalized
and cannot be taken for granted anymore. As in all other times, changes
and continuities coexist, but there is a general experience of living in an age
of insistent change, so that the modern present is experienced as sharply
separated from the past. David Harvey (1990, pp. 240ff) talks about a
process and experience of 'time–space compression', resulting from the
speed-up in the pace of life which shortens time horizons and expands the
present, as well as the overcoming of spatial barriers that shrinks the world
to a global village. This is induced mainly by the expanding communication
technologies made possible by the Enlightenment project, but it affects
people's very deepest experiences of time and space in everyday life.

In spite of all this, the importance of traditions increases within certain
social or geographical areas – religious fundamentalism is only one extreme
example. Hobsbawm and Ranger (1983) argue that traditions are invented
and used particularly in conditions of threatening social change and
insecurity. Benedict Anderson (1983/1991) similarly thinks of nationalism

---

[3] This passage has been discussed by Berman (1982, p. 21). Compare also the way that
Foucault (1969/1972, pp. 3ff and 166ff) stresses how modernity has opened our eyes to the
discontinuous aspects of history: its interruptions, fractures and holes.

[4] Cf. also Bender and Wellbery (1991) concerning the modern temporalization of
experience.

in terms of imagined communities, and Anthony P. Cohen (1985) argues that the symbolic behaviour of traditional rituals tries to reconstitute boundaries and habits which social change threatens to dissolve or problematize. Arato and Cohen (1988, p. 44) state that modernization dissolves not traditions but only 'a traditionalistic relationship to tradition', and Ricoeur (1981) stresses that modernity and emancipation have their own accumulated traditions. All this would make modernity a reinforcer rather than a destroyer of traditions. Traditions are 'reproduction in action', representing 'not a necessary but a *desired* continuity', actively selecting among received and recovered elements of the past (Williams 1981, p. 187).

This seeming paradox of tradition in modernity might be dissolved by separating two different concepts of tradition. The word 'tradition' derives from the Latin *trādĕre* (deliver, hand over), composed of *trāns* (across) and *dăre* (give). A tradition thus hands something over through time, from one generation to another. This handing over can either be a consciously thematized ritual or a semi-automatic habit. Modernization may induce a ritualization which installs new traditions that react to the decline of the non-reflexive prejudices and routines of pre-modern 'lifeworld' horizons that the denaturalizing thrusts of modernization have triggered. There is then a dialectic between traditional *rituals* and traditional *customs*.[5] New rituals gradually sink into the unreflected habits of everyday life, experienced as natural facts of life, while old habits may suddenly again be questioned and drawn into the reflexive whirl of modernization. Times of rapid change increase feelings of insecurity, which makes habits less self-evident but may simultaneously bring old and new rituals to life, in order to master this insecurity.

The interplay between continuity and change is very complex. Processes of modernization are sometimes manifest as clearly visible landslides, but they more often appear as a slow and hardly discernible erosion of traditional structures. Oskar Negt (in Brückner et al. 1981, pp. 183f) talks of a recent 'erosion crisis' of bourgeois society and culture, which since around 1960 has affected the core both of subjectivity and of societal institutions. Ziehe and Stubenrauch (1982) have similarly discussed modernization as causing a crisis of erosion of traditional values and norms, of which youth culture may function as a sensitive 'seismograph'. It is by no accident that seismic and geological metaphors are repeatedly used in this context. Just as wind and water may, almost imperceptibly, eventually erode whole mountains, social and cultural erosion wear away structures in everyday life and mentalities that were apparently firm as a rock. And while most adults are stuck in habits and routines that make it difficult to notice what has changed, certain mobile groups (e.g. artists, scientists,

---

[5] Hobsbawm and Ranger (1983, pp. 2ff) distinguish between traditions and customs in a similar manner, but instead of restricting tradition only to invented and reactive rituals, excluding habitual, inherited customs, it is better to separate it into two forms.

immigrants and young people) function through their flexible and sensitive cultural expressions as seismographs for such faults and displacements in the deep 'ground' – signalling very strong and irresistible forces before their final effects reach us.

> . . . immense plates, entire sections, slide under one another and produce intense surface tremors. No longer in the form of a devouring fire in the sky that strikes us down, a generative lightning that was (at) once punishment and purification, and which regenerated the earth. Nor is it in the form of a deluge, which is more of a maternal catastrophe at the point of the origin of the world. . . . The sky is no longer falling on your head; it is the terrain that is sliding. We are in a fissile universe; a universe of erratic icebergs and horizontal drifts. Interstitial collapse: this is the effect of the seismic rupture that awaits us, and of mental seismic ruptures as well. (Baudrillard 1988, p. 195)

These seismic metaphors activate a dimension of surface and depth, but if the basic ground and inner core of the earth are no longer a fixed and solid foundation, then the dichotomy of surface and depth loses its earlier polar quality. This dichotomy is frequently invoked when swift changes are opposed to stubborn structures. Such a duality is misleading, and in at least three different ways. It binds its poles to highly problematic metaphorical connotations, it hides other temporal process-types than these two, and it over-simplifies the process of modernization.

The first problem is that there is an uncontrolled aura of metaphors circulating around this dichotomous pair. As metaphors of change, processes of modernity *can* sometimes be opposed to stable structures, but it is false to collapse this dichotomy into other dichotomies suggested by the metaphor of *surface versus depth*. That which is deep below under our feet is often felt as stable, while what is on the surface changes. The surface is often thought of as fluid, visible and superficial, while the depth is conceived as static, hidden and more important. In this way the surface/ depth metaphor produces a false equivalence-chain between *change, the visible* and *the superficial*, on one hand, and *reproduction, the hidden* and *the important* on the other (see Figure 2.1).

A common diagnosis suggests that on the surface age, gender, class and ethnic roles might change, but this is just an inessential appearance which masks a deeper truth of reproduced traditions and structures of domi-nance. In another typical form of the argument, a basic linguistic structure is contrasted with changing semantic contents of concrete utterances, as a hidden essence beneath superficial illusions of a dialogic human agency. In subject theory, the topographic model of psychoanalysis may induce similar connotations: in much Jungianism, the tendency to conceive of the unconscious as a parallel sub-world under the surface of the conscious ego implies that this 'subconscious' is an almost eternal archaism, as opposed to time- and culture-bound conscious ideas.

Much effort has been made to deconstruct and modify these problematic dualist metaphors emanating from the pair of surface versus depth. Many tenacious traditions are certainly important but unrecognized, in need of unmasking by critical research. It is often easier to notice that which

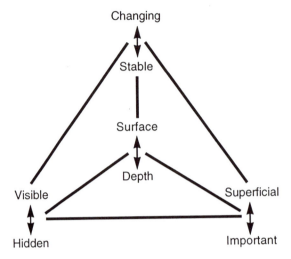

Figure 2.1   *The surface/depth complex*

changes than that which has become a daily habit, and reflection is induced by social changes making old habits dysfunctional. Still, there are also very important changes, some slow and gradual, others fast and sudden. Many such transformations first pass without much notice and can only be traced through reflection, aided by the 'seismographs' offered by time-sensitive cultural practices. A clearly visible phenomenon – whether a change or a tradition – is not automatically less important than a hidden one, even if many fundamental ones are hidden away. A change can be both as hard to trace and as important as a constancy. Not all traditions are more essential to people's lives than are all changes. The visible can sometimes be as important as that which is hidden, and the fluid can be both as invisible and as important as the solid. If some cultural patterns like artistic styles, age, gender or class relations change, while others remain intact, it is an open question which of them are of highest relevance, independent of whether they are unrecognized or acknowledged by the people involved. Some clearly visible changes of fashion or mentalities are just as significant for people's lives as are some candid traditions.

> To philosophers, the most ardent interest of fashion lies in its extraordinary anticipations. It is well known that art in many ways, for example in images, forestalls the perceptible reality by several years. . . . And yet fashion has a much more constant and precise contact with the emerging, due to the exceptional scent of the female collective for what awaits in the future. In its newest creations, each season offers some secret semaphore of coming events. The one who could read them would know in advance not only of new currents in art but also of new codes of law, wars and revolutions. – Herein lies no doubt the greatest incitement of fashion, but also the difficulty in making it productive. (Benjamin 1983, p. 112; author's translation)

The use of geological metaphors for the modern erosion of old traditions, and for the detection of this erosion by youth cultural seismographs, offers a hint that the depth is maybe not so stable after all. Modernity theory is interested in those hidden but extremely important changes which take place in spite of the apparent reproduction of traditions in everyday life – processes of change which are sometimes hidden, sometimes undisguised, and which are neither more or less momentous than are surviving traditions. All these frozen equivalences should be split up, so that the degree of flexibility, of visibility and of importance are conceived as independent dimensions, even though they all may in different ways be associated with surface and depth.

The second problem with the dichotomy of changes and continuities is that it hides the much greater complexity of actual historical processes. To equate change with modernization is not enough. All three initial approximations of modernity – recent times, the present now and the changing new – are insufficient. Modernity is already old and can, as a deep temporal process-structure of our world, as well be opposed to more occasional events as to static traditions.

The whole dichotomy of stability versus change needs to be decomposed. One way is to realize that historical understanding needs more than these two extreme poles. Modernity is composed neither of rigid, tenacious structures nor of rapid, random changes. Time flows in many different ways. Within a certain time-span, it is possible to discern at least four different historical process-types. *Stubborn structures* can be opposed to swift and unpredictable *accidental events*, as when the stubbornly reproduced routines of everyday life are contrasted with the eventfulness of news or fashion reports. But 'between' these two extremes there are at least two other modes. One consists of wavelike *periodical cycles*, caused, for example, by the regular shifts of generations or by the cyclical curves of capitalist economy. The *directional processes of modernization* is then a fourth historical mode. All four modes coexist within the modern epoch, and while modernization may affect the three others, they should be kept apart analytically.[6]

The by now aged modernity has its own traditions, and not all changes can immediately be identified with modernization. On the other hand, most traditions are also changing, if only slowly and covertly. There is a long historical tradition of modernity, and a modernity of traditions in present societies. The idea that modernity has to do with the new and changing is therefore only half-true. Modernization concerns changes that are comparatively stable: a set of historical processes which combine to shape a specific temporal logic of fundamental transformations in the development of social, cultural and psychological patterns. Modernity induces an enduring experience of swift time-shifts, but such a generalized transformation-consciousness is only truly modern when it is structurally bound to a certain developmental logic. Many historical periods of rupture have produced similar cultural symptoms of openness, insecurity and self-

---

[6] Cf. Bjurström and Fornäs (1988, pp. 455f).

reflection. These can be caused by accidental events or by cyclical turns, or by other structural changes than those connected to modernity. Modernization only amplifies, makes permanent and spreads these traits in widening circles.

Natural disasters and wars change people's lives drastically, through the insecurity and re-creation of enforced exile and mobility. This may accelerate processes of modernization but is still not identical with changes produced directly by the structural trends of modern society. Cyclical generational shifts are likewise often confused with long-term modernization, when for example apocalyptic conclusions are drawn from the conflicts between baby-boomers and their precursors or successors. Such conflicts may be effects of modernization, but accidental events and cyclical processes may also play an important role.

The third 'structural' problem with the simple polarity between that which changes and that which is stable is that it over-simplifies the modernization process itself. Studies of media and popular culture often invoke images of the modern versus the pre-modern, but seldom go into detailed analysis of these temporal flows and their more exact phases. The vague and simple old/new dichotomy needs to be qualified by a differentiation of dimensions of the modern, which will be specified below.

Modernity is not a heading for any type of historical transformation processes, but for those which are directed, in that they are to some extent *irreversible*. If they have a direction, they might be interrupted but cannot easily be undone or reversed. There is no way back to pre-modern conditions. If the atomic bomb has been invented, it can never again be undone or forgotten, even if it might one blissful day become banned. And if people have started differentiating between aesthetic expressions in art and normative statements in law, reactionary fundamentalists or nostalgic romantics may try to mix them again, but it is unlikely that they would in any stable way once more become an undifferentiated whole. One will always be able to think of beauty and rightness as two separate dimensions, though it may be attractive to try to reunite them.

This does not mean that nothing modern can ever disappear again – that would be a highly un-modern form of modernity! While the growth of the welfare state resulted from a certain phase of modernization, its presently attempted destruction by neoliberalism needs to be understood not as a demodernization, but as a (destructive) answer to recent crisis phenomena of modernity. Fundamentalist movements within Christianity and Islam react against modern cultural tendencies but cannot themselves avoid being deeply influenced by the modern project, which they even push forward, albeit unwillingly. They do not effect any real return to pre-modern life forms, in spite of their active efforts to restore traditions. If modernization is stopped on one level (as neoconservatives try to turn the cultural clocks backwards), its continuing march on other levels (an expanding capitalist economy) will effectively prevent any return to a pre-modern condition. Even if a natural or social catastrophe should suddenly interrupt the historical process, memories of the twentieth century would make a new 'innocence' impossible.

All historical changes are in one sense irreversible, since nothing can ever be undone or repeated in exactly the same way – at least the fact that a similar thing happened before will lend its repetition a slightly different meaning. When learning processes are involved, this is particularly true, since human experiences can to some extent be accumulated in artefacts, language and other symbolic forms. Modernization relates to evolution mechanisms that are like learning processes for human societies.[7] It not only moves but has a directional logic, more like an accelerating spiral than a straight line, as expressed in the tendencies towards rationalization, differentiation and universalization.

Ambivalent rationalization

The changes summed up under the heading of modernization are related to what has been discussed as *rationalization* processes. This polydimensional growth of reason has long roots in human civilizations, but was definitely accelerated by the Enlightenment. A famous text by Immanuel Kant has defined enlightenment as 'man's release from his self-incurred tutelage': '*Sapere aude!* "Have courage to use your own reason!" – That is the motto of enlightenment' (Kant 1784/1963, p. 3).

Michel Foucault (1983/1984) has argued that two very different critical traditions can be traced back to Kant. One is an analytic of truth, asking how true knowledge can be possible, searching for more basic foundations than the ones inherited from tradition. The other is an ontology of the current present, asking about the characteristics of its own time, seeking to historicize and relativize all seemingly fixed foundations. Foucault placed himself in the second of these philosophical traditions – the reflection on the modern condition – stretching from Kant and Hegel through Nietzsche and Weber to the Frankfurt school.

Based in this same tradition of critical theory, Habermas (1984/1989 and 1988/1992) instead finds it important to recombine the two streams. A structural analysis of truth, judgement and communication is needed to clarify the normative criteria used to criticize modern forms of power. The critique of power has to gain a reflexive insight into its own foundations and conditions of existence, in order not to disintegrate into nihilistic cynicism or nostalgic pessimism. Like the philosopher Paul Ricoeur, the sociologist Anthony Giddens and many others, Habermas therefore tries to reconnect the two critical traditions by opening continental critical theory, based in Marxism, hermeneutics and psychoanalysis, to Anglo-American system functionalism, speech act theory, cultural studies, semiotics and anthropology.

---

[7] Habermas (1981/1984–8) thinks of this phylogenetic evolution as related to the ontogenetic stages of individual moral and cognitive development elaborated by Kohlberg and Piaget.

Modernity introduces an condensed discourse around its own temporality, as it is an epoch where human society has to create its self-consciousness and its norms by itself, instead of relying on gods or pre-given traditions. There is an important historical dialectics in the continuing debates between these two lines of critical thought. They sharpen each other, as the structural analysis of truth elaborates normative criteria needed to found the critique of contextualized power systems and avoid its fragmentation into cynical or pessimist nihilism, while processual reflections upon the historical constitution of knowledge-forms force this critique to be sensitive to a range of differences and to respect the Other.

The goal of this reformulation of modern rationality is to let the critique of reason, inherited from early Romanticism, Nietzsche, Adorno and the postmodernists, radicalize the modern project of enlightenment, rather then liquidate it. Continuously intensified processes of and in modernity have directed the critical power of reason towards itself and forced it to become reflexive. Many have tended to reduce rationality to its instrumental, technocratic, manipulative and authoritarian forms, caught in a trap where critical reason has to abandon itself. It is certainly necessary to criticize the dangers of modern reason, but in order to develop it in better ways, not to destroy it. The dark sides of the dialectic of enlightenment can only be counteracted by enriched and intensified enlightenment of a more diversified kind. What is needed is more rather than less reason – but of a richer, more differentiated and reflexive kind, which can localize its own basis and enter communicative processes where it may itself be tested and refined. Instrumental reason and the critical tradition of suspicion towards it are born out of the same modern process, and instead of choosing one or the other, it seems necessary to reconnect them into a more complex and self-critical understanding of rationality, which is able not only to attack limited and one-sided forms of reason, but also to understand why it is possible even to formulate or argue for such a power-critique in rational terms rather than by exactly such manipulative power-games as are attacked. An updated critical theory must try to 'formulate an idea of progress that is subtle and resilient enough not to let itself be blinded by the mere appearance [*Schein*] of emancipation. One thing, of course, it must oppose: the thesis that emancipation itself mystifies' (Habermas 1979, p. 56).

Habermas has distinguished two main forms of rationalization. On one hand, a growing, goal-oriented or instrumental rationality is pushed forward by the economic and political systems, market and state, with money and administrative power as the main tools. The *systemic rationalization* leads to an increasing effectiveness and complexity in the allocation of resources. It develops a *goal-oriented rationality* which can be instrumental (directed towards external nature) or strategic (aimed at social relations). While being effective and necessary to release the lifeworld from overwhelmingly many decisions, which would annihilate any space for cultural creativity or social relations, the systemic rationalization process can be destructive if it goes too far and colonizes lifeworld areas where mutual communication is indispensable. Commercialization and bureaucratization are typically modern threats to the likewise truly modern potentials for communicative rationality.

On the other hand, there is an ongoing *lifeworld rationalization* creating a growing potential for a *communicative rationality*, anchored in the use of meaningful symbols, differentiating between aspects of symbolic interaction which are geared towards mutual understanding. Rationality is much wider and more differentiated than is recognized by the more totalizing critiques of instrumental reason. It does not only concern effectivity, neither does it only thematize cognitive truth. Communicative rationality means that actions can, if needed, be explicitly motivated by arguments of either cognitive truth, normative truthfulness, subjective sincerity or aesthetic well-formedness. It is a 'procedural rationality' which offers forms for an open-ended process of criticism and self-reflection where old certainties may always be problematized when needed. Its basic source is in intersubjective communication through symbolic forms, which puts the theory of culture in a very focal position. Various social institutions have historically formed to specialize in these different aspects of communication: science, law, socialization and the arts. But through their use of speech, writing and other symbolic modes they all remain anchored in the daily life interactions from which they emanate.[8]

It is this nuanced analysis of knowledge and reason which makes it possible to clarify important foundations of social critique of modernity, without falling back on irrationalism. Modern rationality has several sides. Its incessant demystifying and self-reflexive questioning permeates mentalities and institutions, specialist activities and everyday life. It is necessary to understand modernity as fundamentally *ambivalent*. While 'equi-valence' refers to two things of equal value, the prefix *ambi-* means 'both', so that the ambivalent has two (opposite) values simultaneously. It does not denote a general vagueness, but rather that one singular force has two precise but contradictory implications.

Modern processes may be irreversible, but they have various and even contradictory effects and meanings in different contexts and from different viewpoints. Modern rationalization has emancipatory and repressive potentials at one and the same time. Therefore, monocular, totalizing pessimism is as futile as is a naïve and ethnocentric optimism of development. Many theories of modernity have lost sight of ambivalences and are caught in dramatic but misleading models that totalize certain trends without seeing important nuances and counter-tendencies. Such grand 'post-'narratives about the death of history, of sociality, or of the subject may be useful heuristic tools for catching sight of tendencies within

---

[8] See Habermas (1981/1988, pp. 113–98 and 283ff, or 1985/1987), Nørager (1987), White (1988) and Calhoun (1992). The concepts of system and lifeworld will be further discussed in Chapter 3, whereas the aspects of communicative action and symbolic modes are thematized in Chapter 4 below.

modernity. But they have little explanatory value, since they are themselves as one-sidedly totalizing as are the simple-minded instrumental
reason which they attack. Instead, a more complex analysis is needed to
distinguish the very complicated interplay between the progressive and
regressive moves of modernity on various levels and areas. Its inner
contradictions create a transcendent dynamics and make possible a critique
which is immanent, based on the utopian elements born out of its own
measures, rather than searching for something totally new, pure and
different, completely outside of past or present reality. This relates to the
productive interplay between understanding interpretation and distanced
critique mentioned in the previous chapter. Understanding opens up
critical perspectives immanent in existing social forms, while critique leads
to a deeper understanding. There is a tradition of critique and a critique of
tradition, because modernity is basically and self-reflexively ambivalent.

Differentiating universalization

Modernity has a *universalizing* tendency, stretching itself all over the world
and imposing its forces globally.[9] This globalization process does not mean
that modernity looks the same everywhere. The differences between
regions, social strata and subcultures are as enormous today as they ever
were. But certain features of life, culture and society installed by the
modern project are today discernible everywhere in the world, in isolated
villages and in old cities. Intensified and accelerated communication
systems, of people, goods and messages, have spread modern traits widely
and made the whole world more accessible than ever. Those irreversible
rationalization processes that were earlier confined to the industrialized
Western sphere are now obvious all over the world, through the spread of
migration, travelling, trade, media and computerized information technologies. On the other hand, modern traits that have developed in
peripheral regions have also been dispersed and generalized, not least in
the aesthetic sphere. Modernization is not a one-way process from a given
centre to the retarded margins, and it has many more different faces than
those that have hitherto been experienced, but whatever its routes and
concrete forms, it can clearly be experienced all over the world today.[10]

  Modern universalization, however, has to be understood in the typically
modern, historicizing manner. The new, universal categories are historically produced and anchored, rather than absolute or logically necessary.

[9] Cf. Featherstone (1990) and Hannerz (1992a). Melucci (1989, pp. 74, 185 and 206) talks
about a 'planetarization' and a new 'planetary consciousness'.

[10] Some studies argue that oppressed people of the 'third world' were the first to be
modernized. 'These two features, the rupture from tradition and the pure form of a peripheral
economy, make the West Indies perhaps the first and potentially clearest example of a
"modern" society' (Miller 1990, p. 51). 'It is being suggested that the concentrated intensity
of the slave experience is something that marked out blacks as the first truly modern people,
handling in the nineteenth century dilemmas and difficulties which would only become the
substance of everyday life in Europe a century later' (Gilroy 1993b, p. 221).

This is something which Foucault emphasized with his idea of a 'local critique', but which is also implied when Habermas uses Marx's concept of real abstraction to understand the basics of communicative action as emerging out of history and not existing a priori. This historicizing and constructive understanding does not make modernity less universal.

> The presuppositions of modernity are historical in origin, our reconstructions of them are fallible, yet their validity is transcendent. This is also true of modernity as a whole; although it arose only a few hundred years ago, it is not merely one of many historical traditions which we can voluntarily adopt or discard; modernity, too, is universal and thus irreversible, intractable, unavoidable. (Kelly 1994, p. 388)

Modernity does not imply a universal standardization, however, but rather a growing universal *differentiation* in society, between state, market and lifeworld, between individual and society, between spheres like art, science, religion and politics, and between different types of human action and social interaction like work and leisure, reason and emotion or production and reproduction. The concepts for stratifying modernity are themselves historically created by processes of modernization which make it possible to think of culture, society and individual as different categories.[11]

Modernization provokes strong counter-forces which alter modern conditions, but cannot escape them. Once differentiations have been constituted, they are hard to forget or cancel. Separated aspects and areas may again be combined, but such post-differentiated totalities are radically different from pre-differentiated ones, in that there will always remain the latent possibility to think of their elements as separate again. One can, for example, experiment with border dialogues between art and science, but there is no escape from remembering the possibility of keeping them apart. Their reunion presupposes that specialized competences have developed which make this recombination much more attractive than was ever any original pre-differentiated unity.

Counter-arguments against theories of modernity have pointed at the present blurring of the borders between high and low, art and politics, childhood, youth and adulthood, or state, market and civil society. If differentiations are really dissolved again, the result is not pre-modernity, since there will always remain traces of the modern separations in between. But is there really a postmodern de-differentiation and de-rationalization? Or is there rather a super-differentiation which dissolves simple and rigidly dichotomous polarities into freely floating networks of multicultural pluralities, in a complex interplay of instrumental and communicative rationality fulfilling the modern project by turning it reflexively upon itself? There seems at least to be a need for more rather than fewer differentiating concepts and categories today.

---

[11] On modern (hyper-)differentiation, see Melucci (1989, pp. 19–28, 45 and 178) or Crook et al. (1992).

Dimensions of the modern

Modernization thus is a configuration of ambivalent rationalization processes of systems and lifeworld, spreading new differentiations globally by
means of escalating communications, irreversibly and intensely changing
the world.

There are at least three dimensions along which a differentiation of the
phenomenon and concept of the modern is needed for clarification.
'Horizontally', there is a diachronic or temporal dimension of *phases* and
stages of the modern era (e.g., early, high, late). Synchronically, there are
two other dimensions. 'Laterally', a conceptual dimension separates
various *modes* of the modern (e.g., modernization, modernity, modernism). 'Vertically', there are a series of *levels* or aspects of the modern (e.g.,
social, cultural, subjective). Keeping these dimensions apart makes it
possible to join ideas from various discourses, disciplines and directions
into a more consistent and necessarily polydimensional theory of
modernity.

Phases

Along the 'horizontal', diachronic or temporal dimension, it is obvious that
modernity is not one homogeneous bloc, clearly separated from pre-
modernity by a strict line. Modernity has a long history and pre-history
through various stages and phases.

In everyday thinking and in discussions of modernity, stereotypical
dichotomies of 'past' versus 'present' are often used, in phrases like:
'Before there was a pre-modern traditional lifeworld; now everything has
changed and is continually changing.' But when is 'then' and when is
'now'? It is neither possible nor necessary to give modernity a fixed
birthdate, but the usual vagueness on this point sometimes leads to
difficulties. When modern traits are discussed, it is often not very clear
whether they apply to the whole modern era of capitalism and industrialism, or if they are distinctive of its later phases, say, from the 1960s
onwards. This vagueness is common to many texts on modernity, including
those by Habermas or Ziehe.

The pre-modern should not be regarded as static or natural. Modernization is not the first or only dynamic process in human history, and all
traditions are basically historical and social constructions. But modernity is
one of the epochs where changes are intensified.

It is also problematic to assume that each phase of modernization only
attacks age-old pre-modern forms and additively replaces them with new
ones, so that modernization becomes a simple cumulative process where
the old is successively made new. Modernity also acts reflexively, on itself,
so that what was fresh yesterday becomes old-fashioned today and may be
eroded by still newer modern forces tomorrow. Later phases dissolve not
only pre-modern life forms but also modern forms that in earlier phases
were shaped through compromises between old and new tendencies. This

creates a complex pattern with surprising offshoots and contrastive intermediary stages, resulting from the superimposition of parallel, different but connected processes that together form modernization. A constant push towards secularization, technologization and commercialization would, for example, acquire a quite different meaning depending on what religions, technologies and commodities look like in each phase.

Phases and epochs do not 'exist' in any evident way – they are ways to order historical memories into meaningful narratives. This ordering does not only take place in the imagination of academics, but is also a collective, intersubjective process taking place everywhere in all societies. It is not completely random, since there are actual changes that can be experienced and that sometimes pile up to form distinctive moments of transition.

Accidental events, cyclical oscillations and linear developments at some instances, in some places and on some levels co-operate to condensate gradual changes into fundamental breaks. Such breaks are unevenly spread between different places, strata and cultures. Social, cultural and psychological conditions, on different levels of the nature/culture/society/individual totality, are often transformed in a certain phase-displacement, resulting in phenomena of 'uncontemporaneity'. Modernization processes take different forms and have various rates of speed in different geographical and social areas, related to age, gender, class and ethnicity. Particular processes such as a growing ethnic plurality, secularization or expansion of the mass media may but need not be related to modernization. This can only be decided by an analysis of the contextual relations between different processes.

Sometimes a series of specific displacements co-operate to form a general break in the history of larger social and geographical areas, shaping a series of epochs and phases. Each single characteristic element of a new phase can mostly have a very long pre-history, but their sum and precise constellation is new.

Which of these breaks and phases are considered most important is decided by human agents with particular interests and in particular contexts. The meaning of history, as formulated in linearized narratives of epochs and phases, is, first, not totally subjective but rather intersubjectively constructed, and, secondly, not completely random but the result of a definite interaction between actual historical events and active historical interpreters. Phases are no objectively fixed linear and basically atemporal stages, but rather a pragmatic tool or frame of interpretation to shed light on the way the temporal dimension differentiates modernity. They do not define and classify a series of sharp ideal-typical stages of modernity, following neatly upon each other. It is important to delinearize history and instead search for its overlapping tendencies, forces and logics. It would be as problematic to reify historical formations into homogeneous structures which are superimposed upon actual temporal processes. Each phase is a fluid construction, loosely connected both to linear chronology and to an only faintly outlined structural typology.

Traces of modernization can be found far back in history, for example in classical Greek and Roman antiquity, in early Christianity or in the Italian and Flemish Renaissance, with their growing money economies, circulation of commodities, differentiation of social spheres, increasingly individualized identities and germinating abstract thinking. In Europe, the Reformation was a phase where modern traits grew intensely, but their definite breakthrough on a large social and cultural scale came with the establishment of capitalist society, as manifested in the Enlightenment, the bourgeois revolutions, imperialism and the industrial world order. The growth of markets, cities, state powers, technology and communications spread social and cultural institutions and patterns of socialization, identity and everyday life from the European metropolitan merchants to most parts of the world, thereby modifying them into more generalized forms.

Depending on country and perspective, that is where a step from premodernity to modernity may be localized, that is, somewhere between 1500 and 1800. Within this span, a step from nascent to early modernity may be located around the modern breakthrough signalled by industrialism, Enlightenment and the French Revolution in the second half of the eighteenth century. In a West European perspective, high modernity was established somewhere around the year 1900, when certain political, economic, social, cultural and psychological forms were stabilized into a full-fledged bourgeois, industrial society, with capitalist forms of production and distribution, industries and wage labour, parliamentary democracies, a differentiated public sphere for political and cultural activities, aesthetic codes and genres, specific age, gender and class life forms, socialization institutions and generalized normative models of personal identity. By then, philosophers, sociologists, historians, artists and writers had found ways to formulate the typical traits and problems of modern life.[12]

In other parts of the world, other phases and chronologies can be constructed, but the spatial effects of imperialist trade and warfare, market economy, transportation and communication technologies eventually made modernity an evident fact all over the world. Capitalist modernization created an effective world-system, analysed by Marx and others, including Wallerstein (1974 and 1990). After the Second World War, a new phase was entered. Its date of emergence is debated. Some first signals can be detected as early as in the 1920s, but the fascist war did to some extent cause a delay. In the 1950s, a renewed development of modern processes took place, and there is much evidence of a definite phase-shift somewhere around the year 1960. Many of the social and cultural forms that had been crystallized as modern then started to be seriously questioned and eroded

---

[12] Berman (1982) sees Rousseau, Kant, Hegel and Goethe as starting-points, but thinks that the generation of the 1840s, with Marx and Baudelaire, are the ones who finally manage to formulate a vocabulary for the experience of modernity, followed by founders of sociology like Durkheim, Weber, Simmel and Mead.

by the continuing modernization process itself. The 1960s was also the decade when many old 'truths' were attacked, in science, philosophy and reflections on aesthetic praxis.

How should this new phase be characterized? Some critiques have called both the differentiation, the irreversibility and the universality of modernity into question. They have depicted it as an outdated and ethnocentrically Western affair, superseded by a contrasting epoch of 'post-modernity', where differentiations disappear and modernization is reversed.[13] This claim that we have passed from the modern epoch into a new condition of 'post-modernity' underestimates the continuities between high modernity and the current phase of development. Our times have seen a radicalization and intensification of modernization rather than its dissolution. On a global scale, modernization seems to accelerate and multiplicate, and opposing forces like religious fundamentalism or aesthetic postmodernism depend on and augment it rather than reverse it. Modernity has spread globally and into most pores of social life, and has turned reflexively onto itself, dissolving its older forms and creating new crises and new possibilities. Increasing global mobility and electronic media, changing social relations and identity forms, and an intensified modernity critique have all resulted from a generalization of modernity rather than from its inversion. This new phase is still typically modern. 'Postmodernism' might be a relevant term for artistic currents that react against earlier avantgarde movements, but the last decades sometimes labelled 'postmodern' should rather be seen as an intensified and accelerated reflexive, ultra-, super- or late phase of modernity.

The term 'post-modernity' is a problematic construction. Even though it contains a temporal prefix, it is hard to place on the temporal axis. Many postmodernists talk apocalyptically about the end of history and the death of modernity.[14] At the same time they often shun periodizations altogether, as belonging to the logic of totalizing meta-narratives that is to be overcome. Care should be taken when discussing temporal successions, but there is a much less productive reason behind this problem with phases, namely, that the hypothesis that modernity has been succeeded by something completely different is mistaken. For most allegedly 'postmodern' traits, it is easy to find early parallels within or even before classical modernity. One example is the famous table proposed by Ihab Hassan (1985, pp. 123f), opposing allegedly modernist purpose, hierarchy, distance, semantics, metaphor, signified and metaphysics to the play, anarchy, participation, rhetoric, metonymy, signifier and irony of postmodernism. On closer inspection, all such crudely dichotomous catalogues of modern versus postmodern characteristics dissolve into opposed but

---

[13] On 'postmodernity', see Lyotard (1979/1984), Foster (1983/1985), Hassan (1985), Jencks (1986/1989), Baudrillard (1988), Featherstone (1988), Hebdige (1988), Harvey (1990), Lash (1990) or Jameson (1991).

[14] See, e.g., Baudrillard (1988) and Fukuyama (1992).

parallel aspects of the modern itself. Modernity has from its very start cherished linear goal-orientation as well as polydimensional fragmentation, Enlightenment rationalism and Romanticist anti-rationalism.

One of the main postmodernist theorists, Jean-François Lyotard, has felt this problem:

> What, then, is the postmodern? . . . It is undoubtedly a part of the modern. . . . A work can become modern only if it is first postmodern. Postmodernism thus understood is not modernism at its end but in the nascent state, and this state is constant. (1979/1984, p. 79)

But if the 'post-modern' does not come after but before the modern, then the choice of prefix is misleading. Paradoxical, self-contradictory concepts may be thought-provoking in cultural debate, but counter-productive for developing a useful cultural theory.

> To say 'post' is to say 'past', hence questions of periodisation are inevitably raised whenever the term 'postmodernism' is invoked. There is, however, little agreement as to what it is we are alleged to have surpassed, when that passage is supposed to have occurred, and what effects it is supposed to have had. (Hebdige 1988, p. 183)

It thus seems impossible to connect the ideal-typical dichotomies of modern/postmodern traits to a historical periodization.[15] But if it rather refers to parallel streams in modern culture, none of which comes temporally after the other, why keep the prefix 'post' at all? And, secondly, how then are we to deal with the need to discern a new and intensified phase of modernity, which does not abandon the modern but heightens and restructures it? Intensified, heightened, super-, reflexive or *late modernity* is a more relevant label for recent developments. This concept makes it possible to avoid the historical vagueness in an undifferentiated perspective on the whole modern epoch (which blinds us to the differences between the late eighteenth and the late twentieth century), as well as the self-contradictions of a 'post-modernity' (which is after all neither opposite nor subsequent to modernity). Late modernity dissolves some prevailing remnants of pre-modern traditions, but also erodes some early modern life forms, in a reflexive dialectics. Some of the traits characterized as 'postmodern' actually belong to this late phase of

---

[15] In spite of an awareness of its problems, Hebdige and many others have unfortunately stuck to this problematic concept. '[Postmodernism] is a space in the very heart of modernism. . . . Instead of being named modernism, this localization should be called modernism/postmodernism or preferably (post)modernism. Then (post)modernism can be considered as the period/Topos replacing tradition in Western history. Postmodern awareness is the periphery of modernism and emerges simultaneously . . . . The "post" of the term certainly does not translate a temporal succession, it rather indicates the margin or the hidden face. It does not signify "after" but "beyond" ' (Seguin 1994, p. 68). This somewhat desperate effort to save the term postmodernity could as well lead to the conclusion that one should skip this problematic term and instead use insights won in the debate to understand that modernity and its modernisms have always had a thematically double edge, as well as several different temporal phases.

modernity, and can be diagnosed not as a total break with modern tendencies, but rather as their radicalization. Other 'postmodern' traits belong to a self-critical side of the always ambivalent modernity, a 'sub-modern' tradition which runs back to the early dialectics between Enlightenment and Romanticism, in which both sides are inseparably modern. Modernity is intrinsically split into two dialectically related discourses: a 'master discourse' of modernity as liberating autonomy versus a 'counter-discourse' of modernity as constraining disciplinization (Marin 1994; Wagner 1994). What characterizes late modernity will soon be discussed in greater detail, but what will then come after modernity is not yet possible to conceive, since it seems to await in the distant future.

I first used the term 'late modernity' in a text published in 1987, from where it has spread widely.[16] There are also many forerunners and parallels. Fredric Jameson (1991) called postmodernism the 'cultural determinant of late capitalism', the latter term borrowed from Adorno and Horkheimer (1944) and Ernest Mandel (1972/1975), referring to the socioeconomic forms of capitalism after the Second World War. A periodization of aesthetic modernism into early, high and late phases, thus introducing the concept of late modern*ism*, had been carried out in 1981 by the architect Charles Jencks (1986/1989, p. 32, note 32). Luthersson (1986) and others have thought about literary modernism in similar ways. But these texts did not yet argue for 'late modern*ity*' as a general epochal concept. Ulrich Beck (1986/1992) suggests the term 'reflexive modernity' for a new stage of the modern, characterized by a growing problematization and critique not only of pre-modern remnants but also of modern processes themselves. This road into another, 'second' modernity opens up a self-critique towards the risks of industrial technologies, implying a fulfilment of the earlier only semi-modern project, more than its collapse.

Time was ripe for the concept of late modernity as a way to discuss new facets of modernity that have resulted from a real qualitative and quantitative change effected by the consecutive accumulation of modernization processes rather than their reversal. Such a concept also offered a way to integrate some crucial elements of the postmodernist time diagnosis within a more ambivalent and open conceptual framework based on modernity theories like that of Jürgen Habermas. Several others soon developed similar thoughts, such as Lawrence E. Cahoone (1988), Paul Willis (1990) and Anthony Giddens (1990 and 1991).[17]

The concept of late modernity thus has two aims. One is to avoid the vagueness of those who talk about modernity as almost a historical constant, not discriminating between its historical phases. A need for historical specification might have driven the 'postmodernists' to their theories in the first place. The other aim is to understand this new phase

[16] Fornäs (1987), further developed in Fornäs et al. (1988/1995).
[17] Willis (1990) gives no references but seems to be inspired by our Swedish work, through discussions as well as through stencilled English translations of my texts.

more as a radicalization and an intensification of modernity than as its
demise, as has been stressed by modernity theorists like Thomas Ziehe,
Marshall Berman and Jürgen Habermas. While 'postmodernity' stresses
the break too much and leads to inconsistencies, 'modernity' alone is too
general to conceptualize important contemporary processes. It is problematic first to say that modernity dates back several centuries and in the next
moment without qualification use the term 'modern' to refer to new traits
of the last decades. '

One problem with concepts like late modernity is that they make it hard
to label still later phases of the modern era. All epochal concepts have this
problem, with their underlying organic metaphors of birth, growth,
maturing and decay. Alternative terms like super- or intensified modernity
do not escape this problem, and these periodization constructions at least
suffice to underline some important features of our time.

Late modernity carries within it seeds of something different, which can
today only be divined. Theories of 'postmodernity' are a mixture of
characterizations of late modernity and images of a possible future after
the present epoch. The global and vertical universalization of modern
tendencies do not lead to any homogeneous and self-reproducing totality.
Instead, there is a radicalization of the contradictions and openness
inherent in the modern project. Late modernity has a transitional character, but its final outcome cannot yet be decided. The tension between the
strategically oriented system rationalization and the communicative lifeworld rationalization – both of which are gradually intensified, with a
radical step taken in the late modern turn – contains an unspent potential
into which critical movements and thoughts must tap.

Modes

This discussion around the temporal dimension of modern phases has
already indicated a need for differentiations along at least two other axes.
The second, 'lateral', dimension is of *modes* of the modern, different
inflections of the adjective root 'modern'. The terms modernization,
modernity and modernism come from different intellectual traditions:
social sciences, philosophy and aesthetic theory. These fields of discourse
have met and mixed in recent interdisciplinary debates, with the result that
these terms are used in many different ways.

As will soon be shown, other ways can be used to differentiate between
the various aspects or levels of the modern that have been thematized by
different disciplines. There is therefore no need to continue to reserve the
term 'modernization' for social phenomena or think of modernism as the
aesthetic aspect of modernity. These terms could instead better be used in
the way they literally suggest, as modes rather than levels of the modern.
Modernization then sums up the various processes leading to modernity as
a state or condition, and modernism is not an epoch but a heterogeneous
group of collective ways of relating or reacting to these processes and this

state, in social or cultural movements. Modernization is the process, modernity the state, and modernisms are movements of response to that state.[18]

The roots of these terms in different discursive traditions threaten to interfere dysfunctionally with their application as three modes of the modern, creating inconsistencies. The processual should, for example, not be limited to the socioeconomic field, and it would be good to avoid the repeated confusion between modernity and modernism. The dimensions ought to be kept strictly apart, so that this modal dimension only refers to the distinction between processes, states and responses, nothing else.

There are several ways to combine this dimension with the first, temporal one. As for the processes of *modernization*, a term formed out of the verb form 'modernize', these are actually a combination of several conjunctional processes (commodification, industrialization, secularization, etc.). It can be debated whether the combined result is a single process which leads societies and cultures through a series of different stages, or whether the process itself also changes its character. The fact that modernity functions as an overarching term for the whole epoch indicates that there is a certain continuity over time in the abstract process form of modernization. On the other hand, the way this process is realized in concrete forms of change is successively transformed through time. Modernization is a slightly different process today than it was in the 1790s, even though there are some continuities in the connecting modern project.

If modernization is a directed process, its successive impact results in a condition of *modernity*. This term is a substantivation of the adjective 'modern', similar to the alternative noun 'the modern'. Modernity is both a stage or phase in history, and something that some phenomena can possess: people live in modernity and their lives are characterized by modernity. Since the process can be slow, continuous or unevenly distributed, it may be hard to specify exactly what condition deserves the name of (early, high or late) modernity. Misunderstandings arise when some people think of modernity as a delimited chronological phase of historical development while others define it as a certain qualitative state: the former may then think of everything happening in a certain time interval as a priori modern, while the latter use specific criteria to analyse which phenomena are modern, irrespective of their date. To some, the 1980s were, per definition, late modern, while others will think of them as consisting of simultaneous late, early, pre- and post-modern elements in a 'simultaneous uncontemporaneity'.[19]

As for the *modernisms*, they are movements that actively respond to the modern condition by expressing its problems and formulating possible

---

[18] Cf., e.g., Berman (1982), Featherstone (1988, p. 197) and Hebdige (1988, p. 195).

[19] The term *Ungleichzeitigkeiten* derives from Ernst Bloch (1935/1991).

routes of action. Modernity moves, that is, it changes and develops in various directions. These directions are not decided in advance, but only through the web of actions in which human beings respond to their life conditions. People are not helpless victims of modernization, but individual and collective agents able to react and shape their own future, though in conditions they cannot choose. In a very wide sense, modernisms refer to all such answers or reaction forms. People make moves in modernity which determine the direction it will take. Modernity is less a fate than a human product.

It is not clear which responses shall be classified as early, high or late modernisms. Does it suffice that they react to a certain stage of modernization, or do they also have to give answers which are typical of that stage? Was fascism a high modern movement, like futurism or dadaism, or was it, rather, a political anti-modernism? Modernist terms are often restricted to those responses that are principally positive in relation to a certain stage of cultural modernity, so that neoconservative or reactionary formulations are excluded. These are then counted as regressive reactions against the modernist currents themselves. But each movement is coloured by its particular time, and it can be hard to decide which of all simultaneous '-isms' are true responses to recent conditions and which are 'uncontemporaneous'. It might be useful to distinguish between two main types of modernisms: one very wide collection of all movements that in any way answer to their own time, and one more narrow subfield consisting of the movements that explicitly define themselves as (early, high or late) modernist. These last are (early, high or late) modernisms proper, while the first ones are just (early, high or late) modern movements.

Another problem is that these responses do not fall outside of modernity but are in their turn also its constituents. Modernization produces a modernity in which the existence of modernisms is a crucial feature, to which other (anti-modernist) movements may respond. Literary modernism, for example, is an integrated part of the modern condition – it doesn't really point at it from any outside position. And different modernisms react not only to a general social condition but also to each other. Responses may be reflexive: just as a person's self-image is both part of his or her identity and answers to it, so the various modernisms are both parts of and reactions towards modernization. They constitute the sometimes critical, sometimes affirmative self-reflection of modernity.

Are specific phenomena caused by modernization, or are they part of it, or both? Modernization is often said to produce effects like urbanization, secularization or aesthetic modernism, which are at other times seen as its parts. While modernity is the result of modernization that provokes modernisms, modernity is also the condition in which modernization appears and of which modernisms are necessary constituents. The interrelations between the modes of the modern are certainly very complex, but even to discuss them, they have first to be kept apart.

Levels

A third, 'vertical', dimension is of aspects or *levels* of the modern. Modernity shows different faces: it is not one single thing, but internally differentiated. The levels structuring this book also differentiate modernity, which is basically an intersubjective, sociocultural phenomenon, but with implications in three or four basic directions: externalized institutional spheres shaped by objectifying social practices, inner subjectivities formed through modernizing socialization practices and the essentially intersubjectively shared (and simultaneously inner and outer) levels of social norms and relations, on one hand, and cultural or symbolic forms, on the other.

Some of the mechanisms and effects of modernity are *objective* or rather objectivized and externalized in technologies and institutions related to the economic and political systems of market and state. New technology and environmental changes, capitalist markets and bureacratic state apparatuses appear to acting individuals or groups as reified pseudo-natural forces.

Technical modernization includes industrialism and computerization, the invention and spread of agricultural, manufacturing, warfare, information and communication techniques which feed people and create wealth while simultaneously threatening survival on earth by ecological pollution and accumulated overkill capacity. Technology is extremely forceful within modern culture, but is no ultimate cause of modernization processes. It is no primary 'basis' for social and cultural 'superstructures', but as much a product of those social and cultural conditions that give it significance. Still, this aspect exists and has important repercussions on culture.[20]

Technology and science have both positive and destructive potentials, and they produce a self-reflexive spiral oscillation between optimist technocratization and dystopian anti-rationality. The increasing reflexivity and constructionism in science affects the meanings and effects of the technologization and increasing intrusion of science in societal institutions and in everyday life. In high modernity, technologization and 'scientificization' (*Verwissenschaftlichung*) usually meant scientific experts telling truths and solving problems with simplifying machines. Science and technology were means for goal-rational models and systemic demands to colonize the lifeworld. Self-critical and more relativistic late modern

---

[20] Cultural theorists with a background in structuralist Marxism sometimes relapse into seeing technological, demographic or economic processes as the only and ultimate foundation or cause of cultural shifts. Already Williams (1974) questioned that type of techno-determinism that repeatedly surfaces in British media and cultural studies. Examples may be found in Frith's otherwise extremely valuable studies of the rock industry (e.g., Frith 1989, pp. 92, 126 and 129f). Attali (1977/1985), Frith (1981 and 1988), Frith and Goodwin (1990) and Goodwin (1993) discuss the technology and institutions of music. Political-economic studies of mass communications like Murdock and Golding (1977) and Garnham (1979), and the tradition of 'production of culture', with Peterson (1976), DiMaggio and Hirsch (1976) and Crane (1992), study this institutional level.

science tends to change the functions of expertization: using science *can* today also mean questioning simple solutions and pointing at complexities, when this science understands itself in more problematizing and constructivist ways, inviting rather than replacing public communication.[21]

Economic modernization includes a generalized private ownership of goods and means of production, a general but divided wage labour creating a modern social class/age/gender power system, and an expanding unequal capitalist world market for the accumulation of profits in increasingly centralized and concentrated transnational companies. This capitalist economy is an effective machine for distributing commodities and expanding material wealth, but it also creates inequality, exploitation, poverty and powerlessness among great masses of people, and leads to deep and repeated crises that throw people into the insecurity and impoverishment of unemployment. Economic modernization rationalizes and expands the market system as a strong and influential determinant of social and cultural life.

Political modernization includes the formation of a global network of nations where formally democratic, parliamentary state systems with a specific series of bureaucratic/administrative institutions for legislation, government, military, socialization and social services interact with the ('civil') society of the lifeworld in matters of public interest and concerning international relations between nation-states. These political processes install secular forms of legitimation and make possible certain democratic procedures for collective decisions, but they also produce strong and potentially dangerous apparatuses for control and supervision. The expansion of this modern political state system also creates its own crises of legitimation, leading to a combination of increasingly complex federations of states and disruptive regionalist separatisms. Both market and state will be further discussed in the next chapter.

Modernization also affects psychic and bodily forms of subjectivity. Some changes are internal or internalized in individuals, making them experience *subjective* modernity in the form of new and changing inner psychic structures. New forms of subjectivity result from changing socialization patterns, giving rise to a *psychological* modernization process. They can only be studied indirectly, through cultural expressions, but inhabit a separate analytical level.

Early and high modern forms of subjectivity have been thematized both by classical psychoanalysis (though sometimes in a de-historicized manner) and by phenomenological accounts of modern forms of life and perception. Both abstract concepts of individuality in general and the whole psychic structure suggested by Sigmund Freud in particular are basically historical products of modernization, even though many of their elements go much further back or seem almost universally valid. The early Frankfurt school of critical theory (Adorno, Marcuse, Fromm, et al.) anchored 'super-ego'

---

[21] Cf. Beck (1986/1992), Giddens (1990) and Beck et al. (1994).

structures of authority in intimate socialization practices which arose with the early modern, originally 'bourgeois', but gradually generalized nuclear family.[22]

Simmel (1900/1990 and 1908/1992) and Benjamin (1968 and 1983) described new forms of experience made possible by high modern urban life in large cities and by new media and cultural forms like film or radio. The mobile, distanced, anonymous and intensely observant *flâneur* was emblematic for freely floating identity forms, resulting from the dissolution of pre-modern of social structures. Socialization (*Vergesellschaftung*) and individualization combine to create a tension between levelling homogenization and separating differentiation which characterizes a typically modern lifestyle.[23] This emergent spleen touches upon new aesthetic styles and social patterns, but also concerns new personality forms on an inner level.

This development has tendentially eroded not only pre-modern but also the high modern forms of subjectivity, particularly in the late modern phase. Chapter 5 below will discuss some recent transformations of psychological modernity, including the breaking up of fixed ego boundaries through 'narcissistic' tendencies.

The *intersubjective* aspects of modernity divide into two main subtypes. On one hand, there is a *social* modernization of norms, groups, relations and actual interaction forms. On the other hand, there is a *cultural* modernization of meaningful symbolic forms, both in everyday aesthetics and in artistic practices.

Modernization processes lead to what Thomas Ziehe (1975 and 1991; Ziehe and Stubenrauch, 1982) has called a 'crisis of erosion', where traditional values have been denaturalized and partly worn down. The apparent self-evident naturalness of conventional identities has been questioned in more and more life areas by deepening changes and transformations of everyday life. People are released from the rigid confines of older horizons and at the same time exposed to an intense bombardment by new impulses. Both these sides of the process are ambivalent. To be released from older habits is potentially a liberation or emancipation from traditional bounds and a freedom to form one's own life in new ways, but it is also a loss of security.[24] And to be exposed to a crossfire of ideas for how to form one's life offers an access to rich languages for ideals but simultaneously a threat to one's feeling of authenticity.

[22] For introductions, see Freud (1930/1961), Sohn-Rethel (1970/1978), Dahmer (1973), Rudolf Wolfgang Müller (1977), Erdheim (1982), Giddens (1991) and Elliott (1992).

[23] Cf. also Simmel (1911/1983), the Simmel issue of *Theory, Culture and Society* (1991) and Gisela Müller (1992).

[24] The term 'cultural release' Ziehe and Stubenrauch (1982) is inspired by Marx's talk in Chapter 24 of *Capital, Vol. 1* (1867/1976) of how early capitalism released the proletariat doubly: from feudal bounds and from their own means of production. It should not be interpreted as only a positive liberation.

If non-questioned traditional norms and life forms may be visualized as walls surrounding the growing individual, and if these walls are partly eroding, this opens new spaces for identity experiments but also leaves people without the support that stable traditions offered. When deciding what to do with one's life, it is a relief to be able to rely on certain habits that are handed over from older generations, even though overly rigid norms may at the same time be experienced as imprisoning. And if these 'walls' are tumbling down, there is no completely free space to rush into. There are a growing number of offers of how to lead a good life, presented in mass media and popular culture, but also in face-to-face interaction with others. Late modern society offers a rich language for wishes and desires in various life areas, compared to the previous relative scarcity of symbolic formulations. This is a resource in people's life choices, but it is also a kind of expropriation of the mind by pre-formulated images. If people were 'before' boxed into rigid self-evidences, they are 'today' living in a crossfire of contradictory messages.[25]

If cultural, social and psychological release and expropriation are parts of the historical processes of modernization, then individualization and reflexivity are resulting tendencies of the modern condition. They are all inherent in modernity from its very beginning, but have been radically intensified and transformed in late modernity.[26] No one can escape them and return to a quasi-natural collective rootedness or to an innocent self-forgetting naïvety. All have in some way to deal with a state of individual-ized and reflexivized being in the late modern world, whether they like it or not.

The historical process of individualization should not be confused with individuation (a psychological concept for the gradual achievement of an adult identity), nor with individualism (an ideological or philosophical tradition which prioritizes the individual before the collective). It can be either social or cultural. It is social if people really act separately in a more multicultural, pluralistic and heterogeneous society, whatever they think they are doing. It is cultural if they first of all think of themselves and make their choices on individual rather than collective grounds, whatever the actual result of these choices may then eventually be.

[25] Ziehe's term 'cultural expropriation' (*Enteignung*) is too negatively charged: it is important to remember that it implies both colonizing and communicative possibilities. While often stressing the ambivalence of each term, Ziehe sometimes equates release with freedom and treats it as the polar opposite of expropriation interpreted as if it was only constraint. But just as release has negative sides (a loss of security and an increasing load of identity-work), expropriation has positive ones (opening communicative means for formerly tabooed or non-communicable experiences). An opposite polarity could therefore as well be between the enriching communicativity of expropriation and the impoverishing uncertainty of release. The colonizing side of expropriation can be associated with Foucault's (1974/1979) ideas of surveillance. Cf. also Keniston (1970) and Koselleck (1979/1985).

[26] Cf. Habermas (1981/1984–8, 1985/1987 and 1988/1992), Beck (1986/1992), Mitterauer (1986/1992), Melucci (1989) and Ziehe (1991).

Reflexivity is a cultural way of mirroring (individual or collective, subjective, social or cultural) selves or identities through symbolic images in media, verbal language or face-to-face interaction. It has several facets: individual or group self-mirroring through symbolic practices (with or without communication media); media texts mirroring people mirroring themselves (problematizing identities); texts mirroring themselves and their own construction (often in ironic ways); and researchers reflecting upon their own way of constructing their findings. All these together add up to a general sociocultural reflexivity, which is reducible neither to intellectual or even verbal self-reflection (but may also be pictorial and embedded in ordinary everyday life practices), nor to narcissism as a psychodynamic concept (which involves a confirming self-mirroring, but of a particular kind), nor to mediatization (the intensified presence of mirroring media in culture which is again only one facet of an increasing reflexivity), nor to the colonization of the lifeworld by systemic demands (one of them being the demand for self-definition in formalized categories) – though there are interesting relations between all these, to be further discussed later on.

There are reasons to believe that both individualization and reflexivity have been extended and generalized in our time. Thomas Ziehe has added a third tendency, towards what he calls 'makeability': a demand and a capability to regard more and more things – like one's own or one's children's selves – as possible to shape and produce according to a project or a plan rather than as an outcome of natural developments or given traditions.[27]

Not only can modernization and modernity be analysed on different levels, but so can modernisms. It is possible to react to modernity either negatively or positively, but in practice most responses are mixed and ambivalent. Ziehe (1991) distinguishes two triads of general attitudes to modernization. A conventionalist response is to continue old habits as before and pretend nothing has happened. Neoconservatives or reactionaries acknowledge that things change but strive to turn time backwards again by resurrecting the past against the present. 'Seeking movements' (*Suchbewegungen*, collective strivings to look for new ways of life), thirdly, affirm at least some aspects of modernity and test its creative possibilities. In reality these two last forms are not as easy to distinguish, since most reactionary movements affirmatively make use of some modern traits (like fundamentalists using video and commercials to spread their message), while the most radical modernists usually criticize at least certain other modern traits (like rappers shunning urban anonymity).

Ziehe's second triad concerns different emphases in the value and legitimation structures of modern currents. First, some groups and individuals have a subjectivizing tendency – they react primarily against the

---

[27] Cf. Ziehe and Stubenrauch (1982) and Ziehe (1991).

coldness of modern society and strive for closeness and intimacy. Examples are found in therapy forms or authenticity-oriented rock culture. A second type of attitude is the objectivizing or 'ontologizing' tendency to avoid chaotic contingency and strive for meaning and certainty, as in socio-biology or age-old religions. A third type is the potentiating tendency to avoid emptiness and strive for intensity – it can be noticed in forms of play, sports and entertainment.[28] The first anchors values in the inner, subjective world, the second tries to find their legitimation basis in the external, objective world, while the third stresses the autonomy of the cultural or aesthetic dimension of the intersubjective world. None of these can escape the conditions of individualization, reflexivity or makeability which make the choice between the attitudes a personal, problematized and calculable matter.

On the social level, there are movements and groups reacting to modern transformations and pushing in various directions. Some of them act on the economic and political systems and on established, objectivized institutions, some relate to socialization and personality forms, and all use cultural means of communication. They are all engaged in normative and relational issues and forming new types of networks of social interaction, reacting to the way modernization affects relations to nature or the dimensions of age (children's and youth movements), gender (women's movement), class (workers' movements), ethnicity (anti-racist movements) or geography (regionalist movements).

On the cultural level, there is a wealth of aesthetic or symbolic treatments of the experiences of modernity, in artistic '-isms', popular culture, everyday styles and expressive forms. Many studies have depicted such new cultural traits in popular culture, media use, youth culture, art, music and literature. It is here the term 'postmodernism' has mostly been used, meaning primarily aesthetic currents with a secondary reflexivity towards the earlier modernisms or cultural avantgarde movements. Cultural responses to late modernity can also be found within trends of popular culture and within everyday self-images and world-views. New cultural moves in late modernity have been discussed as a growing intertextuality between works, styles, genres and historical times, a heterogeneous and pluralist aesthetics avoiding closure and looking for enjoyment in dirty, unorthodox combinations of 'high' and 'low' traditions, in reflexive hybrids, bricolage, montage, irony and pastiche.

Some responses (like this book itself) use philosophical and theoretical tools to formulate experiences of modernity. Others use aesthetic tools, as in the artistic currents of 'postmodernism'. Still others use political or ethical discourses. They have many interconnections, mutual influences and similarities: theories use metaphors and symbols, artistic works

---

[28] Cf. how Cohen and Taylor (1976/1992, pp. 118ff) mention three goals of escape attempts from the confines of everyday life: to seek the true self, to seek meaning, and to seek progress and novelty.

formulate understandings of the world. Still, they are different types of currents, and 'postmodernist' art styles should not, for example, be reduced to exponents of poststructuralist theory, even though they might inspire each other.

There are many simultaneous uncontemporaneities at play between these levels. Different individuals seek varying solutions to similar problems, and similar social phenomena have varying cultural or psychological backgrounds. A revived interest in old rituals can be either the result of a searching for fixed values in a fluid world, or of an almost opposite demand for intense aesthetic enjoyment instead of an everyday, grey, ascetic and functional effectivity. A partial release from traditions might become blurred by such efforts of re-ritualization in everyday life, but even when people act (socially) in traditional ways, they might think (culturally) in new ways. A culturally modernized self-image can hide behind conventional social actions or the other way around. The moves *in* modernity are as complex, shifting and diverse as the moves *of* modernity.

The differentiation between external, objective aspects of technological, economic and political modernization, the internal, subjective aspects of psychological modernization and the intersubjectively shared aspects of social and cultural modernization is itself produced by modernization processes separating formerly inseparable aspects. It is in modernity that the social world severs an external nature, an inner subjectivity and a symbolic order that were all previously integrated in intersubjective practices. Whatever initiated the modernization stream, there is a complex interplay of aspects and levels once it is running. Objective facts are formed by social, cultural and subjective forces and can never appear as such to us, but only as symbolically coded and represented. Social and cultural forms develop through objective and subjective detours, and the inner life through external and sociocultural processes. There is no need to think of subjectivity as just a side-effect of language systems, of symbolic forms only as delayed reflexes of collective practices, or of social relations as totally determined by material factors. The separation of aspects makes it possible to thematize much more intricate interrelations.

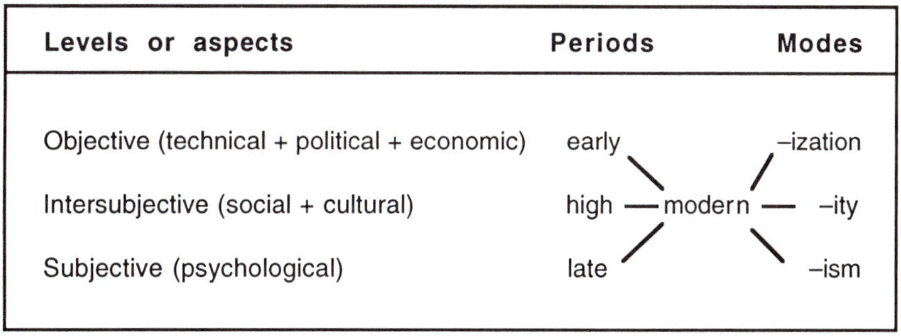

Levels or aspects	Periods	Modes
Objective (technical + political + economic)	early	–ization
Intersubjective (social + cultural)	high — modern —	–ity
Subjective (psychological)	late	–ism

Figure 2.2 *Modern dimensions*

Complex temporal processes

The three dimensions of horizontal phases, lateral modes and vertical levels are separate from each other but related (see Figure 2.2). All phases can be studied on each of the different levels, and in each of the three modes. One can, for example, discuss social late modernization as well as subjective early modernity or modernisms. With these differentiations in mind, and with the modernity perspective as an unspoken framework, it is possible to develop more elaborate theoretical concepts for analysing, in turn, objective, social, cultural and subjective aspects of culture, which structure those modern temporal flows that have now been presented in a general manner.

3

Spheres

The temporal dimension may be contrasted with aspects of culture that are usually conceived in spatialized terms: the social spheres which simultaneously frame and enable cultural activities. The time-flows of modernization run into spatial spheres formed by order structures in the physical and social spaces of modernity: relatively fixed structures and institutions which, like sluices, delimit which human actions are possible.

All cultural phenomena have roots and meanings pointing in these objective and social directions. Cultural phenomena both originate from and refer to objective things and structures of an external world, and to social norms, relations and groups in an intersubjectively shared world. Every media text is, for example, partly conditioned by economic, political and social forces, and it always implies a representation of such structures. Cultural practices and communicative actions also move and transform the objectivized spatial frames within which they are born. By thematizing structures of power and money, cultural texts can make them less solidly reified and more open to change.

This chapter investigates these objective and social levels. A general introduction to a series of concepts related to the sphere theme is offered as a means to reflect upon how they can be used to express various aspects of these framing structures. It is important to develop a sensitivity for how terms are used, not in order to regulate them, but to appropriate the knowledge inherited through the symbolic form of language. This is followed by a discussion of the central concept of power. A series of key theories on the social level will then be worked through, starting with its most objectified sides and ending with its interfaces with the cultural level. The chapter concludes with an outline of a theory of resistance.

Disharmonies of the spheres

The time-waves of modernization are channelled, concentrated, split and refracted by various spatial spheres of modernity, framing human actions. People live in different spheres, between which the relations are far from harmonious. Identities are produced by practices located within public institutions like school, services or leisure organizations, in private institutions organized by the commercial market such as industrial workplaces, shops or the mass media, or in more informal entities like families or peer groups. The borders between such spheres give rise to conflicts, in a play between power and resistance. The demands and rules of different spheres collide, strategies confront each other, polarities of dominance and opposition are continuously reshaped in new contexts.

Spheres constitute a (physically or socially) spatial dimension, a network of ordering structures that the temporal streams of modernization unavoidably break against, but also gain momentum from. Temporal processes are framed by the spatial boundaries of spheres, but they are also given speed and direction by them, just as floodgates block but also direct torrents. Structures are both obstacles to and prerequisites of changes. And, conversely, it is movements that create and reproduce boundaries. Both aspects are needed in cultural theory.

In this chapter, structures, frames and institutions will be focused on, in their continuous interplay with processes, actions and life. These societal aspects of culture contain what relates to the social level of actual intersubjective interaction, norms, communities and regulating systems. *Society* can be defined as the combination of territorial organization, institutional structure and temporal continuity. A society consists of individuals living in an organized community that controls a certain territory, locality or place; that is structured by institutions that distribute positions, roles and statuses to these individuals; and that is reproduced over time.[1] Thematizing *spheres* is a way to focus on the various webs of socially effective institutions that are inevitably also power structures.

Some types of spheres encircle individuals and groups, so that each of them 'belongs' to one sphere or another. Their discords then imply contradictions between different categories, subcultures or groupings, as, for example, between men and women, rich and poor, urbans and rurals, or between conflicting ethnic communities.

But spheres can also be positions or areas that people can inhabit without completely or definitely belonging to them. Each person moves between the spheres of family, leisure and work or school, meeting a series of separate rule-systems, demands and resources. These often collide, with positive and negative effects. Each human being lives in a crossfire of contradictory sphere-related discourses, but can in favourable conditions manoeuvre within and between them.

A sphere is a globe, a ball – the simplest conceivable three-dimensional space, that, like the two-dimensional circle, encloses all within a certain distance from its centre. It thus has a centre and a uniform rule to decide

---

[1] This definition of society is suggested by Ricoeur (1983/1984, pp. 195ff), inspired by the historian Mandelbaum. '[The social] has more to do with the roles ascribed to us within institutions, whereas the cultural involves the production of works of intellectual life. . . . The political focuses on the institution of the constitutional, the sharing of power, and so on, whereas the social encompasses the different roles ascribed to us by varying institutions. The cultural, on the other hand, has more to do with the medium of language and the creation of ideas' (Ricoeur 1986, p. 323). Geertz (1973, pp. 3–30, 144 and 361) has a similar, 'semiotic' concept of culture that could as well be labelled 'hermeneutic', and he also makes similar points about the relation between culture and society.

what is inside or outside its periphery. Spheres may be hierarchically ordered, if they are placed concentrically inside each other, with approximately coinciding centres but varying radii (i.e., extent). With separated centres, they may instead overlap each other in more complex ways, lie completely apart or just touch each other's boundaries at one single point.

This description of physical globes can be metaphorically transferred to social spheres as well. Geographical, political, economic, social, cultural or psychological spheres are of course not necessarily perfectly ball-shaped, but they should in some respect be continuously connected around a centre and be delimited by one simple rule, in order to deserve that name. A district or town (like Stockholm), a country (Sweden) and a continent (Europe) can mostly be hierarchically/concentrically ordered, while regions or territories like the European Union, Western Europe, Christianity, Scandinavia and the Germanic language area may overlap in more complex ways.

The relation between centre and periphery may be viewed in two ways: either the envelope encloses its content; in the way that a soap bubble is held together by forces in its exterior; or the central core is the most determining factor, in the way that the biological cell is governed by its nucleus.

The concept of *field* structures space slightly differently.[2] It implies an area or a space with some sort of specific order or direction. The word has West Germanic origin and first denoted a bounded land area used for cattle pasturage. The directionality was then only in the third, vertical dimension, through gravitation, the growing grass and the standing cattle. The horizontal order produced by the fences or by the movements of the animals was much more vague and accidental. If this pasture or cultivation field is, like the sphere, also a bounded area, it does not as obviously have a centre.

The field concept has, however, gradually been enriched by imported meanings: battle-field, magnetic field. Here, yet another directionality is added: a dichotomization between two poles that seem to compete in trying to order the field between them, thus creating a hierarchical inner structure where each point in the field has a definite position in relation to these two main poles (the commanders or north/south). The sphere has a centre and a periphery, the cattle-field has an earth and a heaven, magnetism and the battle-field have two separate but mutually dependent and opposite centres. Adding a time dimension, the grass can be seen growing or cut and swallowed, the troops move and the filings wander.

In metaphorical uses, these associations are mingled. Spheres and fields may vaguely denote bounded areas, but may also imply a certain inner structure of dominance relations within these areas, between centre and periphery, in steady growth processes or among competing forces. Some think of fields more in terms of cultivation and growth, where something

[2] Cf. Lewin (1951).

germinates, sprouts and flowers, is born, fertilized and crossed, and where living agents ramble in various unpredictable directions. Others gather their metaphorical associations much more from a male world of war, conjuring up positions, bastions and trenches, armies, attacks and defences, vanguards and marching masses, strategies and tactics. This military (or magnetic) field imagery has been particularly promoted by the influential French cultural sociologist Pierre Bourdieu.

None of these lines of interpretation is right or wrong, but it is important to notice that both are possible, and that each of them opens and closes certain uses of the field concept. It is worthwhile in each particular case to consider in what respect a specific sphere really has one centre and one periphery, is continuously connected and defined by a simple and uniform rule, or if it should be thought of as a more vaguely defined space. And is a certain field more like a cattle-field or a battle-field?

The distance to the centre of a sphere may not be the only important characteristic of a specific point or element within it – there might be other ordering principles crossing the sphere with another logic. And some fields may be intersected by magnetic forces and grass roots, or used by both animals and armies. The different associative spheres may thus be actualized simultaneously, giving rise to really complicated interpretations of a social sphere. It might be crucial to forget neither the strict polar directions nor the heedless roaming of the sheep. All elements and events of some social space need be reduced neither to free play or the satisfaction of needs, nor to a struggle for power and status.

A series of other terms belong to the same conceptual sphere, uncovering some crucial aspects of spheres in general. The seemingly innocent term *area* originally refers to a vacant ground, while the almost synonymous *domain* implies an ownership of a master (*dominus*), and a *territory* is a piece of land that is occupied, demarcated and guarded by someone. Here, power relations are closer than one might have expected; positively, as fields controlled by someone, or negatively, as fields freed from such control or ruled jointly by everyone. In any case, an area is a space that has been staked out and demarcated, and is thus at least mentally mastered through knowledge and surveillance.

A *space* is a stretch or an extension containing something. It is here used as the most general concept for three-dimensional expanses. A *place* was originally a flat and even area but today mostly refers to a particular location, whatever its form. A *room* is an enclosed place or a three-dimensional area.

Concepts like places, spaces and spheres are filled with sometimes confusing metaphorical connotations. While some distinguish between social and physical spaces, others talk about the physical aspects of social life as spatial aspects of society. The result is a complicated mixture of metaphorical and polysemic spheres of meaning. When concepts like space, place and room are used parallel to but separate from concepts like sphere, field and arena, they usually refer to concrete physical aspects.

In other contexts, they may have wider and more abstract meanings, more synonymous with these other general concepts.

An *aspect* is a way to look at something in a certain *direction* or from a certain *perspective*. Spaces may also in themselves be clearly directed, that is, put straight or ordered in a linear fashion. A perspective in a general sense is something (an aspect or a direction) through which spaces and things are viewed from a certain *position* in which one is put. Some spaces have discernible *levels* – balanced, even surfaces that stratify them horizontally into layers. Such a layered or levelled space thus has a hierarchical, vertical dimension, an up/down polarity, making it possible to distinguish ascending and descending movements from movements within a stratum that is defined by a certain altitude.

Sometimes spheres and spaces have diffuse contours, but sometimes clear *borders*, *boundaries*, *frames* or *walls* shield, screen, confine, order and separate. While the power in spheres and fields relies on forces working over distance, such framing implies a firmer, but perhaps also more passive, steering – a distinct and rigid limit against which one may bang one's head.

Orders and *structures* are shaped through hierarchizing and polarizing forces working in spaces, fields or areas. The concept of structure is deeply imbued with the tradition of structuralism, but should also be possible to use in a more general sense. Whether a structure presupposes a singular centre or can be open and dynamic is a much debated issue within poststructuralist theory.

A *system* is something composed of several pieces, but has through sociological functionalism often received a more specific meaning: something that is delimited, well ordered and in some aspect autonomous or self-reproducing, like a working mechanism or organism. In the theory of Habermas, the concept of system has mainly been restricted to the political and economic spheres of state and market. But others talk about many different types of system: school, gender, symbol systems, etc. They are always orders with a structure and fixity, often also clearly demarcated with frames and centres.

Patterns, *schemata*, *models* and *recipes* are inner orders that, more than structures, hint at a pre-formulation or at any rate a possibility of distilling them as maps of or prescriptions for sociocultural practices. Models are simply measures, manners or means for doing things. A pattern is like a father (the term derives from *patron*) giving rise to scions in the form of concrete realizations of itself, while recipes are devices for effecting something, received or taken from tradition. Related terms are the theatrical *roles* and the somewhat militaristic pair *strategies* and *tactics*, which all tend more towards processual practice than external frames. In some cases such prescriptions exist in social reality, in other instances such basic codes are merely analytical constructions made by the observer.

The term *formation* is often preferred to structure as a way to stress the temporal dynamics that may disappear in the more solidifying spatial metaphors.[3] A formation is a complex that has received or developed a certain form or shape in a historical process. In actual theoretical practice, however, this term is often used in a very similar way to structure or system. Formations are mostly thought of as relatively stable constructions rather than as types of temporal flows. The time/space tension is to be continually reworked rather than to be avoided. Spatial structures are certainly not as rigid as they are often thought to be, but the tension between events, actions, flows or 'software', on one hand, and settings, structures, orders or 'hardware', on the other, remains a useful way to conceptualize cultural phenomena.

Some fields, places or spaces are called *stages* or *arenas*. The classical role-theory and Erving Goffman's (1959) dramaturgical sociology are important traditions here. Stages and arenas are where actors act to audiences. There are front- and backstage regions, visible places of performance and hidden rooms for rest and preparations. This implies not only social practices, but also an aesthetic dimension with scrutinizing glances, self-representation and prescribed parts or roles.

Yet other sociological traditions can be associated with the term *institution*: symbolic interactionism, ethnomethodology and sociology of knowledge.[4] To institute is to establish, to put in place, and the spheres, fields or spaces that are institutionalized are organized in a more formal way: they are established by effective decisions with a collective legitimacy that makes them socially acknowledged, and they have more or less explicit purposes and rule systems. Besides such social institutions one can conceive of cultural institutions – not only as social institutions dealing with cultural affairs (like national theatres or local councils), but also as aesthetic genres or symbolic modes. A language or an art form might, for example, in itself be thought of as instituted, but the term will here be reserved for specifically social phenomena.

Texts, cultural items or phenomena are surrounded by *contexts*, which are all that comes 'with' the text. Contexts may themselves be textual configurations of texts that precede, follow or relate to a certain passage and fix its meaning, in which case they may also be named intertexts. But they can also be conceived as not necessarily textually organized social frames of various kinds.

It might finally be noted that the use of the term *culture* as a delimited phenomenon, which can have an indefinite or plural form (a culture, cultures), also stresses the spatial aspect of cultural processes. A particular culture is like a specific cultivation field with internal structures and external limits which give it the shape of a sphere, distinct from other surrounding or overlapping cultural spheres. Speaking of '*a* culture' is to

[3] Cf. Murdock (1993, pp. 524 and 529).

[4] Berger and Luckmann (1966/1984) develop a sociological understanding of institutionalization from Gehlen's anthropologically based theories.

distinguish a specific area that is kept together and marked off by certain cultural patterns. But culture may as well stand for symbolic or communicative aspects of all human praxis in the more general and abstract sense developed in the next chapter.

There is thus a large spectrum of concepts that thematize the spatial, material or objectivized aspects of social life and the relatively solid orders in and through which people act, move, struggle and create. 'Sphere' will here be used as the most general term, signifying any collection of social or spatial elements held together by some principle. 'Space' and 'area' denote something more clearly confined, while 'field' refers to a space with a more dominant inner order.

Objectivizing sociality

To all of humanity, only nature is external. There is a radical polarity between subjectivity, society and culture, on one hand, and material nature, on the other. But even this cleavage is not quite so clear. Our own biological bodies are in some ways natural organisms, in other ways highly (inter)subjective creations. That which for one individual or group is internal can be experienced as very external by another. And many societal institutions appear to us as objectivized and externally 'given', in spite of the fact that they were once intersubjectively created and are socially maintained.[5]

Does exteriority 'exist'? Such a discussion moves on to the limit of all language and theorizing, since that which is truly external to us can only be understood as inconceivable – what we understand and conceptualize has been made 'ours' by being pulled into a shared, sociocultural world. It is therefore often thought that reality is only what people know of or give meaning through language. But reality is much more than what is understood and given meaning, even though it can only be known through meaning-production, used to construct an external, objective world for us. To say that external phenomena are only real if they are meaningful to us is a mistaken reduction of *the* world of reality to a phenomenology of *our* world. Even though we cannot understand it, we cannot avoid assuming that there is an exteriority in the world we inhabit. This not only includes things far away from us but also aspects of our own praxis that exceed the meaning-production of our multifarious symbolic languages.

An objectivizing perspective on cultural phenomena is always possible, since culture itself has objective, objectivized and objectivizing aspects. Cultural practices create new objectivized forms, institutions and products, which in their turn then function as frames for future praxis. Each cultural

---

[5] Cf. Elias (1989/1991) and various anthropological work on the interfaces between nature and culture, which are only briefly mentioned here.

production objectivizes human praxis in material traces: physical objects or movements, light- or sound-waves. This physical aspect of culture – the materiality of symbols – is manifest in the discussions of the texture and tenacity of raw materials in artistic work. Cultural phenomena are caused by objective factors and they have their own objectivity as material things or movements.

Symbolic utterances can also thematize objective matters, just as external frames (nature, materiality, etc.) are continuously referred to in symbolic discourses. And the validity criteria of efficiency and truth touch upon the relation between cultural texts and objective structures. The criterion of efficiency is emphasized by established institutions that are geared towards the goal-oriented success of strategic interests. Commercial industries value cultural phenomena for their ability to return profits, while bureaucratic apparatuses want them to fulfil ordering or administrative tasks. The criterion of truth can be applied to any symbolic representation of an external reality, including both everyday verbal language-use and artistic visual or musical work. It is a foundation for the critique of ideology and propaganda, and a positive value in works disclosing hidden injustices.

In many aesthetic genres the importance of cognitive truth (as a criterion for validating the relation between a symbolic expression and the external world) is, however, deliberately reduced. Debates on mimesis and realism in art and literature have indicated the weakness of one-dimensional theories of culture as mirroring external reality. Cultural expressions do not faithfully reflect or copy reality but create new realities that use direct references to reality to indirectly say something more important about the conditions of human life. Aesthetic expressions often avoid or distort direct representation, in order to destroy usual simple and direct refer- ences to liberate the words, sounds and images from their primary significations and instead let them create 'deeper', secondary truths, which can seldom be judged by any simple truth criteria.[6] If the demand for truth may be too narrow and flat on a naïve, direct level, it may aquire a new relevance in a deeper and more mediated perspective. Such evaluations are also made by audiences and critics, discussing how works of art manage to catch relevant aspects of current problems. Other criteria discussed below, like socially normative truthfulness, subjective authenticity or, most importantly, aesthetic well-formedness are, however, often at least as important.

The objective aspects are partly truly objective traces of natural forces in human life, and partly objectivized social ones: systemic forces which originally emanate from social interaction but have been autonomized through reified ordering structures. To all of humanity, these latter are only temporarily externalized, while they are experienced as definitely

---

[6] Ricoeur (1985/1988, pp. 100f and 158f) therefore abandons the concept of reference in favour of refiguration, to make clear that references are secondary, reshaping and productive rather than simple, copying and reproductive.

external to most of society's single individuals and interpretive communities. Other parts of the social order are much more obviously intersubjective, forming the genuinely social level of relations, groups and norms, shaping webs of praxis and interaction. Symbolic forms are produced in and by such intersubjective relations, which they also thematize.

The term 'social' derives from the Latin word *socius*, friend and companion, which in its turn is formed of *sequor*, follows. The social thus concerns human communities shaped by intersubjective relations of nearness, belonging and solidarity. The focus here is on actual interaction between people. An important aspect of the social level is how the use of symbolic forms and of communication media is involved in markings of status and identity, and in the shaping of internal relations of community through concrete interaction within groups.

Cultural praxis is always also social praxis: the joint production of meaning is not clearly separated from the co-operation of individuals or the normative rules regulating this interaction.[7] Cultural phenomena always have a social side, besides their social sources and social references.

Modernization tends to produce a growing differentiation between individuals and between subcultures, a growing plurality of coexisting (ethnic or self-chosen) groups in society, with differing norms and traditions, collectivity forms and relational patterns. While globalization increases people's mobility and enhances communication between subcultures, an exploding range of lifestyle offers and a fragmentation of old collective communities prevents this from leading to any universal homogeneity. Early and high modernity disintegrated pre-modern localities and opened up new roads to a more uniform lifeworld, while alternative currents were marginalized and pathologized. In late modernity such normative hegemony is no longer so easily upheld. Normality is being denaturalized in a world where few traditions or values are experienced as self-evident. The result is a norm-crisis of insecurity and confusion which breeds a nostalgic longing for a world of clear-cut shared norms.

Symbolic forms have a series of different social functions. On one hand, they transgress borders and create communities. Through communicative praxis, cultural forms can create social bounds between people and mediate between separate groups. On the other hand, they mark differences and boundaries that deepen social rifts by producing and elucidating distinctions. A rap group may, through tours and record sales, transgress some geographic and social borders, for example, while simultaneously creating a difference between idols and audiences, and widening the gaps between generations and between subcultures, that is, between their fans, on one hand, and their parents or persons of the same age who prefer other genres, on the other. Each cultural phenomenon includes communicative actions that in various proportions blend fusioning with fissioning, uniting

---

[7] Anthony P. Cohen (1985), Clifford and Marcus (1986) and Marcus and Fischer (1986) mention symbolic aspects of how social communities are constructed.

with separation. No symbolic languages are limitless – genres of image, music and dance may just be able to draw lines that run in other places than those between verbal languages.

The way cultural phenomena point to the social dimension actualizes issues of normative righteousness. Each community develops ethical norms that regulate interaction and make some degree of justice and well-being possible. An internal differentiation is sometimes made between *ethics* as the ideal and praxis of a good life, and *moral* as social rules for justice and rights. Cultural praxis is used to negotiate between various interests and formulate contracts about which values, norms and relations are to be intersubjectively legitimated. Again, as with truth, normative judgements on cultural phenomena are repeatedly made and discussed, as one of the polydimensional aspects that may be thematized.

Social relations are often regulated by (usually unwritten) mutual agreements or 'con-tracts' – rules 'drawn together', agreed on and signed jointly by two struggling parts.[8] Some of these contracts may sometimes be renegotiated in explicit or implicit reflexive acts that temporarily cancel, thematize and reformulate these agreements. Those social contracts that are up for negotiation rise to at least partial consciousness, while other intersubjective rules for interaction may rest for centuries deeply embedded in the horizon of the lifeworld. Negotiations are a kind of meta-discourse where the rules for interaction are reflexively discussed and adjusted. They are often inseparably united with the social acts themselves, so that regular interaction successively redefines social relations. But sometimes they are carried out in specific forms, not least through cultural images and argumentation in verbal language. Aesthetic practices often function as such processes of negotiations of social relations and identities, for instance concerning gender roles or ethnic conflicts, where mediated formulations can be important tools for posing or opposing social claims and for testing life forms or patterns of interaction. But there are also contracts on the cultural level (rules for symbolic practices) and negotiations made on the social level (the use of force or other forms of effective interaction rather than symbolic communication to solve problems), so that a set of transferences appears between these levels. Negotiations are also of many different kinds, from the strategic action of business treaties where exchange of values or brute force is used to regulate relations, to the communicative rationality of reflexive argumentation aiming for consensual agreement and mutual understanding.

A late modern trait seems to be that a whole range of formerly naturalized social contracts have become opened and thematized through increasingly intense negotiations, as a result of cultural release from traditional norms and of increasing cultural reflexivity. Discourses of negotiation make the conditions of social action explicit: 'discourses, treating as they do problematic validity claims as hypotheses, represent a

---

[8] Cf. Haavind (1985), Hirdman (1988) and Drotner (1991a).

reflective form of communicative action (Habermas 1983/1990, p. 201). Since negotiations are communicative acts elevated to a discursive and reflexive level, there is a tight connection between negotiations and modernization.

Power

The whole social dimension is particularly closely knit to questions of power. The spatial, material, objectivized and institutional spheres create power structures that induce social actions that under certain conditions may condense into emancipatory critique and various forms of resistance. Power is a term that goes back to a Latin term for being able.[9] Power can be directed towards anything: nature, the self or others. But it is usually associated with social, intersubjective dominance, a word that derives from the Latin *dominus*, master. Subordination is the relation of the dominated to the dominating, in being placed under their rule. Power, then, implies coercion and oppression (being pressed or squeezed). A weaker relative is influence, originating in the astrological belief that a flow from the stars could affect people's actions. Social power is thus a mastering, dominance, coercion, oppression of or influence over (other) people. It is both restricting (to its victims) and enabling (to its bearers). It gives capability to those in power, but can sometimes also let the dominated learn through resistance. Power agents may be individuals, groups, social categories or autonomous and abstract social or cultural mechanisms (embodied in institutions or symbolic systems). Its forms include physical violence, economic extortion, political force, aesthetic seduction and psychic manipulation.

Resistance means standing up against something or somebody.[10] It therefore presupposes power, to which it constitutes an answer and a reaction. Those who resist try to prevent something that tries to influence them. Resistance is connected to critique and criticism, and answers to a more or less consciously experienced lack, a want. It is therefore also connected to the creation of positive utopias, more or less developed wishes and dreams of a better, more free and happy state where the influence of certain powers has been reduced and that which these powers obstructed can be freely developed, so that the lack is cancelled. A society without lack or power is impossible – they are necessary conditions for human action and change. Power breeds critique and a hope for resistance, needed to make those transforming actions possible which make humans into true subjects. 'At a time when everything is blocked by systems which have failed but which cannot be beaten – this is my pessimistic appreciation

---

[9] A similar etymology applies for the Germanic *Macht*, while *Herrschaft* parallels domination and mastering.

[10] 'Resistance' derives from the Latin word for 'standing again', while the German *Widerstand* means 'standing against' or 'counter-standing'.

of our time – utopia is our resource. It may be an escape, but it is also the arm of critique' (Ricoeur 1986, p. 300).

All human beings are involved in relations of power and resistance, only with a varying balance between being a victim and an agent of dominance, and in more or less conscious, intentional, focused, consequent, collective or organized ways. Categories like age, gender, ethnicity and class form quasi-objectivized frames that support dominance structures and feed multidimensional resistances.[11] Some of these power relations are supported by the hard systemic structures of the market and the state. But there are also subjective aspects: subjects who are subjected to the execution of power and subjects who execute power. Abstract systems may influence each other, but do not exert power or resistance until these influences pass through wanting, acting and experiencing human beings.

To think of power and resistance as Siamese twins is not as trivial as it might seem. Autonomous self-determination implies a 'mastering' of living conditions, but the 'resistance' that this 'power' meets is either the mere passive inertia of the material context over which control has been recovered or a competing power striving to regain its dominance. If this then seems to exemplify power without resistance, is there not also resistance against forces other than social powers? What about a diffuse inertia, mental or ideological defences that resist insights and change, but where these resisted transformational forces cannot be said to be related to social power? Neoconservatives, traditionalists and lazy conventionalists may be resisting, but what they resist is change more than power. Still, it seems as wrong to conclude that power and resistance are independent concepts.

A solution to this dilemma is to distinguish between wide (general) and narrow (truly social) versions of power and resistance. Both of these conceptual pairs are mutually connected: power in general presupposes resistance in general, and vice versa. *Some* type of resistance can always be found where some sort of power exists. Resistance towards change need not go against any social power structure, but in a wider, non-social sense, change itself is a kind of force that exerts power over people. And the inertia of material conditions may be said to offer a general resistance to people's efforts to master their own lives. Similarly, power and resistance as social forces are always coexistent, and it is such social interplay between them that is focused on in the following. The paradox of a disjunction between power and resistance appears if a wide power concept is combined with a narrow concept of resistance, or vice versa.

The material coercion to which natural 'laws' expose us forms an 'objective' power aspect that is only relevant to the discussion of social

---

[11] See Beck (1986/1992 and 1991), Peter A. Berger (1987), Schulze (1992), Frankenberg and Mani (1993) and Frow (1993) for relevant thoughts on tendencies within the late modern class system and its relations to other power hierarchies in society.

power when it is deliberately used by people and institutions. The physical and spatial structures formed by technology are also coercive and can be relevant to this discussion if they are used by human beings or social systems.[12]

Power/resistance is an asymmetrical relation, associated with tensions between *centres and peripheries* in spatial and social spaces, where places, territories and borders are crossed by various flows and movements. In the complex global network of such centre/periphery relations, various centres exert dominance across distance over multiple peripheries.[13] A first asymmetry in these patterns is that centres are different to peripheries – above all, they have more power. A second asymmetry is in the flows between centre and periphery: it is not the same money, commodities, people, information, etc., that flows from centre to periphery as in the opposite direction. A third asymmetry is that there are more peripheries than centres. A sphere has a centre but innumerable surface points, and even though there are several cultural or social power centres, they tend to coincide and each of them relates to many more highly diverse peripheries. These peripheries cannot be reduced to the single function of being margins of some centre. There are a multitude of margins (associated with geography, race, class, gender, sexuality, age or any other category) which have similar relations to some norm that institutes a centre, but these margins are mutually very different and cannot be collapsed into just faces of a constant Other, though that is what the One centre strives for.

These issues have been much discussed in late modern theories of gender and race. Feminist theory has thematized sociocultural gender as a discursive construction of positional differences and domination in critique against essentialist models of gender as a biologically or socially pre-given substantial identity.[14] Theories of ethnicity have discussed how cultural identities interact with geographical places through nation-states, exile, migration, tourism, travel and media. Benedict Anderson (1983/1991) has analysed nations as imagined communities, constructed by discursive practices. Edward Said (1978/1991) shows how stereotyped images of other ethnic groups are formed through the dichotomizing practices of orientalism, where negative aspects are projected onto the Other. Ulf Hannerz (1992a and b) talks of creolization as a new mixing of collective identities pushed forward by multicultural meetings, particularly through intensified communication processes. This concept generalizes the Afro-Caribbean experience to most modern cultures, where mixed identities have become increasingly normal. Stuart Hall (1990, 1992a, b and c), Dick Hebdige (1988), Iain Chambers (1990) and Paul Gilroy (1987, 1993a, b and c) have

---

[12] Harvey (1990, pp. 226ff) discusses the control over space as a source of social power.

[13] Kirshenblatt-Gimblett (1992) argues that the concept of boundary problematically implies bounded, substantial and unitary entities, while margins and peripheries are positionally related to centres and imply asymmetrical power relations.

[14] Cf. Chapter 5 below.

developed the Biblical–Jewish idea of diaspora as a model for how cultural identities are formed not around or inside bounded territories but instead disseminated like spores over the world. This was true of the Jews in many historical phases, and it has been true of several oppressed people like the Gypsies or the large and enormously influential Afro-American cultures that were dispersed by slavery and have constructed mobile identities through hybridizations with other cultures and certain transatlantic connections between the exiled groups. Again, these dispersed, scattered cultures offer a model of identity that is mobile, open, composite and impure, which is more appropriate to late modernity than some other traditional models of petrified rootedness. Jewish thinkers have formulated the experience of living in chronical exile and homelessness, and now black philosophers and cultural theorists have added new dimensions (not least of scale and cruelty) to this experience. Migration is a process that constructs ethnicities without territories, homeless identities. They are 'constituted from two directions at once' (Hall 1992c, p. 28): rooted doubly, both in an absent source of historical inheritance – since the site of origin has been irreversibly transformed – and in the specific 'diasporic conditions' of (mostly but not only oppressing) connections with dominating cultures – a painful history of hybridization. The increasing global mobility of urbanization, travelling and mass media have made such identity forms relevant not only for a growing number of refugees and immigrants, but for virtually all late modern people.[15] Traditional spatial routines are dissolved into, on one hand, a search for 'roots', which may be artificially constructed, and, on the other hand, an exploration along 'routes' towards new and often hybrid positions (Gilroy 1993a and b). Thus cultural identity is woven in crossings – understood both as transgressions of borders and as montage-like mixes of various elements.

Most such theories try to get away from any essentialist ideas of pure origins. Even though the level and speed of the mixing process increases, all historical cultures have been the result of hybridizing communication processes. Still, every discussion of peripheries, margins, diaspora, hybrids, mixes or crossings seems to imply an idea of something in the centre that is or once was originary and pure. If some cultural phenomena are placed outside of the dominating sphere, others are implied to exist within it. Changing concepts never helps much, since each new term that is used to emphasize impurity drags with it its potential obverse of purity. A radical solution would be to declare that there are no centres at all, only a totally fragmented plurality of marginal subcultures in an unpredictable

---

[15] Hall concludes that 'there are no pure forms [or ethnic identities] at all' (1992c, p. 28). The Norwegian Anders Johansen (1994), inspired by Salman Rushdie, argues that national identity in general is shaped by politically motivated symbolic affiliations rather than by any historically rooted cultural homogeneity: 'Men have no roots. Identity cannot reasonably be anchored in the distant past', and 'the insistence upon confirming our modern sense of identity in the distant past' implies an untenable 'reification of culture' (pp. 247f).

global flow. But then total heterogeneity turns into its opposite, an undifferentiated homogeneity where all are equally peripheral. Instead of abandoning these concepts, they can better be critically reinterpreted. De-differentiation is a problematic strategy, in research as in social life, for subcultures as for ethnic groups, as well as concerning the relation between spheres like ethics, aesthetics and politics or school, work, family and peer groups. To cross boundaries is interesting, productive and often rebellious, as is reflecting on them, problematizing them and moving them in opposition to frozen power structures. But to remove them completely is either futile or tendentially totalitarian. Spheres may be compared to rooms in a house – doors and windows are needed, some walls need to be moved and others torn down, but some walls, separations and differen-tiations are also needed for orientation or protection.

The deconstruction of binary patterns need not be conceived of as a romantic and very traditional dissolution of borders that unites everything that was separated, but rather as a critical reflection on difference and interplay that makes it possible to use the differentiated terms in a more flexible way. A reflexive differentiation is preferable to the de-differentiation wished by some postmodernists.[16] It is important to discuss the problematic connotations and limitations of concepts like margin (that the centre is fixed), hybrid (that the origins were pure) or diaspora (that most others still simply inhabit their confined spaces of home), but this deconstruction need not lead us to abandon them, since structural models are necessary to critical thinking and no other terms can permanently evade such problems. The futile search for pure concepts is in itself an expression of the same dread of hybrids that motivates it. The world society should be reduced neither to free flows nor to fixed units. A model may heuristically emphasize either side, but routes and flows get their meaning only in their interplay with roots and places, and vice versa.

Antonio Gramsci's Italian prison notebooks have greatly influenced how power and ideology have been theorized among later Marxists such as Althusser, Laclau and Hall.[17] Like Adorno, Benjamin, Brecht and Bloch in Weimar Germany, Gramsci emphasized the subjective factor and the cultural aspects of politics and power, against economic determinism. Many have found this useful as a way to enhance the feeling for the multidimensionality, changeability and relative autonomy of ideological struggle and political praxis. Gramsci's key concept of 'hegemony' in particular, related to 'consent' in 'civil society', and contrasted to the 'direct domination' within 'political society' or 'the State' (1971, p. 12), has

---

[16] One example is how Haraway (1989) affirms the dissolution by cybernetics of the difference between human being, animal and machine. There is a certain agreement between the stress of the differentiations of modernity against identity-philosophy in Habermas (1985/ 1987 and 1988/1992), and the war against totality and will to activate differences in Lyotard (1979/1984, p. 82).

[17] See Gramsci (1971); cf. Althusser (1965/1966), Althusser and Balibar (1968/1970), Laclau and Mouffe (1985), Hall (1986a), Laclau (1990) and Kenneth Thompson (1992).

been much used in later critical cultural studies. In this theoretical tradition, it refers to a type of ideological domination in which the ideological apparatuses of civil society (church, family, school, media and various organizations) act to legitimate class power among the dominated classes themselves. Economic forces or political constraints alone do not create consciousness in modern, complex societies; cultural and ideological hegemony is instead shaped by processes of 'articulation' in which various forces and discourses are tied together. In political and ideological struggles, flexible alliances are to be forged between critical intellectuals and different other social groups, particularly of the subordinate classes, in order to conquer hegemony and transform society in an emancipatory way. Old economistic models of static dominant ideology are thus put into motion, as a praxis of active articulation, disarticulation and rearticulation of cultural discourses can effectively change hegemonies.[18]

However, there still lingers a somewhat traditional and superficial concept of culture here. Culture easily tends to be reduced to a superstructural layer and a carrier of moral values or political contents, as the specific aesthetic forms of symbolic orders are neglected. Hegemony is an indispensable concept for analysing political power, but cultural processes cannot be seen only through this lens. Moreover, in spite of the wish to understand the late modern diversity of political struggles, the structuralist tradition persistently tends to look for ideological totalizations like 'the people' or 'the power-bloc' (Hall 1981).

Power is in various ways thematized by all of the theories discussed in this chapter, and here only one much discussed example will be given. In a series of investigations into the geneaology of social institutions, the French philosopher Michel Foucault has shown how modern human subjects are formed by practices involving micro-power, working on the human body. He stresses that power is not only constraining and restrictive repression, it is also mobilizing and enabling production: power not only prevents people from doing things, it also forces them to creative actions. The 'juridical model' of repressive power as flowing from a centralized source is only relevant within the more systemic sectors of society, whereas the 'disciplinary model' of power as exercised rather than possessed, coming from the bottom up and primarily productive rather than repressive, is of crucial importance in modern societies (cf. Kelly 1994, pp. 30ff and 374ff). Power involves a multiplicity of force relations immanent in a sphere, the struggling process which develops them, their mutual relations in chains, systems or contradictions, and the strategies in which they take effect, institutionally crystallized and embodied in the state apparatus and social hegemonies (Foucault 1974/1979, p. 17). Power is exercised both in intersubjective relations and through objectivized institutions: the micro-

---

[18] 'Hegemony' is a Greek term for leadership. It is related to the word 'seek', which also has to do with the act of tracing, directing, etc. Hegemony is possessed by those who show others the way.

powers of everyday life and the institutional macro-systems mediate each other. These social institutions and everyday practices are further integrated with communicative and cultural discourses. The will to knowledge is for Foucault always a will to power: compounds like 'discourse/practice' underline that knowledge-practices and power are inseparably united.[19] And while domination is a situation where resistance of the subjected has been effectively blocked, power relations are constantly called into question in struggles, so that power and resistance mutually imply each other.

While this perspective has been much used in recent cultural studies and is certainly usefully provocative, the formulations of the early, 'structuralist' Foucault and his later adherents are problematically totalizing and induce an unprecise oscillation between incompatible positions. If symbolic communication is so strongly bound to power, then no dialogic rationality seems possible, and it becomes hard to defend one's own theory as a critique of that all-encompassing power. On one hand, there is a tendency to sweepingly characterize 'The Power' as a ubiquitous hydra, whose observant eyes and disciplining organs leave no room for real communication or effective resistance. On the other hand, Foucault offers a very useful thematizing of the discursive or cultural aspects of decentred and dispersed micro-powers, stressing that power is no unidirectional force that can be possessed, but is an always concretely situated, mutual but asymmetrical, intersubjective relation. It is hard to reconcile theories of how societal discourses overdetermine subject positions that direct individual actors with ideas about resisting, transgressive counter-cultures. In later texts, Foucault avoids the total denunciation of reason in an effort to make space again for communication, subjectivity and resistance, retreating somewhat from the Nietzschean position and instead linking up with the Enlightenment tradition, especially with Immanuel Kant's ideas of autonomy.[20]

While disciplining (Foucault) is always the obverse of the civilizing process (Elias), it is important to understand these as ambivalent processes. The tools of supervision may serve power but can also be used for a lifeworld-based self-reflexivity that may increase the ability of individuals and groups to resist power by understanding how it works.

The Foucauldian analysis of power, thus, is paradoxical, but contains many useful elements which may productively be related to critical theory. Habermas and Foucault are often seen as antagonistic advocates of, respectively, a modern and a postmodern perspective, but in the 1980s a

[19] This view is directly inherited from Nietzsche and close to Adorno and Horkheimer (1944). Cf. Foucault (1969/1972), Millot (1988) and Sholle (1988).

[20] See Foucault (1982 and 1983/1984). De Certeau (1985, pp. 185ff) and many others have mentioned this inner tension between Foucault's earlier thesis of an all-seeing 'panoptical' system of surveillance and his own subversive writing. Giddens (1992, pp. 23f, 28ff and 172f) is critical of Foucault's overemphasis on the repressive aspects of modern sexuality and his neglect of the emancipatory potentials of reflexivity.

kind of convergence emerged.[21] Instead of rejecting the one or the other, it is possible to link their theories, not by just combining them, but by using the strengths of each to rework the other's weaknesses.[22] Habermas has, for example, been accused for being too universalizing in his search for intersubjectively valid rational foundations of normative judgements. But debates with feminists, anthropologists, communitarians and poststructuralists have led to an important sharpening of his awareness of how deeply divided the lifeworld is. He has increasingly emphasized the irreducible differentiations of modern society and the necessity of parallel life forms each with its specific norms for the content of a good life, and declared that the ethics of communicative discourse is positioned on a formal meta-level, concerning the coexistence of such life forms rather than their inner values and contents.

Systems and institutions

The modern distinction between lifeworld and systemic forces is crucial to the understanding of cultural practices. It has already been mentioned in relation to the corresponding twin set of rationalization processes, but the model deserves a closer inspection here. The following presentation is based on the writings of Habermas (e.g., 1981/1984–8 and 1992b).

The concept of lifeworld derives from phenomenology (Edmund Husserl and Alfred Schütz), and has been further developed both by sociology and hermeutics. The lifeworld is like a horizon or a hidden context for human thought and action. While a 'world' is that which people thematize in their communicative interpretations, the lifeworld is that which each such communicative utterance necessarily has to take for granted as its tacit and unconscious foundational support. It consists of the pre-understanding or the set of prejudices and background suppositions which is always culturally transmitted through tradition and from which one cannot wilfully escape. Inspired by hermeneutic and linguistic insights into the communicative and intersubjective character of understanding, Habermas defines the lifeworld as a culturally transmitted and symbolically organized stock of interpretive patterns, constituted by language and culture. It consists of the symbolic structures that make everyday communicative practices

---

[21] 'Now obviously, if I had been familiar with the Frankfurt School, if I had been aware of it at the time, I would not have said a number of stupid things that I did say and I would have avoided many of the detours which I made while trying to pursue my own humble path – when, meanwhile, avenues had been opened up by the Frankfurt School' (Foucault 1983/ 1994, p. 117). Cf. also Foucault (1982), Habermas (1984/1989 and 1985/1987) and Kelly (1994).

[22] See, e.g., Poster (1989) and Steuerman (1989), who both also add elements from Lyotard (1979/1984). Richters (1988) argues that the shared interest in processes of power and resistance motivates a dialogue between the theories of Habermas and Foucault. White (1988, pp. 113ff) compares their positions in relation to new social movements.

possible, and which rest on a material substratum that has to be reproduced through labour in order for people to survive. It thus combines work or production with interaction and communication.

The lifeworld is not only a delimiting horizon but also a resource which is used in each communicative act and has to be continuously reproduced in order to avoid serious disturbances or crises. It is a seat for that communicative action and understanding which its reproduction itself presupposes, in a delicate complexity. As a resource, it has three main components. First, it includes a stock of knowledge which has to be handed over by the cultural reproduction processes of tradition. Secondly, it is a society consisting of norms, institutions and other legitimate orders necessary for interpersonal relations, group formations and mutual solidarity, reproduced by processes of social integration. Thirdly, it contains individual persons: the identities, needs and competences for interaction inherent in each human being and reproduced through socialization. These components of the lifeworld are not fully separated systems, but crucially interconnected through sharing the same everyday language (and other symbolic modes) as their medium of interaction. The lifeworld is anchored and realized in various institutional settings (family, associations, etc.), but is not itself only the sum of these – it is a horizon and a resource for human interaction rather than a particular area or space for it.

Processes in the lifeworld can be analysed by close ethnographic studies or text analyses. But they are as incomplete without any concept of the overarching structures inherent in societal institutions as are macro-studies without some understanding of the practices of everyday life. The lifeworld is not all of human society. Human agents are not completely autonomous, but framed by externalized structural forces. Symbolic orders are challenged by economic and administrative ones which often blur and distort communication and block understanding. Society also has systemic features. A long evolutionary process has separated two subsystems from the lifeworld-flows: the market and the state apparatus, with money and administrative power as their respective main regulating tools. The commercial laws of commodity production have installed a logic of exchange-value which no late modern cultural activity can escape. This is also true for the pervasive administrative control mechanisms installed by the state apparatus and extending their influence deep into the sociality and identity formations of everyday life.[23]

These two systems are organizing forces more than clearly circumscribed areas. They do not constitute any 'world' in the phenomenological sense, but externalized systems outgrown from the social world. Their sometimes

[23] Foucault (1969/1972, pp. 68 and 162) talks of 'a field of non-discursive practices' and 'non-discursive domains (institutions, political events, economic practices and processes)', which neatly covers what Habermas identifies as systems. Kelly (1994, pp. 262 and 379) notes that Foucault's three-dimensional model of knowledge, normativity or power and subjectivity parallels Habermas's tripartite model of relations to the objective world the social world, and ourselves as subjects.

overlapping, sometimes conflicting demands structure a series of institutions like the media apparatuses, schools, work-places and leisure
organizations which frame everyday life. It is unfortunately common
among other social theorists to speak about lifeworld and 'system world' as
if they constituted two antithetically symmetrical spaces (cf. several
contributions in Calhoun 1992, e.g., pp. 340, 370 or 404). This creates a
misleading image of systems as social spaces, while they are more like sets
of rules for regulating interaction. While the lifeworld is like a universe in
which people live, and while the objective, social, cultural and subjective
fields of experience may also be described as a series of worlds, the market
and the state do not in the same way encircle people and should better be
described as externalized systems than as a 'world'.

Moreover, it is also crucial to remember that these subsystems are *two*
different ones, even though they share a goal-oriented efficiency, in
contrast to the lifeworld. To see them as one single, unified mega-system is
to underestimate their mutual contradictions and to overestimate their
corporative lack of animosity. They have some interests in common, but
their differences and mutual conflicts are of great importance also for
cultural politics and counter-cultural movements.

The capitalist form of modernization both develops and distorts the
potential for rationality inherent in intersubjective communication.
Western social evolution, building upon multidimensional learning processes and the capability for institutionalization, has differentiated systems
and lifeworld from each other and internally, bringing about systemic
growth and an increase in rationality of both kinds, with complicated
patterns of interference. This historical modernization process can be
summarized in five main steps.

First, the lifeworld is rationalized by means of a differentiated institutionalization of its constituent elements. Separate institutions start to
grow around the main types of strategic and communicative action. This
differentiation and condensation of communication processes enables
language to reflect upon these constituents as separate abstract categories,
open to criticism. General lifeworld structures are abstracted from the
concrete plurality of actual life forms, creating a stock of culturally
transmitted knowledge. Formal, discursive procedures arise for debating
social norms. Mental structures and identity forms are generalized,
enabling an acknowledgement of the abstract individuality and subjectivity
of human beings. In all these dimensions, general forms are successively
abstracted from concrete embodiments, as embryonic institutions for
production, distribution and power, knowledge, ethics and socialization
develop each of these action areas and open roads towards increasing
reflexivity, universality and individuation.

This process starts early in history, though it reaches its peak with late
modern globalization, connecting the lifeworlds of separate societies into
one continuous lifeworld, a joint human horizon of habits, prejudices,
basic ethical patterns and subject forms. Simultaneous differentiation

processes fragment this lifeworld into multiplying but coexisting life forms, ways of living or subcultures. Society becomes universal but like a divided macro-subject: a decentred network of interlacing life forms. The lifeworld is an aggregate of several particular but connected 'lifeworlds', whose mutual interlacing through communicative action binds society together, in spite of all its diversity.[24] This simultaneous process of homogenization and pluralization starts already with communication itself.

In a second step on a certain evolutionary stage, the steering means of money and the delegation of administrative power are institutionalized as relatively autonomous from communicative lifeworld practices, resulting in the formation of separate systems for market economy and state government. This triggers an accelerated systemic rationalization which makes them increasingly effective, complex and disengaged from the lifeworld.

These systems relieve the pressure on the lifeworld and release its communicative potentials for issues other than the allocation of material resources and collective steering. If there were no economic or administrative systems, complex societies would have to spend immense time and energy on discussing which needs to fulfil and how to make joint decisions. No room would be left for developing knowledge, norms, subjective experiences or aesthetic play. The systemic rationalization through money and power enables the lifeworld to develop its communicative rationality still further, in a process that both erodes traditional life forms and makes possible modern, more flexible and reflexive ones.

This whole process involves a dense interplay between the complexity of communicative practices in everyday life and the specialized lifeworld institutions for science, law, socialization and art. These areas each produce their own expert structures, but they continue to be connected back to everyday communicative forms, particularly through their use of verbal language. Scientists, for example, intensely develop forms of understanding external nature, but this search for knowledge is never completely cut off from the similar quest for knowing in daily life. Scientific concepts build upon symbolic tools emerging in the lifeworld, which they simultaneously further enhance and rationalize.

In a third step, the capitalist form of modernization has a problematic tendency to let the twin systems grow enormously and colonize the lifeworld. The logics of money and power intrude in areas where communicative processes of understanding are indispensable for the reproduction of lifeworld constituents. Their goal-oriented strategic rationality becomes more and more effective, and tends to impose principles of efficiency,

---

[24] Cf. Habermas (1981/1984–8) and Thyssen (1991, pp. 9ff and 116f). Habermas (1992a, pp. 444f) explicitly talks about 'particularized forms of life and lifeworlds' in the plural, especially 'in posttraditional societies in which a homogeneity of background convictions cannot be assumed and in which a presumptively shared class interest has given way to a confused pluralism of competing and equally legitimate forms of life.'

profit and control on areas of understanding, ethics, aesthetics and identity. But 'meaning can neither be bought nor coerced' (Habermas in Honneth and Joas 1986/1991, p. 259): symbolic communication aiming at mutual understanding of shared meanings is necessary to reproduce the constituents of the lifeworld. The colonization process gives rise to social reproduction crises and pathologies: deficits of legitimation of authority, motivation for political action and education, identity distortions, etc. There is an irony in the modernization process in that the rationalization of the lifeworld makes possible a heightened systemic complexity and hypertrophy which in its turn threatens the very reproduction of this lifeworld.

In a fourth step, this problematic twin tendency towards excessive commercialization and bureaucratization then gives rise to defence mechanisms of the lifeworld, in the form of counter-movements resisting the expansive systemic demands and intensifying the development of a communicative rationality in the lifeworld. Such lifeworld resistance includes political pressure on the state to guarantee citizens' rights, in the form of waves of juridification – the institution of individual rights; the democratization of the political order with constitutional parliamentarism and free elections; and the rise of the social welfare state protecting freedoms and rights against the economic system. New social movements such as those around issues of feminism, youth, peace or ecology have shaped counter-institutions and autonomous public spheres where cultural practices are crucial, since the development of richer communicative forms implies experiments with alternative forms of life, interaction and meaning-making. Such movements are sometimes problematically particularistic or even regressively anti-modern, but they often try out important emancipatory steps towards a richer and stronger communicative rationality. In any case, they are necessary means to increase society's reflexivity around the disproportions between lifeworld and systems.

This accumulated complex of processes increases the rational potentiality of the lifeworld by means of those insights and the reflexivity which are provoked by the problems as such. It might be this fifth step that for the first time in history makes the lifeworld as a whole discernible to us, even though it of course can never become fully transparent, but must in principle remain a hidden horizon for our actions and thoughts. Social processes have created totalizing problems for the reproduction of the lifeworld as a whole, which in its turn makes people acknowledge the existence of its general structures as such. Modern society develops reflexive interactional forms that are used to disclose the rules and logics of communicative action itself, as a result of the provoking threat that systemic colonization presents to these symbolic structures in the lifeworld as a whole. With this conclusion, Habermas (1981/1988) also sketches out a historicizing explanation for the possibility of his own theory as a real abstraction, emerging out of actual social practices rather than invented out of thin air.

The relation between lifeworld and systems should not be confused with the polarity between traditional and modern. It is a mistake to think of the lifeworld as a linear reproduction of pre-modern structures of meaning and life forms, while simply identifying modernization with the growth of systemic rationality. The systems have long historic roots back towards commodity exchange and state formations in pre-capitalist societies. And modernization also resides within the lifeworld, through the chiselling of a differentiated communicative rationality. The whole division between systems and lifeworld is a modern phenomenon that dissolves previous unities and creates new differences and interrelations. Modern culture cannot be reduced to an increasingly system-oriented goal-rational communication, but also contains normative, aesthetic and expressive potentials that were previously inconceivable. The colonization of the lifeworld by the systems through tendencies of commercialization and bureaucratization is only the one, dystopian or authoritarian, side of modernization, mediatization and reflexivity – the other, emancipatory side is a rising communicative capacity and rationality.

One of the two systems, the state with its bureaucracy, has developed a particular institutional sphere for the execution of political decisions. Here, power is a specific tool for steering and interaction. In democratic societies, the citizens elect their parliamentary representatives, delegate their decisions to them and must then obey their injunctions. On the basis of a shared acknowledgement of legitimate power distribution for common, societal issues, a special bureaucracy is built up. This system is necessary for the regulation of common affairs, but its modern rationalization has dysfunctional sides in that its emphasis on instrumental and strategic action forms has a tendency to spread outside of the areas where it is legitimate. Its power structures tend to invade the lifeworld.

Administrative power is the particular steering tool of the state system, while the other, economic market system uses money as its specific tool of co-ordination. The influence this commodity order has on people runs primarily through the workings of economic mechanisms. In practice, other kinds of dominance and power are often also used, and the two systems are sometimes hardly separable. Yet, there exist societal rules and codes that regulate the principal spheres and limits of these systems, and the fact that people are usually alert to when these limits are overstepped indicates that these rules are at least to some extent efficacious, both as ideals and as real functioning principles.

Castoriadis (1989/1992, p. 282) emphasizes, however, that power and the state should not be completely identified: 'Neither explicit power, nor domination need to take the form of the State.' He warns against 'the mixing up of *the* political, the dimension of explicit power, with the overall institution of society'. To him, politics is about 'explicit power' and the striving for autonomy through created institutions. This is only a section of social life, but it touches more than just the state apparatus. But even if various other public spheres are also involved in politics, it seems clear that the state has a particular position within the political field, and that it develops specific forms of power to regulate society.

Power also cuts through the lifeworld, in the form of personal, social and cultural relations of dominance. These can either exploit individual coercion or be bound to and legitimated by social hierarchies associated with categories of age, gender, ethnicity, race or class.[25] They are not differentiated out the lifeworld but deeply embedded in it, cutting through all everyday social interaction. The lifeworld is no system, but neither is it any wide-open, homogeneous, conflict-free or equal flow of communicative actions. Both the systems and the lifeworld contain tensions between dynamizing actions and stabilizing structures (and between negotiations and contracts that regulate them). The lifeworld also contains its own institutional arrangements that strive to regulate interaction. But in contrast to market economy and state administration, they are primarily directed towards communication and use money and power only as a secondary tool.

Habermas (1992b, pp. 182ff, 208ff, 351, 400 and 622) differentiates between four types of power. *Administrative power* is the systemic form executed by state professionals. *Social power* is a dominance by individual or collective, spontaneous or organized interests within lifeworld practices: the general capability in social relations to have one's own way, even against the resistance of others. Social power can but need not be illegitimate, strategic or goal-oriented. If it is instead a form of influence based on the force of better arguments, in rational debates on validity claims where people aim at convincing others, it becomes *communicative power*, which is essential for any democratic decision processes.[26] *Political power* finally works as a transmission between social or communicative power, on one hand, and the administrative power system, on the other, as a collectively organized form of social power in political parties or movements, directed towards affecting and controlling the state. It does so with the aid of justice and judicial procedures which are meant to institutionally guarantee that social power is not allowed directly to steer the administrative power of the state. Such differentiations make it possible to avoid a problematic abstract choice between naïvely idealizing the lifeworld as the opposite of (administrative) power or almost cynically accepting that (social) power is everywhere. Power in general comprises all these forms, but will here denote its non-communicative forms: the specific context of each instance of the term will hopefully make it clear whether it is administrative power or social power which is not communicatively

---

[25] Thyssen (1991) argues that the systems cannot be distinguished by money and power, since both these steering mechanisms are used by both systems and in the lifeworld as well. Both money and power also presuppose communication and meaning: it is necessary to understand that money symbolizes value and that decisions have to be followed. Still, each system develops a specific order around each of these steering tools, and their use in the lifeworld constitutes an interface between everyday interaction and systemic forces.

[26] This concept is inspired by Arendt (1958).

legitimated that is implied. Whereas resistance to non-legitimate social and administrative power is necessary, it cannot ultimately avoid using political power and should in fact *strengthen* the communicative power of language use and symbolic interaction.

In the lifeworld, individuals, thus, are positioned in a plurality of dominance forms. Some of them are supported by systemic forces, as when white men occupy the high positions in state or market institutions. But everyday communication is also in itself permeated with various domination efforts, intimately connected to strivings for knowledge, justice and well-being. The micro-powers of the lifeworld relate to systemic forces but cannot as easily be delimited to specific institutions or steering mechanisms. They evolve through language itself and presuppose that symbolic forms manage to create meaning and understanding. Otherwise neither threats nor manipulation would function at all.

The relations between the systems and the lifeworld involve not only power but also resistance. Resistance is needed within the lifeworld itself, since it is no peaceful oasis of community and benevolence, but crisscrossed by sexism, racism and other dominance relations. This gives rise to complex nets of intersecting and often contradictory power/resistance patterns, inviting a multifront strategy of flexible alliances. Either system may be used as a tool to counteract injustices and unfreedoms created by strategic actions in everyday life.

Some social groups criticize commercial interests, others revolt against the state apparatus. Their critique cannot always be defended, since both systems seem to be necessary in modern, complex societies, and since some such movements of resistance suffer from a potentially oppressive puritanism and/or a 'terroristic' aggressivity. But they are important symptoms of systemic colonization tendencies and the need to keep both market and state in their place. Even common daily life contains micro-resistances against commercial and bureaucratic mechanisms, including alternative learning processes partly outside of the goal-oriented apparatuses of established institutions, playing with cultural forms that give rise to knowledge, meaning, community, identity, autonomy, new normative ideals and unforeseen pleasure. These critical and utopian potentials elaborate the emancipatory sides of communicative action.

State institutions have a problematic tendency to circumscribe the freedom of citizens by normalizing and disciplining practices. An unhampered market mechanism only offers freedom to the few who can pay for what they need, at the expense of the poorer majority. Similar threats are directed towards equality and justice, both from unfair market rules and from a central state apparatus dominated by societal élites. The school system is, for example, an enormous resource for the acquisition of knowledge, but it is simultaneously engaged in disciplining the working classes and sorting pupils into an unequal labour market.

Resistance against oppression is as important as struggle against injustices. To identify market with freedom and state with equality is to short-circuit. The capitalist market has a historical tendency to dissolve traditional fetters, but it also re-creates certain lacks of freedom, for example in the way it forces the majority to sell its labour-power in order to survive. Letting the market loose will therefore not increase people's freedom, if it is not hampered by a continuing social and political engagement within the lifeworld, assisted by the civil rights and liberties guaranteed by the judicial system of the state apparatus. While the laws and measures of the state can be used as instruments for increasing equality, they are not in themselves sufficient. They need to be accompanied by actions in other spheres, concerning norms and relations in social movements and everyday life, etc.

Equality and freedom condition each other. Freedom from oppression is needed if nobody is to live at the expense of others, and equal life conditions are needed if nobody is to be unfree. Freedom without equality would be a slaughter-house, equality without freedom a prison. The freedom of an unequal society is only for the few, and in the long run not even for these élites, because of the hate born in the marginalized masses. The equality of an unfree society is a similarity worth nothing.

It is essential to distinguish between equality and similarity: equal rights are only possible if differences are respected. Studies of youth, women and ethnicity have emphasized the need to separate justice from standardization, and to avoid being stuck between separateness and likeness. Both institutions and movements may lose their respect for differences, for the Other, for the stranger. There is a general need for learning to endure the insight that one's own way of life is far from the only legitimate one.

Around the systemic spheres of state (politics) and market (economy) are spread a series of institutional spheres between and within which people move and which function as social arenas for struggles of power and resistance. These institutional spheres are primarily social in their definition but they also have spatial aspects. Some rooms and spaces are erected and dominated by certain institutions: in a school building other rules of behaviour apply than in a shopping centre. Institutions constitute spatial spheres, networks of localities and places that are permeated by their more or less systemic codes and principles. They frame fields of action for interacting individuals. Their rules and resources both make actions possible and limit their scope. They are often influenced by the economic and political systems, but they also have lifeworld aspects. They are arenas where people act and communicate around knowledge, norms, identities and meanings. Institutions mediate between systemic demands and lifeworld horizons and thus are no pure systemic organs. They are dependent on the ordering principles of both systems, but also on communicative action based in the lifeworld. While some institutions (like the stock exchange or the ministry) are very close to one of the systems, others (like the critical journal, the rave club or the family) are closer to the lifeworld. The concept of *civil society* denotes the institutional dimension of the lifeworld, that is, the non-systemic (relatively autonomous of state and

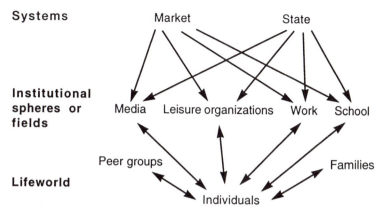

Figure 3.1   *Institutional spheres*

market) part of society.[27] Civil society is thus also the social aspect of the lifeworld, rather than the cultural one of symbolic communication flows. Such more or less spontaneously emerging lifeworld groupings, associations, organizations and movements collectively organize the reproduction of traditions and knowledge, solidarities and community, identity and socialization. Ideally, they are independent of the systems, but in practice there is always a mixture of systemic and lifeworld principles, in varying proportions (see Figure 3.1).[28]

Institutions often collide. There is a main opposition between those which orient themselves towards the market and those which are mainly state-supported. State interventions in cultural life are sometimes motivated by a wish to counteract the negative effects of commercialism, while the supply of the market is frequently offering compensation for and liberation from the gloominess and coercion caused by school and other state-oriented spheres. But there is also much co-operation and exchange between institutions, including those that lean on opposite systems.

Mutual conflicts between institutions are not only created by differing systemic demands. Their organizational principles and goals may collide for other reasons as well. There might be unclear borders or overlappings between their spheres of activities, which can cause confusion or conflicts. It is sometimes unclear when to leave one type of institution and enter another, the boundaries between social strata are unprecise, and different activities may collide in their needs of space, localities, economic resources or their clients' time.

Institutions are not obedient tools of the systems (mainly the state). They do not only discipline and control, but also frame social life, care and

[27] Cf. Gramsci (1971, pp. 207f and 257ff), Cohen and Arato (1989/1992 and 1992) and Habermas (1992b, pp. 443ff).

[28] Cf. Berger and Luckmann (1966/1984) and Habermas (1981/1984–8 and 1992b).

the creation of welfare and justice. State organs have an important task in counteracting problems in the market system (including the labour market). Politically decided state interventions are ideally tools of the lifeworld to regulate society. It is, for example, important that social institutions act against oppression and inequality both within the market and within the lifeworld, through legislation and active support of threatened minorities. The model of systems and lifeworld should thus not fool anyone into regarding the former as evil and the latter as good. Neither should one rally to the uncritical support of any of the systems as a purely good force against the other, evil one. The relevance of all this for cultural policy will be discussed at the end of the section on public spheres below.

The market sphere is continually expanding throughout modernity. The neoliberal offensive of the 1980s and the inclusion of the post-communist nations in the capitalist world-order gave extra momentum to this trend. The cultural industries constitute a crucial factor for cultural theory. The state sphere has simultaneously increased its engagement in various processes of culture and socialization, through the general prolongation of education and an expansive sector of leisure provisions. In both these ways, systemic forces invade the lifeworld, with positive and negative effects. This double systemic rationalization offers people more resources and practical solutions to social problems, but it also breeds crises of legitimation and motivation. Both a commercial profit-orientation and a bureacratic control-orientation threaten to impose instrumental regulations on the production of sociality, meaning and identity that must use communicative means.

Four late modern tendencies can be discerned in the interrelations between systems and lifeworld. The first two can be summarized in the formula of 'systemic colonization of the lifeworld', while the last two concern the relation between the systems.

First, a continuous commercialization process pulls more and more life areas into the economic market sphere. Capitalist mass media, cultural industries and consumption supply leave few areas of life untouched. This opens new possibilities for attaining goods and services that were formerly inaccessible to most. But the expansive commodity form also has three problematic constraints. First, it only distributes use-values to those who can pay for them and thus reproduces inequalities. Secondly, it induces the dual phenomena of alienation and fetishization: commodification reifies living social relations while producing a magic aura around dead products. Thirdly, the private ownership of means of production and the exchange mechanisms create an opacity and a separation of consumers, producers and owners, where direct influence is concentrated in the latter and where the ones who make and who use the products know little of the total process and have only indirect influence over it.

The second tendency is that state institutions have increasingly entered areas that were formerly left to the dialectics between market forces and the spontaneously formed socialities of the lifeworld (families, peers, etc.).

One example is the growing amount of organized cultural activities in state-supported organizations, schools and clubs, especially aimed at children and adolescents. This leads to institutionalization, formalization and bureaucratization, making cultural practices more fixed and regulated. It also leads to a pedagogization in that cultural activities become more similar to schools, with leaders/teachers, handbooks or written goals and plans. There is, thirdly, an instrumentalization in that culture is subsumed under external goals when, for instance, young people are offered music festivals mainly to counteract drug-use or to keep them off the streets during noisy weekends. All elements of this second set of tendencies are probably strongest in those European countries where the state and the old popular movements (like trade unions, Free Churches or the temperance movement) have traditionally been relatively strong and centralized, particularly within the extensive apparatus for public and professional socialization (day-care, schools, higher education, social services and public service media).

A third late modern tendency is that tasks and resources that have belonged to the state sphere are privatized, mainly to diminish the pressure of taxation and clean up the state finances. A neoliberal ideological offensive has argued that this also increases people's freedom of choice, and it may in some instances be true that there has been a substantial widening of the scope of services that are offered by the market, in comparison with the sometimes more uniform state provisions. But this is far from always true – privatization gives free space for monopolizing market mechanisms that may equally threaten the diversity that a public organization at least has the potential to uphold, depending on its choice of organizing principles and ideology. And the exchange-value mechanism of commercialization always implies a reallocation of resources from the poor to the rich. Without any patronizing morality, cultural industries may offer products for every taste, but they are only attainable by those who can pay.

If, then, there is a general movement from the lifeworld to both systems and from the state to the market, a fourth tendency is for the boundaries between the systems to become more permeable. The struggle against commercialism seems to have lost its role as a central motive for state cultural policy, and there is more and more collaboration between state authorities and private sponsors. It would, however, be premature to say that the two systems have become one, and while they have in fact always grown in mutual co-operation, important differences and conflicts persist. As with the other tendencies, there are also plenty of counter-tendencies.

Movements

Some institutions are explicitly constituted in opposition to established structures, for example to resist some demands from one or both of the systems. Such counter-institutions may later be integrated and subsumed under systemic demands, if they survive at all, but what gives them life and force is their anchoring in social movements.

Movements are collective formations that move, try to re-move power structures and move society. They are characterized by collective action in deliberate co-operation between people to change the prevailing social order, and by the activity and will of each participant to realize these goals.[29] Movements produce and use more or less institutionalized organizations, through which they form and move, and with which they move social power relations. Movements react against unsatisfactory states of things, they resist power structures, and they contain a progressive, utopian moment as they contribute to societal change that emancipates and liberates people from oppressive constraints. Sometimes movements converge and collaborate in their critique of prevailing conditions and in some of their strategies and utopias. But in many cases they collide with each other, by being moved by differing interests and raising opposing demands.

Many social movements try to push systemic demands back, as defensive reactions to the tendencies of both systems to colonize the lifeworld. But they also have offensive traits that point towards alternative solutions and test the potentials of a wider, communicative rationality that is not only turned against destructive systemic forces but is also an autonomous development of the emancipatory potentials of the modernized lifeworld. By explicitly aiming at problematic social issues and thematizing them in symbolic forms, movements help to make power structures more visible. Anonymous or concealed forms of dominance become more manifest as a result of concrete counter-actions against them.[30]

> The actors become visible only where a field of public conflict arises; otherwise they remain in a state of latency. Latency does not mean inactivity. Rather, the potential for resistance or opposition is sewn into the very fabric of daily life. It is located in the molecular experience of the individuals or groups who practice the alternative meanings of everyday life. Within this context, resistance is not expressed in collective forms of conflictual mobilizations. Specific circumstances are necessary for opposition and therefore of mobilizing and making visible this latent potential. (Melucci 1989, pp. 70f)

Melucci thinks of social movements as 'nomads of the present', that in their mobility make the forms of power visible and that mobilize those hidden resistance potentials within everyday life without which these movements would not exist. He further argues that more recent social movements tend to let the present acitivities be more than just means to a distant end, that they construct more invisible networks than the publicly visible mass

---

[29] Friberg and Galtung (1984, p. 13). Negt and Kluge (1972/1993) and Fornäs (1979, 1990a and b, 1993) study how movements create alternative institutions and public spheres.

[30] Cf. Habermas (1981/1984–8, 1985/1987 and 1992b), Dowe (1986), Eyerman (1987), Arato and Cohen (1988), Cohen and Arato (1989/1992 and 1992), Melucci (1989), Eyerman and Jamison (1991), Henrik Kaare Nielsen (1991), Thörn (1991), Carle and Peterson (1992) and Fornäs and Bolin (1992).

organization of the old movements, and that their collective actions are more tolerant with regard to internal differences and diversity. New social movements do not function like unitary subjects – they converge and crystallize as collective actions out of a plurality of different motives, perspectives and relations. New movements are more than ever giving attention to information and culture, as an expression of general late modern tendencies towards reflexivity, mediatization and aestheticiation of politics, economy and daily life. They also become more and more mediated themselves, which makes it increasingly hard to define them in any simple way. When the collective action of movements can take place through mediated communication, it becomes hard to distinguish unambiguously between movements and the subcultures that will be discussed below.

The growth of nationalist, separatist, fundamentalist, neoconservative and/or racist movements complicates the situation still further. They are certainly symptoms of societal problems, power relations, etc., but how can they be classified? If only movements with emancipatory and power-subversive traits are labelled social movements, then there will be unending discussions on where the line is to be drawn. The most authoritarian and reactionary movement may contain some moment of critique against other power centres, as when today's racist rhetoric attacks the central democratic government or parts of international big business in the name of local community. If, instead, all such movements are joined under the same label, it becomes very vague indeed. What is valid for youth, feminist, ecology and leftist movements is seldom correct for neo-fundamentalism and only partly for ethnic or regionalist movements. A differentiation of the concept seems necessary, and a separation of reactionary or conservative from progressive, radical or emancipatory movements does not suffice, since there are also important differences within each camp.

As with public sphere theory below, theories of social movements and civil society cannot avoid normative issues. Their ideal-typical models, where the theorists often strongly sympathize with some of the demands put forward by the movements in question, tend to blur the distinction between how social spheres really work and how they ought to function. But this opening towards the normative dimensions of political and ethical issues is also a strength. After all, cultural theory has to find some terms to discuss the crucial question that also motivates itself: What *is* emancipatory?

> I define emancipatory politics as a generic outlook concerned above all with liberating individuals and groups from constraints which adversely affect their life chances. Emancipatory politics involves two main elements: the effort to shed shackles of the past, thereby permitting a transformative attitude towards the future; and the aim of overcoming the illegitimate domination of some individuals or groups by others. The first of these objectives fosters the positive dynamic impetus of modernity. Emancipatory politics is concerned to reduce or eliminate *exploitation*, *inequality* and *oppression*. (Giddens 1991, pp. 210f)

Public spheres

That which is public is open and accessible to everyone, or the common
affair of in principle an all-inclusive number of people, in contrast to the
private: that which is intimate, closed to the unwarranted or the business of
only a strictly limited number of persons (down to only one single
individual).[31] Public spheres in reality create their own groups and
boundaries, but if they are to be considered public, they should at least in
principle have the crucial double openness that everyone may enter them
and that new themes may always be raised in the communication they
organize. Private spheres may involve a group of people, but they are
essentially not open to all. The public and the private are logically,
etymologically, historically and juridically each other's opposites.

A theory of public spheres was developed in the early 1960s by Jürgen
Habermas, developing ideas of Immanuel Kant.[32] In pre-capitalist
societies, the boundaries were diffuse: neither the private nor the public
existed in any clear, modern sense. The feudal, 'representative' public
sphere had not yet installed institutions for an open public of citizens, and
it often mixed the public with the private, for example in the role of the
ruler. The aristocratic ruler presented himself to the people, representing
power by his own symbolically enacted personal appearance. No democratic system protected the common interests of all citizens, and no clear
rules separated them from the private sphere of the individual.

The rise of the 'bourgeois' or 'civic' public sphere also created the
private. As fora and channels for public debate and activity evolved, walls
were also erected around the private enterprises, on one hand, and private
family life, on the other. All this modern public/private polarity evolved in
a dialectical process, together with the growth and generalization of
capitalist industrialism, the working class and the modern state. The new
public sphere functioned as mediator between state, market and individual, that is, systems and lifeworld. Its main form was civic and bourgeois
at once, in principle open to each citizen but in reality dominated by the
rising bourgeois middle classes. As civic, it appears as the collectively
communicative part of civil society, which in its turn is the institutional
aspects of the lifeworld. Other public arenas, anchored in popular or
working-class social strata, interacted with this dominant bourgeois one,
and they were successively amalgamated into a wider general public

---

[31] The Latin term *pūblicus* does not, as might be expected, derive from *pŏpulus* (people),
but from *pūbēs* – mature, adult or, more precisely, adult male youth; cf. 'puberty': to reach
manhood. It therefore denoted the affairs of the adult men(!) who constituted the free citizens
of antique society. The term 'publish' has the same roots. In Germanic languages the
corresponding term *öffentlich* simply means that which is open, and is thus not gender-biased.
The Latin *prīvātus* denotes individual affairs which are outside the reach of the common
affairs of the state, originating in the word *prīvus*, separate, which is interestingly enough also
the root of 'privilege' by addition of *lēgis*, a form of *lēx* (law).

[32] Habermas (1962/1989); cf. also Arendt (1958), Calhoun (1992) and John B. Thompson
(1993).

Lifeworld	Exchange relations	Systems

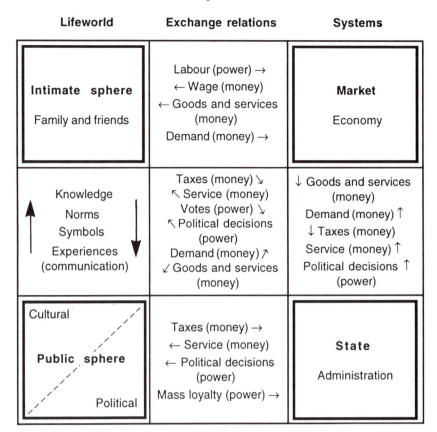

Figure 3.2 *Exchanges between spheres*

sphere, internally differentiated into various subpublic spheres, which are often related to class, gender, age and ethnic divisions in the population.

As soon as the modern public sphere was born, it started to transform. There is a continuous struggle on the borders between public and private, a struggle that constitutes and reproduces them both. As the result of this struggle, the private and the public are sometimes clearly distinct areas, sometimes overlapping tendencies.

Figure 3.2 outlines some relations between the main societal spheres, including some typical examples of their mutual exchange flows.[33] The distinction between private and public spheres is strictly separate from the one discussed earlier between systems and lifeworld. The private/public distinction cuts across the lifeworld by separating the intimate sphere from cultural and political public spheres (i.e., a division within the left part of

[33] The figure combines and extends the ones in Habermas (1962/1989, p. 30, and 1981/ 1988, p. 320). Exchanges also take place inside each sphere, as when money circulates in the market or opinions inside public discourses (and may travel between its cultural and political branches).

the figure). It also runs between the two systems (the right part of the figure). The *intimate sphere* or inner space of the more or less nuclear family and personal friendships is the private sector of the lifeworld. Here, people are individual persons in kinship groups and close communities. The *market* consists of economic interests accumulating capital through wage labour in private enterprises and publicly exchanging commodities and services with money as equivalent. Here, people are owners, workers and consumers. The *state* is a particular apparatus of public, administrative power for organizing common affairs, in which people are citizens and clients. It is ideally publicly controlled but should in its systemic and bureaucratic nature be distinguished from the public institutions of the lifeworld which organize communication around political or cultural issues. This genuinely *public sphere* is thus basically a network for communication, using communicative action to create a social space for individuals and groups to exchange meanings. It can be separated into one political and one cultural branch, with parties, movements, organizations and journals, on one hand, and publishers, theatres, concert houses, museums and all other cultural institutions, on the other. Mass media work in both of these branches. Here, people act as communicating subjects. The public and cultural spheres function as mediators between the private intimate sphere of the lifeworld and the two systems. While the political public sphere relates more to the state, the cultural public sphere also scrutinizes the market. It is highly unfortunate that the cultural branch of the public sphere has not been as intensely discussed and theorized as the political one. The forming of a general but often divided 'public opinion' is only one half of the story; it is quite as important to study how various publics use symbolic modes of expression to share aesthetic ideas, tastes and lifestyles. It is this cultural segment of the public sphere which stands in focus here.[34]

The usage of terms like public, society and state is characteristically diffuse in modern discourses. They are often confused in ideological formulations. The so-called 'public sector' of state institutions is something other than the true public sphere of the lifeworld. In most social theories the distinction between state and ('bourgeois' or 'civil') society is crucial. Society in this sense has more to do with the sum of the market and the two (intimate and public) spheres of the lifeworld than with the state apparatus.

Actors close to the state system are particularly apt to make these simple identifications, which make legitimation problems and power aspects of state authorities in relation to the lifeworld invisible. Actors closer to the market instead tend to make the distinction between the intimate sphere and the private economic sphere diffuse, as when the privatization of services is motivated by families' and individuals' rights of self-determination. The varying interpretations of the public/private distinction

---

[34] Habermas always (from 1962/1989 to 1992b) tends to focus on the political aspects of the public sphere: its functions in the making of political opinions, checking the state, etc.

in different times, countries or interest groups give valuable clues to strong ideological figures that use such conceptual slippages. In theoretical models, a much clearer use of the concepts is needed, in order to avoid paradoxical self-contradictions.

The public sphere in a strict sense is thus a particular set of lifeworld institutions for organizing discursive communities or socialities. But the term 'public' can be used in a much wider and more general sense as well. First, the democratic state has a certain public character in standing in principle for the common interests of its citizens rather than representing special private interests. Secondly, working in a larger private company usually means participating in a collective community that does not belong to the public sphere, nor to the 'public' (state) sector, but certainly feels more public to the individual than the family at home or the closest circle of private friends. Thirdly, within the intimate sphere of the lifeworld there is also a micro-phenomenological gradation in degrees of publicness, from the most intimate and secret rooms of one's own to the living-rooms where family members interact with each other and with friends and visiting strangers. Similar experiential gradations may exist in other localities as well, for example between the toilets, fitting rooms, staff localities and counters of a shopping centre. There are thus a range of different ways to apply the terms 'public' and 'private' to social phenomena, and it is important not to confuse them.

The public/private distinction is often mixed with the system/lifeworld relation. When one expresses a wish to protect a space of one's own from public view or instead to break isolation and meet others in open communication, this may relate to the basic private/public division. But a wish to be left alone may also express a need to protect the lifeworld from systemic colonization by state authorities or market tentacles; in this case one may try to avoid public visibility in certain system-oriented institutions (like school or media) while simultaneously moving freely in various (counter-)public spheres (like city streets or rave parties).

Public discourses lodge communicative processes. There must always be a dialogue of different voices in order to produce discussions. Discourse, communication and public spheres are not only about producing consensus, but also about letting differing sides formulate themselves in relation to each other. Public debates use linguistic and symbolic forms of expression to argue about facts, norms, styles and identities. Different individuals and groups have differing ideals and views which meet and confront each other in public spheres, without necessarily becoming one. Public spheres do not make subjects alike or even necessarily united – they also thematize differences and make them explicit. They open spaces for polyphonous dialogues of separate voices more than for a chorus. Dialogues do not erase differences. Reasoning and resonance, rational argumentation and concordant harmony are not synonymous terms.[35]

---

[35] 'Reason' derives from the Latin *ratiō*, 'resonance' from *re-sonāre* (resound).

Habermas has been accused by some critics of over-stressing the consensual aspect of communication in the lifeworld, including the public sphere.[36] To some post-modernists, this is a reason to dismiss these theories totally, while other authors think it is a good motive for improvements. Ricoeur has, for example, questioned Habermas's 'over-estimation of the power of persuasion by discussion . . . the assertion that finally the extension of discussion will be enough to change things' (1986, p. 298) The theories of public spheres and communicative action may well be developed towards a stronger emphasis on dialogicity.[37] Public discourses are hybrid processes where communicative action aiming at understanding is always mixed with strategic action aiming at success through manipulation of the other. Thyssen (1991, pp. 190f) mentions three possible results of communication. Conflicts may dissolve and consensus arise. Or conflicts may endure but consensus be reached on how to handle them, for example in negotiation, voting or compromises instead of violence. A third possible outcome is that no unity is reached at all, neither on the content nor on the form of the conflict. The resulting 'open war' still involves communication with certain game-rules, but interaction is then based more on strategic action than aiming at understanding. Against all consensualist idealizations of actual ongoing communication, it must be emphasized that as a mixture of strategic and communicative action it always both manipulates and strives for shared understanding.

As shown by Habermas (1992b, pp. 201ff), compromises reached through negotiation are still to some extent based on rational discourses aiming at consensus, in that they presuppose a normative agreement on which techniques for measuring interests are legitimate. This also implies that the formation of political opinion cannot be reduced to the strategic making of compromises, but also includes crucial communicative processes of testing validity of social norms. Modern politics is thus a complicated net of discourses, negotiations and power plays, rather than a plain exercise of strategic force.

The specific organization of the public sphere in modernity is crucially biased by the fact that this modernity is capitalist, bourgeois, patriarchal and Eurocentric. Like modernity itself, its public sphere is ambivalent – it contains emancipatory potentials but also intrinsic limitations. Negt and Kluge (1972/1993) stress that the public sphere is 'bourgeois', since it evolved in capitalist society and mainly engaged the young bourgeoisie. Its expansion to include the working class and in principle all the population created a series of problems and contradictions that indicated certain limitations in this bourgeois public sphere. As a result, various 'counter-public spheres' appeared, as institutional arrangements that are constituted

[36] E.g., Negt and Kluge (1972/1993), Steuerman (1989) or Berg (1990).

[37] Habermas himself repeatedly stresses the importance of irreducible diversification and differences in our time. There are very useful perspectives on dialogicity in the work of Bakhtin (1963/1984, 1981 and 1986). Cf. also the discussion in Hoy and McCarthy (1994) on Habermas's critical theory, Gadamer's hermeneutics and Foucault's poststructuralism.

by social movements and that criticize the dominating bourgeois public sphere and experiment with alternative organizational structures for political discussion, information exchange and cultural activity. They are related to counter-movements and counter-cultures, as their alternatively constructed organizational apparatuses and institutionalized networks for collective communication in political or cultural areas. They are certainly not anti-public (as little as counter-movements are against movements or counter-cultures anti-cultural), but instead create public structures designed to be richer and more open than the established ones, as a reaction to the fact that these have been colonized by systemic demands or hegemonic social classes, ages, genders or ethnic groups. While the concept of counter-movement emphasizes dynamic, social and political aspects, and the concept of counter-culture focuses on cultural stylization, the concept of counter-public spheres emphasizes institutionalized forms of interaction and discourse.

Negt and Kluge then analyse the actual efforts to build counter-public spheres, particularly around the workers' movement, where they found recurrent tendencies towards the closures of a 'camp mentality', where separate organizations attempt to structure the whole life of their members while disconnecting other important spheres of society and often unintentionally importing negative aspects from the bourgeois adversary, undermining their own emancipatory attempts.

Talking about counter-public spheres seems to assume the existence of an 'ordinary' bourgeois public sphere to oppose. The late modern segmentation of public arenas and differentiation of communicative communities has, however, made such an assumption problematic. No single public sphere connects and summarizes everyone and everything. No discussion forum reaches all spheres of society, but, on the other hand, no one is totally separate from the others anymore: pro- and counter-public spheres are intertwined in a web of discursive games into which all communicative fora are woven. The public sphere is fragmented yet the fragments are not separated into a broken mosaic, but continuously interrelated in processes which no counter-movement can stay outside. A weaker concept of counter-public spheres may, however, still be useful, to label organized communicative efforts to counteract other, more hegemonic institutions and construct more lifeworld-oriented alternatives to them.

The plurality of public spheres is not only a late modern phenomenon. Parallel to the bourgeois public sphere, there were from its very beginnings a whole range of other and alternative forms of public discourse, for example within various social movements and popular cultural forms.[38]

---

[38] This is the first of the four main neglects in Habermas's theory of the public sphere that John B. Thompson (1993) discusses: of other forms of public discourse than the bourgeois ones, of gender aspects of the public/private distinction, of the activity of media-users, and of the importance of communication media. Cf. also Calhoun (1992, pp. 33ff, 109f, 117f, 136f, 303ff, 359f and 421ff), John B. Thompson (1990, pp. 119f and 238ff) and Peters (1993 and 1994).

Later counter-public spheres often connect back to such non-bourgeois precursors which have strongly influenced the development of public discourses but often been repressed by their dominant actors. So, modern public spheres should always be thought of in the plural, consisting of a range of variously institutionalized discourse fora. They embrace at least three subtypes: the dominating, bourgeois, white, Western, adult and male-dominated classical public sphere, the marginalized variants of popular, working-class, ethnic, youth or female alternative public spheres, and the openly oppositional counter-public spheres.[39]

Besides the class domination built into the bourgeois public sphere, there is also an important gender dimension.[40] The formation and history of the bourgeois public sphere and the very definition of private/public dichotomy is deeply connected to a gender order of male domination and marginalization of women. The intimate sphere as the core of the private is generally viewed as a female territory, while the market, the state and the public sphere are all dominated by men. Women are associated with home and family, intimacy and emotional life, while men are associated with politics, war and stage performances in cultural arenas or on urban streets.

A feminist critique of Marxism and other economic models regretted the neglection of the mostly female reproductive care-work in the intimate sphere and the prioritizing of the mostly male 'productive' industrial work. This is, however, not just a theoretical mistake, but a real mechanism within capitalist society, where only commodity production is valued fully by the market system, while the reproduction of human life and of the capacity for work is relegated to a hidden backstage position. To regard the intimate sphere of home and family life as only a (the) reproduction area is nevertheless a very traditional, male perspective. To many women the family is as much a place of work, while other public arenas (cafés, theatres, etc.) may offer more relaxation and satisfaction of their own needs.

Janet Wolff (1990) has criticized the literature on modernity (Baudelaire, Simmel, Benjamin, Sennett and Berman) for treating the male *flâneur* as the archetype of modern life, thereby identifying modern experience with both the public and the male one. She argues for a feminist sociology of modernity that catches women's experiences and also the

[39] Cf. Fraser (1992a) and Miriam Hansen's interesting foreword to Negt and Kluge (1972/ 1993). Habermas has fully accepted these ideas of both 'a greater internal differentiation of the bourgeois public' and 'the coexistence of competing public spheres . . . the formation of several arenas where, beside the hegemonic bourgeois public sphere, additional subcultural or class-specific public spheres are constituted on their own and initially not easily reconcilable premises. . . . The exclusion of the culturally and politically mobilized lower strata entails a pluralization of the public sphere in the very process of its emergence. . . . I must confess, however, that only after reading Mikhail Bakhtin's great book *Rabelais and his World* have my eyes become really opened to the *inner* dynamics of a plebeian culture' (1992a, pp. 425ff). Cf. also Habermas (1992b, pp. 435–67).

[40] This is evident in its historical and etymological origins, where the public primarily consisted of adult men (see n. 31 above).

more intimate and private aspects of modernity.[41] Bocock and Thompson (1992, p. 2) want to erase the border between public and private spheres altogether, since the most intimate aspects of life are in fact genuinely social. Haraway (1989, p. 212) argues that the public/private divide between factory or market and home, and between political and personal realms of gender existence, is 'a totally misleading ideology', and prefers the image of a network of spaces, identities and bodies with permeable boundaries. She then enumerates various 'idealized social locations' within such a network, like market, paid work-place, state, school, clinic-hospital and church.

It seems clear that a gender-oriented rethinking of these categories is needed. Others have, however, voiced strong critiques in a similar vein without wanting to erase the modern public/private distinction totally.[42] Indeed, it seems strongly gendered, but cannot be reduced to simply a male/female dichotomy. Some public spheres are in fact densely populated with women, and some function as refuges for other marginalized or oppressed categories (like children, youth or certain ethnic minorities). Women have, for example, constituted the largest part of the audience in many cafés, shopping centres and department stores, libraries, museums, concert halls, theatre salons, public spectacles and other spaces of popular entertainment. To say that women are invisible in modern urban street culture is also false: women are the most frequent window-shoppers and 'womanliness as masquerade' is an important aspect of the female role to make oneself a public object and especially to attract the male gaze.[43]

There is also much empirical evidence that contradicts the common view in traditional mythologies and ideologies of women as home-bound and men as extrovert and mobile. Today women travel as much as men and they start travelling on their own earlier in life than men do; moreover, they are the first to move from home to a place of their own and from the sparsely populated countryside to the large cities.[44] That women leave their parental home earlier may partly be explained by their traditional earlier marriage and thus dependence on a new man, the husband. But they also move out to form single-households, which, like the earlier and more extensive female travelling, is a historically new, late modern phenomenon. They also seem to conquer more and more public arenas, in art, politics and youth culture, while men make new moves into the private sphere, for example in the home-based computer culture. It is true that women have been kept away from public power positions, but they have

---

[41] Bjerrum Nielsen and Rudberg (1993 and 1994) have developed a gender-sensitive analysis of socialization. As Berman (1982) used the Faust-figure as a type model of modern man, so they investigate the fate of Gretchen and the new possibilities that open up for young girls through modern and late modern history. Cf. also Jenny Ryan (1994).

[42] Cf. Fraser (1987 and 1992a), Halonen (1991), Landes (1991), Benhabib (1992), McLaughlin (1993), John B. Thompson (1993) and Marshall (1994).

[43] Cf. Riviere (1929/1986), Modleski (1986b) and Ganetz (1992/1995).

[44] Cf. Mitterauer (1986/1992) and Czaplicka (1987).

therefore not been isolated in their homes during the whole modern epoch. The public sphere is internally differentiated into variously gendered subspheres, so that the public/private distinction as a whole is genuinely separate from the male/female one, even though there are influential interconnections between the two.

The public cannot be understood apart from the private, whose core is individuals and their inner subjectivity. The demands to pay attention to women, private spaces and the psychological dimension are often voiced together. Many recent trends in psychoanalysis and other subject theories have definitely abandoned all biologistic essentialism and conceptualized the symbolic and interactive aspects of subject formation. The most intimately private – our unique personal inner core – is deeply embedded in symbolic discourses and communication processes. While public spheres are constructed and inhabited by living subjects, these subjects are themselves inhabited by symbolic orders that are intrinsically public. Again, the public/private dimension needs to be separated from the ones of individual/society and subject/community.[45]

Public spheres constitute and are constituted in public spaces, rooms where people meet and interact. But communication technologies have already in early modernity made possible mediated interaction in imagined rather than copresent communities. Communication creates an inter-subjective, social space which need not necessarily be a physical space (cf. Habermas 1992a, pp. 436f).

In late modernity, there is an increasing mixing of public and private spheres, particularly as an effect of mediated communication and popular culture. Old distinctions between public and private become blurred as television and computers open direct roads from the most intimate private room out to, in principle, the whole world. News and entertainment programmes open windows between the viewer's private living-room and the public network of the media, to the public political arena and to the portrayed private lives of other people. The media are part of the public sphere, where systemic and lifeworld elements are mixed and mediated. The late modern interplay between market, state and media also blurs the borders between the private and the public, so that specific activities can no longer as easily be classified as belonging to either sphere. These develop-ments were formulated by the New Left and the women's movement, which in the 1970s raised the slogan 'the personal is politic' which politicized the private and thereby made it a public affair. They appeared in the New Right's reverse programme to privatize the public sector. And they can be traced in many recent cultural phenomena. With a Walkman, the underground public space can be aurally privatized with personal musical sounds, just as in book-reading or territorialized corners of open squares.[46] Weekly magazines, computer networks and video-swapping

---

[45] For critiques of the concept of community, see Young (1990) and Fraser (1992a).
[46] Cf. Hosokawa (1984).

conversely open public spaces inside even the most carefully locked doors. To be home-oriented need no longer imply having little contact with the surrounding world. Hackers can shape new open fora or hide behind secret codes. In open mirroring chains people's private identity work relates to mediated images that are in their turn modelled upon private experiences of others. New technologies for cultural production, like sampling or advanced photocopying, make it difficult to maintain the strict rules of private ownership that have been codified in copyright legislation, causing great problems for courts, cultural industries and artists' trade unions.

Habermas (1962/1989) and Negt and Kluge (1972/1993) talked about a refeudalization of the public sphere, through a corporativist fusion of state institutions, commercial conglomerates and mass media, which threatens to dissolve the public sphere. This pessimistic account, much in line with the analysis of the cultural industries in Adorno and Horkheimer (1944), has later been problematized by other critiques and denied by Habermas's own work. It certainly remains a risk in late modern capitalism, but is no fact. After all, differentiations persist, and communicative processes are still strong enough to form nets and social spaces which manage to resist the efforts of systemic forces to co-opt them.

Richard Sennett (1977/1986) thinks that 'the lack of a strong, impersonal culture in the modern city has aroused a passion for fantasized intimate disclosure between people', thus 'destroying the essence of urbanity, which is that men can act together, without the compulsion to be the same' (p. 255). Myths of an absence of community have been spread by an ideology of intimacy, creating a crisis of public culture that robs society of its 'civility'. 'Electronic communication is one means by which the very idea of public life has been put to an end' (p. 282). To Sennett, the mass media have a logic of passivity, a paradox of visibility and isolation where one sees more and interacts less (p. 284). He advocates a new kind of sociability, where the city can again be 'the forum in which it becomes meaningful to join with other persons without the compulsion to know them as persons' (p. 340). However, Habermas (1992a, pp. 426f) has pointed out that Sennett's nostalgic argument tends to collapse the modern public culture into the type of staged and stylized presentation of oneself in front of others which belongs to feudal, representative publicness. And his basically conservative ideas of media use as passive and isolated cannot be sustained in view of recent reception studies.

With Thomas Ziehe (1991), this can be related to a subjectivizing attitude towards modernity, in combination with the reflexivity enhanced by mediatization. Between the grand institutionalized political or cultural arenas and the closest intimate circles there is a lack of the sociality that is a crucial part of the public sphere. Similar ideas have been formulated in much critical media research, wishing to open more spaces for collective debates and communicative dialogues.

The nostalgic refeudalization thesis and its often more neoconservative alternative formulations are, however, not tenable. They build on an overly idealizing image of the classical bourgeois sphere and a diagnosis of late modern tendencies that is too one-sidedly pessimistic. The work of Negt and Kluge, Janet Wolff and others has shed light on the limited class and gender character of the early bourgeois public sphere. As Giddens (1992) has argued, the developments of late modern intimacy cannot only be seen as oppressive: the new forms of pure relationships between people in the intimate sphere form important elements of a richer democracy as well. While men dominated the democratization of the public sphere, women have thus far played the main role in the democratization of personal life (p. 184). In his later work, Habermas (1981/1984–8) questions pessimistic conclusions by stressing that new media can never avoid the communicative potential that resides in its audience's ability to interpret what is and say no to it. Late modern public spheres may have unclear borders towards both the state and the market, but public life – certainly not as organized by the media – is not therefore devoid of meaning-producing dialogues. This is in line with studies of popular culture and media reception which show what strong dialogic and active moments there are in the use and interpretation of mediated texts.[47]

Thompson (1993) also thinks that the refeudalization thesis exaggerates the passivity of individuals in media reception and misses the discursive and interactive aspects of electronic communication. But even if late modern media are thus still communicative rather than manipulative tools, he also argues that mediated communication is neglected in the way Habermas analyses the public sphere and its relations to democracy within modern, internally differentiated societies. In contrast to the classical Greek conception of public life, its modern versions rely much more on de-spatializing communication media as crucially modifying extensions of personal, face-to-face speech acts. This was true already in the early, bourgeois public sphere, where the press and the publishing houses were important factors. The advent of electronic media, starting with telegraph and radio, was more a difference of degree than of kind.

In fact, to make something public is always to present private experiences in an open arena. In the classical public sphere, the bourgeois citizens developed fora to ventilate their personal opinions. All intersubjective communications to some extent have always bridged the private and the public, for example in the production of styles. The reflexive interplay between individual identity work, collective social formations and extrovert symbolic forms freely crosses this border. People take the most private out into the public light as they let personal lifestyles express their identities through public signs. Like all intersubjective communication, styles have the capacity to partly transcend gaps between inner and outer, private and public. The private lives of individuals are always partly open to the public eyes of state supervision and commercial mass media communication. The public and the private are not two diametrically

---

[47] Cf. Hall (1973/1980), Hobson (1982), Radway (1984) and Morley (1992).

opposed and clearly separated areas, but extreme points on an increasingly complex and multi-layered continuum. The differentiating processes of modernization have fragmented the public and the private into a series of sub-spheres with varying kinds and degrees of public character. The public and the private have not been abolished but differentiated and multiplied. Media have not erased the spheres but increased their mutual dependence, making it more difficult to discern unambiguously private or public zones or spaces. The public and the private always and increasingly penetrate each other. They should be understood less as mutually exclusive spaces than as opposing efforts of making public and making private. Public phenomena do not gradually penetrate an originally private sphere, or vice versa; they are constituted together and develop as inseparable pair-wise tendencies.

Modernization and mediatization processes have tended to separate spatial from social aspects of private and public. It has become more difficult to classify concrete physical spaces into either public or private. On one hand, there are certain public spatial places, localities where people physically meet face-to-face. On the other hand, there are public social spaces, rule-bound arenas for open communicative interactions. These may or may not be identical. A public arena can be formed or even be bound to a certain room, like a square, a café, a stage or a club house. All media technologies have always made it possible for social public spheres to loosen such bounds to direct physical interaction and therefore to spatial limitations. Electronic media have accelerated this trend by crossing time and space, potentially freeing public communication from most spatial and temporal borders. This process of cutting off the links of public spheres to physical (co-)presence does not necessarily erode public spaces in the more abstract and general sense. Communicative practices continue to create public spaces in the social form of interpretive communities, even when they do not form homogeneous spatial areas.[48]

As with all politics, *cultural policy* is based in organizations and movements of civil society, based in the lifeworld but directed towards the state, striving to steer its systemic engagement in cultural processes, in particular those connected to arts and aesthetics in a more narrow sense, that is, the activities of the institutionalized forms of art, including both its 'high' and its 'low' forms. From a communicative perspective, it should primarily aim at the creation, maintenance, deepening and expansion of cultural public spheres, through identifying, debating and attacking the obstacles to this. Such hindrances are located on three levels.

The cultural industries and commercial media are institutions particularly oriented towards the market system and often (but not exclusively)

---

[48] Giddens (1990, p. 18) also talks of a modern separation of space from place, of social spaces from physical localities. Cf. Meyrowitz (1985), Skogerbø (1990), John B. Thompson (1990), Calhoun (1992, pp. 359ff, 436ff and 473), Habermas (1992a and 1992b, pp. 435ff), Reimer (1993/1995 and 1994) and Dahlgren (1995).

dealing with popular culture. This market sector of cultural institutions has a double problematic. Its profit logic in some respects makes possible an increase in both equality and freedom by the mobility and neutrality between differing interests which money offers in its continuing dissolution of some older privileges and restrictions. But it simultaneously creates new injustices and unfreedoms. Groups with few resources cannot get their needs satisfied or their voices heard in the established cultural public sphere. Dominating mechanisms of market competition often lead to standardization of the supply, restraining controversial avantgarde experiments as well as a sufficiently rich wealth of amateur activities at grassroots level. This is not only true for 'serious art'; commercialism is as bad at providing sufficient local arenas for activities within popular culture, including, for example, dancing, rehearsal rooms for pop bands, media workshops and possibilities for amateur writing.

Public service media and other publicly supported cultural activities are more dependent on the state system, and have a tendency to care more for so-called 'fine arts' and (at least ideally) other not immediately profitable tastes of various minority groups. The state is partly a guarantee for freedom and equality through its fundamental and constitutional laws as well as its actions to secure justice and care, while simultaneously threatening both of them. Overly rigid central regulations easily cumulate into a dysfunctional bureaucracy which inflicts unnecessary limitations on cultural activities and impairs the capability to develop new understandings. State support and legislation are also often injust. Many cultural state institutions are steered more by the interests of social élites to retain old privileges and reproduce their cultural capital than by the communicative interests of larger, non-propertied strata. A much too rigid boundary between high and low induces a double crisis within the institutionalized arts: a creativity crisis nourished by a relative lack of vitalizing impulses between 'fine art' and popular culture impoverishes the former by reducing its contacts with ongoing tendencies in late modern everyday life; and a legitimation crisis occurs as the majority of the population manifestly lacks interest in what the majority of state cultural support is, concerned with arguments that cannot be rationally and legitimately defended.

Cultural practices in the lifeworld – in everyday life, in social movements and in genuine public spheres – have to manoeuvre between these two main sectors. The lifeworld is affected by the colonizing tendencies of the two systems, creating problematics of commercialization and bureaucratization in cultural matters. But it also has internal obstacles to the development of a well-functioning cultural public sphere. Social cleavages and dominance patterns between ages, genders, classes, ethnicities and geographical regions decrease the freedom and capability of action of the weaker parts of the population. A multidimensional cultural policy should find ways to strive for more equal opportunities, to vitalize and extend the public spheres which emerge in civil society, outside the control of systemic institutions, and in general to strengthen the communicative power of symbolic practices, against all illegitimate forms of social or administrative power and oppression.

All these deficits need to be counteracted by an active cultural policy which does not favour any genre or taste category but is, rather, allocated according to the needs of the ages, genders, social classes, ethnic groups and geographical locations within the population, with a bias in favour of those with less social power and economic resources. There is no option but to anchor cultural policy among those whom it concerns, through a functioning public debate where large efforts must be made to include as wide a number of groups as possible, so that all sorts of cultural interests are drawn into the decisions. With communicativity in focus, a main aim for cultural policy is to enlarge and deepen the multifarious public spaces needed for making richer and more satisfactory life forms possible in the lifeworld, and forcing the systems to aid rather than to counteract this emancipatory process.

To sum up, theories of the public sphere thematize how information and communication is institutionally organized in discursive arenas for the staging of conflicts. The public is a useful critical concept for counteracting overly homogenizing and static understandings of community (cf. Fraser 1992a). Cultural practices always cross the borders between public and private, and let them interact. The communities of shared meanings shaped by communication are of a dynamic, temporary and in principle open kind, even though they sometimes seal themselves off and try to become rigid fortresses. Sometimes subcultures or movements actively construct open fora for political or cultural communication, sometimes individuals or groups equally actively try to withdraw and protect closed spaces of their own for fragile experiences and intimate relations. Media developments are an important aspect of how modernization successively influences the relation between these two main directions, and the types of places and spaces they shape.

The distinctions between classical, alternative and counter-public spheres and between social spaces and spatial places should make it possible to use these concepts in a more fruitful way. Late modernity has differentiated public social spaces from public physical places, particularly through new communication media. The 'bourgeois' public sphere has also been differentiated into a range of various degrees and types of public spheres that sometimes marginalize, counteract or even attack each other. Some are biased towards certain classes, races, ethnicities, genders or ages, some are dominant and others marginal, some powerful and others oppositional, some institutionalized and others spontaneous, some political and others cultural, some strongly system-related to either market or state and others closer to the lifeworld, some localized and others mediated. All these separate publics of a society are interwoven through their function as communicating arenas. Each differentiated public sub-sphere is in principle open or porous towards the others, and they together form an overarching, general civic public sphere of which the classical, bourgeois is only a variant (Habermas 1992b, pp. 452f). Those counter-public spheres that emerge in opposition to the established one still communicate with it and gradually tend to be drawn into it, such as has been the case with the workers' movement and with feminism. This is a sign not necessarily of their decay but as much of the vitality of public debate in modern society. Just as mechanisms of symbolic communication open the horizons and contexts of particular individuals and social groups onto each other and connect them into one general lifeworld of modern society, so do the same communicative networks knit different public sub-spheres together into one heterogeneous and largely mediated modern public sphere, a delicate network for multidimensionally rational societal self-reflection. In this way, publicness becomes a highly differentiated concept instead of a completely unified entity.

Taste hierarchies

Ricoeur (1965/1970, pp. 507ff) mentions three spheres when discussing how human praxis has to objectify itself in external objects in order to develop subjectivity and social identities. In his model, the first sphere is the economic one of exchange value, money, capital and markets, where work and private property give rise to products, commodities and owner-ship. The second one is the political sphere of the state apparatus, where power relations are objectivized and crystallized in public institutions, forming a structure of dominance, identifications and group constellations. These two objectivizing processes relate to the systemic spheres of market and state. Ricoeur's third sphere is, however, seated within the lifeworld. Taste patterns, tendentially organized in value hierarchies, here constitute the objects of the cultural sphere of symbols, texts, works of art and artefacts, which are used when people mutually recognize and evaluate each other and themselves. This is the type of sphere that has been thematized as taste fields by a series of cultural sociologists. These taste spheres are hierarchized in a polarity between high and low culture that might be fragmenting today, but still seems effective, functioning through a set of highly material cultural institutions (schools, councils, publishers, journals, museums, cultural industries, etc.).

Ludwig Wittgenstein (1945/1976, §§ 7, 19, 23 and p. 226) sees language games, the uses of language, as embedded in activities or forms of life, which are what must be taken for granted as given. Life forms are the horizons within which people live, constituted by language-use and social interaction. Life forms can be seen as specifications of the lifeworld, its particular form for individuals or groups in specific temporal, spatial and social contexts. They consist of sets of social and symbolic actions or patterns of praxis, shaping local cognitive, normative, cultural and emotional horizons in which people live their lives.

Life forms can be classified in many different ways. Individuals, groups, subcultures or social categories may all share certain horizons, so that a life form may be located on each of these levels, from micro- to macro-. It has become customary to define life forms or forms of life as structurally determined ways of living, related to social categories of class/gender/ethnic/age positions. Lifestyles then are considered to be more self-chosen individual constructions, with 'ways of life' often situated somewhere between these two.[49] This is not the only possible solution, but it seems reasonable to think of life forms as ways of living that follow from the social positions people inhabit, so that a life form is more grown into rather than momentarily chosen. Wage labourers, housewives, academics, lesbian feminists or Somalian immigrants may live in different life forms, but they then do so in various ways, shaping many more individualized lifestyles. If a lifestyle is, like other styles, a particular and observable way to elaborate a certain genre, which is in this case the 'genre' of life forms, then lifestyles may either be shared or individual, but they in any case are the symbolic, signifying aspects of life forms that offer other people clues to one's personal taste and way of life. A lifestyle is the particular way one chooses to inhabit one's life form, including the symbolic tools with which one shows to others one's personality, an individual identity that may or may not be (deliberately or unconsciously) shared by many others. There are thus types of taste subjects: individuals, groups or larger interpretive communities, social categories or even regional, national or supranational population clusters, each contributing aspects of lifestyles that may be personal or belong to microcultures, subcultures, etc.

Various cultural sociologists have analysed taste spheres, from a series of sociological or ethnological work on lifestyles and life forms to the Birmingham studies of subcultures. While Herbert J. Gans and George H. Lewis have developed models of taste cultures, the most complex and debated work on taste, power and status is that of Pierre Bourdieu.[50]

Bourdieu generalizes the concept of *capital* from economic capital to all sorts of values and resources. Symbolic capital is all that social groups recognize as valuable. Cultural capital is that symbolic capital which relates to higher education, refined taste and high cultural competence. Educational, informational and scientific capital are other terms for branches of this general symbolic capital. Social capital consists of personal connections and relations through kinship, friendship or other forms of supportive ties to other people with some sort of power. The accumulation of economic and cultural capital necessitates long-term strategies for fruitful investments. These are anchored and reproduced in various groups and families, who make use of the possibility of converting one type of capital into another. The value of all these capitals is decided in a mutual social

[49] Cf. Højrup (1983) and Johansson and Miegel (1992).
[50] See, e.g., Bourdieu (1972/1977, 1979/1984, 1980/1993, 1992 or 1993), Broady (1986 and 1991), Roe (1987), Skovmand (1988) and Reimer (1992/1995). Other studies of taste, lifestyles and/or life forms are Gans (1974), George A. Lewis (1978), Lenz (1986) and Bois-Reymond and Oechsle (1990).

play of recognition, distaste and misrecognition, where certain symbolic resources are recognized as valuable while one's own material interests are masked and denied as such.

In *habitus*, the bodily coded system of enduring and transferable dispositions to act and think in specific ways, people store experiences for future use in social, economic and cultural strategies. The distribution of habitus among different individuals and groups creates parallels or homologies between the space of lifestyles and the social space of class positions. While this concept of habitus may be read as an effort to analyse the subjective traits of individuals in materialist terms, the concept of field is used to analyse their objective, social conditions. A social *field* is a system of relations between positions inhabited by specialized agents and institutions that struggle over something they all find important. Literature and literary criticism, for example, form a reasonably autonomous field with its own goals, values and rules, institutions and agents, orthodoxies and heterodoxies. All those who take part in its struggles at least have to agree that their values are worth this fight. Bourdieu has analysed fields of production (authors, critics, publishers, galleries, museums, etc.) and of consumption (readers, audiences, etc.). A field is here clearly a well-ordered structure: economic and cultural capital may be seen as two competing poles, and for all capital types there is an unambiguous hierarchy between high and low quantity. All individual positions in the field are determined by their mutual relations within this structure. This is more similar to the way iron filings line up between the magnetic north and south poles, or the way troops line up on the battle-field, than to how the seed grows in a corn-field.

Broady (1991, p. 291) mentions that Bourdieu's field concept can be related to Marx's concept of classes and relations of production or to Habermas's concept of public spheres, provided that dominance aspects are acknowledged as fundamental and unavoidable, and not seen as pathological exceptions. He also argues that it is close to theories of the literary circuit of institutions, but that it is important to respect the relative autonomy of each field instead of thinking of the accumulation of economic capital as a totally determining factor. In spite of this, Bourdieu's interest in relations between fields, through the homologies between the space of lifestyles and the social space, sometimes makes him tend towards reductionist formulations.

Collective lifestyles and cultural gaps are to a certain extent reproduced by socialization processes in family and school. This reproduction of tastes has a power aspect through the ordering of tastes in status hierarchies between what is considered high and low by dominating groups and institutions in a society, and by most of its citizens.[51] Such dichotomies are

---

[51] On the history of the gap between high and low culture, see Burke (1978), Chambers (1986), Huyssen (1986), Collins (1989), Ross (1989) and Boëthius (1990/1995). Radway (1989 and 1992) illustrates how the cultural legitimacy of élites is maintained.

repeatedly transgressed by new styles, as in the mix be^r
high culture (with self-reflexive forms that problematize
languages) and pre-modern folk culture (with functional
and carnivalesque joking and role-reversal) within lat
culture. But such transgressions are fascinating only b
between spheres are alive in public consciousness: tra...
limits, however relative, dynamic and temporary they may be.

Commercial, state and scientific interests meet in trying to classify and
overview the complex plurality of people's individual ways of everyday life
by systematically constructing a number of typified lifestyles. People are
not a priori living in well-ordered boxes but are divided up by various
actors with specific motives and perspectives.

All such instruments of classification are based on generative principles.
Different aspects of daily life may be regarded as sorts of overarching
genres within which individual lifestyles may be distinguished, forming
rule-bound patterns of and within these genres. In too many studies, the
basic principles used for the classification of lifestyles are unclear. In many
maps constructed by commercial or institutional interests highly different
criteria are mixed, creating patterns of dubious value. If a field of lifestyles
is relatively autonomous it does not have to be based upon external factors,
but if it is a real field there must exist some sort of ordering principle which
gives it a non-arbitrary structure.

Marxist theory generates its class concepts by using the relation to wage
labour and to the means of production as instruments. Other social
classifications use a mix of income and other properties as generating
principles. Besides such objectivized positional factors based on class,
gender, age or ethnicity, the choice of forms of identity or activity may
generate very complex patterns of lifestyles. The choice of a leisure activity
like sports may, for example, enforce certain lifestyle patterns, including
ways of living, political attitudes, etc. Conversely, resources, attitudes or
psychic dispositions may induce certain leisure activities.

Lifestyles imply sets of habitual actions in daily life and of reflexively
expressed attitudes of taste. They can be related to general value-
orientations that may be distilled out of these contextualized practices of
everyday life. It may be thought that the basic values, rooted in identities,
must be the motor behind the development of patterns of attitudes and
action, taste profiles and habits. But there is also a reversed logic of
determination, where the choice of action forms creates experiences and
routines that gradually restructure basic values and social or subjective
identity forms. Again, the surface/depth metaphor seduces one into seeing
the most inaccessible (values) as more fundamental and essential than the
most visible (attitudes and habits). It may or may not be so.

Different aspects of lifestyle relate to political, economic, social, cultural
and psychological levels and to various life spheres like family, work,
school or leisure. Specifying the generative principles on which a lifestyle-
mapping is based makes it much more useful than just lumping levels and

ects together in an arbitrary and unclear manner. Instead of totalizing, y to explain all lifestyle patterns from one single principle (whether it be class, gender, ethnicity, value structure or action forms); each model should be regarded as a partial tool which sheds light on some but not all effective generative mechanisms. Lifestyles are constructions and tools for orientation in various fields of dynamic social praxis rather than means for reproducing objectively existing facts.

Tastes are always related to power. Each act and each symbolic discourse has an aspect of dominance which should be recognized. That is not all there is to say about cultural phenomena, however. Other motives and mechanisms are also relevant, and though one side always has to do with social status, this is never the only side. Cultural praxis cannot be reduced to a will to power. The strategic rationality of the profit motive alone – whether aiming at accumulating economic or symbolic capital – is inadequate to explain why human beings engage in intellectual or cultural work, which is always co-motivated by moral, ludic and expressive interests (cf. Mander 1987, p. 446).

To a certain extent, taste and activity patterns can be related to class and life forms, as has frequently been done by Bourdieu and in the 1970s British studies of youth cultures. But there is always a remaining scope both for other generating factors (like gender, age and ethnicity) and for individual variations.[52] The homologies between the taste and the social class field exist but are always only partial, and increasingly so. The forms and contents of tastes and lifestyles always have multiple determinations. They are never only effects of power-games: they have a range of other use values that also have to be taken into consideration. It is not only status factors that determine what becomes legitimate taste for someone, but also political, social, psychological and aesthetic qualities related to other needs than the will to be recognized and to dominate. The use value of symbolic forms should not be reduced to their exchange value on the status 'market'. They are always more or less consciously used by people to position themselves in relation to others, in the extrovert social type of use value which could be called 'ex-positioning'. But there are many other use values: to develop social groups by internal interaction, to form and reflect on one's subjective identity, to transmit information, to learn about the world or to enjoy aesthetic pleasure. That something has been adopted by the dominating, legitimate culture does not imply that legitimating power

---

[52] Bourdieu (1990) thematizes gender, but Broady (1991, pp. 222 and 434) finds that his basic anthropological hypothesis is that man(!) is a bartering and struggling being inclined to seek other men's acknowledgement and to dominate them. Cf. Moi (1991). Roe (1992) emphasizes that both class and gender are necessary basic dimensions in mapping tastes. By reducing gender relations to the use by men of women as exchange objects in their competitive pursuit of status, essential aspects are neglected – for example the active tension between mother and father that has been analysed by psychoanalysis and is a crucial factor behind the conflicts between men and women in both the intimate and the public sphere. Not everything can be reduced to the quasi-economic sphere of sociocultural status.

is its only function, as little as the popular culture of subordinate strata is just an expression of submission or rebellion.

There is no simple linear or even bi-polar (cultural/economic capital) hierarchy of social power which can explain more than some trends in actual tastes, as is evident when gender and class are combined. It is mostly agreed that working-class women are at the bottom of the social hierarchy, exposed to a double oppression. But it turns out that in many matters of young people's taste and lifestyle, it is middle-class women and working-class men that are the opposites, while working-class women are closer to middle-class men. The hierarchies of power and taste here obviously do not quite overlap, and it seems difficult to choose either class or gender as the most fundamental dimension.

Bourdieu sometimes has problematic structuralist tendencies: a reductionism which sees only class and status; a totalism which avoids internal differences; a determinism which is biased towards reproduction as against transformation; an objectivism which makes no space for acting subjects; a miserabilism which does not understand the potentialities of resistance.[53]

To reduce culture to 'nothing-but' stakes of status and power offers few openings for inner contradictions and resistance. The result may be a monolithic, one-dimensional theory of power.[54] The consumption of popular culture is not a passive copying, simply reproducing prevailing taste norms, and the 'legitimate' taste may therefore not reign as supreme as might first be thought. These theories are simply best fit for the study of élites, and other perspectives are needed to understand the tastes and lifestyles of subordinate or subversive groups. Bourdieu has chosen to study culture from its most dominating viewpoint, and while this is fully legitimate, it is problematic that there does hardly seem to be even an empty space for resistance in his theories, open to others to fill. Such a space thus needs to be opened up. 'Resistance occurs on terrains altogether different from that of culture in the strict sense of the word – where it is never the possession of the most destitute, witness all the forms of

---

[53] 'Bourdieu's perspective, however, is rationalist and economistic, insofar as it reduces all practice to the accumulation of cultural capital, i.e., of specific forms of power' (Friedman 1990a, p. 103; cf. also 1990b, pp. 312f and 327). 'Social positioning is, however, only one element in the construction of identity' (Miller 1987, p. 9; cf. also p. 213). Gesser (1987, p. 283) argues that Bourdieu sees everything as a rule-bound game but says too little about the specific content of 'honour', 'education', etc., engaging so much in exchange values that he forgets the use values of culture. And Broady (1991, p. 476) concludes that the specific 'matter' of each cultural area seems to disappear in Bourdieu's analyses.

[54] Such a critique has been directed at both Bourdieu and Foucault by de Certeau (1974/ 1988, pp. 45ff). Frow (1987, p. 72), Stauth and Turner (1988, p. 522) and Huspek (1993, pp. 5, 7 and 14) all argue that Bourdieu totalizes dominance and leave too little space for subjectivity, resistance and change. Jenkins (1992, pp. 97, 123 and 149) finds Bourdieu conformist and reductionist, leaving little room for innovation, deviance or individual psychology, treating power almost as a natural force, underestimating the role of knowing, decision-making actors and seeing culture as a wholly arbitrary historical and social construction. One of the few places where resistance and counter-culture is mentioned is in Bourdieu (1980/1993, pp. 2f).

"counter-culture" that, as I could show, always presuppose a certain cultural capital', writes Bourdieu (1987/1990, p. 155). Counter-cultures can surely not do without some resources, but it seems problematic to think that all real resistance must reside outside the cultural arena. This echoes the old basis/superstructure metaphor which reduced symbolic forms to secondary reflections of more essential socioeconomic factors. It could instead be argued that precisely cultural resistance has a determining role in the formation of power-critiques and counter-movements on all levels.

Social class conflicts are acted out on the cultural field when established élites try to dominate others by erecting absolute and uniform norms of good taste. Counter-cultures then try to break these hegemonic taste norms and make space for other aesthetic forms. In such struggles, the two systems, market and state, often are engaged on different (though changing) sides. Sometimes state institutions are used by dominant social groups to enforce their taste norms against the 'low', commercial, mass culture. At other times avantgarde subcultures get support from similar institutions in their fight against established mainstream popular tastes.

Bourdieu's former collaborator Jean-Claude Passeron (1991) has argued similarly against the reduction of culture to its power and status dimension. He opposes both the 'miserabilist' account of working-class popular culture as marked only by subordination and the 'triumphalist' perspective of it as only a site of resistance (Grignon and Passeron 1985; cf. Rigby 1991, pp. 127ff). Culture is often engaged in domination and rebellion, but it is also frequently 'at rest', in a state of autonomy which must be studied in its own terms. This is an important point, for whereas it is important to understand how resistance is born, it is as crucial also to thematize other aspects of cultural practices than those related to either power or resistance. High culture is not only a tool of class domination; popular culture is neither only marked by its subordination nor a pure source of resistance – it is both and simultaneously much more.

In transformational periods like late modernity, taste spheres are displaced by the pluralization tendencies that have arisen from late modern individualization, reflexivity and makeability. This has made it increasingly difficult to reduce cultural distinctions to social classes. Correlations will probably always persist, but they are not in any way total. What exists are general tendencies for different social groups to make specific lifestyle choices, but few absolute rules. Social structures have not been dissolved, but fluidized and fragmented. While standards of high and low remain effective in important institutional settings, different subcultures tend to define them increasingly differently. Traditional social contexts are partly disintegrated, the plurality of life forms grows, the range of possible actions is widened for most individuals, and identities may be chosen or at least thought in less collective ways. Individualization does not imply that all forms of collectivity disappear, it only gives community new, late modern forms. The need for ordering structures to orient oneself in daily social life makes people invent restrictions for their actions even where they are not given a priori. Collective schemata therefore appear even where everyone must choose by her or himself, which is increasingly the case in late modernity.[55]

There is a principle of 'misrecognition' in the tendency not to see one's taste as related to one's social position, but as a purely individual and aesthetic affair. This mechanism was stronger in closed élites and in more static times than it is in late modern popular culture, where it is counteracted by growing reflexivity. While individualization and make-ability tend to make the belief in one's individual responsibility for life choices more real than illusory, reflexivity conversely tends to make people more self-conscious of how their lifestyles are connected to social relations. People may well know the legitimate high culture and express their distaste for it. Mander (1987, p. 436) argues that Bourdieu writes from an élite perspective when he (falsely) 'assumes the working classes *do* recognize the culture of the élite as legitimate'. People also more often view their own taste as typical of their position. Taste and distaste are not as obviously regarded as natural. Instead, they are more often relativized and seen as what they are and have always been: socially, culturally and psychologically anchored constructions. There is a late modern struggle between individualization and reflexivity that makes it necessary to carefully analyse each group and context to see which of these tendencies is the stronger, resulting in a varying balance between demystification and misrecognition. And while it is true that there is always some misrecognition, it is as important to develop an understanding of the processes through which recognition arises, in processes of learning and self-reflection.[56]

The distinction between economic and cultural capital offers a fruitful way to differentiate the élites of modern societies. Broady (1991, pp. 303ff) argues for a third capital form, related to careers within the various popular movements and organizations that have been so important in the political life of the Nordic countries, and which are relatively independent of both economic and traditional high cultural capital. It might be possible to proceed in several steps to include a number of other distinctions related

---

[55] 'First and foremost, it no longer seems tenable to try to establish strict correspondences between cultural cleavages and social hierarchies, creating simplistic relationships between particular cultural objects or forms and specific social groups. On the contrary, it is necessary to recognize the fluid circulation and shared practices that cross social boundaries' (Chartier 1988, p. 169). Frow thinks the construction of unified class-bound aesthetic systems is essentialist, since 'cultural forms are understood as non-contradictory expressive unities rather than as sites of political tension' (1987, p. 66). Rigby (1991), Johansson and Miegel (1992) and Reimer (1992/1995) also emphasize that there is no exact correlation between taste and class structure. Cf. Beck (1986/1992) and Giddens (1990) on social individualization, and Schulze (1992, pp. 18ff and 76f) on its relation to community.

[56] Cf. Fornäs et al. (1988/1995, 1990a and b), Johansson and Miegel (1992, pp. 294ff) and Malmgren (1992, p. 221). Fowler (1994) complains of Bourdieu's bleak, abstract and reductionist treatment of the popular aesthetics of mass culture and his closing off of the space for resistance in both high and popular culture.

to other hierarchies, not least the gender dimension. The continuous fragmentation of taste hierarchies threatens to make this a never-ending process which completely shatters the initially simple model.

Rudi Laermans (1992, pp. 256ff) has argued that there is still a power centre in society, but that this centre is now surrounded by an intricate web of peripheral subcultures, each with its own legitimating hierarchies and canons. This creates 'a polyhierarchichal but still "centred" situation', where internal distinctions between 'high' and 'low' are formed within each autonomized field. While some of these subcultural value-scales are backed up by institutions supported by one of the two societal systems (e.g., schools, cultural authorities or mass media), others are in opposition towards some of those that are more established and dominating.

Voices have been raised calling for the widening of the concept of cultural capital to include a popular cultural capital, with its specific status positions and value hierarchies.[57] This is directly against the ideas of Bourdieu himself, who has repeatedly declared the whole concept of popular culture to be dubious (e.g., 1979/1984, p. 395; and 1980/1993, pp. 4f). But to those who want to understand modern popular culture it has been impossible only to choose between high, half-, non- and anti-culture. To conceive the lifestyles of workers and other subordinate groups as primarily a lack of culture seems insufficient. And the newly discovered activity of mass cultural media audiences, in fan and everyday creativity, makes it hard at least quite so strictly to oppose high culture as the field of restricted cultural production, destined for a public of cultural producers, to popular culture as a field of large-scale cultural production, destined for the non-producing public at large.[58]

The experiments with this new popular subtype of cultural capital do, however, seem to create more problems than they solve. While there are subcultures that value and accumulate alternative cultural competences to those legitimated by dominant institutions, this popular cultural capital is rarely recognized by actors outside the subculture and is often harder to convert to social positions or economic capital. Only in combination with regular academic or commercial investment does pop fandom give convertible dividends. To talk of popular culture as a variant of cultural capital is to use a concept of culture which is quite different from Bourdieu's, and can hardly be reconciled with his models. It would be more appropriate to think of popular culture as a quite different type of symbolic capital than that which Bourdieu labels cultural capital. He simply has an extremely traditional and narrow concept of culture and doesn't share the wider definition used by most who discuss media and popular culture. This wider definition cannot immediately be joined to more than a very heuristic use of the model of cultural capital, far from the determined homology schemata which it originally supports. If such contradictions pass without

---

[57] Cf. Fiske (1989a), commented on by Reimer (1992/1995).
[58] See, e.g., Bourdieu (1993, pp. 53, 115ff and 185ff).

notice, the juxtaposition of theories from cultural sociology and studies of popular culture becomes a self-destructive eclecticism.

There is in fact a weakness already in Bourdieu's concept of economic capital, which is much more 'flat' than the differentiated and dynamic one of Marx. When income, property and power over means of production do not completely overlap, it becomes hard to reduce them to a single scale of material resources. In the cultural sphere, the problems multiply, as the discussion of the taste patterns of dominated classes shows. This capital form is even less quantifiable on one hierarchic scale, and it seems unlikely that two or three scales would suffice. That implies that there is no 'general equivalent' comparable to money within economy, and no straight way to translate between economic and cultural capital (cf. Frow 1987, p. 67). The economic metaphors are good at showing some aspects of cultural life, but they do not fit completely and cannot be taken as more than partial truths. Experiences and competences can be accumulated and utilized in status careers, but if there is no reliable way to compare or translate between different subcultures, then the capital metaphor is definitely limited.

The measuring and accumulation of taste which the concept of cultural capital presupposes is supported by the reification of cultural processes which takes place within many cultural institutions, but it hides more dynamic, open and creative aspects of culture and communication. Bourdieu's analyses aim to thematize transformations of taste structures but in practice mostly tend to stress their reproduction. To understand the main 'conditions of production of habitus', Bourdieu constructs 'a space whose three fundamental dimensions are defined by volume of capital, composition of capital, and change in these two properties over time (manifested by past and potential trajectory in social space)' (1979/1984, p. 144). His studies of struggles in various fields and of the trajectories of individuals within and between them hint at possibilities of resistance and of change, but mostly the emphasis is on the integration within existing power relations and their reproduction.[59] To stick with (Marxist) economic metaphors, the reproduction of taste hierarchies is not only simple (a copying of existing orders) but 'expanded'. It includes a quantitative growth and successive qualitative transformations of these hierarchies, for example, as a result of individualization, reflexivity and makeability.

This model of taste hierarchies and lifestyles, habitus, fields and cultural capital thus has its limitations but is a forceful tool for analysing certain aspects of culture. It is particularly useful to understand phenomena close to the dominating élites of society, where systemic demands are internalized and where strategic action predominates. There are forceful homologies between cultural tastes and social class or status, but culture may not be reduced to only this dimension – no cultural phenomenon is 'nothing-but' instances or investments of cultural capital. Overarching

---

[59] Rigby (1991, p. 109) thinks that while Bourdieu attempts to deal with changes, most of his work 'gives the impression that he is treating the cultural system as relatively static'.

patterns exist, but they do not annihilate micro-variations. Old structures are reproduced, but they also change. There are objectivized institutions, but rather than creatng culture as automatic mechanisms, they do so only in conjunction with acting human subjects whose internal motives include but cannot be reduced to a will to recognition or domination. Subordinate groups are caught in a self-restricting submission to dominating forces, but their cultural practices are more than just submission – there are also elements of resistance and aspects that are neither the one nor the other. Improved by such an opening, dynamization and differentiation, the theory of taste hierarchies and their relation to social structures is an extremely useful tool for understanding how culture and power are interrelated in ways which no one, and certainly not the researcher, can avoid.

Subcultures

Taste groups and lifestyles have been studied differently in another tradition, using anthropological ethnography and semiotic text analysis to interpret youth subcultures. This theme has been developed within many British and American cultural studies.

The analysis of lifestyles moves between the social and the cultural level. A taste is a pattern of aesthetic value judgements about cultural genres, but the theories discussed above are mainly concerned with how tastes are distributed socially among the groups and categories of a society. Lifestyles concern meaningful symbolic forms, but lifestyle theories tend to focus on who share which lifestyles, why and to which effects. Subcultural theories also study the meeting-points between the social and cultural levels, as they thematize how symbolic expressions are related to social forces of various kinds (classes, genders, races, ideologies). They tend to go one step further towards the truly cultural, by scrutinizing the stylistic forms in greater detail through semiotic or hermeneutic close readings. Yet, they retain a social emphasis in that social structures and the actual use people make of symbolic forms remain in focus, rather than these forms in themselves. Subcultural studies, further, have thematized resistance much more than have Bourdieu's more power-oriented taste studies.

In choosing lifestyles, people form not only concrete groups and locally bound taste or lifestyle patterns that can be termed microcultures, but also patterns transcending the local environment. Such 'subcultures' are collective sociocultural patterns in a given society, and are thus another name for lifestyles, viewed from another angle. In cultural studies, they have been explored and interpreted semiotically and semantically as magical texts, as carriers of secret, coded messages, as 'maps of meaning' (Hebdige 1979, p. 18). The use of text analysis methods in studying social youth phenomena was part of a general theoretical turn towards the cultural level within many disciplines, to which linguistic semiotics and literary hermeneutics have offered important tools. While 1970s British cultural studies developed influential models that interpreted youth subcultures as meaningful textual structures, similar connections between social and cultural structures and methodologies were suggested in many other places and areas as well.[60]

At the Centre for Contemporary Cultural Studies (CCCS) in Birmingham, British cultural studies developed highly influential models of youth subcultures, using concepts and methods that had earlier been elaborated in the Chicago school of criminology, Gramsci's hegemony theory, the structuralist anthropology of Claude Lévi-Strauss, and in newer semiotics and poststructuralism. Instead of describing in detail the successive development of subcultural studies, this section will more systematically present useful and problematic aspects of it by first introducing some general ideas and then in turn focusing on the problematic key concepts of homology, intentionality, visibility, marginality and oppositionality.[61]

Within the CCCS tradition, three influential polarities may be distinguished. In the early 1970s, a tension developed between the 'culturalism' of Raymond Williams or E. P. Thompson and the structuralism advanced by Stuart Hall and others, who imported Althusserian ideas of economic overdetermination in the last instance, structural totalities and ideological state apparatuses.[62] In the late 1970s, there was a methodological difference between ethnographic work (e.g., Cohen or Willis) and semiotic media readings (e.g., Hebdige or Hall).

One basic idea was to read subcultural styles as linguistic expressions of real and wished-for identities, and as meaningful messages about various youth groups' relation towards the dominating institutions of hegemonic cultures. Youth subcultures were seen as symbolic attempts to solve problems in adult culture, caused by social transformations associated with modernization. These subcultures could be read as symptoms of such crises, but also as symbolically formulated utopian proposals for alternative solutions, and thus as germs of resistance towards power structures. Because of their symbolic or cultural rather than political nature, these resisting 'solutions' were, however, seldom regarded as particularly effectual.

This resistance was first thematized in relation to age, generation and class, as Phil Cohen, Paul Willis, John Clarke, Tony Jefferson and others

[60] In the early 1950s, Bakhtin (1986, pp. 60ff) analysed how social spheres are connected to cultural (speech) genres. In an essay from 1971, Ricoeur (1981, pp. 197ff) argued for meaningful action considered as a text.

[61] See Hall and Jefferson (1975/1976), Hall et al. (1980), Brake (1985), Punter (1986), Brantlinger (1990), Turner (1990/1992), Grossberg et al. (1992) and Storey (1993) for overviews. Critical evaluations from a Marxist position have been made by Gudmundsson (1984 and 1992) and from a feminist perspective by Franklin et al. (1991).

[62] Hall (1980) mentions the semiotics and linguistics inspired by Lévi-Strauss, Lacanian psychoanalysis and discourse theory, the theories of Foucault and political economy as alternatives to the two main paradigms, but all except maybe the last one are currents that can be placed under the structuralist umbrella.

studied young working-class implicit critiques of adult life, the school system and middle-class culture, their responses to a structural and ideological crisis within adult working-class culture, and the dialectics between proletarian subcultures and middle-class counter-cultures. This last pair of concepts was borrowed from two earlier American traditions. The criminology of the Chicago school delivered the concept of subculture, which came to be used mainly for working-class youth cultures like the teddy boys, mods or skinheads.[63] In style and behaviour, they reacted to class-based dominance patterns, but only with a partial and non-reflected resistance which seemed hard to transform into political struggle and organization. From the 1960s studies of rebellious youth generations, the concept of counter-culture was imported, used for middle-class youth cultures like the hippies.[64] These cultures explicitly formulated a social critique and almost organized social movements, while their bounds to their own parental class produced an ambivalent relation to class domination and, again, a limited form of resistance. By the end of the 1970s, other lines of resistance were also thematized, mainly in relation to gender, race and ethnicity.

Subcultures were thus positionally defined in relation both to each other and to larger social categories. In the early formulations, they were outlined as class-based generational patterns between subcultures and their parent cultures. The latent function of subcultures was to work out in terms of generational conflict and magically solve internal, hidden and unresolved conflicts of the parent culture. Subcultures were seen as 'a compromise solution to two contradictory needs: the need to create and express autonomy and difference from parents and, by extension, their culture, and the need to maintain the security of existing ego defences and the parental identifications which support them' (Phil Cohen 1972/1980, pp. 82 and 84). This made them both similar to and different from their parental class-cultures.

When other dimensions were recognized, like gender and ethnicity, and the often heterogeneous class origins of subcultures had been noted, these formulae could be modified. For Hebdige (1979, p. 80), (subcultural) style was 'a coded response to changes affecting the entire community', not only defined in terms of class. Such a generalization converged with the interpretation of youth phenomena as symptoms of processes that are

---

[63] Hannerz (1992a, p. 277) traces the concept of subculture back to Sapir (1932, p. 236), but it was criminology that used it specifically for youth groups, and CCCS that generalized it to non-criminal youth styles.

[64] While Parsons introduced the concept of youth culture in social science in 1942 (cf. Parsons 1951/1964 and 1961), Hollingshead (1949) was the first to discuss how socioeconomic conditions shaped a series of plural youth cultures. Coleman (1961) stressed the generation gap and the separation of a general youth culture from adult society, inspiring a flow of American studies of such a generational youth culture. Keniston (1968), Roszak (1968/1970) and Martin (1981) analyse generational tensions and resistances within middle-class counter-cultures as reactions to the crisis of this hegemonic culture itself.

related not only to particular youth experiences, but also to overarching historical tendencies, the way in which American and German socialization theory used youth cultures as sensitive seismographs to decipher the spirit of the times (Ziehe and Stubenrauch 1982).

This seismographic function may be questioned. Subcultures have lost some of their avantgarde role, as both they and the definitions of 'normality' have been increasingly fragmented. When 'normality' is less obvious, 'deviance' also becomes more difficult. This has forced subcultures to adopt a greater flexibility, and blurred their borders towards non-subcultural lifestyles. But ageing subcultures have always tended to become petrified into rather conservative traditionalist positions, however avantgardistic they once were. Today's seismographs are not to be found among the old and established subcultures, but in the new and more fluid ones that experiment with punctual transgressions and subtle plays with a constructed normality (Ziehe 1991). In a more differentiated and heterogeneous lifeworld with a spectrum of many coexisting lifestyles, these late modern subcultural formations still function as tools of orientation for young people's identity work, and as instruments for registering certain general social tendencies.

The idea that subcultures symbolically work out the problems of their parental culture was further formalized by Hall and Jefferson (1975/1976). Subcultures were thought only to transfer the material or macrosocial contradictions of a parental culture to a cultural or microsocial level of magical, imaginary or symbolic relations, and their defensive function, which cements ego boundaries into subcultural ones, can never constitute any 'real' solution to these societal problems and crises. The only effective solution would be a higher degree of autonomous political organization of the working class, resolving generation conflicts into class struggle.[65]

Two problematic ideological mechanisms are active here. On one hand, age and generation are regarded a priori as less important than class. Later discussions of the relative importance of class, race and gender have made it harder to uphold such simple hierarchies, and the age dimension should not be an exception to this rule. The British subcultural theorists were right to correct the 1960s American models of youth culture by stressing the persistent relevance of the class dimension, since the apparently homogeneous generational youth culture is actually diversified along many axes and filled with internal contradictions, some of which are continuous with overarching societal conflicts (of class, gender, race, etc.), others of which are specific to the youth category (related to structures in the education system or to certain semi-independent subcultural patterns of taste/

---

[65] Cf. Phil Cohen (1972/1980, pp. 84f), Hall and Jefferson (1975/1976, pp. 47f) and Cohen and Robins (1978). Cohen (1986a and b) critically reviews British youth culture research that opens up certain psychoanalytical aspects.

distaste). But as empirical taste and lifestyle studies indicate, generation cannot always be dismissed as only a secondary factor.

The other mechanism is deeply rooted in much cultural theory, namely, a false dichotomy of illusory symbols and material reality, which amounts to a reduction of culture to a side-effect, reflection or diversion of the social level. Just as the cultural level in general must be recognized on its own terms, rather than being reduced to a subordinated effect of social or psychological processes, the symbolic aspects of subcultures and lifestyles have an autonomy and an importance not to be underestimated. To understand the multiple and mutual determinations between symbolic forms and external or internal forces, it is first necessary to acknowledge differentiation between these dimensions and to avoid reductionism. The classical British cultural studies had a weakness in this respect, in adhering to a problematic model of basis and superstructure dating back to some simplistic Marxist formulations that have been criticized with the help of those much less mechanical models that the Marxist legacy also offers.[66] This hierarchical model is echoed in the formulations of imaginary symbolic solutions to real social problems, and the idea that subcultures are almost without material importance and should instead be substituted by true class struggle. This traditional base/superstructure model under-estimates the role of stylization, discourses and symbolic structures in society. Youth cultures have not made the revolutions some of them dreamt of, but they were more than deviations from the essentialities of life and politics. Some of their cultural experiments have contributed to important mental and ideological transformations in society, with wide but diffuse effects far beyond those people who were directly involved in them. Their contestation of 'normal' lifestyles invented new possible forms of identity, in processes that do not compete with trade unions or political parties since they are in a quite different field, but that strongly affect emancipatory potentials of future social movements.[67]

Ricoeur (1986) uses a close reading of Marx to criticize the Althusserian base/superstructure model. He finds it more useful to contrast ideology with praxis than with science, while emphasizing that ideology and praxis are always closely linked (pp. 9f). Praxis contains an ideological com-ponent (p. 223), and all action is symbolically mediated. 'Therefore, we can no longer say that ideology is merely a kind of superstructure. The

---

[66] Mechanistic interpretations of basis and superstructure find support in *The German Ideology* (1846/1970) and in some later works by Engels, while both the young and the mature Marx had a less reductionist view on the interrelations between material and mental processes.

[67] McGuigan (1992, pp. 12f) is wrong in arguing that Bourdieu's view that real resistance is never on cultural terrains is opposite to those of Bennett and Hall. They all share a problematic standpoint in exactly this respect: their structuralist basis lead them to conceptualize culture as only a derived, secondary phenomenon with no material force of its own.

distinction between superstructure and infrastructure completely disappears, because symbolic systems belong already to the infrastructure, to the basic constitution of human being' (p. 258).[68]

This critique also hits the 1970s British subcultural theories, as well as many later positions in cultural studies. The Gramscian theory of ideological struggle and hegemony was welcomed as a way to overcome the rigidity of Althusserian structuralism, to explore concrete contexts and political practices, and to take cultural practices more seriously.[69] It is easy to find works where a very narrow concept of culture is used to neglect the importance of symbolic forms and reduce culture to expressions of social group identities only.[70]

There are several ways to distinguish between components of lifestyles. 'Vertically', explicit behaviour, actions and habits may be separated from attitudes and tastes expressed in consumption patterns or reflexive verbal statements but also from more profoundly hidden values that can only be analysed indirectly.[71] None of these levels can be granted priority, since they may well influence each other in all possible directions. Habitual behaviour may sediment into deep values as much as values may appear in visible actions. One may also ask whether values are components of lifestyles or something else, and how tastes differ from actions if not by being precisely values.

John Fiske (1992, pp. 37ff) has suggested three areas of fan productivity that might be useful here. He first defines semiotic productivity as characteristic of all popular culture uses, as a 'making of meanings of social identity and of social experience from the semiotic resources of the cultural commodity'. Such semiotic productivity is essentially interior and private. Next, enunciative productivity is 'when the meanings are spoken and are shared within a face-to-face or oral culture', thus taking an intersubjective and public form. Such enunciations include not only verbal talk but also hair-styling or choice of clothes. Real fans often go one step further, to textual productivity, creating externalized texts like magazines, pictures or even films, making these audiences evolve into (amateur) producers and thus blurring the line between reception and production. The differences between these three areas are not quite distinct, as they seem to relate to degrees of both publicness, collectivity and exteriorization, which are not always coincident.

Bjurström and Lilliestam (1994) have suggested yet another trio of concepts that are relevant here. First, there is the simple selection of pre-existing items that can most easily be measured as consumption patterns. Next, tastes (and distastes) form a structure of habitus and attitudes.

---

[68] Cf. Thompson (1990) for a critical conception of ideology in modern culture as meaning in the service of relations of power and domination.

[69] Cf. Gramsci (1971), Hall (1986a), Turner (1990/1992, pp. 213ff) and Harris (1992).

[70] See, e.g., the otherwise inspiring Hall (1992b, p. 274) or Bocock and Thompson (1992, p. 5).

[71] Cf. Johansson and Miegel (1992).

Finally, stylization refers to the process of active style production where values, meanings and artefacts are connected. These three dimensions of the way people orient themselves towards subcultures, genres or cultural arenas constitute a third way to discern vertical levels of lifestyles. Other levels and dimensions may also be constructed, pointing at the highly complex and flexible character of the lifestyle concept.

'Horizontally', there are several parameters, modes or subsystems within each lifestyle, related to various human senses and cultural forms of expression. Four such modes concern appearance (dress, hair-style and attributes), performance (gestures, movements and rituals), taste (extrovert use mainly of music but also of other consumed or produced expressedly aesthetic forms) and argot (slang, vocabulary and speech patterns).[72] While appearance and performance mostly refer to visual aspects, music taste and argot mainly (but not exclusively) concern auditory aspects. Appearance is what can be seen on a still photo, performance is what can only be seen on a moving film. Appearance and (music) taste mostly relate to the selection and consumption of pre-fabricated items, chosen from what is offered on the market of the cultural industries. Performance and argot cannot be bought but are self-produced in each moment. However, all these differences are only approximate, and it is easy to find exceptions (music has visual aspects, clothes may be self-made, etc.).

Styles are thus not only bound to youth, subcultures or even collective groups. Practices of stylization take place in subcultural identifications, but also in specific group communities and in so-called 'mainstream' fashion. Stylization creates decipherable lifestyles on all levels, from large collective cultures down to microcultures and even the personal habitus of each individual. We all have style, both individually and as parts of several social constellations, but each such style can be more or less consistent, collective, reflexive, intentional, deviant or oppositional.

Each human being creates a unique personal lifestyle, but never in isolation. Even individual lifestyles result from intersubjective practices. Societal patterns of communication and social interaction give rise to supraindividual configurations. These collective lifestyles or cultural identities form sub- and microcultures. A subculture is a specific lifestyle pattern which is shared by more people than one single concrete group and recognized in a social sphere wider than a single local community. Subcultures gather a number of individuals but are not simply their sum. Individuals consecutively or even simultaneously participate in several different subcultures, seldom identifying totally with any of them, but by semi-attachment using their stylistic patterns as raw materials used to

---

[72] This division derives from Phil Cohen (1972/1980, p. 83), who mentions dress and music as 'plastic' forms which subcultures give meaning by selecting them for consumption, while argot and ritual are more tenacious 'infrastructural' forms produced by the subculture itself. Brake (1985, p. 12) distinguishes image (appearance), demeanour and argot.

construct a personal lifestyle. And while a group is inevitably changed if one person moves in or out of it, a subculture like the mods is not immediately dependent on the exact composition of those who identify with it. Subcultures are primarily symbolic patterns to which people may more or less completely relate their individual lifestyle, even though such identificatory mechanisms make it possible to relate them to specific groups of people. Microcultures, on the other hand, are the lifestyle pattern shared by some specific group of people interacting face-to-face and sharing specific experiences in a particular context or setting, like the culture of one family, peer group or school class. Compared to micro-cultures, subcultures are larger and relatively more generalized and decontextualized.[73] There is a complex and open-ended hierarchy from subcultures small enough to converge with microcultures to large units associated with societal categories like ages, genders, classes or races, or even comprising whole regional, national or supranational cultures. Sub-cultures are segments of some larger culture, defined in contrast to some others, but such segments can be constructed along many different axes. Subcultures develop continually and criss-cross in various ways, which makes it impossible to map them exhaustively.

Like literary genres and styles, subcultures are thus styles within the genre of ways of life that should be regarded as sets of generative principles whose application in cultural praxis may produce concrete groups and communities of people in certain settings, just as books can be written in certain genres or afterwards be classified by them. Subcultures are markers in mobile fields, and just as individuals walk in and out of subcultures, these change their forms and contents continuously, interacting with each other and with other objective, social, cultural and subjective factors.

The prefix 'sub-' thus mainly denotes that a lifestyle is analysed as a segment of some larger one, but it actually has a wider range of connotations that have been implied in cultural studies, deriving from the fact that 'sub' literally means 'under' or 'below': 'does 'sub' make this type of culture simply a segment of a larger culture, or is it something subordinate to a dominant culture, or is it something subterranean and rebellious, or is it substandard, qualitatively inferior?' (Hannerz 1992a, p. 69).

Subculture is here used in the widest possible sense, including all types of collective lifestyles, whether they are consistent, fragmented or even contradictory, conscious or unconscious, deliberate or unintentional, visible or covert, small or large, marginal or central, subordinate or dominant, rebellious or integrated, progressive or regressive, youthful or

---

[73] Phil Cohen (1972/1980, p. 83) stresses that 'subcultures are symbolic structures and must not be confused with the actual kids who are their bearers and supports'. Wulff (1988) emphasizes that several subcultural styles may coexist within the concrete microculture of one single peer group. Widdicombe and Wooffitt (1995) analyse how individuals talk of their relations to subcultures. Hannerz (1992a, pp. 68–99) relates subcultures and microcultures to modern globalization processes and to 'the cultural apparatus'.

adult. Some subcultures are non-reflexive lifestyles that can be traced by an observer but are not intended as such by those who are identified with them. Stylistic traits are then only secondary results of life choices in other areas, such as profession, or of categories into which people are born or cannot easily deliberately change (age, gender, ethnicity). In other, self-chosen subcultures, extrovert visibility is of crucial importance to the construction of one's cultural identity, and they are not only segments of a larger culture but often also subordinate, marginalized and oppositional to the more dominant segments of this overarching culture.

Homology and heterology

One problem with earlier subcultural studies was their exclusive focus on homologies, on the ways in which subcultural styles fitted together into homogeneous totalities. This has to be counteracted by an attendance to the inner differences, tensions and contradictions within subcultures and groups, which newer studies of social relations show as an increasingly important element in late modern lifestyles and life forms.

If the concepts of psychical, social and cultural identity imply diachronic consistencies over time in the structure of an individual, a group or a symbolic formation, the concept of homology primarily indicates a synchronic consistency between different elements or levels of subjectivities, groups or styles. A homology is a concordance between two structures. On one hand, homologies are sought horizontally, as coherencies and uniformities between the elements and modes of a (subcultural or life)style. On the other hand, vertical homologies can be constructed between stylistic behaviour and deep values, or between a cultural style and other levels, mainly the social positions or psychological structures of those who carry this style.[74] These two variants are often combined, but may be separated. It is possible to study the internal aesthetical logic of a style as independent of all social patterns. Conversely, non-coherent, contradictory or fragmented styles may be homological with equally heterogeneous social or psychological factors. But when an inner logic is discovered in a style, the tracing of homologies with extra-cultural levels becomes more urgent.

Homologies found between style elements or levels demand explanations that do more than just enumerate them without searching for their inner connections or causes. Such explanations may be sought for historically in the way style elements or levels have been gradually constituted in a process of stylization, or logically in the way elements or levels determine

---

[74] The term 'homology' derives from the Greek word for accord or concordance, something sounding with the same (*homo*) voice (*logos*) or functioning according to the same logic. Willis (1978) introduced it into subcultural theory, probably fetching it from Lévi-Strauss (1962/1966, pp. 36, 104 and 115). Like Bourdieu (1979/1984, pp. 175ff), they both discuss homologies between symbolical elements within a lifestyle as well as between the symbolical lifestyle and a social position.

each other in the present. On some occasions, one term of the homology may be traced back to another one. Horizontally, orientation towards a certain musical genre can give a subculture admission to a series of dress codes associated with this genre. Vertically, some dance pattern may be seen as an expression of social, class-based conditions in a group. But even when such direct homological relations are found, one has to explain in what way they arise, and why this and not any other possible homology is realized.

Homological relations are based on a specified dimension or aspect in which the two phenomena are similar, indicating the existence of a 'third term' in which they both share. A dance style and a working-class context may, for instance, be homological with respect to preferred patterns of bodily movement, that is, sharing this body paradigm. (It is not correct to say that the homological terms are homological with this third term – it is more of an aspect or a constituent of both of them.) And if elements within two style modes are found to be similar, one should look for a common cause or source behind this homology, so that they both may be traced back to some genetic or diachronically generic third term.

Willis (1978) finds that the style elements (dress, dance movements, musical taste, etc.) of a group of motor-bike boys are internally homological, in that they all point towards a need for direct control (over one's body, girlfriend and life circumstances). In the boys' life histories one may then trace experiences that show how their socialization has created this need. Family socialization may, for example, have mediated a general crisis and lost control in working-class culture that the bike-boys had felt and tried to compensate for by stylistic control-marking of the body and the territory. In this way, internal horizontal style homologies interplay with homologies between cultural, social and psychological levels.

Homology analyses have been criticized for using problematic ideas of iconicity or motivated signs, where signifier and signified are held together by relations of similarity or causality. But one has to understand that the parallels denoted by homologies are not exact identities, only relative similarities. It is therefore possible to construct several different homologies of a phenomenon, irrespective of whether these relations are founded on social conventions or objective facts. Each phenomenon contains many different aspects and dimensions, each of which may form the basis of a different homology through a different 'third term'.

If one style element A (e.g., safety-pin through the chin) is homological with element B (e.g., black dress), they are in some way similar (both may express a feeling of despair and 'no future'). If A is also homological with C (e.g., neon-dyed hair) through another 'third term' (an artificial identity-montage), then B and C need not be similar to each other, other than by both being similar to A (but in two different ways: black clothes and dyed hair are not obviously homological, and neither are despair and montage). One may find a whole series of elements that are all homological to A without being obviously similar to each other. Similar complexities may be found vertically, in that one psychological category D (like aggressivity) and one social category E (say, proletarian maleness) may each be homological with two different style traits F and G (thrash metal music and shaved heads), while there need not necessarily exist perfect homologies between D and E or F and G.

Homological similarity is no equivalence. That two things are alike does not imply that they are exactly identical. In contrast to equivalence, homology is no transitive relation, even though it is symmetrical. With equivalence denoted as $=$, homological 'family resemblance' as $\approx$, symmetry means that if $A \approx B$, then $B \approx A$ (if safety-pins are homological with black clothes, the reverse is also true).[75] The transitivity of equivalence means that if $A = B$ and $A = C$, then $B = C$. But if $A \approx B$ and $B \approx C$, it is not necessarily true that $A \approx C$. This is valid also of numbers or colours. One may think that $10 \approx 8$ and $10 \approx 12$ without accepting that $8 \approx 12$, and even though one might think that red$\approx$orange and red$\approx$violet, few would see much similarity between orange and violet. Homology has to do with voices sounding in concord, and a voice A may sound harmonically with both voice B and voice C while B and C form a very dissonant chord. Concordance is not identity.

If homologies are thus logically possible, it is not, however, always methodologically appropriate or useful to choose homology-based analytical models. The classical Birmingham works of the 1970s put the search for structural homologies at the centre of subcultural studies.[76] But styles and subcultures are filled with inner contradictions and tensions that force them to develop and thus provoke a historical dynamic. Style interpretations can therefore not be satisfied with seeing homologies, but must also thematize heterogeneous and conflictual traits in subcultures. Like identities, styles have diverging facets. The construction of homologies needs to be supplemented by an even more important look for '*heterologies*' and '*antilogies*'.[77] A heterology is an internal differentiation and diversity that fragments any identity, including the cultural identity encoded in a style. An antilogy is that heterology that is sharpened into an explicitly oppositional counter-logic, producing inner contradictions that propel change. No identities can be reduced only to homologies – they always include heterologies that make the homologies only relative and partial.

---

[75] The concept of family resemblance derives from Wittgenstein (1945/1976, § 67).

[76] Phil Cohen (1972/1980, p. 83) distinguishes between three levels in the analysis of subcultures: historical, structural/semiotic and phenomenological analysis. In a reverse order, Willis (1978, pp. 190ff) mentions indexical, homological and integral analysis as three methodological steps. In both cases, structural patterns of homology are at the centre. This focusing of homologies has been criticized by Hartwig (1980), who wants to substitute 'cultural praxis' for the overly reified concept of 'style', as well as by Clarke (1981/1990) and Redhead (1990).

[77] Cf. the musical concepts of homo-, hetero- and antiphony. The term 'heterology' is used by Bataille (cited by Levy 1991, p. 34) and by de Certeau (1985), as the science of the Other, that which breaks the unifying logic of a structure.

Sometimes the homological relations are strong enough to effectively hide inner contradictions, but that is only possible in limited moments.

Subcultural style studies could become much more dynamic and fruitful if heterological aspects were accepted as fundamental to the analysis. Horizontally, two elements in one style may diverge by pointing towards two quite different potential spheres of meaning. Vertically, two diverging style elements may each be homological with totally different class positions or subjective formations, so that the total style ensemble is a form of negotiation or compromise between differing interests. Different members of a subculture can then emphasize different parts of the shared stylistic stock but remain within the same frames. Even one single element (or set of mutually homological signs) may point towards two divergent spheres of meaning at the same time, offering different potential interpretations and functions. Different signs and symbols joined in one subcultural style can point in more or less different directions, and single symbols can also carry different meaning-potentials. Heterology is thus related to the necessary polyvalence, polysemy or polylogy of symbols and texts.[78]

Each personal or collective lifestyle thus contains more or less homologies, but also varying degrees of heterology or antilogy. Both sides have to be thematized by dynamic interpretations. There is a definite danger that subcultural analyses fixate 'the meaning' of a style in one particular image, saying, for instance, that hiphop means multiculturalism. Styles and identities construct certain coherences, but never only a single one, and never an all-encompassing one. Different homologies move on different levels, develop through time and contradict each other. Different interpretations may thematize different aspects, and a style is therefore never definitively understood.

Intentionality and consciousness

Subcultures are more or less (self-)conscious or reflexive formations, which the individuals to a varying degree know that they are involved in. One extreme is subcultural patterns that are only recognized by researchers or other external observers, another is those that everyone is familiar with. People may not spontaneously classify themselves in such terms, but they would perhaps acknowledge certain collective identity traits on closer reflection. There is no sharp limit between conscious and unconscious subcultural belongings, but one could argue that some minimal degree of consciousness is necessary, since culture as symbolic communication and

---

[78] 'Polyvalence' is the term Willis (1978) uses for style elements that carry a wide but not completely arbitrary spectrum of potential meanings. 'Polysemy' is a semiotic term for the ambiguity of signs and symbols. *Polylogue* was the title of a book by Kristeva (partly translated in Kristeva 1980), and where 'polylogy' indicates the necessarily open and diverging expressions of the split human subject, an idea that resonates with the psychoanalysis of Lacan, Derrida's thoughts about *différance* and decentering, and Kristeva's own concept of intertextuality. Cf. also Burgos (1988, pp. 23ff) on openness and contradictions in narrative identities, and see also the next two chapters.

meaning-creation presupposes a certain degree of interpretive effort and purposeful action. Non-conscious collective patterns may better be named social categories or para-communities.

Subcultures are not only potentially conscious but also to some (but again varying) extent intentional, in that individuals make certain deliberate choices of symbols and behaviour that define their communities. At one extreme, some subcultures are the effects either of inherited traditional characteristics or of conditions or life choices that have nothing to do with any will to distinguish oneself in terms of lifestyle. An example may be the cultural traits shared by age, gender, class or ethnic groups, whether they know and want it or not. The other extreme is exemplified by most common youth cultures, which seem to be very calculated constructions that are relatively easy to enter or leave.

Like homology, intentionality presents deep problems. Who are the actors to which the intentions belong that lead to the creation of a subculture? Many studies have shown that subcultures are created in an intricate interplay between various forces, so that the young people on their own are not themselves their sources or ultimate causes.[79] Neither historically nor structurally have subcultural styles been produced out of simple conscious decisions by individuals or groups. One cannot be sure that a skinhead had the intention to acquire such a label, given instead to him by peers, parents, teachers and the media. He might only have wished to have short hair and join the peer group, while explicitly protesting against all subcultural classifications.

Similar arguments have been made of the historical emergence of subcultures through a complex interaction between parents, teachers, the police, the media and young people inside and outside of a group. Stanley Cohen's (1972/1980) classical study of how the chain-reaction of an adult moral panic contributed to the spread and consolidation of youth cultures (mods and rockers) clearly demonstrates this complicated interplay between collective identity work and public media discourse.[80]

Vološinov (1929/1986) argues, against individualistic subjectivism and psychologism, that 'intention is always a lesser thing than creation' (p. 33); since consciousness is basically a materially anchored social fact, but he still retains a concept of expression (pp. 28f, 36 and 84f). Poststructuralism and deconstruction from Lacan and Derrida onwards have radically problematized the idea of subjects as autonomous sources of symbolic expressions. This inspired Hebdige (1991, p. 132) to distance himself from earlier definitions of subcultural styles as 'intentional communication' (1979, pp. 100f), based on visible constructions and deliberate choices. He argues that the term 'subculture' does not fit those floating identities that are formed through the consumption and use of popular culture and have

---

[79] Cf. Phil Cohen (1972/1980) and Cohen and Robins (1978).

[80] Moral and media panics are further discussed by Roe (1985), Drotner (1992), Boëthius (1993/1995) and Wistrand (1992). Cf. also Chapter 4 below.

nothing to do with original communities. He prefers to discuss 'affective alliances' of active media-users, a concept developed by Grossberg (1988 and 1989), or 'interpretive communities', a concept developed in the so-called 'reader-response-critique' reception theory by Fish (1980, pp. 14 and 171) and used in Radway's study of the meaning networks created by female romance readers (1984, pp. 11, 96f, 212 and 242f).[81]

In a similar vein, Willis (1990, pp. 141ff) discusses potential communicative communities or 'proto-communities' that may sometimes be 'serial', that is, not organically formed in direct communication but rather by shared media-related tastes. This goes back to the discussion by Sartre (1960/1982, pp. 642–54) of 'outer-directed praxis' and seriality in relation to the audience of hit-lists.[82] Sartre regarded this media-related collectivity as inauthentic and alienated. This aversion against seriality might today be broken. Communities constructed over distance by media-use may build upon experiences of face-to-face-interaction and widen them. Since subcultures should not be identified with microcultures or concrete groups of individuals, there is no problem in allowing them to include proto-communities where the participants never meet. Such communities may be non-intentional byproducts of media-use, or they may be actively sought for. The late modern expansion of media and communication has increased the number of serial proto-communities, but at the same time reproduced a wide interest in global, mobile and heterogeneous social communities such as those shaped by new social movements and public spheres like rave parties or computer networks (cf. Hebdige 1990).

The necessary insight that subjects are never completely self-conscious does not make intention, motive and will impossible. Human action is characterized by being 'teleologically' motivated, while other physical events only have 'archaeological' causes; human beings differ from things by having ideas of and motives for what they do. Subcultures may thus have differing degrees of consciousness and intentionality, even though none of the total extremes of fully transparent and autonomous or totally unconscious and outer-directed subcultures exist.

Visibility and publicness

A minimal degree of visibility (or audibility) is necessary to each subculture, since styles as cultural phenomena must be sufficiently objectivized to

---

[81] The concept of interpretation is further discussed in the next chapter. Much earlier, Peirce (1940/1955, pp. 99, 162f, 229 and 247) analysed how truth is 'made' by the indefinite interpretive and communicative community of scientists. Jensen and Jankowski (1991, p. 42) prefer 'interpretive repertoires' to 'interpretive communities' in media studies, since audiences seldom are integrated formal groups. Fish's definition is not quite clear. 'Interpretive communities are made up of those who share interpretive strategies not for reading (in the conventional sense) but for writing texts, for constituting their properties and assigning their intentions' (Fish 1980, p. 171). This primacy of 'writing' does not necessarily contradict the importance of reception, since what Fish seems to mean with 'writing' includes the productive activity of reading itself, as a construction of meaning.

[82] Bradley (1992) also develops these concepts from Sartre.

be perceptible by the senses of observers. Otherwise, they would not function as extrovert languages for and parts of identities. But while some subcultures are widely visible in the public sphere, others hide behind signs that are hard to decipher or even recognize for an outsider. Hackers or extreme video fans, for instance, might prefer not to be so easily recognizable by extrovert identification markers. Their specific behaviour seldom reaches public spaces, and the lifestyle traits they share may therefore be hard to discern on the street. Anne Krogstad (1990, p. 250) distinguishes between declarative and regulative symbol aspects. The former are extrovert identity markers, while the latter are used to regulate the inner life of a group. The importance of declarative symbols varies between subcultures.

The issue of visibility has been related to the male dominance in the early British subcultural studies.[83] The neglect of women as subjects was related to a neglect of 'mainstream' youth, the intimate sphere and family life, and inner or psychological aspects of cultural practices. Young women were neglected because they were less publicly visible, while troublesome or extrovert young men attracted the attention of adults and researchers. However, as with the discussion of public spheres, this critical thesis has to be slightly modified. Not only are gender differences subtly changing in this respect, but there is also a crucial difference between the style parameters. The behaviour, movements, rituals and perhaps also music and argot of men fills and dominates public space more than that of women, while the appearance (dress, hair, etc.) of women is hardly less visible than that of men. This makes it problematic to state generally that men are more 'visible' than women, especially in the discussion of fashion, where the opposite might often be the case, as indicated by the converse discussion of the male gaze and the aestheticization of the female body.

Some degree of visibility and publicness is thus needed for each subculture, but different lifestyles and communities vary in this respect too. It is important to see how the public and the private parts interrelate, instead of only studying the extrovert arenas. This implies a need to connect cultural interpretations with close studies of social relations and subject formations.

Marginality and subordination

Some subcultures are small and marginal, others are much larger and more central or dominating in society. Most subcultural studies have dealt with clearly deviant subcultures while those that are considered more 'normal' have been thought of as constituting a diffuse 'mainstream' culture. Just as psychoanalytical theorizing builds general subject theories from studies of single aberrant cases, general cultural models may be developed through such studies of deviant margins. The normal often becomes more visible

---

[83] McRobbie (1991) has underlined the lack of a gender perspective in the early works of Willis and Hebdige. Cf. also Hudson (1984).

when it is explicitly transcended. But this is no uncomplicated method, and it is important to relate such studies also to studies of the less marginal subcultures that also exist.

Many have called for style studies of 'common', non-subculturally identified youth.[84] But if everyone participates in various subcultural formations, this request should instead be reformulated as a plea for studies of less marginal or deviant subcultures. It can be questioned whether 'mainstream culture' exists at all, or if this normality is just a discursive and symbolic construction against which different subcultures profile themselves. But the varying distance between subcultures and institutional power centres does seem to make it possible to distinguish between subordinated and dominant subcultures.[85] Subcultures may thus be contrasted with either mainstream (majority) culture, dominating (élite) culture or (middle-class) counter-culture.

The first of these contrasts is problematic because individualization makes it difficult to see any specific cultural lifestyle pattern as shared by 'the masses' in late modernity. The second contrast needs to be further specified, since dominant cultures have also been diversified, and the discussion of hegemony inspired by the reading of Gramsci has shown that dominance is more complicated than a straightforward influence of the ruling classes. The prefix 'sub-' indicates that a subculture is in some way below another culture in status, which was often thought to imply that subcultures were age-specific variants of working-class culture. 'I do not think the middle class produces subcultures, for subcultures are produced by a dominated culture, not by a dominant culture', wrote Phil Cohen (1972/1980, p. 85), while Dick Hebdige (1979, p. 2) defined subcultures as 'the expressive forms and rituals of . . . subordinate groups'. Gary Clarke (1981/1990, pp. 89ff) criticizes this romanticization of working-class culture and points at the 'semiotic guerrilla warfare' that goes on as much in 'common' everyday stylization, in school, at home or in the work-place.[86] He thus dissolves the absolute polarization of subcultures versus normality, arguing instead for a complex multiplicy of increasingly flexible and reflexive lifestyles.

The third contrast, that between sub- and counter-cultures, is conceived either as a class difference between working and middle classes, or as a modal difference between implicit-partial and explicit-total critiques of society expressed in styles, or both at the same time. This leads to the next point, that of opposition, rebellion and resistance.

[84] E.g., Hartwig (1980), Clarke (1981/1990) or McRobbie (1991 and 1994).

[85] Hannerz (1992a, pp. 80f) has questioned the concepts of mainstream and dominant culture, arguing instead that the world is filled with subcultures. Yet, he makes relative distinctions in terms of 'more dramatically distinctive subcultures' and 'the dominant people, the political and economic élites', who need not coincide with the dominant (most widely spread) culture: 'a mainstream culture can be seen as a subculture in command of a more widely reaching cultural apparatus' (p. 92).

[86] 'Semiotic guerrilla warfare' is a phrase that derives from Eco (1967/1987).

Oppositionality and rebellion

British subcultural studies of the 1970s tried to deconstruct the earlier American concept of a general youth culture, with reference to differences and class conflicts that give rise to dominating and dominated cultures. Subcultures take part in a class-related ideological struggle over cultural and political hegemony in society.[87] The shifting degree of opposition and social critique in different subcultures has led to various theoretical modifications. While some explicitly resist dominating institutions and ideologies, others are more integrated and affirmative, at least on the surface. Unfortunately for a simple Marxist model, the most formulated and overtly rebellious ones (like hippies) seemed to consist mainly of middle-class youth, while working-class groups mostly appeared as rebels without any explicit cause.

A first solution was to differentiate between sub- and counter-cultures (Hall and Jefferson 1975/1976). The subcultures of the subordinate classes dealt with problems within their parental class culture and did not formulate any general critique of the dominant culture. Middle-class counter-cultures, on the other hand, confronted the crisis of their hegemonic parent culture, provoking them to attack central institutions in society and develop alternatives that went beyond the leisure sphere. Resistance was found in both types, but whereas subcultural resistance was split between a cultural class struggle (based on an identification with the parents) and a generation conflict (blurring the class identity by symbolic upward-striving), counter-cultural resistance could develop opposition against parents more directly into social critique.

The problem with this dichotomy was that, at least outside of Britain, the mods were already class-mixed in the 1960s, and as Hebdige (1979) noted, punk dissolved this strict boundary in Britain too. Many youth cultures simultaneously possess both sub- and counter-cultural traits in varying proportions, using leisure styles as well as written words, and engaging people from several classes. Hebdige used the concept of subculture in a more general way, interpreting subcultural style experiments as a subversive semiotic guerrilla warfare in terms of class, race or gender norms.

Those subcultures that approach the form of social movements may then be named counter-cultures, irrespective of their class basis, as they actively resist the prevailing social order. Counter-cultures are subcultures that have developed into movements, or movements that have developed their own subcultures. Social movements as conscious and intentional associations for effecting social change may coincide with subcultures, but are often much wider and more heterogeneous, as their members can have highly varying lifestyles that only converge around one single issue. Most subcultures are vague in regard to political and social issues, and they

---

[87] Hall and Jefferson (1975/1976), Hall et al. (1978).

seldom organize purposeful action for specific transformative goals. But the limits between these types are floating. Subcultures have more or less counter-cultural traits, and those that have such traits can be more or less movement-like, while movements may be more or less subcultural.

Dominated social groups are often associated with resistance against dominating powers, but subcultures may be subordinate without being very oppositional, and vice versa. It has also become more widely recognized that subordination as well as resistance exist along many diverging axes. The border between deviance and normality has been problematized as more diffuse and perhaps even less interesting than was earlier imagined. Resistant stylizations could appear in more places within everyday life than only in movements or subcultures. All this has released the discussion of resistance from its immediate ties to collective patterns of subordination and to youth. The result was new debates in the 1980s between critical and affirmative studies. Some found resistance everywhere, others completely abolished the concept, and against both these affirmative camps still others tended to restore rather crude normative values. A more nuanced position was to retain a critical capacity by developing more precise models of power structures and types of resistance.

Many continued to stress resistance potentials in youth and popular culture.[88] Inspired by Hall, Foucault, Deleuze and Guattari, Grossberg distinguishes between 'empowerment', pleasure, struggle, resistance and opposition in the various 'affective alliances' and 'articulations' of popular discourses and everyday practices:

> Empowerment refers to how cultural formations in daily life make possible particular sorts of practices, commitments and relationships. . . . Empowerment – having a certain control over one's place in daily life – is not the same as struggle, the attempt to change one's conditions. And struggle is not always resistance, which requires a specific antagonism. And resistance is not always opposition, which involves an active and explicit challenge to some structure of power. (Grossberg 1992, pp. 73 and 95f)

When late modern discourses like French and American postmodernism argued for the dissolution of symbols, dichotomies, subjects, communities and reality in an infinite linguistic play of 'simulacra' (Baudrillard 1988), some came to the conclusion either that resistance is everywhere or that it is nowhere. According to Oldfield, power has slipped away and made resistance vain:

> The subversion that pop culture has often imagined, the subversion of activity, infiltration, revolution, eruption of repressed desires, can be forgotten. All that's

---

[88] Bloomfield (1991, p. 80) argues that 'mass-cultural forms of music' contain 'resistances to commodity culture' and a generational 'resistance to socialization into routine adult practices in societies that are fundamentally undemocratic'. Street (1986), Garofalo (1987 and 1992), Ullestad (1987), Denselow (1989) and Bradley (1992) all emphasize politically radical elements in rock, pop and rap.

possible today is the renunciation of *agency*, varieties of refusal to recreate power, to be yourself: simply *disappearance* from or discrediting of the places where power and resistance keep propagating each other. (1989, p. 265)

Foucault would have found it hard to accept such a cynical or romantic belief in renunciation and disappearance from all power/resistance relations. Others have instead found subversion everywhere in popular culture. Dick Hebdige (1988) is ambivalent, as he, on one hand, abandons his old (1979) model of subcultural negation and resistance, while he, on the other hand, uses Gramsci, Foucault and Baudrillard to search for insubordinate moments in wider forms of media consumption and lifestyle. Willis (1990) outlines the 'common' (ordinary and shared) culture with its 'grounded aesthetics' based in everyday life as an oppositional alternative to the dominating institutions of élite culture, using ideas of symbolic creativity and identity-work in media-use. His earlier work had stressed the internal contradictions in youth cultures like the bike-boys, hippies or the noisy lads at school, where emancipatory potentials were curbed by limitations like sexism, racism and anti-intellectualism. Now, all daily life seems unproblematically liberating while all high culture appears as conservative.

To John Fiske, 'Popular culture is the culture of the subordinated and disempowered' (1989a, p. 4). Even though it is said to contain both power and resistance, his main model is a revised version of the old triangle of dominating high culture, reactionary mass culture and emancipatory folk culture. Mass culture (i.e., the 'preferred' readings of media texts) is reactionary but opens spaces for the homogeneous 'people' to formulate alternative, critical interpretations in its own, genuine, authentic 'popular culture' (i.e., the people's cultural practices of meaning-making in reception and production), which primarily opposes élite culture as an aesthetic and institutional unity. This transformation of the old contrast between the false mass culture and the true culture of the people makes popular culture as a whole in principle a progressive tool of 'the people' in its struggle against 'the power-bloc' – two unhappily stereotyped concepts that Fiske (e.g., 1993, pp. 9ff) has borrowed from Stuart Hall (1981), in his turn influenced by Gramsci. In such a model, both the people, with its resistance and popular culture, and the élite, with its power and high culture, are homogenized and idealized into fixed essences, in spite of all efforts to make these categories more fluid by defining them as dispositions or sets of social forces rather than as social categories of people. In whatever way these concepts are defined, this stereotyping polarization tends to collapse the complexity of cultural phenomena, and cannot fruitfully be combined with an insight that some groups or practices in one respect express resistance while in other respects exercising social domination. It also tends to blur contradictions and conflicts that appear within popular culture (between different genres or social groups) or within high culture (between different institutions or aesthetic avantgardes). The result is a wavering between structuralist determinism and populist voluntarism.

Fiske has been intensely criticized both outside and inside cultural studies, both for his own sake and as a typical example of problematic tendencies or uses of the models of Gramsci, Barthes, Foucault, Bourdieu, Hall and others.[89] The binary polarity of popular versus high culture conjures away the internal differences within each of these two poles. The people is no fixed essence that creates its own cultural forms, but is itself constituted in cultural practices, and is crucially divided, as the old critique against the concept of mass showed. And 'high culture' cannot be reduced simply to 'the dominant culture', without discussion of its other meanings and of its internal divisions between conservatives and avantgardes. The wish to construct homogeneous blocs has to be resisted. And the reduction of culture to strategic power-games of subordination and subversion neglects other aspects of communication, as was argued against Bourdieu above. Even if the extended concept of resistance in everyday popular practices is accepted, clearer differentiations between types of power and of resistance are needed, in order to recognize the difference between cultural industrial and alternative media production and to avoid an inflated concept of resistance that, paradoxically, becomes affirmative towards the market system. The power of audiences, media producers and counter-cultures is not the same, and the resistance of wide media audiences, particular categories, subcultures and movements also differs in both degree and kind. Power and resistance are not fixed and unitary essences that individuals or groups may simply possess. 'In short this power is exercised rather than possessed' (Foucault 1974/1979, p. 16). The celebration of the pleasures of counter-reading in media reception tends to idyllicize and trivialize resistance by forgetting the hard work, struggle and pain that is needed to assert one's difference against dominating patterns of meaning (Bordo 1993). This points to the need for a reformulated resistance theory, which is the concluding theme of this chapter.

Resistance

A model of the network of resistance potentials can use elements from all the discussed theories. Power and resistance are always present but not always central or focused in social life. Not all cultural phenomena are primarily instances of domination or opposition, but the incessant presence of power relations in interaction as well as institutions induces germs of resistance in all everyday life practices, including popular culture. Each effort towards explicit and offensive mobilization has to start with such

[89] Cf. Budd et al. (1990), Carragee (1990), Lembo and Tucker (1990), Morris (1990), Turner (1990/1992), Frow (1992), Harris (1992), McGuigan (1992) and Bordo (1993). Some of these critics mention critical theory and particularly Habermas as an alternative, but they unfortunately often fall back to the older ideology-critical and too one-sidedly pessimist versions of this tradition – Adorno and Horkheimer (1944) and the early Habermas (1962/ 1989) rather than the more ambivalently open Walter Benjamin and late Habermas.

profane germs, and cultural analysis has to develop a capability to understand the ambivalences of such phenomena, instead of looking for essentialist and totalizing explanations that categorize everything into good and evil substances. The hierarchical structures of institutions placed between systems and lifeworld intersect other types of power and domination orders, related to categories like gender, age, class and ethnicity, all provoking different attempts of resistance. Such relations of power and resistance can sometimes aggregate to form larger social movements or counter-cultures, but they often contradict each other, so that it becomes impossible to generalize them into pure versions of bad and good. For example, what is resistance to class domination might simultaneously be an example of gender or race domination. Some resistances are directed against one or both of the systems to counteract their colonization tendencies, while others use them to counteract dominance relations within the lifeworld. A political goal might be to form alliances between various resistance seeds, but an analysis of actual popular culture can never totalize all such practices into a common camp of the people against the power élite. Such reductionist models only conceal the delicate dialectics of power and resistance that take place not only between the popular and the educated, or between the lifeworld and the systems, but also within popular culture itself, on all levels, from its production to its use.

A 'prismatic' cultural theory is needed that is able to distinguish between various aspects of domination and opposition, and to see old and new diversities as well as patterns of dominance.[90] It must be able to relate to three important theoretical turns that have taken place in our century. First, the increasing interest in the mobility, flexibility, dynamics, historicization and change of modernization processes that have become focal themes within most cultural and academic fields. Secondly, the problematizing of symbolic forms, language, communication and the whole cultural dimension that is manifest in the rise both of new subcultures or taste debates and of cultural theory within various disciplines. Thirdly, the necessity of differentiation, diversity, distinctions and polydimensionality in late modern complex society, politics and theory.

The new emphasis on dynamics, openness, crossings and hybridity as a normal identity condition implies that the social world consists of a series of interlacing webs, each with its centre and peripheries. These networks are superimposed on each other, shaping intricate interference patterns. When one pattern hides another, critical reflection is needed to disclose the concealed domination forms. Structures of nation-states may, for example, hide regional, class or ethnic relations, or political hierarchies may veil economic ones.

---

[90] In their discussion of the Madonna-interpretations of various ethnic groups, Nakayama and Peñaloza (1993) attack the traditional binary thinking in black/white and argue for a 'prismatic' perspective. Yet, they discern a white interpretive dominance even in non-white interpretations, just like white light is a composite 'centre' for the colours of the prism.

The wielding of power in late modernity is forced to become more flexible, but each power still has a certain rigidity, a tendency to freeze in space and to erect fixed structures that strive to defend the status quo. The resistance towards such power structures always has to be dynamic, even though it sometimes builds its own trenches. These relations have been theorized in various ways. While Gilroy (1993a and b) talks of crossing, hybrid, diasporic identities, Melucci (1989) discusses how oppositional potentials in daily life can be mobilized by nomadic social movements. Michel de Certeau (1974/1988) outlines a difference between the strategies of power and the tactics of resistance. He analyses the everyday life creativity of the practices of consumption and reception which actively use and give meaning to the commodities and media offered by the economic system of cultural industries. Like Hebdige, he argues that in cultural consumption and stylistic bricolages, Others' products may be used to open spaces for play and for critical or utopian manoeuvres against dominating rules and norms.

Dominating powers use centralized strategies to order and control space, and divide it into spheres to prevent changes that would threaten their own positions. Dominated groups can only rarely launch any corresponding counter-offensive. In everyday life, they instead have to develop temporally and transformationally oriented tactics: 'strategies pin their hopes on the resistance that the *establishment of a place* offers to the erosion of time; tactics on a clever *utilization of time*, of the opportunities it presents and also of the play that it introduces into the foundations of power' (de Certeau 1974/1988, pp. 38f). Strategies and tactics should not be frozen into any over-simple polarity of two unitary camps, but instead be conceived as interacting processes that may be abstracted from the complex mix of manoeuvres in all cultural spheres.

These ideas may be connected to the distinction between two types of resistance suggested by Umberto Eco, inspired by Michel Foucault: 'this technique of opposition to power, always from within and widespread, has nothing to do with the techniques of opposition to force, which are always external, and specific' (1979/1987, p. 252).[91]

> Where there is power, there is resistance, and yet, or rather consequently, this resistance is never in a position of exteriority in relation to power. . . . These points of resistance are present everywhere in the power network. Hence there is no single locus of great Refusal, no soul of revolt, source of all rebellions, or pure law of the revolutionary. Instead there is a plurality of resistances, each of them a special case . . . . Are there no great radical ruptures, massive binary divisions, then? Occasionally, yes. But more often one is dealing with mobile and transitory points of resistance, producing cleavages in a society that shift about, fracturing unities and effecting regroupings, furrowing across individuals themselves, cutting them up and remolding them, marking off irreducible

---

[91] Eco reads Foucault differently from Barthes, whom he explicitly attacks. Harvey (1990, pp. 45ff) uses Foucault and Lyotard to describe how society contains plural sources of oppression and multiple focal points of resistance.

regions in them, in their bodies and minds. Just as the network of power relations ends by forming a dense web that passes through apparatuses and institutions, without being exactly localized in them, so too the swarm of points of resistance traverses social stratifications and individual unities. And it is doubtless the stategic codification of these points of resistance that makes a revolution possible, somewhat similar to the way in which the state relies on the institutional integration of power relationships. (Foucault 1976/1990, pp. 95f)

Resistance can be defined as all forms of actions that challenge some established force or power structure and is thus potentially transformative rather than just reproductive of dominating positions or structures. Young (1990) shows that resistance has to oppose five different forms of oppression: exploitation, marginalization, powerlessness, cultural imperialism and violence. And while such a fight for freedom or emancipation must always also strive for equality, it must also acknowledge, respect and affirm differences. Aggleton and Whitty (1985, pp. 62f) find it important to make a series of crucial distinctions: (1) between resistant *intentions* and resistant *effects*; (2) between acts of challenge or '*resistances*' against overarching power relations and those '*contestations*' that are directed against localized principles of control; (3) between the resistant *subjectivity* of personal insights into the nature of power and the resistant *behaviour* of social collectives; and (4) between the *experiential site* in which resistant intentions arise and the field of practice where it results in resistant actions, since a *displacement* may take place from one area or sphere to another (e.g., from school to family, from class to generation or from economics to culture). They argue that studies of resistance need to investigate ethnographically how various aspects are distributed and articulated across different sites of experience and within different sets of power in specific contexts.

A differentiated analysis of resistance should ask *who* resist *what*, *how*, *why* and with *which results*. Some aspects of the agents, enemies, means, causes, intentions and effects of resistance will now in turn be mentioned, to indicate how some of the theoretical models discussed so far may be inserted in such a polydimensional sphere-related resistance theory.

Agents

The resistant agents may be single individuals, groups, subcultures or whole social categories (genders, generations, classes, ethnic groups or geographical regions). Resistance may thus be individual or collective, resistant subjectivity or resistant communality. It may also in both cases be either territorially localized or nomadic and diasporic. But a first condition is that its agent (whether one person or a group, and whether fixed or mobile) acts like a subject, equipped with will, affects, reason and responsibility. Resistance involves conflicts between subjects and some goal-oriented order that tries to force these subjects to do something which they do not themselves want. Power is not (social) power until the plans and wishes of some subjects are subjected to foreign forces and rules. Our tendency to think of non-human processes in terms of resistances and colliding forces is a constructed projection of experiences in social life onto nature. Ricoeur (1986, p. 131) argues that Althusser's and Foucault's wish to bury the philosophical myth of the human being as a subject makes it impossible to protest against encroachments on people's rights. 'I do not see from where we could borrow the forces to resist the apparatus if not from the depths of a subject, having claims that are not infected by this supposed submissive constitution' (Ricoeur 1986, p. 150).

Why would people resist oppression if they and the whole sociocultural world were just a structural-functionalist, behaviourist or discursive mechanism? There must be a human will to resist power, whenever power exists. The neo- and poststructuralist debate inspired by Lacan, Derrida and Foucault has problematized this intentionalist perspective for its reduction of institutionalized power to relations of personal dominance. Power does not have to be defined as based upon the individual subjective will. In an extended sense, power can also flow from intersubjective or even objectivized forces. But in order to be power, it still has to be break against the will of subordinated subjects, thus engaging in a dialectic relation with their latent or manifest resistance.[92] The psychoanalytical critique of the subject does not necessarily erode its intentional aspects. The ego is no master in its own house, since the unconscious as a social product prevents us from deliberately steering our thoughts and actions or even know all about ourselves. But the fact that every subject is a sociocultural and opaque construction does not make it an illusion. Subjective will is necessary for human life and society, and thus for resistance, even though it is never totally controlled by each self.[93]

Targets

The primary targets of resistance may be of different kinds. In relational resistance, they are of the same kind as its agents, that is, human subjects. This type is completely embedded in the intersubjective level of the lifeworld. In structural resistance, the oppressing enemy may be objectivized institutions or systems, in which case resistance may aim either at lifeworld structures (like institutionalized patriarchal, ethnical, class or generational hierarchies) or at the commercialism and bureaucracy of the economic or political system. Single actors may exercise power through direct force or by creating structural frames and rules that provokes resistance, but power is also stored in inhuman systems that exceed the subjective interests of their representatives.

Only by contextualizing cultural practices can their degree and type of opposition be estimated. An oppositional rhetorical gesture or self-

[92] Mathiesen (1982, pp. 9, 32f and 74) sees power as intentional, relational and enforcing, and argues that its dependance on intentional decisions is what makes resistance possible.

[93] Cf. Elliott (1992) for a critique of Lacanianism's tendencies to regard the subject as totally determined by the language system, thereby neglecting the potential for creativity.

understanding must be judged in relation to its targets and motives.[94] Each act of meaning production in cultural practice should then be related not only to what is the normal interpretation pattern in the specific social group in question, but also to those preferred readings that are foregrounded by established societal institutions (critics, teachers, politicians, etc.) and/or by older normative interpretive traditions. One act may be oppositional within a certain group, another may oppose what leading authorities prescribe, a third one may break with inherited norms. These three may coincide or not, depending on the status of the group in society and the rate of cultural change within established institutions. And what is critical towards a class rule may be affirmative towards a gender or age hierarchy, or vice versa. All this calls for a precise specification of the target of each act of resistance, in order to understand its long-term transformative and emancipatory potentials.

Means

The means of resistance are manifold – counter-identities, counter-cultures, counter-public spheres, counter-movements, counter-institutions and counter-powers form a sliding scale from the subjective over the cultural and social to the political and objectivized level. While manifest resistant acts explicitly attack power relations, the latent resistant potentials in everyday life grow in inner subjectivities, in social relations and cultural communication forms or as objectivized material or institutional resources.

Within the subjective level, one may distinguish between imaginary resistant fantasies and real resistant acts, but that line is mostly blurred, since cultural symbols are necessary both to mental conceptions and to social actions.[95]

On an external level, resistance may sometimes build institutional organizations that form strong counter-powers. These organize material resources and shape spaces for oppositional practices both of a critique and defence against oppressive powers, and of experimental and offensive utopias. Counter-movements and counter-cultures may create counter-public spheres where commercial and bureacratic systemic demands can be

---

[94] Evans (1990) argues that if adolescents are normally rebellious, then only non-rebellious adolescent interpretations would be oppositional to that norm. Schulze et al. (1993) mention that some Madonna-haters think of themselves as oppositional towards the allegedly dominating discourse of Madonna as subversive.

[95] Cohen and Taylor (1976/1992) discuss how identity work contains elements of resistance from the routines and constraints of everyday life, using fantasies and free spaces related to the media and popular culture. They tend to deem these 'escape attempts' as ultimately integrative and individualistic, advocating instead a resistance that is more organized and anchored in concrete historical and social contexts. A more hopeful view on utopian elements of daily life and popular culture is offered by Bloch (1959/1986) and Reyher (1975).

resisted and alternative social and cultural forms can be tested, with differing norms and values, styles and expressive means, relations and identities. These may simultaneously rebuild problematic new dominance forms on the ruins of the old ones, but they may also contain elements of justice, solidarity, autonomy, pleasure and communication that transcend narrow special interests.

It may be useful to distinguish four levels. Resistant potentials are the latent possibilities that are created in each site where subjects are subjected to the exercise of power. Resistant germs grow where subjects start to act in their own interest. Resistant hearths are formed in collective clusters of such individual counter-actions. Finally, resistant movements are explicit, target-oriented and unified collective processes.

The struggle against power is often a fight for autonomy in free spaces for wilful interactions. Physical rooms of one's own and social spaces where others may not intrude with control demands may be strictly protected side-areas, but they may also be constructed in the middle of power structures through cunning manoeuvres that outplay them against each other to clear the space for resistant subjectivities and socialities. New mass media affect social counter-movements and counter-cultures by changing the coordinates of time and space. Late modern de-localized subcultures and mediated communication make it possible to form communities over distance between people who are not in the same time or space. The spatial co-spatiality or territoriality of a particular place or locality is no longer necessary to create contacts, movements or resistant networks, even though intersubjective communication (the sharing of meanings) remains an inescapable precondition.[96]

Causes and intentions

The question of 'why' resistance appears has two aspects. The ultimate *cause* of social resistance is social power – oppression, coercion, dominance – and the lack, suffering and frustration it creates in human subjects. The precise type of power defines what type of cause lies behind a specific resistance. Besides the differences covered by the aspects already discussed (agents, targets and means), one may also differentiate between direct violence and indirect influence as possible causes.

The motives or *intentions* of resistance may also vary. Some resistances are unintended side-effects of other intentions, appearing as such only from the perspective of power. Some are unconscious protests intended but never reflected by the subject. Others are conscious and intentional, some of them even reflexive, where the subjects not only know that they wish to resist but also formulate and actively relate to their own motives

[96] Cf. Hebdige (1990) and the discussion of the public sphere above.

and goals, by intersubjective discourses within some counter-public sphere.[97]

An intention of the dominated is often to take power (over one's own destiny, over the old rulers, over resources), but even if this succeeds, the struggle against the old master is no less resistance. Power is no fixed essence but a fluid and shifting relation. Nobody can avoid all power, but a radical resistance strives to deconstruct power structures.

Gilroy (1993a, p. 37) distinguishes two dimensions of critical culture. While 'the politics of fulfilment' tries to fulfil the social and political promises left ungratified by today's society, mainly using verbal and textual means, 'the politics of transfiguration' invents qualitatively new desires, social relations and communality forms, striving for the sublime, present-ing what cannot be represented, in mimetic, dramatic and performative modes. Here, a difference in means is thus connected to one in intentions, but the model is not quite convincing. The connection of fulfilment/ transfiguration with textual/dramatic modes is not quite necessary. The politics of fulfilment seems somewhat like the bricolage of a Jack or Jill of all trades or do-it-yourself person that rearranges objects at hand into a new signifying montage, thus realizing hidden potentials in these existing objects. The politics of transfiguration is like the work of an engineer, who invents from scratch.[98] But it is the *bricoleur* rather than the engineer who uses mimetic and performative means to reach the sublime, while the engineering dream is more bound to certain currents within literate modernist aesthetics.

Hegel, Marx, Adorno, Benjamin, Bloch and Habermas all seem to stress the politics of fulfilment in their views of capitalism as containing its own utopian potentials to be uncovered by revolutionary praxis and 'immanently' critical theory. But this does not necessarily make all of them always forget the transfigurative. If capitalism or modernity is understood as deeply cut through with diverging promises, then fulfilment and transfiguration are not so wide apart as might first be believed. And an overly rash transformative voluntarism is dangerous, since it takes too little care of the actual potentials and needs of the present while simultaneously being weighed down by disastrously unconscious remnants of the past. Fulfilment and transfiguration need to be put into a dialectical motion of critique and utopia, rather than strictly separated.

Effects

Some intentional or unconscious resisting acts succeed in keeping oppressors back or transformating power relations. Others fail, either by

---

[97] Cf. the discussion above of intentionality and consciousness in relation to subcultures.
[98] Lévi-Strauss (1962/1966, pp. 16ff) discusses the pre-modern myth-making *bricoleur* versus the modern constructing 'engineer'. Clarke (1976, p. 177) and Hebdige (1979, pp. 102ff) study the stylistic bricolage of late modern youth subcultures.

meeting over-strong power-defences or by using the wrong means and unvoluntarily leading to integration and adjustment rather than to transfiguration.

It is problematic to separate partial contestations from general resistances, since no position allows us to judge all effects of an act and no resistance can presumably be total. But it is true that resistance can be displaced between different levels, spheres and experiential sites (Aggleton and Whitty 1985, p. 63). This sometimes helps to spread critical actions, while at other times diverting resistant flows into ideological blind alleys by losing sight of the roots of power.

Objectively, resistances may or may not succeed in really breaking down the powers they attack. But even when the resistant intentions are not fulfilled, resistance is not necessarily wasted. Institutions may have been indirectly affected, social relations and norms may have been displaced and cultural discourses in public media may have been changed in a possibly not intended but nevertheless welcome direction. Subjectively, individuals may have to give up the struggle in which they were involved, but they may retain inner traces and memories that keep critique and hope alive.

A resistance to one power dimension may (even intentionally) result in the strengthening of another one. Resistance to class domination is not always innocent in relation to age, gender or ethnicity, and a social movement may have quite different consequences on political, economic, social, cultural and psychological levels. An alternative experiment that fails institutionally or socially may leave inspiring symbolic marks in the cultural public sphere, and the fate of a single individual after participating in a counter-culture need not coincide with its collective or symbolic function.

Willis (1977) has analysed the anti-school culture of a group of working-class lads, and found it highly ambivalent. Their opposition to middle-class values and power structures within the school institution is an overly partial resistance. The peer-group culture contains devastating limitations in its relation to the division of labour (reflection), women and immigrants. This leads its resistance to anti-intellectualism, misogyny and racist xenophobia that prevents the rebellious germs from developing into any emancipatory movement. It is in fact the very resistance of the gang that prepares it for accepting a future subordinate wage labour position. The partial character of the critical potentials and the fundamental inner contradictions of this working-class culture prevent its seeds of emancipation from maturing. There is no simple line between power and resistance: opposition is often intimately mixed with hidden repression, adjustment and subordination, and the frontiers run in much more complicated ways than expected. An effective resistance on one level may be conservative on another level, and this may in the longer run make the victories on the first level useless.

Radway (1984) discovers similar complex ambivalences in adult women's romance reading that keep utopian hopes and anti-patriarchal critique alive while simultaneously reproducing restricting self-definitions.[99] A similar ambivalence runs through the whole literature on the carnival and on popular culture, where the safety-valve function of a play with the world turned upside-down may even inspire effective revolutions, but also is a temporary escape that may make it easier to adjust and accept the usual subordination (cf. Bakhtin 1965/1984). What effects each instance of resistance has is decided by its specific agents, targets, means, causes, intentions and contexts. It is an empirical, political and contextual question whether or not a set of different resistant germs can form tactical or strategical alliances that effect emancipatory transformations.

Conflicting social agencies

All spheres are filled with disharmonies. They are seldom attuned, and each carries plural power-hierarchies that create manifold resistances whose liberating aims sometimes may be successful, if always only partially and in non-intended sites or ways. A model of some important types of social agencies that exercise power and/or provide resistance in various ways concludes this chapter.

(1) People set up various *institutions* which are objectivized and more or less formalized apparatuses, networks, fora or channels for collective action and interaction. Some such institutions are like circuits for the exchange of cultural texts like books, magazines, records or images. Some of these are related to the established forms of art, while other media circuits relate more widely to the various public spheres that organize communicative interaction of the lifeworld in relation to both state and market. Some of these public spheres are large and general, like the bourgeois public sphere, others are alternative or oppositional, like the popular and the working-class subpublic spheres or like various counter-public spheres that are connected to social movements with explicit transformative goals and forms of collective organization. Every human being necessarily takes part in many institutions, by being a crucially social animal.

---

[99] Cf. also Blix (1992, p. 67) on the 'small places for resistance and alternative readings of their lives through moments of excess' in women's readings of magazines around 1950. Thurston (1987) finds that historical transformations of the romance genre has later offered larger spaces of critique against patriarchal power, and McRobbie (1991, pp. 135ff) comes to a similar conclusion for teenage girls' magazines. Aggleton and Whitty (1985) use Willis and Bourdieu to analyse the problems for kids of the new middle classes to politicize their local oppositions into a general resistance. Laing (1985) and Baron (1989) show how the subcultural resistance of punk revealed shortcomings in society but also contained deep inner fractures and limitations. Rasmussen (1989/1990) studies how young working-class boys' collective watching of action videos creates and upholds internal power structures. Malmgren (1992) highlights several aspects of class- and gender-related resistance in teenagers' relation to school, media and literature.

(2) In different *communities*, people share certain interests, modes of interpretations or constructions of meaning, forging specific relationships towards the texts that circulate within various institutions and networks. Several interpretive communities may share one single public sphere.[100] Communities may be divided vertically (between specialist insiders and amateur outsiders), or horizontally (between various special sub-interests). They shape dialogic discourses functioning like symbolic orders or horizons that define what interpretations are possible in each setting. While everyone uses interpretive repertoires or schemes, only some take part in conscious, explicit and organized interpretive communities.

(3) Specific *cultures* are based on collectively shared lifestyles or taste patterns, mutually recognized within themselves as well as by surrounding others. Some such cultures are large and comprehensive, others small and marginal, in a range from general cultures to subcultures. The ones explicitly oppositional to some ruling powers may be called counter-cultures. All these cultures can develop or inhabit various interpretive communities. We cannot avoid living in cultures, but only a minority is actively engaged in reflexive subcultures, and still fewer in transgressive counter-cultures.

(4) Concrete *groups* of people, with their respective microcultures, are based on regular and close face-to-face-contact within specific contextual localities or settings. Each group may or may not be socially and culturally unified. Each culture, community and institution thus consists of a series of interacting groups, but single groups mostly also inhabit and are intersected by a series of interacting subcultures, communities and public spheres.

(5) Individual *subjects* are the minimal units of agency, even though they are never unitary but always internally split and fractured. Interacting subjects construct and inhabit all the various social forms above.

All these types of spheres and socialities are sites of power and resistance, arising through communicative interaction which generates, uses and modifies that range of symbolic tools and orders which is the core of the cultural level itself. People share social belongings of various kinds, but they also share meaningful symbolic forms, which are next to be discussed.

---

[100] Thus, folk and rock music fans gathered in the 1970s Swedish music movement (Fornäs 1993).

4

Symbols

The core of culture is symbolic communication: the dialogic flows and textures of meaningful forms. Symbols presuppose subjects and social spheres, but are also necessary for their formation. In opposition to reifications of the symbolic order of language systems, what Vološinov says of verbal language is true of all modes of communication:

> In actual fact, however, language moves together with that stream [of verbal communication] and is inseparable from it. Language cannot properly be said to be handed down [from generation to generation] – it endures, but it endures as a continuous process of becoming. Individuals do not receive a ready-made language at all, rather, they enter upon the stream of verbal communication; indeed, only in this stream does their consciousness first begin to operate. (1929/ 1986, p. 81)

This chapter will study the symbolic rivers on which we move, in life as well as in cultural theory – including the writing and reading of this text. Within this level, all the other levels turn up again, as discourse types and as style aspects. Symbolic or cultural forms mirror, represent and thematize other parts and aspects of human life, society and the external world. This is no transparent reproduction but a symbolically coded reconstruction which is never the same as what it depicts or points at. And it does not imply that the whole cultural sphere is only a reflex of material, economic, political, social or subjective levels. Culture represents or refigurates these other 'realities' while simultaneously opening an intersubjectively shared symbolic dimension of its own. Cultural texts mirror society but simultaneously take part in its formation.[1]

There is a deepening insight in late modernity that this cultural level is relatively autonomous, in need of specific theoretical models and modes of interpretation. It is through webs of symbols that we enjoy, suffer, love, hate, know, value, judge and understand, and specific interpretive means are needed to reveal how these symbolic webs work. Models of symbols in action have been suggested by various types of hermeneutics and semiotics, developed within the humanities, particularly the aesthetic disciplines, but the functioning of languages, images and other symbolic representations has also been increasingly central among social scientists,

---

[1] 'The representations of the social world themselves are the constituents of social reality. Economic and social relations are not prior to or determining of cultural ones; they are themselves fields of cultural practice and cultural production – which cannot be explained deductively by reference to an extracultural dimension of experience' (Hunt 1988, p. 7).

sociologists, anthropologists, psychologists and historians. Culture is intimately connected to social spheres and personal subjectivities, but its own
order is also to be respected. Culture is more than a mediating membrane
between objects and subjects, society and individual. A traditional thinking in a dichotomy of inner versus outer or individual versus society misses
the fundamentally shared nature of symbolic forms and makes them
transparent mediators of social or psychological forces.[2] Neither should
culture be reduced to ethnic identity. Instead, ideas of cultural forms
within philosophy, linguistics, literature, art and musicology will here be
used to construct a model of symbolic forms, as the very heart of cultural
theory.

Culture and communication

Culture is the aspect of human interaction that concerns how meaning is
created by the use of symbols, involving various modes of style production
and communicative action.[3] The term derives from a Latin word for tillage
or productive use of the earth. Already the ancient Romans spoke of
cultura animi, cultivation of the soul. This metaphorical use has since the
seventeenth century become dominant in a secularized meaning, distinguished from religious 'cult' but closely related to both individual
formation or *Bildung* and societal civilization. Among the hundreds of
definitions, two main senses have been refined.

One is the 'narrow', aesthetic concept of culture, enclosing the fine arts:
the aesthetic works and their traditional institutional settings. This definition dominates discourses of state cultural policy, mass media cultural
journalism and the aesthetic disciplines. It may be criticized for being too
narrowly bound to institutional art forms and neglecting popular culture
and other cultural practices in everyday life. Most cultural forms circulate
outside of the art institutions which belong to the bourgeois public sphere.
It is true that the separation of art institutions and activity forms from
spheres like politics or religion has created a degree of autonomy that has
made it possible at all to think of cultural forms as something distinct from
scientific knowledge, ethical norms or subjective emotions. In modern
society, some professions and institutions are specialists in creating and
evaluating cultural forms. But they are also made and used by everyone in
daily life, and culture is therefore more than these specialized art circuits.

The other main definition of culture is the wide, 'anthropological' one of
a life form or 'a whole way of life' (Williams 1958/1966, p. 16), which is

---

[2] Simmel (e.g., 1908/1992 or 1911/1983) belongs to the many social scientists who get stuck
in a dualism of subject and object, inner and outer, and reduces the cultural level to the
mediation between them.

[3] Cf. Kroeber and Kluckhohn (1952/1963), Williams (1958/1966, 1976/1988 and 1981),
Geertz (1973), Cahoone (1988), Hauge and Horstbøll (1988), Hannerz (1992a) and Jenks
(1993).

implied when whole local or regional communities or societies are thought of as cultures. This alternative is valuable in turning attention to practices rather than artefacts, but it seems too wide, making it hard to distinguish cultural from social aspects of human phenomena, identifying culture with society or community.

An 'intermediary' third definition of culture as symbolic communication – more than just the institutionalized arts but less than all social life – has therefore been developed, influenced by the functionalist sociologist Talcott Parsons and the hermeneutic philosopher Paul Ricoeur.[4] Clifford Geertz (1973) advocates a 'cutting of the culture concept down to size, therefore actually insuring its continual importance' (p. 4), and defines 'a semiotic concept of culture' as 'webs of significance' (p. 5). He distinguishes analytically between 'the cultural and social aspects of human life' and sees culture as 'an ordered system of meaning and of symbols, in terms of which social interaction takes place', while social system is 'the pattern of social interaction itself' (p. 144). Therefore, 'cultural structure and social structure are not mere reflexes of one another but independent, yet interdependent, variables' (p. 169). 'Society's forms are culture's substance' (p. 28). Raymond Williams (1981, p. 207) comes to a similar conclusion, proposing to 'specify and reinforce the concept of culture as a *realized signifying system*', as a necessary part of (but not identical with) the whole social system. 'For modern societies, at least, this is a more effective theoretical usage than the sense of culture as a whole way of life' (p. 209), since 'in highly developed and complex societies there are so many levels of social and material transformation that the polarized "culture"–"nature" relation becomes insufficient' (p. 210). Social anthropologist Ulf Hannerz has noted that 'in the recent period, culture has been taken to be above all a matter of meaning' (1992a, p. 3). He defines culture as socially organized productions and flows of meaning and meaningful forms, related to likewise socially organized forms of power, material resources, time and space, and consisting of three dimensions: ideas and modes of thought, forms of externalization and social distribution (p. 7; cf. also Hannerz 1992b).

This late modern hermeneutic-semiotic concept of culture has been created in a dialogue between the humanities and the social sciences, where the narrow and the wide concepts have met and modified each

---

[4] 'Culture . . . consists . . . in patterned or ordered systems of symbols which are objects of the orientation of action, internalized components of the personalities of individual actors and institutionalized patterns of social systems' (Parsons 1951/1964, p. 327). Cf. Kroeber and Parsons (1958). Habermas is influenced by this line of thought, including Durkheim, when he defines culture as 'the stock of knowledge from which participants in communication supply themselves with interpretations as they come to an understanding about something in some world' (1981/1988, p. 138). This sociological concept of culture is, however, too reified and geared to reproduction. Culture is not only a common stock of knowledge, but also intersubjective and creative processes of play with symbolic artefacts where new and unexpected things and meanings may occur.

other. It both breaks with and bridges the aesthetic and ethnographic traditions, by being of intermediary specificity and by emphasizing the interplay of action, consciousness, intersubjective communication, symbolic forms and social institutions. Culture is the necessary interplay between contextualized creative practices and ordered sets of symbolic forms. In a wide sense, it describes the meaning-aspect of all human activities. In a more narrow sense as a specialized set of practices it refers to 'all those practices whose principal or specialized function is making meaning, the institutions that organize such practices, and the agents that initiate and receive them', including both the arts, popular culture and other signifying practices primarily aiming at making meaning (Lury 1992, p. 369).

Cultural phenomena or symbolic processes are intrinsically *intersubjective* – between human beings – and in two respects. They are shared twice: by the inner worlds of several human beings, and between the internal and the external world.

First, cultural processes demand more than one subject's consciousness: several human individuals in social interaction and communal associations. Symbols intervene or mediate between subjects by connecting them around certain meaning-contents. This is a social aspect of culture: it is in some ways necessarily shared by several people.[5]

That culture is shared, common or joint knowledge, values, experiences and ideas does not mean that it must be shared by all. An over-emphasis on this joint sharing may create an image of culture as only consisting of consensual meanings, marginalizing conflicts and individual differentiation. Culture presupposes certain shared codes and experiences, but also gives room for distinctions. It involves what is common but also what separates people. Understanding is not equalizing. What is common is not necessarily single ideas, but rather the general shapes of the languages in which they are expressed. Even a unique insight, judgement or experience is cultural, provided it is formulated in an intersubjectively valid symbolic mode. This is particularly important in the late modern times of rapid changes, differentiated norms and multicultural mixtures.[6] Shared habits, values and ideas may better be called life forms, mentalities or lifeworlds than cultures, except when their symbolic aspect is to be emphasized. It is not expressions of collective identity or things collectively shared by groups that define culture in general, but rather that which is communicated and thus shared between subjects through symbolic forms.

[5] Vološinov (1929/1986) notes that signs are interindividual, 'located between organized individuals', as their medium of communication (p. 12), that 'the organism and the outside world meet here in the sign' (p. 26), that 'every sign, even the sign of individuality, is social' (p. 34), and that language and meaning are therefore intersubjective and social rather than subjective (pp. 46f and 93).

[6] Similar arguments were made above concerning dialogues in the public sphere. Hannerz (1992a, pp. 11ff) also questions the traditional anthropological idea of culture as collectively shared and homogeneously distributed in society, and emphasizes the pluralities and differences that partly arise from the operation of market, state and social movements.

A second aspect of intersubjectivity is that cultural meanings not only reside inside individual beings and are shared by several subjects, but also have an objectivized materiality, so that they exist both inside and outside of the subjects and their minds, as materialized textual expressions. Symbols are thus in two ways *between* subjects. They consist of external things, traces or tokens which are conferred meaning by the process in which we learn to make them point at something else. Symbolic forms are needed in social interaction because there can be no immediate, unmediated union of human minds. Culture is more than just shared flows of consciousness – it always involves an external medium, a code or language system of some kind. It might be statues and inscriptions, writings and images, flows of light from extrovert bodily gestures or just sounding airwaves of speech and music, but an exteriorization in objectivized artefacts, movements or sounds is in any case crucial. Culture, symbols and languages are literally inter-subjective forms of ex-pression:[7]

> language is itself the process by which private experience is made public. Language is the exteriorization thanks to which an impression is transcended and becomes ex-pression . . .. Exteriorization and communicatibility are one and the same thing for they are nothing other than this elevation of a part of our life into the *logos* of discourse. (Ricoeur 1976, p. 19)

If culture is defined as collective consciousness carried by communication, two mistakes should be avoided. One is that communication can be misconceived as a neutral and secondary tool to create contact between pre-existing conscious subjects. But subjective consciousness is not primary, but produced by communicative processes, and can only be reconstructed by interpreting cultural symbols. The term 'consciousness' should, secondly, not hide the unconscious sides of culture and subjectivity in a cognitivistic manner. 'Meaning and consciousness are separable; something may be meaningful without being recognized' (Ricoeur 1986, p. 229). Meanings created by the use of symbols are not always explicitly acknowledged or reflected.

Culture thus has several dimensions: one psychological dimension of individual minds and senses, one social dimension of interactive communication between subjects in groups and societies, and one objective dimension of material objects and externalized institutions. But what is specifically cultural is that these expressive, interactive and externalizing processes are based on an intersubjectively shared symbolic order of some kind, consisting of tripolar constellations of signifying marks, signified

---

[7] To Winnicott (1971), cultural symbols constitute a third, intermediate or transitional area, opening up between primary and secondary processes as well as between internal and external world or between subject and object. Vološinov (1929/1986) stresses that 'verbal interaction is the basic reality of language' (p. 94), that each sign has 'some kind of material embodiment' which makes it objective and external (p. 11), and that 'expression organizes experience' (p. 85). Lacan (1966/1977) emphasizes the exteriority of the symbolic order, as does Derrida (1967/1976 and 1967/1978), whose parallels with Ricoeur are shown by Peter Kemp (1981/1990).

meanings and interpreting subjects. Cultural artefacts can only be sufficiently understood in their social contexts of production and use. Symbolic forms get their meanings by being used in the communicative encounters between people. Symbolic objects and practices must be understood in their mutual interplay.

All social life has symbolic dimensions, and can therefore be seen from a cultural perspective. This wide view of culture borders on the earlier discussion of social life forms, lifestyles and subcultures. But some activities, artefacts, processes and forms put this aspect in focus, and are often labelled as cultural in a more narrow sense. Cultural analysis can scrutinize the symbolic dimension of every part of society, but is particularly interested in those fields where symbolic forms are explicitly central: in the cultural institutions of the arts and the media, where aesthetic discourses are enacted that evaluate and reflect on rules and patterns within such forms.

The relation between culture and *communication* is obviously dense. Most of what was said about culture also applies to communication as a particular form of intersubjective exchange. In fact, culture *is* communication – of symbolic forms and meanings. Neither culture nor communication is a classification of things, but rather aspects of human, intersubjective processes; aspects that may always be actualized but are only in certain cases in focus within these processes themselves. Culture and communication are always present in human life and society, but their relative weight varies between contexts and instances. Just as culture can be seen as communication, communication can also be studied as culture. Communication models can be applied to all cultural phenomena, and cultural theory is always useful in communication studies. Communication in general is wider and has many non-symbolic forms, for example, the transportation of people and goods. But here it mainly refers to symbolic communication, that is, interaction by means of meaningful sign-structures, that is, culture. Human communication presupposes shared cultural meanings, and no culture can exist without communication. The difference is only in perspective: whereas 'culture' stresses the ensembles of symbols and actions, 'communication' emphasizes the interactive processes as such: symbols in action.

Signs may, like symbols, be defined as units of material marks that stand for something else (meaning) to some people (interpretive community) in a certain setting (context). Symbols are sometimes defined more narrowly as signs with an aura of indirect or secondary meanings, as in religious and mythical symbolism.[8] But there is always a possibility of finding extra, indirect meanings for each sign, which blurs this distinction. The idea of

[8] This is how Ricoeur (e.g., 1969/1974, p. 12) defined symbolism in his earlier work, before he discovered the necessary polysemic and potentially metaphoric character of all linguistic signs (cf. 1976, p. 45). Baudrillard (1988, pp. 90ff) regards the symbol as transcendently 'beyond the sign' or even subversive of signification, through the ambivalence of symbolism as analysed by Lacan.

signs as tokens with univocal meanings is an ideal abstraction which is contradicted by the ambivalent polysemy induced in every act of interpretation. 'Communicative', 'cultural', 'symbolic', 'signifying' and 'meaningful' will therefore be used as approximately synonymous terms, which only emphasize different aspects of the same basic symbolicity.

There are many alternative perspectives and process-types. Economic and political systems can, for example, be described in terms of communication, where money and power connect and mediate between people. But that which is then circulated is not primarily meanings but economic values and effective influence. The market and the state apparatus demand that buyers, sellers and citizens can understand meaningful symbols – read the text on commodity covers, interpret metal pieces as coins and understand official documents. And culture and communication may again be focal in the use of bought commodities or the lifeworld phenomena which are regulated by official decisions. Financial and political operations may be studied as cultural phenomena, since they cannot do without processes of understanding. But this is not their essential goal as such, as they substitute more than focus upon symbolic communication. A cultural perspective may therefore contribute much to the study of money and power, but it does not replace specifically economic and political analysis.

The Latin term *commūnicātiō* means making common, sharing something with others.[9] Communication is such human interaction which involves some sort of sharing, connection or making common, for example around messages or meanings. Even in its widest sense (including forms of transportation), it implies both something that is transferred and some who are joined. If I communicate something to you, I share it with you and let it momentarily bind us together. It is no coincidence that to communicate may also mean to partake of the Holy Communion, which unites believers through the sharing of bread and wine with its significant message of faith, hope and love. Theology here uses a communication-metaphor that is as useful for profane interactions.

Symbolic communication can be viewed from two different sides. It may be seen, first of all, as a transportation of embodied meanings from sender to receiver – a special case of the transmission of goods and people. Or it may be conceived primarily as a shaping of shared meanings in communal rituals.[10] These two competing perspectives are actually both valid and in fact both necessary for a full understanding, as they highlight two different sides of communication processes. On one hand, something is transmitted from someone to someone else. On the other hand, shared, common

---

[9] This is explicit in the German word for message: *Mit-teilung*, sharing-with.

[10] Cf. Wilden (1987), Joli Jensen (1990, pp. 124ff) and John B. Thompson (1990). Carey (1989/1992) discusses these aspects as the transmission versus the ritual view. He sees communication and culture as two sides of the same phenomenon, viewed either as process or as structure. They surely coincide, but it is problematic to delimit culture to artefacts and structures, excluding processual aspects, or to argue that all structural studies of communication are cultural studies.

meanings are thereby created, as people interpret these transported symbolic forms, to understand what they signify.

Habermas (1981/1984, pp. 273–337) makes a distinction between communicative and strategic action as two main ways of intersubjective coordination. While strategic action is aimed at success through goal-oriented efforts to influence others, communicative practices co-ordinate actors through the creation of understanding, that is, shared meanings. Human agents can to a certain extent choose between the two, but most actions contain elements of them both, so the choice is rather between which aspect to emphasize. No symbolic action can definitely avoid creating some form of understanding: even the most manipulative social practices must be to some extent communicative, making others understand at least what they are told to do. Conversely, there are at least unconscious manipulative goals hidden even in most communicative acts. Observers may focus upon either strategic or communicative perspectives of social actions, depending on whether their effects or meanings are emphasized. By making a similar focusing, the actors themselves may choose which type they prefer to use as a matter more of emphasis than of exclusive choice. Communicative action arises when all the involved actors intentionally aim at mutual understanding, and if it succeeds, mutual understanding becomes its main effect.

Media and popular culture

'Let us communicate' is an invitation to interaction with the help of meaningful symbolic forms, to gather around a text and jointly explore its meanings. It may take place in listening to, reading or watching anything audible or visible, but particularly in relation to someone talking, writing, music-making, dancing, gesticulating or image-making. Each such communicative mode involves a specific code, a flexible, intersubjective rule system or symbolic order that regulates how symbols may be understood. There is always also a material medium involved, an external, mediating link of some kind. In some cases a man-made technological apparatus is used. Those technologies that not only assist and enhance face-to-face interaction but also replace it are *media* in the common, more narrow sense of the word. The media are thus technologies of communication and of culture that substitute direct, face-to-face interaction with the help of a man-made apparatus of some kind. Hannerz (1992a) defines the media as 'cultural technology' (pp. 85f), or, more precisely, as 'the use of technology to achieve an externalization of meaning in such a way that people can communicate with one another without being in one another's immediate presence; media are machineries of meaning' (pp. 26f).[11]

---

[11] Cf. Williams (1974) and John B. Thompson (1990) on connections between media, culture and technology.

While many media are mainly used for dialogues between two people only (letters, telephone, etc.), those that communicate between larger groups of subjects are often called 'mass media'.

> We have mass communication when the Source is one, central, structured according to the methods of industrial organization; the Channel is a technological invention that affects the very form of the signal; and the Addressees are the total number (or, anyway, a very large number) of the human beings in various parts of the globe. (Eco 1967/1987, p. 140)

The Latin term *medium* refers to something situated in the middle, mediating between people and thereby both uniting and separating them, like arbitrating mediators. A medium is in the middle between sender and receivers or between communicating parts, as that around which they gather to (re-)construct webs of meaning.

Like communication, media may be variously widely defined. The widest definition corresponds to the widest sense of communication as transport, where media are all that mediate between people, including money or vehicles. If only cultural or symbolic communication is concerned, media usually indicate technological systems that replace rather than simply amplify direct interaction, that is, where the other can only be perceived through a man-made apparatus. The fact that material channels in the form of sound- or light-waves are always mediating face-to-face communication, and that late modern technologies are ubiquitous in everyday life, tends to blur the lines between media and direct communication. Still, there are crucial differences between two sorts of media:

> on one hand, steering media, via which subsystems are differentiated out of the lifeworld; on the other hand, generalized forms of communication, which do not replace reaching agreement in language but merely condense it, and thus remain tied to lifeworld contexts. . . . The mass media belong to these generalized forms of communication. . . . These media publics hierarchize and at the same time remove restrictions on the horizon of possible communication. The one aspect cannot be separated from the other – and therein lies their ambivalent potential. Insofar as mass media one-sidedly channel communication flows in a centralized network – from the center to the periphery or from above to below – they considerably strengthen the efficacy of social controls. But tapping this authoritarian potential is always precarious because there is a counterweight of emancipatory potential built into communication structures themselves. Mass media can simultaneously contextualize and concentrate processes of reaching understanding, but it is only in the first instance that they relieve interaction from yes/no responses to criticizable validity claims. Abstracted and clustered though they are, these communications cannot be reliably shielded from the possibility of opposition by responsible actors. (Habermas 1981/1988, p. 390)

The steering media money and power tend to replace symbolic communication in dialogues and other cultural forms aimed at mutual understanding, while communication media only condense and supplement it, as technologies of communication and culture over distance.[12] Habermas

---

[12] These communications 'media tied up with natural language are open to retrieval by any agents for reassessment, retranslation, rereception; they are open for and even rely on face-to-face communication and interactions. This is what totally distinguishes this type of

(1992b, pp. 435ff) returns to the ambivalent effects of the mass media, noting that media professionals develop specific ethics to neutralize their own power and to prevent its subsumption under either administrative state power, commercial demands or the social power of partial interests.

Mass media in capitalist societies are highly dependent on the state and market systems. Systemic demands compete with communicative needs of the lifeworld for power over these institutionalized technologies of communication. Certain media sectors are strongly subsumed under profit interests, while others are heavily state-controlled. These processes of subsumption go in two steps. First, a 'formal subsumption', where pre-existing communications are drawn into a context of either capitalist accumulation or administrative power, as when someone starts to charge a fee for attending a concert or a theatrical play. The second step is a 'real subsumption' whereby the processes of communication are transformed to fit these systemic demands, such as when cultural industries develop new genres.[13] This second step is the most problematic one. Subsuming work under capital increases its productive efficiency while making it instrumental, goal-oriented and technocratic, which produces problematic side-effects for human beings as well as for the ecological environment. A not only formal but real subsumption of communication under systemic rules is still more problematic. It threatens to destroy the communicative core which is its raison d'être, transforming communicativity into strategic manipulation. Communicative practices can never be totally subsumed in this way, but have to retain non-systemic elements, which is also what can be noted in the workings of late modern mass media. The cultural industries deeply transform our ways of shaping meaning, but do not subsume them totally under the logic of profit-making. They have to keep open crucial channels back to lifeworld interaction of a non-strategic kind. Agents within civil society continue to be active in mediated communication, contributing to the regeneration of a public sphere, if only through intense struggles to keep it autonomous from both systemic forces and partial social powers. Mass media continue to open up public spaces, in their processes of production as well as in those of reception. Non-systemic communicative processes take place among those who work in the cultural industries, within their mediated products and in their uses within the interpretive communities formed by their audiences. Even the most commercial or administrative medium retains connections back to interpersonal communication, if it is at all still a medium of communication and has not simply developed into money or administrative power.

communication from money and administrative power' (Habermas 1992a, p. 473; cf. also Habermas 1981/1988, pp. 181ff and 269ff). The structural functionalism of Parsons and Luhmann describes money and power as interaction media in line with communication media, and does not sufficiently distinguish the social and symbolic structures of the lifeworld from the societal systems of state and market.

[13] This model is an extension of Marx's (1933/1969) analysis of the formal and real subsumption of work under the logic of capital.

Media and communication may be studied from various perspectives. The cultural aspect is only one of many options. It may be delimited in at least three different ways. The widest area comprises all perspectives that focus the understanding of meanings in symbolic forms – how meaning is created when subjects meet symbols. While other perspectives may analyse news media as economic, political, technological or social systems, studying *media culture* is to focus cultural aspects on any media phenomenon. With the increased general interest in meaning aspects within media studies, the border-line is not so clear any more, but it may still be used as a matter of emphasis.

A second definition concentrates on those processes, products and uses that themselves focus the cultural aspect and are therefore commonly interpreted as *cultural media* in a more narrow sense. Here, entertainment, fiction and the arts are studied, rather than the communication of information, news or other contents. Mixed forms like faction or infotainment make it hard to sustain any strict limit, but it is at least sometimes useful to indicate an interest in media oriented towards culture, whether high or popular.

The most narrow delimitation frames the largest and most widespread media culture and culture media that is usually thought of as *popular culture* – products and uses that in our society are conventionally classified as popular or mass culture. Distinctions between high and low, élite and mass, have been codified in societal taste and value systems, anchored in certain institutions and circuits for the production, distribution and evaluation of cultural forms. What is seen as low culture is often (but not necessarily) produced by cultural industries, spread through mass media and used in broad population strata. The term 'popular' derives from Latin and denotes what belongs to the people, related to plebs and plebeian. The culture that is popular may have three qualities: it may derive from common people's everyday practices, it may be loved by the people, and it may be made for the people (whoever they are). In historical studies popular culture is close to folk culture.[14] In media studies, it is mostly associated with the makings and uses of products of cultural industries in modern capitalist industrial societies, as a less derogative alternative to the term 'mass culture'.[15] Popular culture is the sum of popular music, popular arts, popular literature, popular press, popular fiction, etc.

[14] The relation between the popular, folk and mass culture concepts varies greatly between languages. To Scandinavians popular culture is mostly almost identical with modern mass culture and clearly different from folk culture, while Mediterranean languages retain more of the old associations between the popular and that of the people.

[15] The concept of mass problematically implies that consumers or audiences of popular culture are homogeneous and easily manipulated. Cf. Hall and Whannel (1964/1990), de Certeau (1974/1988), Gans (1974), Reyher (1975), Cohen and Taylor (1976/1992), George H. Lewis (1978), Prokop (1979), Gurevitch et al. (1982), Waites et al. (1982), Modleski (1986a), Brantlinger (1983 and 1990), Bennett et al. (1986), MacCabe (1986), Carlsson (1987), Kausch (1988), Collins (1989), Ross (1989), Shiach (1989), Hermansen (1990), Ericson (1991),

Like culture in general, popular culture consists both of symbolic artefacts (texts in the wide sense) and of signifying practices (ways of doing things, creating and interpreting texts), and just like subculture, it is a generic rather than classificatory concept. We use it to differentiate between products, but single works may actually move between high and low spheres, depending on the time and context of their use. Referring to Michel de Certeau (1974/1988), Meaghan Morris therefore defines 'popular culture as a *way of operating* – rather than as a set of contents, a marketing category, a reflected expression of social position, or even a "terrain" of struggle' (1990, p. 30). Modern society orders cultural processes into different communicative circuits to which taste values are attached, but this is a flexible process of normative construction and cultural practice rather than any once and for all fixed classification.

The hierarchical dichotomy of high/low goes far back in history. A series of dichotomization processes led to the establishment of its modern shape in the nineteenth century. First, the priestly, aristocratic and bourgeois élites withdrew from the formerly communal folk culture typified by the carnival. Then, the bourgeois public sphere was dichotomized in entertainment versus serious arts by the simultaneous growth of cultural industries and the commodified mass media, on one hand, and, on the other hand, the bourgeois élite culture (including not only the production of literature, art and classical music, but also the whole system of reproducing education and consecrating criticism) together with new avantgarde aesthetic movements culminating in various modernisms.[16] In our century, the formerly repressed cross-currents between high and low have again surfaced, signalling at least a partial fragmenting or possibly erosion of these hierarchies. Late modern culture mixes high modern avantgarde traits with traditions from older folk culture, as, for example, punk culture mixed futurism, dadaism, expressionism and surrealism with carnivalesque jesting games, or in the so-called postmodernist aesthetics of art, architecture, literature, film or television. Today it is difficult to say what is *not* popular culture, as mass media and cultural industries organize most professional cultural practices. Taste hierarchies have been further differentiated so that various groups have quite dissimilar criteria for what is and what is not popular culture. But even if more people are today more often reflexively aware that all dichotomies of high/low or art/popular culture are socio-historical constructions, they continue to be effective in much cultural life. The crossings that blur distinctions do not synthesize them into one quite continuous field. In some fields of culture the dichotomy is weaker than

Keppler and Seel (1991), Naremore and Brantlinger (1991), Frow (1992), Gripsrud (1995) and Kellner (1995).

[16] Burke (1978) describes how the upper social strata in seventeenth-century Europe withdrew from the formerly common and shared popular culture – typified by the carnival, analysed by Bakhtin (1965/1984) – and started to attack it. Habermas's theory of the public sphere (1962/1989) gave new impetus to analyses of the following dichotomization of bourgeois culture in the modern society; cf. Bürger et al. (1982) and Boëthius (1990/1995).

elsewhere, and hierarchies are variously defined by different social agents, but if there were not still active borders, the outspoken aesthetic transgression of them would be less attractive than it seems to be.

With these reservations, all of these concepts retain analytical value. Interaction, communication and culture are three concentric spheres. Human interaction encompasses everything people do together or in relation to each other, including struggle, love and labour of all kinds. Communication comprises those interactions that involve a transmission and a sharing or making common of something, including all forms of transportation. Culture concerns that communication which primarily relates to the transmission and sharing of meaningful symbolic messages of any kind, involving interacting subjects and a recognized symbolic order or code. Through these three concentric spheres crossing distinctions can then be made. In one dimension, that interaction, communication and culture which uses mass media or other media may be distinguished from those that are more or less directly interpersonal. Along another dimension, those that are considered 'low' or popular may be contrasted with those that are recognized as 'high' or legitimate.

Signifying practice

Culture and communication are the production of shared meanings by way of symbolic forms. To signify is to mean, to produce signs which convey meanings to others. 'Now this human phenomenon, culture, is an entirely symbolic phenomenon. . . . It is definitely the symbol which knots that living cord between man, language, and culture' (Benveniste 1966/1971, pp. 26f).[17] Symbols are things which unite in three ways.[18] They join interacting people in a shared understanding of meanings, as in the ritual view of communication cited above. They integrate the internal with the external, subjective consciousness with material objects. And they join physical signs with references or meanings. Symbols are marks, tokens or signs which 'point at' something outside themselves, by possessing the intersubjectively constituted capacity to make us think of something else. Symbolic phenomena are objects, movements, sounds or words that, to interacting human beings in specific lifeworlds, in one way or another, represent or stand for something else, which is their meaning: that which they mean, make us think of or have in mind.

Symbols form objectivized structures obeying formal rules codified as symbolic systems or (understood in a generalized sense) language systems.[19] A structural analysis of such systems is indispensable, but has to

[17] Cf. also Pochat (1983), Blonsky (1985), Hodge and Kress (1988) and Israel (1992).

[18] The term 'symbol' derives from the Greek word *symbállein*, which literally means throw together, related also to 'ball' (which is thrown) and 'ballet' (where legs are tossed).

[19] Saussure (1916/1974) distinguishes between *langue* (the language system) and *parole* (living speech). His structuralist followers tend to emphasize, autonomize and reify the structure side, as was already noted by Vološinov (1929/1986, pp. 52–82), who instead emphasized the historical mutability and generative process of language, the dynamics of

be integrated with a deep semantics and pragmatics that uncovers what is being signified and how these signifying acts displace and renew the symbolic structures themselves. Symbolic orders are no fixed and self-reproducing systems. Even the rules of sport, games and mathematics are changed when people use them to create new patterns. Verbal vocabularies and grammars are stubborn but not static structures. A dialogue uses existing linguistic codes but can also invent new ones and its unique event adds some new aspects to the meanings of the words used. A new tune uses given musical genres but can also subtly move genre boundaries by certain unusual and innovatory combinations of the inherited rules. Fantasy, imagination and creativity are psychological terms used to catch this inventive force, which is actually intersubjective in character, anchored in the symbolically mediated and meaning-making interaction between human subjects.[20]

Text and action are knit closely together. Texts are both produced and apprehended by a work of signifying practices. Social action can, on the other hand, also be understood as a kind of text. Like texts, actions are realized temporally and in the present, but leave marks that are fixated over time. Both texts and actions relate self-referentially back to an author or agent, however indirectly, and even though this source can also be a collective agent, it is nevertheless a unique, contextualized individuality. They symbolically point out towards a universe of meanings. And as intersubjectively anchored, they pragmatically relate to an open set of addressees or to those other human beings whom the act affects.[21]

Three different aspects are present in all communication, whether by writing, speech, images, music or any other symbolic mode, only with shifting characteristics, functions and mutual relations. First, there is a *materiality* of any visual, aural, verbal, pictorial or musical sign – the material substrate of physical existence and sensuous presence, which can be as solid as monumental stone or as volatile as sound- or light-waves. Both black ink on a piece of paper and transient air vibrations have that type of a graphical, phonetical or acoustical force which is a necessary basis for symbolic forms. But it can only be conceived as a limit of our

speech and the concrete utterance, and the living multiplicity of meaning (p. 77). For Lévi-Strauss (1958/1963 and 1962/1966), structures are conceived of as almost timeless, as determining events and as consisting of a strictly limited number of basic elements and rules that are constant over time and space and for all subjects. Ricoeur (1969/1974, pp. 39ff) argues that Lévi-Strauss gives the structure too much weight, and that the unique event always contains a 'surplus of meaning' in relation to each structure in which it partakes. Frank adds: 'Linguistic differentiality – the linguistic code, convention – forms the *condition*, without which there could be neither speaking nor understanding. But the agency that sees to it *that* meaning can in each instance be produced and understood is subjectivity as individuality' (1983/1989, p. 408).

[20] On imagination, cf. Kearney (1988) and Kristensson-Uggla (1994, pp. 343ff), showing how Ricoeur's ideas here transcend the limitations of both Kant and Sartre.

[21] Ricoeur (1981, pp. 197ff); cf. also Geertz (1973, pp. 448ff) and Volosinov (1929/1986, pp. 85f).

understanding, since all efforts to understand this materiality as such must use ordering and signifying devices that involve the other two aspects as well.

Secondly, there are *form-relations* between symbols: their mutual, grammatical or syntactic configurations and relational structures. Symbols are positioned in specific temporal and spatial relations to other symbols, forming ordered units on various hierarchical levels, for example, from letters over words, sentences to works in writing; from phonemes over words, utterances to conversations in speaking; from sounds over motives, themes and sections to whole pieces in music.

Thirdly, *meaning* is their semantic content, sense, references – their pointing towards something else: to phenomena in the external, social or internal world, or to other cultural phenomena. An utterance in a dialogue is and does something in itself through its own material sound and relational form in time and space. But its connected signifiers also say something of something by evoking signifieds in the conversing subjects, in processes of signification that offer themselves for interpretation.

All texts thus include materiality, formal relations and meanings. The pop tune works by the force of its sounding energy, its musical form structure, and the meanings it implies. These three symbol aspects are interrelated but analytically separable. The materiality of what symbols are and do adds to the formal relations of how they are composed, to make possible what they say or mean by pointing towards something else. The form-relational play of differences presupposes and transgresses the materiality of the sign-embodiments, but these form-relations are themselves also presupposed and transcended by the meaning-aspects in their pointing from language to subjects and worlds. The three aspects cannot be reduced to one another, and they are all present in any cultural phenomenon.

A fourth aspect might be added: the *pragmatics* of uses and functions of symbols in meaning-making acts (speech acts, musical or visual gestures) interwoven through interaction into webs of discourse. An analysis on this level considers how subjects make use of verbal utterances, arguments and narratives, musical sounds, forms and themes, or visual gestures and images in a dialogic taking of roles according to codes and rules set up within specific intersubjectively ordered genres. This pragmatic aspect embeds all symbolic texts in social contexts, and will be further discussed below in relation to how meanings are made in practices of interpretation.

These symbolic aspects have been formulated in various ways.[22] Tzvetan Todorov (1970/1973, p. 20) distinguishes a verbal, a syntactic and a

---

[22] Cf. how Hegel (1812/1969) discusses the relations between matter, form and content. John B. Thompson (1990, pp. 138–45) distinguishes intentional, conventional, structural, referential and contextual aspects of symbolic forms.

semantic aspect of literary works. The verbal aspect consists of the concrete sentences of a text, and can be connected with the pragmatic function of signs, that is, their relations to their users. The syntactic aspect concerns how the parts of a work are logically, temporally and spatially related to one another, just as the syntactic function of signs concerns their mutual relations. The semantic aspect points at the themes or contents of a text, as the semantic function of signs is about their relation to that which they signify or to which they refer. Materiality, form-relations and meaning are an extension of this model from verbal literature to all symbolic modes.

Text, work, discourse

Intersubjectively anchored signifying practices combine meaningful signs into complexly structured and ordered symbolic units. These are referred to as *texts*, whether they consist of spoken or written words, images, sculptural or architectural forms, musical sounds, body movements or any combination of these or other symbolic entities. This wide and general text-concept must be kept apart from the more narrow concepts of verbal texts and of written texts. Verbal texts are ordered symbolic units in the verbal mode, while written texts in a wide sense are any materially fixed symbolic webs (including, for instance, painted images or CDs). Verbal, written texts may then in fact include the fixated sung or spoken words on a record. But written texts (or writing) in the most narrow sense of written words is the most common usage of the term 'text'. In many contexts, one of these alternative concepts is implied by the general term 'text', but here it will often be used in the widest sense, if it is not qualified as verbal or written.

This may seem to be a problematic extension of a literary or linguistic term, but originally it does not imply anything verbal at all. It derives from a Latin term for to weave. Texts are like webs, where symbols are interwoven to form meaningful networks, in which the textual totality enriches and modifies the significance of each of its symbolic constituents by simultaneously focusing and widening its signifying scope. They are complex totalities that are more than the sum of their constituents (a document is more than the sum of its letters, words and sentences, the painting is more than the sum of its colours and lines, etc.). Texts are entities on a higher order than the symbols of which they are composed, and they are to some extend fixated and rounded-off as complex wholes. Ricoeur (1981, p. 145) defines a text as 'any discourse fixed by writing', which is true in the narrow sense of the word. It is also relevant in the wider sense used here, but only if the concept of writing is extended in the way suggested by Derrida (1967/1976), to include speech, music and indeed any symbolic mode where symbols may be fixed in any element, including the human mind. The main point is that a text is an ordered and fixed symbolic compound that appears as a totality (however fragmented and inconsistent it may be), and thus structures not only discourse but also (through the meanings and references produced) our world itself.[23]

Texts must contain symbols with materiality, form-relations and meaning. All these symbol aspects are often man-made, in any cultural artefact, including utterances, gestures, subcultures, media products and art works. But even when natural objects are understood (interpreted, 'read') as texts, at least one piece of work has to be done: the construction of meaning that is always necessary to make an object into a text. Nature may have given things a texture and a formal structure, but only interacting human subjects can constitute their meanings.

With each text there is always a context, surrounding it in time and space both with configurations of other (inter)texts that relate to it and with other types of social structures. As the meaning of one symbol depends on its position and use within discourse, the meaning of one text is delimited by the various contexts which surround it.

Texts where not only the meanings but also the materiality and form-relations are produced by human subjects are often called *works*, especially when clearly perceived as (composite) wholes and belonging to the institutional sphere of the arts. Works are texts that have been worked on and where the traces of work as intersubjective activity and creative practice – as toil, labour, deed, production, making and creation – cannot be erased. No text can in fact be understood only as a reified structural object, but must be inserted in a pragmatic dimension of signifying practice, at least in the necessary dimension of meaning. Each cultural phenomenon – from single symbolic units to complex texts – involves the work of giving meaning. In a very wide sense, all texts are therefore works, but the notion is mostly used more narrowly for (materially and formally) constructed text-totalities within the cultural art sphere. Each tune or image is a text and may be understood as a work: a polyphonic web that smells of the work and life that has given it materiality and form and of the never-ending work of giving it meaning.

Julia Kristeva (1974/1984, pp. 86f) distinguishes between two main aspects of texts. 'Genotext' is the semiotic and proto-symbolic processual aspect of the practices in which subjects channel drive energy and generate texts, while 'phenotext' denotes the structural aspect of textual products within transmission chains of communication. To study a text as genotext is to focus its nascent and transcendent process of becoming-text, while to study it as phenotext is to freeze it as a finished unit. Conceiving texts as

---

[23] Cf. Vigsø (1993, p. 48). The narrow sense of text is of course opposite to speech dialogues, while the wide one bridges both these modes and the non-verbal ones. Ricoeur's (1981) model of action as text and text as action implies such a wider text-concept. Landow (1992) describes computer-based 'hypertexts' which blur the border between author and reader, and offer network-like multiple openings, endings and linear orders. Still, they remain structured and meaningful materialities which (like books, paintings or songs) appear as (however open and vague) entities allowing for narrativizing interpretive moves.

works is compatible with both these perspectives, depending on whether the creation or the completion connotation of the concept is stressed.

In a text from 1971, Roland Barthes (1977, pp. 155ff) argues for the notion of the text against the notion of the work, but seems stuck in a simultaneously over-reified and over-romantic perspective. On one hand, he views works as totally closed and institutionalized categories, forgetting the aspect of practice implied in the very term. The subsumption of the subject (author as well as reader) under the text also unduly autonomizes texts. The counterpart to these reified ideas of symbolic orders is a romantic notion of the text as a subversion of all limits and of *jouissance* as a complete pleasure without separation. This model's thought-provokingly incisive dramatization may be productive, but Ricoeur's (e.g., 1976 and 1981) more dynamic and non-reductionist approach to text, work and discourse seems more useful, by dialectically integrating the action, practice, event, discourse and process side with the structure, artefact, object, text and product side.[24]

Texts are produced when subjects in sociocultural contexts combine and use symbols in intersubjective communication acts of *signifying practice*. Human praxis evolves in time and therefore has a certain degree of linearity, while intersubjectivity makes dialogicity an equally necessary condition. Symbolic phenomena are created and interpreted in practices that follow a temporal axis, in movements that do not run directly from intention to insight, but wander about and apart in sometimes contradictory directions, where various voices mingle into composite narrative structures which have a direction, a beginning and an end. A *discourse* is such a concrete – fluidly linear and dialogically interwoven – course of signifying acts; a conversation of voices where symbolic units are lined up into utterances which express propositions and mix in an anti-, hetero- or polyphonic manner. The Latin *discurrĕre* means to run apart or to run about. Symbols are thus woven into discourses: textual webs are compositions of symbols resulting from the interlacing shuttle of discourse running to and fro, and which may always be actualized by interpretive acts that again run through these webs in hearing, watching or reading them.

While symbols throw material signs and intersubjective meanings together, discourses are meaningful voices that run apart. Symbols combine, discourses separate. Symbols are the basic micro-units of the larger constructions of discourses. Symbols constitute texts used in dialogic practices called discourses. Symbols bring meaning-potentials that are realized and in fact made by the work of discourse.[25]

---

[24] Born similarly calls for 'a return of agency in theorizing cultural production, and for acknowledgement of the place of originating creativity or, simply, work' (1993, p. 275). Cf. also Kearney (1988).

[25] While 'concur' and 'concourse' denote a coincidence or confluence of something that runs together, and while the German words for bankruptcy and competition, *Konkurs* and *Konkurrenz*, also indicate something that implodes or collides, in discourse the individual utterances carry the conversation forward by going in varying directions.

However, not every chain of symbols is usually thought of as a discourse. It is common to add two other demands, one of which is less tenable than the other. A very narrow concept of discourse confines it to verbal argumentation only: discussions in words. But musical or pictorial works – and not only verbal references to them – can form or take part in discourses as well, if they also contain meaningful symbolic chains which in certain interpretive contexts and communities are understood as arguments or propositions. One might then instead restrict the concept to reflexive forms of communicative action (Habermas 1992b, p. 663), which, like symbolic utterances, on a second degree thematize symbolic expressions and explicitly argue on validity claims. However, it seems hard to draw the line here, since any symbolic utterance may be interpreted as such a discourse if its implicit arguments and validity claims are sought out. The difference becomes more of a distinction between various ways of appropriation of texts than categories of texts themselves. Discourses are then chains of meaningful symbolic forms which may be read as a series of arguments with a reflexive potential.

Mikhail Bakhtin (1963/1984, pp. 87f and 177) emphasizes that human thoughts and ideas are living events, resulting from dialogic encounters between one consciousness and another. Words, languages, texts and ideas are thus essentially interindividual and intersubjective, born and living in the counterpoint between the dialogic voices of communicating subjects that use them. Bakhtin was therefore particularly interested in such dialogic works that consciously make use of the polyphonic word instead of trying to reduce the many voices of language into homophonic mono-logues. But dialogicity inheres in every text and work, whatever its genre and intentions are. It is sometimes explicitly a mixture of different and divergent voices in a real polyphonic conversation, in other cases an implicit polysemic or intertextual plurivocity of meanings within a unitary work.

Textual meanings are realized in discourses where symbols are encoded and decoded in sequential chains: 'the sign owes its very meaning as sign to its usage in discourse' (Ricoeur 1975/1986, p. 217). Meanings of texts as well as of single symbols arise in that intersubjective work of active interpretation which is invested in their use within specifically situated discourses. The notion of discourse is closer to the crosscurrent symbol-webs of concrete living speech (*parole*) than to the structural codes of an abstract language system (*langue*).[26] Confusion arises if discourse is instead used to denote underlying structures or fundamental themes in texts, like genres, myths, ideologies or lifeworld horizons. The root of such a problematic definition may go back to distinctions between different types or formations of discourse, which are then wrongly identified with the discourses themselves. If a discourse is found to be racist, it may be said

---

[26] Ricoeur (1976, p. 7). *Langue/parole* are terms deriving from Saussure (1916/1974). (Cf. note 19 above.)

that a racist discourse hides in the text, but this should then not be understood as if the racist discourse were an abstract system of beliefs or ideological rules that is hidden inside or under the text itself. Instead, it might be possible to construct a racist reading of the text by running through its signifying elements in a particular order. A text may then 'contain' a racist discourse not as an underlying code but as a (potential) reading that chooses some of its meaning-threads and weaves them into a specific concrete discursive chain. The discourse is not an abstract code system on the level of *langue*, but remains on the concrete 'surface' of the text and its use, on the level of *parole*. A discourse may be racist, political, mythological, musical, etc., but this qualification of its traits is not a definition of itself: myths are expressed and realized in discourses and the discourses that embed texts may be analysed in relation to fundamental themes and codes, but a discourse is therefore not a myth or any other abstract code but always a specific linear and discrete chain of significations corresponding to a text in its concrete totality. Discourses deal with themes but abstract themes are as such not yet discourses until they are developed in concrete communicative chains. Discourses realize themes in spatial or temporal successions.

Michel Foucault (1969/1972, p. 27) also defines discursive events as the completed and temporarily defined set of formulated linguistic sequences. He then makes a distinction between discourses and discursive formations, defined as systems or sets of rules for some discursive practice (pp. 74 and 115ff). He also says that discursive representations function in a field of non-discursive practice (p. 68), but then only wants to accept a concept of prediscursive that paradoxically enough still remains discursive – he cannot recognize any possibility of leaving the dimension of representation (p. 76). This indicates that Foucault here tends to think of the discursive as the communicative in general, which is a wider definition than the one used by Langer or Habermas.

In a qualitative leap, each symbolic order or mode constitutes a certain minimal degree of discursivity through the very birth of the dimension of meaning. Discourses are composed of propositionally argumentative sequences of more or less discrete meaningful units which may in principle order elements of any symbolic mode. Cultural phenomena therefore always have some discursivity that makes them parts of discourses. Yet, texts and works may be more or less discursive, depending on how this discursivity is central to the formal structure of the text itself. Depending on the materiality involved and on the specific way its meanings relate to its signs, different symbolic modes have varying inclinations towards such a discursivity. In verbal language, there is an immediate relation between discourses as processual acts and texts as resulting artefacts, so that enunciations give rise to utterances, the saying creates the said, speech acts convey messages, narrations produce narratives and discourses shape written or spoken texts. Most verbal texts have a configuration of materiality, form-relations and meaning that underpins discursivity in a very focused way, by being composed of sequences of relatively discrete signifying units lined up in time or space. Texts and works in non-verbal symbolic modes, like sculptures or musical tunes, are also always embedded in such intersubjective discourses – both when produced and when interpreted. Their meanings are constructed and actualized in discourses, but their materiality and internal form-relations are often formed by less discursively organized signifying practices. There is for each interpreter, then, a less prescribed order in which to 'read' the symbols (as in pictures), the choice of how to delimit each signifying unit is less predefined (as in music) and/or the range of meaning for each symbolic element is much less standardized (as in abstract painting or instrumental music, but also in poetry). All cultural work and all interpretation is thus embedded in discourses, but individual works and signifying practices may be more or less (explicitly) discursive.

Materiality: symbolic modes

Symbols and texts are not of a uniform kind, but differentiated into several different *symbolic modes*, *modalities*, *forms* or *orders*. Most theories of symbols and signs are based in linguistics and focus on speech or literature, but a more general approach to a wider range of symbolic modalities has to be informed by models developed in other areas as well. In fact, terms like 'text', 'work' and 'discourse', while often primarily associated with literary theory, have much wider genealogical roots. Nothing prevents us from emphasizing that a text may be any web of signification in whatever material form, or that sculptures or gestures may also be seen as works. 'Language' is here used as a composite concept for all kinds of communicative symbolic structures and actions, including musical, pictorial and bodily ones. When only words are discussed, this is indicated by addition of the prefix 'verbal'. Words, images and music are often mixed, used simultaneously and coordinated. But the materiality, form-relations and meaning-aspects of these different symbolic modes differ, so that they obey partly different sets of rules and fulfil varying functions in communication practices.

There are many alternative terms for symbolic modes. While symbolic modes definitely involve differing *codes*, *symbolic* or *language systems* and *discursive forms* or *modes*, many such alternative concepts have much wider significations as well. To discuss them as *modes* or *forms of expression* is to stress the signifying work of an acting subject, but might too 'expressivistically' imply that each symbolic expression is some sort of secondary formulation of something hidden inside human subjects, which is 'pressed out' and materialized in utterances of some kind. It might be wise to avoid conceiving all symbolic practice as expressions of subjective feelings, states or ideas. Even though it is often quite useful to talk of expressions or utterances in this sense, the most general functioning of

	Aural	Visual
Verbal	Speech	Writing
Non–verbal	Music	Images

Figure 4.1 *Symbolic modes*

symbolic modes in communication cannot be reduced to expressivity. The meaning conveyed by a symbolic text is not necessarily any (more or less conscious) expression of a speaking or otherwise producing subject, but rather a construct in the meeting-point between the text and an interpreting subject who might but need not be 'expressing' something in this process. *Means of expression* are something else: stylistic tools and techniques that may or may not be utilized within quite different symbolic modes.[27] When the resources of a whole symbolic mode are used as a means of expression, the two may temporarily coincide, but this is no rule. And *genres* as generative and grouping patterns in cultural fields are again also wider categories that may or may not be confined to single sense modalities, symbolic modes or media forms. Radio theatre, novels or rock may be seen as (relatively large) genres, and romance, crime or action are genres that may exist both within covers and on large or small screens. Single devices or means of expression may be preferred in specific genres or styles. While a symbolic mode may be understood as a particular kind of genre, where the generating principle of the genre is the use of a particular symbolic mode, a genre may also be defined by quite different stylistic criteria.

There is no simple universal model of how to classify symbolic modes, and each categorization creates a number of complicated border cases and mixed modes. There are two common modern ways to differentiate the most discussed symbolic modes. The distinction of *verbal* and *non-verbal* cuts across sense modalities and materiality, since the verbal can be written as well as spoken, and the non-verbal can appear as images as well as musical sounds. On the other hand, texts and images are both *visual* forms primarily located in space, while speech and music are intrinsically *oral/ aural* ones developing temporally. While this latter distinction is based in the material aspect of the symbolic modes, the former one relates to the meaning-aspect. Words as written share visuality with images and as spoken share orality with musical sounds (see Figure 4.1). While writing

---

[27] Cf. what Barthes (1953/1968) refers to as idioms.

and speech are closely connected as verbal modes, writing may also be seen as a particular branch of images (visual signs) and speech as a specific subfield of music (aural signs). The verbal mode is like an ordering and signifying force that may organize visuality into writing or sounds into speech. It thus not only is separate from music and images, but also connects them, as when lyrics bind visuals and music together into a meaningful totality in opera or music video, where written/spoken/sung words are often perceived as the underlying glue.

These two dimensions are often falsely collapsed into one another, but should be kept strictly apart. When, for instance, Deleuze (1988/1994, p. 338) contrasts the 'visual scenes' and 'visibility' of 'Light' with the 'sound curves' and 'statements' of 'Language' as 'two irreducible forms of knowledge', both music (neither light nor language) and writing (both light and language) are forgotten. The contrast may be analytically useful, but it misleadingly mixes these two quite separate dimensions, since sound curves are not necessarily the same as statements or language. Many other examples can be found in theories constructing such over-simple dichotomies.

These symbolic modes are obviously related to different perceptory channels and *sense modalities* such as the seeing eye or the hearing ear. Which senses are activated in symbol-use depends on which material carriers are used by a medium or a symbolic mode. This dimension clearly separates images from music and dichotomizes words into speech (as an acoustic phenomenon directed to the ear) and writing (as a visual phenomenon directed to the eye). Sense modalities are sometimes associated with time and space in a problematic way, since there are in fact both temporal and spatial aspects of both visual and aural forms. Most cultural and communicative practices freely blend different senses, as in dialogues where words are supported with gestures and facial expressions or in art forms like dance, theatre, opera, film and television.

The olfactory (smell), taste and tactile senses are much less attended by symbol theories as well as by cultural media. Still less theorized are other senses than these five classical ones – the senses of balance, temperature, etc.[28] Synaesthetic associations may relate them in memory to vision or sound. Additionally, the tactile sense is, for example, more directly connected to sight through three-dimensional images, reliefs, Braille, etc., and to hearing through sound vibrations that may be felt in the whole body.

Symbolic modes are also related to different, historically constituted *media forms* with differing technologies and aesthetic codes (press, radio, film, television, etc.). Words, images and music are not media forms, but each of them has a central position within certain media, for example books, photographs or records. This is then indicated by terms like 'music-media', 'image-media', etc. Music, for example, is no medium, but a

---

[28] Cf. Classen (1993).

symbolic mode engaged in several media: scores, records, discs, tapes, cassettes, videos, etc. And magazines can contain pictures as well as words (but seldom meaningful sounds or smells), photos may use explanatory or reproduced texts (but again, seldom sounds), records may have texts and images both on the covers and on the discs themselves, a medium like radio mixes words and music (but not images, except for in the visual form of the radio receiver itself), and film and television utilize both writing, speech, images and musical sounds. Various media stress different symbolic modes, but the two dimensions are not identical.

The distinction between media is a complicated affair. Television is different from radio, but are local-TV, cable-TV, music-TV or video separate media or only genres within an overarching TV-medium? It seems to be a pragmatic question where to draw the line where variants become distinct media, and it is also a social decision whether to emphasize the type of technological apparatus, the material carrier of texts, the dominating textual genres, the principal audiences or the social organization of production or distribution as the key classificatory factor.

Symbolic modes are further related to different *aesthetic fields*, *art forms* or *art worlds*. Forms or branches of art are differentiated social institutions within which professionalized specialists produce, disseminate, consume and evaluate works of art, that is, the texts within any symbolic mode which are authorized as such by these interpretive communities themselves. Forms of art are embedded in the *institutional circuits of culture*, *branches of cultural industries*, *public spheres*, *interpretive communities* and *subcultures* discussed earlier. Cultural institutions produce certain conventions and traditions, schools and critics. Like media and art forms they develop certain genres, which are both socially and aesthetically determined.

Both symbolic modes and media forms seem also to be loosely connected to different social spheres and contexts of use. For many young people, books belong to school, TV to family and music-media to the peer group. Tensions between reading, viewing and listening are then superimposed on social and cultural conflicts between such institutional spheres in everyday life.[29] Television and music both combine words with non-verbal modes, but still the teenage searching for an identity of its own leads away from family and television to peers and music. The TV set is mostly placed physically in the centre of the home, which youths tend to avoid. It is also historically associated with family life through childhood experiences and earlier cultural history, and this association cannot at once be erased even when one may have a TV set of one's own. And even music television is often less useful than plain music for combinations with other activities like conversation, dance or reading, because the symbolic mode of music does

---

[29] Fornäs et al. (1988/1995), Baacke et al. (1989 and 1990) and Drotner (1991b) have studied the movements of young people in and between different arenas and media worlds in approximately the way Radway (1988) proposes.

not physically and cognitively fixate attention as much as image media tend to do. Video, satellites, cables and new family patterns may come to change these patterns, but media statistics and programme policies still indicate that teenagers are those who watch TV the least and listen most to music.[30]

Symbolic modes are overarching human ways of communicating – specific cultural constellations of sense modalities, media forms and branches of art that have developed a certain historical stability. Which they are is to a certain extent conventional. The large verbal mode can be subdivided into speech and writing, and forms like dance, theatre, film and television may be regarded either as combination of more 'pure' modes or as full and independent ones. The human senses offer a given biological frame, but as no cultural phenomenon is free from social and historical determinations, the institutionalization of media and forms of art influence how symbolic modes are classified in communicative practices.[31]

The human senses, 'the human nature of the senses, comes to be by virtue of *its* object, by virtue of *humanized* nature. The *forming* of the five senses is a labour of the entire history of the world down to the present' (Marx 1844/1975, p. 302).[32] This applies all the more to the symbolic modes and the art forms. A long historical process has separated music, words and dance out of a complex mixture of gestures, sounds and visual marks. The human voice was differentiated into words and music, visual signs into images and writing. Some gestures came to support speech (in dialogues as well as theatre), others were affiliated to music (dance and the playing of instruments). Aesthetic forms were separated from religious rituals and political debates. New mixtures like opera, film and music television then grew, and all these complex processes of differentiation and recombination make it impossible to deduce an ultimate priority for any symbolic mode. Cooperation of symbolic modes is a normal condition, whether in pre-modern undifferentiated communication patterns or late modern montages or syntheses of already differentiated modes. Portable Walkmans make possible a full separation of the eye from the ear, which, like the far earlier separation of instrumental music from song, dance and religious rituals, has made it easier for us to think of and treat them as distinct. The conglomerate of symbolic modes in opera or in music video is post- rather than pre-differentiated: it presupposes their differentiation, that repeatedly is reactualized by distancing montages, sampling and other techniques that not only combine but also contrast the various modes in question.

[30] Cf. Frith (1981 and 1988), Larson and Kubey (1983) and Roe (1983) on the structural conflict between youth/rock and family/TV.

[31] On interrelations of symbolic modes and art forms, see Jakobson (1968/1971), Goodman (1976), Kristeva (1981/1989), Ellis (1982), Palm (1985), Crisell (1986), Fabb et al. (1987), Sandra Kemp (1992), Lecercle (1992) and Lagerroth et al. (1993).

[32] Marx here builds on Hegel. For Marxist aesthetics on these premises, see Hauser (1951/1962), Fischer (1959/1978), Jameson (1971), Balet and Gerhard (1973), Williams (1977), Laing (1978) or Nelson and Grossberg (1988). Cf. also Freud (1930/1961, pp. 99f).

Each historical epoch shows crucial parallels between the symbolic modes. In modern society, most symbolic modes have, for example, methods for creating and representing a basic distinction between figure and ground, individual and (collectively social or biologically natural) context. In the literary novel, in the central perspective of painting and in the functional–tonal music structures of most Western music since the sonata form, such a figure/ground dichotomy is a shared convention. Its forms have changed and been problematized, but still people search for figures and characters in books and images, or for melodic shapes (*Gestalt*) standing out as individuals against, above and in front of the musical accompaniment's rhythmic web of contextual background sounds.[33]

Most symbol theories are logocentric, scriptocentric or verbocentric: they are primarily modelled on spoken or written words in verbal language and treat non-verbal modes of expression as special cases. For example, Jacques Lacan, Mikhail Bakhtin, Julia Kristeva, Tzvetan Todorov and Paul Ricoeur all primarily deal with words, sentences, utterances and literary texts rather than non-verbal ones. Conventional hierarchies of sense modalities, symbolic modes and art forms place the eye, writing and literature at the top, and most theories of symbols and discourses are rooted in literary studies or rhetorics. Media theories also tend to concentrate first on the written word (print, press and maybe literature) and then on the electronic visual media. They usually neglect music-media (and to some extent also radio), which are hardly even mentioned in the standard works on media and communication. Choosing terms like 'readers' or 'viewers' in studies of media reception hides the communicative role of sounds and hearing.

Derrida (1967/1973, 1967/1976 and 1967/1978) sharply criticizes earlier philosophies for a logo-phonocentrism that hides the importance of the exteriority of material traces behind an ideology of presence and immediacy. While sometimes correctly accepting speech and writing as equals, he mostly focuses on verbal writing so strongly that speech, music and non-verbal images are forgotten. The phonocentric and the graphocentric variants of logocentrism make useful criticisms of each other, but share some biases that have to be counteracted by models of non-verbal symbolic modes.[34]

---

[33] Cf. Márothy (1974), Fornäs (1982), Tagg (1990a and 1994), Björnberg (1991) and Bradley (1992).

[34] Derrida (1967/1978) makes use of a slippage between a narrow concept of writing (in contrast to speech) and a wide one (that materiality and those inscriptions in some exterior element that are inherent in each human symbolic language) for a highly ideological rhetoric. Michael Ryan (1982) couples Marx and Derrida but criticizes the 'semiocentrism' of Lacan. Ong (1982, pp. 75ff and 165ff) makes some strong arguments against Derrida while exposing himself to Derrida's critique of the phonocentric metaphysics of presence. Milner thinks that 'where Derrida, the prophet of *différance*, chooses to privilege writing over speech, it is [Raymond] Williams ironically enough who proves able to register this distinction between speech and writing, word and notation, as quite simply difference' (1994, p. 59).

Verbocentrism is to a certain extent legitimate. Words do have a privileged position in human communication.[35] The development of verbal language in the history both of societies and of all children founds a communicative mode that fundamentally changes human life and affects other symbolic modes as well. While all symbolic modes should not be reduced to incomplete variants of verbality, the central place and crucial presence of words in (modern) culture cannot be denied. There are important tensions between different sides of all symbols, as preliminarily indicated above by the aspects of materiality, form-relations and meaning. Words specialize in an intense development of certain of these aspects, particularly in the elaboration of a discursive system of meaning construction in the form of cognitive, rational arguments. But all verbal texts retain roots in those other symbol dimensions that are stronger and more central in other symbolic modes. The understanding of certain non-discursive material and formal traits in verbal expressions as well as in symbolic texts in general has therefore much to learn from a consideration of non-verbal modes like music and images, where these traits are perhaps more obvious and focal.

The dominance of words and writing is particularly strong in academic discourses such as the one in which this text itself takes part. This can also be 'seen' in how theories are formulated, as they 'read', 'view' or 'regard' phenomena and 'show' their models in printed books. Verbal and graphic modes of expression and visual metaphors are definitely necessary in theoretical work. A certain privilege of the verbal mode is inescapable in interpretive discourses, since it is already privileged in human communication. But it is useful to reflect upon this fact and sometimes try to experiment with other voices.[36] The verbocentrism of symbol theories invites some revision and supplementation by ideas deriving from the analysis of other symbolic modes.

In a quite typical statement, Habermas (1976/1979, p. 1) not only takes 'the type of action aimed at reaching understanding to be fundamental', but also, as 'language is the specific medium of understanding', singles out 'explicit speech actions from other forms of communicative action' and deliberately ignores 'nonverbalized actions and bodily expressions'. Later (Habermas 1981/1984, pp. 15–23), he narrowly reserves the term 'discourse' for such communicative acts where consensus can be reached. He thinks this is the case where knowledge, norms and intelligibility are thematized, but not in discussions of aesthetic values or subjective truthfulness. That is why he talks of theoretical, practical and explicative *discourses* but of aesthetic and therapeutic *critiques*. One can produce arguments for the validity of one's position as being in style or honest, but whereas mutual agreement may be reached in cognitive, normative or

---

[35] Vološinov (1929/1986, pp. 13ff) and Benveniste (1966/1971, p. 23) think of the word as the 'purest' sign that is always present in any conscious human act, thereby being fundamental to the constitution of individual and society.

[36] Cf. Classen (1993) and Clüver (1993, p. 44).

explicative discourses, the discussants cannot be expected to reach the same conclusions in aesthetical or subjectively expressive matters, which rest on conditions which are insufficiently universal, while tied to subjective and personal experiences. Discourse should not be defined quite so narrowly, nor should aesthetics be reduced to subjective expressivity or non-verbal symbolic modes be excluded from communicative action, as Habermas tends to do.

> It seems to me that *strategic action* ('oriented to the actor's success' – in general, modes of action that correspond to the utilitarian model of purposive-rational action) as well as (the still-unsufficiently-analysed) *symbolic action* (e.g., a concert, a dance – in general, modes of action that are bound to nonpropositional systems of symbolic expression) differ from communicative action in that individual validity claims are suspended (in strategic action, truthfulness, in symbolic action, truth). (Habermas 1976/1979, p. 41)

It is true that a poem, an abstract painting or a musical performance should not be interpreted as a cognitive statement about facts in the objective world, but it seems wrong to exclude symbolic modes from communicative action just because they do not give equal importance to all types of validity claims. Truth is after all not completely irrelevant to all aesthetic acts, and they may well strive to create a mutual sharing of collective experiences and a consensual understanding of the stylistic rules which they develop. Habermas's theories of the public sphere and of communicative action have been rightly criticized for focusing too much on the verbal and argumentational aspects of human interaction, neglecting other symbolic modes.[37] They can and should be modified by including other symbolic modes than verbal argumentation. All symbolic modes have other use values than the application of a given set of rules to transmit messages in propositional form, but this is particularly obvious in the non-verbal ones. The use of symbols is a creative process that plays with rules and therefore changes them, and it is far from only cognitive statements that are communicated.

Orality and literacy

Influential and important studies have related the history of media and symbolic modes to technology, social organization and patterns of socialization.[38] One model outlines three grand periods, from pre-modern

[37] 'Such an iconoclastic stance toward the symbolic leaves us with both an impoverished account of how communication in fact works and impedes the imagination of alternative forms of participatory media' (Peters 1993, p. 565). Cf. Crespi (1987), Fornäs (1987, 1990a and b), Fraser (1987), Steuerman (1989), Benhabib (1992), Elliott (1992) and Lee (1992). Frank (1988) instead defends Habermas against Lyotard, and Hellesnes (1988/1991, pp. 42ff) argues that it is Wittgenstein more than Habermas who neglects creativity by reducing action to rule-abiding behaviour.

[38] See McLuhan (1962 and 1964), Attali (1977/1985), Lowe (1982), Ong (1982), Pattison (1982), Goody (1986 and 1987), Eriksen (1987/1989), Fabb et al. (1987) and Lundström and Sahlström (1992).

primary orality (speech before writing) via early and high modern script and print *literacy* to the *secondary orality* of late modern electronic media in the twentieth century. Pictorial and phonetic script, the printing press and electronic information-processing have indeed had a fundamental influence on social, cultural and psychological forms – an influence which is usually invisible because these techniques are taken for granted in everyday life.

These theories are useful, but sometimes make overly romantic assumptions. One such idea is that of a pure origin (in pre-history or in childhood) of full and direct presence in the world of nature and of unmediated community. Derrida (1967/1976 and 1967/1978) is right in arguing that symbolic communication always involves writing in the wide sense of patterned and exteriorized memory-traces. This is also stressed when Ricoeur (1976 and 1981) shows how writing only makes the distanciation that actually inheres in all language-use more evident. The written alphabet is a much later invention than oral speech, but it is less obvious whether oral or visual signs came 'first'. Children talk before they learn to read or write, but this cannot so easily be extended to any hierarchy of sense modalities. Neither are any such historical (ontogenetic or phylogenetic) arguments automatically valid as logical arguments concerning the priority between modes in present adult society. There are good reasons to abolish the hierarchy between speech and writing, rather than either accepting it or just turning it upside-down. Each symbolic mode deserves to be understood in its own terms, instead of being reduced to something else.

The idea that aural symbolic modes are surpassed by visual ones, or that oral culture is succeeded by literary and then image-oriented culture, is too simplistic. Each new epoch does not erase the experiences and traces of the earlier ones. Late modern culture does not substitute images for words, but rather increases the flows and uses of both words, images and music. New media and modes generally interact and cooperate more than compete with old ones, as in magazines for computer games that in their turn generously mix speech, writing, images and music, creating an increasingly complex media interplay that carefully reproduces important moments of earlier phases. Personal computers have in fact expanded rather than diminished the capacities of the written word, and the reading of books and magazines has not decreased. It is true that such innovations make it impossible to relive the innocent naïvety of the times when they did not exist, but the old is actually rarely outdated by the new. Neither the book nor the cinema seems, for instance, to have succumbed to television.[39]

It is also too simplistic to reduce the complexity of symbolic modes into a single oral/literary or aural/visual dichotomy (Classen 1993, pp. 135ff).

---

[39] Feilitzen et al. (1989), Boëthius (1992/1995) and Filipson and Nordberg (1992) show that book-reading has remained pretty constant among Swedes since the 1960s.

Oral cultures (using direct speech as their main medium of communication) are not always aural (emphasizing hearing among the senses), but can as well build their main world-view upon metaphors of smell, taste or touch.

Finnegan (1989) and Berkaak and Ruud (1992) have described rock as an oral music culture, where composition, learning, music-making and listening are relatively independent of musical notation or written words. Since it uses both music, sung lyrics, gestures and image, it is in fact both visual and oral. Its orality is not primary (before writing) but secondary.[40] Its agents can read and write, and even though the practices of written language seem relatively marginal in rock culture, it certainly uses and is influenced by the expressive resources and cognitive patterns of written language. Recordings are inscriptive forms that are not only marginal means of distribution, but crucial tools for composition, learning, music-making, memory and reflection, and often even function as the standard against which live concerts are measured. To the romanticists of pure immediacy, this might seem to deprive rock of its sensuality, but there is no such absolute contradiction between writing and expressivity. Each inscription changes the context of spontaneity and presence, without erasing them. Sensuous 'touch', feeling and empathy are possible in book-reading as well, as can easily be shown by studying romance-readers. The same is true for listening to records at home in comparison with participation in public concerts, which may in fact be a quite distancing experience. Both the importance of recordings and the sensuousness of reading are easily neglected in an overly one-dimensional and romanticist account of the orality of rock.

A related trap is to idealize earlier stages and construct history as a decay. One variant of such a cultural pessimism has a nostalgia for pre-literate orality, seeing literacy as the great Fall that may be healed by a return to a new orality. Another version takes the opposite site and thinks of early literate culture as the ideal civilization that is now corrupted by electronic returns to orality. These variants thus have opposite implications, but they share a similar pattern of nostalgia for a lost world and a linear, reductionist and one-dimensional view of history.

It is also difficult to decide which level is primary in these developments. Media technologies certainly influence social life, but they are also produced by social actions. Some formulations of Marshall McLuhan and others tend towards a techno-determinism which over-simplistically credits technology with too large a power over cultural trends.

The verbal/non-verbal dichotomy is an issue of symbolic form and meaning that should not be misunderstood as a distinction between material sense modalities. To measure these things is probably impossible, but if writing should expand at the expense of speech, this tendency can either be one aspect of a generally increasing dominance of the eye over

---

[40] Cf. Ong (1982, pp. 1ff and 135ff) and Lilliestam (1988).

the ear, or just a process within the verbal mode that may even be accompanied by an increasing importance of music at the expense of images. A conflict in late modern youth culture between music and writing may likewise be read as a struggle either between the oral and the visual or between the non-verbal and the verbal. Such tendencies and conflicts may have various causes, going back to sense modalities, symbolic modes, media forms or social institutions. Systemic demands may, for instance, affect writing more than music, through pedagogic and administrative institutions. A problematization of writing may therefore result not from its own inherent logic, but from a resistance against the demands from state and market for goal-rational control. This is supported by the observation that fiction and poetry seem to have as important a role as music and pictures in the departure from instrumental rationality.

It should be noted that graphic notation is not limited to the verbal mode. Musical notation and the sound-tracks of films or phonograms fixate aural–temporal flows into visual–spatial traces that can be stored like memories over time and transported through space. Just as writing offers verbal expressions other (both more and less) possibilities than does speech, musical (and other sound) notation widens the range of this symbolic mode. It creates a more definite temporal and spatial separation of production and reception and of authorial intention and textual meaning, and it facilitates reflection on symbols and discourses, at the cost of the close and dialogic community that can emerge in live music-making.[41]

Musical notation is music in written form, just as written words may function as a manuscript or protocol of human speech. It works because the form-relations of written notes are homological with those of sounding tones. Notation is a particular visual–graphic language for music, which uses certain elements of verbality in the form of instructive words and letters (specification of tempi, sound levels, instruments, etc.).

While writing/reading is regularly used by most modern people as an independent symbolic mode, and not only as a secondary aid to speech/listening, musical notation and sound-tracks are as a rule exclusively used as a technique for the preparation of true musical sound-flows. Very few people other than musicians read scores without actually listening to the music – musical notation is mainly used as a tool for real music-making. And nobody gets a musical experience out of looking at the tracks on a record disc – the inscription in no way constitutes a separate and independent symbolic mode the way writing does in relation to speech. Therefore, while the verbal mode consists of two equally important sub-modes, music is primarily aural.[42] Images are for similar reasons also a

<hr />

[41] Cf. Jakobson (1968/1971), Ricoeur (1976) and the works on orality and literacy. H. Stith Bennett (1980, pp. 209ff) distinguishes various types of musical notation.

[42] The traditional ideal of western art music has enticed theorists like Goodman (1976, pp. 112ff) to believe that the notated version is the essence of a musical work, that all music is performed from written scores and that the relation between notes and tones is the core of

more unitarily visual mode, in spite of the fact that they may be described for (and felt by) blind people.

Primary orality, literacy and secondary orality can further not be totally identified with social categories like gender, ethnicity or class. Writing is particularly important in the upper strata of the androcentric Western civilization, but this society has also refined musics and images, and while women are the most extensive book-readers, young men are often described as escaping the pressure of patriarchy by preferring electronic image media.[43]

Discursivity, presentationality, symbolicity and semioticity

If care is needed in the use of the forceful categories of orality and literacy, the same is true of the concept of *discursivity*, denoting a particular characteristic of certain symbolic modes or uses of them. This more narrow concept of discourse was elaborated by Susanne K. Langer (1942), who defined discursive symbolic forms as those forms of communication which are based on a linear order of discrete units that allow for the expression of propositions and arguments. Verbal language is discursive, since it contains a delimited number of meaning units (morphemes, words), each with a reasonably fixed set of individual meanings, and where these units can be enumerated, defined, translated and combined in a linear fashion into larger units or sequences (sentences, works). Non-verbal symbolic languages are non-discursive in one or several of these aspects: their meaningful units are not so easily enumerable and definable, their meanings are not as fixed and translatable, etc. Much less consensus exists on which are the meaning units in a painting or a musical piece than in a written text. Such presentational symbols can only be interpreted as contextual totalities. Non-verbal images and instrumental music differ from words in radically different ways. On one hand, images have no evident linear time-dimension. They extend in space as simultaneous totalities, whereas music flows through time and forms chains of aural gestures. On the other hand, while their basic elements are not always clearly definable, and in abstract paintings or designs seem to have no univocal meaning at all, images at least more often seem to let themselves be interpreted with some intersubjective consensus as depicting and thus referring to something else. Music lacks not only clearly definable signifying elements and vocabulary but mostly also all references to anything outside of itself. The meaning music makes is based on internal form-relations, and musical elements are only rarely understood as referring to external objects or ideas. Common to images and musics as

musical semiotics. In genres like jazz, rock or rap various forms of spatial fixation are certainly used – in electronic circuits and phonogram tracks – but musical notation is generally marginal there.

[43] Cf. Drotner (1991a and b).

presentational symbolic modes is that they are not interpreted piecemeal, but only as integrated, presentational wholes.[44]

This polarity echoes in other terms within later semiotic theories that posit the musical and/or the pictorial as an antithesis to the verbal. Langer's concepts have been taken over and reworked by a series of later authors. Alfred Lorenzer (1972 and 1986) anchors them in psychoanalytical ideas of *protosymbols*: vague halos of meaning vibrating around certain objects in early childhood before definite definitions are established. In repressive socialization forms, this protosymbolic richness is depleted as the symbolic order rigidifies into overly fixed meanings, and living symbols turn into dead clichés. Presentational symbolic modes like images, music and dance may then be royal roads to give new life to a petrified language by renewing the symbolization process and drawing previously non-communicable experiences into it. By expressing what words cannot say and working otherwise than verbal discursivity, they may reconnect the whole symbolic order to its hidden protosymbolic undercurrents.[45] Particularly in adolescence, temporary regressions to pre-verbal experiential states through the use of non-verbal symbolic modes may be productive and even necessary for keeping the self and its symbolic creativity alive. Sociological and psychological findings agree that music has a particularly central role in the intense teenage identity work, where an active inner restructuring requires temporary and voluntary regressions to pre-verbal modes of experience. Thomas Ziehe (1975) and a long series of Nordic works on rock music and youth culture have subsequently developed these ideas further.[46]

Similar distinctions have been elaborated within French psychoanalysis, cultural theory and semiotics. One example is how Tzvetan Todorov (1978/ 1983) counterposes symbolic evocation to discursive predication, explanation or argumentation. However, a particularly important line of

---

[44] Meyrowitz (1985, pp. 93ff) relates the discursive/presentational dichotomy to Goffman's (1969) distinction between 'expression' and 'communication' and to the dichotomy of digital versus analogic messages (Watzlawick et al. 1967). Cf. also Lash (1990, pp. 177ff) on Lyotard's discursive versus figural regimes of signification and economies of desire, related to the secondary processes of the ego and its reality principle, on one hand, and the primary processes of the unconscious and its pleasure principle, on the other.

[45] For critiques of Lorenzer, see Menne et al. (1976) or Dahl (1987). Habermas has also used Durkheim's (1912/1976) concept of palaeosymbols – historical precursors to fully developed and differentiated symbols – as a phylogenetic parallel to protosymbols. They are ritual actions that symbolize in a holistic way, not yet differentiating between cognitive truth, normative righteousness and expressive truthfulness (Habermas 1981/1988, pp. 54ff). The relation between Lorenzer and Habermas is discussed by Mylov (1988).

[46] Cf. Elo Nielsen (1977/1984), Fornäs et al. (1988/1995) and Drotner (1991b). Ziehe was inspired by Baacke (1968) and by psychoanalytical theories on adolescence as a second birth or chance (Blos 1962), on regression in the service of the ego (Kris 1952) and on narcissism and creativity (Kohut and Levarie 1950; Kohut 1957, 1964 and 1971).

thought goes from Jacques Lacan to Julia Kristeva and Roland Barthes. Here are useful correctives to some of Langer's weaknesses, but also remnants of some problematic aspects.

Kristeva defines 'symbolic function' as 'a system of signs (first, rhythmic and intonational difference, then signifier/signified) which are organized into logico-syntactic structures whose aim is to accredit social communication as exchange purified of pleasure' (1974/1986, p. 150). This symbolic order is only possible on the basis of a mostly unconscious play with the symbols of language. Below, behind or within this formal and rational *symbolic* order of the syntactic and semantic logic of discourse, Kristeva finds another '*semiotic*' level of drives and their articulations.[47] This can be studied not only in the parapraxis (faulty function) and inconsistencies in communication.[48] It also appears in nonsense, alliteration, sounds, gestures, rhythms and pulses, where the material and sensuous presence of texts interacts with psychological processes before and below the conscious ego, associated with the primary processes of the unconscious and the transgressive id-oriented enjoyment discussed by Lacan, Barthes and Kristeva as *jouissance*, in contrast to the more ego-oriented *plaisir*.[49] There are obvious parallels between Kristeva's and Lorenzer's ideas here.

The non-discursive, presentational, non-semantic, expressive or 'semiotic' traits in poetic verbal language that do not carry definite meanings or tell a straight linear story are often termed 'musical'. Kristeva repeatedly uses musical metaphors (rhythms, sounds, melodies, etc.) for such underlying levels within the symbolic order, connected to aspects of materiality and the subjective unconscious.[50]

> For while music is a system of *differences*, it is not a system of *signs*. Its constitutive elements do not have a signified. Referent/signified/signifier here seem to melt into a single mark that combines with others in a language that doesn't mean anything. (Kristeva 1981/1989, p. 309)

The non-discursivity and emotional presence of music dispose it to stand for and open up to deeply unconscious bodily impulses and desires – the pre-verbal experiential space of protosymbols, the 'semiotic' and *jouissance*. In modern Western societies, music is often regarded as a pre-verbal, archaic mode without semantics, meaning or discursivity – a symbolic mode with particularly strong and direct connections to emotional life; a

---

[47] Kristeva (1974/1984, p. 43, and 1987/1989, p. 65). The term 'semiotic' is problematic here, since semiotics usually is at least as associated with form-relations and meanings as with the materiality of the signifier.

[48] Cf. Freud (1901/1966) and Laplanche and Pontalis (1967/1988, pp. 300f).

[49] Cf. Barthes (1973/1975 and 1977).

[50] See Kristeva (1974/1984, pp. 24 and 63ff; 1980, pp. 159ff; 1980/1982, pp. 178ff and 196ff; 1981/1989, pp. 295ff; 1983/1987, pp. 37, 259, 281ff and 324; 1987/1989, pp. 62ff and 222ff). A critique is offered by Hill (1990, pp. 149ff).

language of feelings, in contrast to the more cool and rational written verbal language.[51]

> We have seen that there is some reason to consider music the primary semiotic practice. Within the process of psychological development . . ., its origins lie in the aural relationship of baby and mother, which, together with the tactile relationship, pre-dates the significance of visual (still more, verbal) signs (dependent as that is on an apprehension of the external world as *other*). The initial connotations of sound-structures (the origins of which may go back beyond the repetitive 'coos' of the mother even into the womb): the (equally repetitive) sound/feel of maternal breathing and heartbeat are prior to any emergence of a subject, locating itself in opposition to external reality; for this reason the basic pleasure of music may be thought of as narcissistic – just as its quintessential structural tendency may be described as infinite repetition, or, everything is combined in a 'great similarity'. (Middleton 1990, p. 288)

A historical hierarchy is constructed where music is ontogenetically oldest, followed by visuality and then verbality. Music's roots in the early mother–child interaction are sometimes also used as an argument for its allegedly strong ability to transgress sociocultural boundaries and unite people. 'Music . . . thus has a unifying power. . . . It unifies a multiplicity of listeners without distinguishing between them', writes Bradley (1992, p. 29), for example, and he gives the parameter of rhythm particular credit for this. The symbolic modalities of the ear make possible a collective communication where different voices may join simultaneously and form polyphonic webs, and where groups can gather and be united in strong emotional experiences of communality. Collective musical activities can bind people together and thus restructure social differences. As a symbolic mode different from verbality music may sometimes be shared by people who do not understand each other's verbal languages. And, like other mobile occupational groups (jesters, preachers, intellectuals, au pairs, travelling salesmen, artisans, etc.), musicians may move and make contacts between different groups. More importantly, music reaches back to early forms of experience with roots in the infant's symbiosis with the mother with no clear boundaries between the self and the surrounding world.

---

[51] The polar contrast between writing and music seems more often to be thematized than the one between image and speech. Hegel (1842/1975) sees music as 'complete withdrawal, of both the inner life and its expression, into subjectivity' (p. 889), with the task of 'making resound, not the objective world itself, but, on the contrary, the manner in which the inmost self is moved to the depths of its personality and conscious soul' (p. 891). Since 'music must express the inner life as such' (pp. 934f), he concludes: 'Music is spirit, or the soul which resounds directly on its own account and feels satisfaction in its perception of itself' (p. 939). Bradley (1992, pp. 19ff) sees music as a material and signifying practice where human work and intersubjective relations are crucial, and he stresses that the listener has to make an identification of the humanness of the music-maker. He thinks music cannot refer, but only affect: it is a non-referential but affective signifying system which symbolizes or means nothing except as an expression of emotions, by which it has the power to produce real changes of state in the listener. Nattiez (1987/1990) and Barry (1987) also discuss music as a signifying symbolic mode.

Still, music is far from alone in this unifying ability. It is shared by religion, love, dance and literature. All human interaction potentially transcends borders, since symbolic communication is a sharing of meaning. In all collective activities (work-places, sport teams, restaurants, etc.), people make shared experiences that transgress at least some earlier social and cultural differences. Even verbal communication can create mutual understanding and community, sometimes even where music fails to do so. Music can in fact give rise to cleavages as well as community – a metal fan and a rapper may find it easier to talk than to share music. 'Musicking is not necessarily a unifying force at all; on the contrary, it can articulate and even exacerbate social divisions' (Small 1987, p. 71). Musicians and various professional gatekeepers are involved in the construction of collective identities but they also help in enforcing distinctions – of genre and distaste as well as between idols and fans. The idea that music is an almost magically universal language is a romantic myth that hides the fact that different generations and groups often develop quite contradictory musical competences and preferences.

Music and words are often joined in songs of various kinds. But music also appears within written texts, in at least three ways. On the level of semantic meaning, texts may thematize or refer to music. This is often done by describing how it is produced, using terms related to musical techniques or instruments and to the work of musicians and composers. Or, metaphors are borrowed from the reception side, via the physical or emotional effects of a sound on its listeners. Texts may thematize all levels of music, by trying to translate or depict what music means, how it is structurally formed or which sensuous force inheres in its material substrate.

On the level of syntactic form, words may be homologous with music. The relations between letters, words and sentences may form patterns that are homological with musical forms. Metres, variational principles, the sonata and the blues forms have all been tried in literature as well, making texts like music, independent of their semantic content. This homological level is often a necessary aid to semantic interpretations of musical form-relations or materiality. It may be easier to explain a musical form by translating it into an analogical verbal form. Saying that a minuet has ABA-form is, for instance, simpler than explaining that it has three parts, of which the last one is a repetition of the first. Habitual conventions for such translations let us easily grasp the idea, skipping the complicated detour through a semantic interpretation. And a poem in ABA-form can be perceived as formally related to the music of a minuet even if it is written in an incomprehensible (foreign or nonsense) language.

On the level of material force, verbal texts may possess a musicality, as poets and literary semioticians, including Kristeva, have so often suggested. Textual materiality here fuses with musical materiality into a pulsating audiovisual substrate, underneath all form and meaning. Kristeva shows how words in poetic works (as well as in everyday speech) carry 'semiotic' openings, so that verbality is obviously more than just a discursive machine that constructs additive chains of well-defined symbols. Much discursive writing may be used in the service of system-oriented societal institutions, but this does not mean that verbality is doomed to be only a tool of power. Literature may well be as subversive of the symbolic order as are musical works, not only by using discursive arguments against power structures, but also by subverting the conventional discursive logics in poetic transgressions that sensuously play with the enjoyment of writing.

Verbal expressions actually are not so completely discursive as Langer seems to think. Words can be enumerated in dictionaries, but in living languages their meanings have an irreducible polysemic openness and context-boundedness, so that no perfectly universal and fixed meaning-units exist. Sentences and larger textual wholes (works, discourses, genres, epochs, etc.) both extend and delimit the meaning of each of their units. The univocality of a dictionary is therefore deceptive, and the discursivity of verbal modes are more of a striving and a tendency than an attained fact. Words contain presentational, emotive and expressive as well as discursive, cognitive and semantic aspects (as does music, as will soon be argued). All symbolic modes have materiality, form and meaning aspects, and are open to unconscious pulsions as well as a conscious symbolic ordering. In poetry and pop lyrics, the expressive and 'semiotic' side is extremely important, offering oceanic feelings of unlimited *jouissance*. The roots back to a pre-verbal 'semiotic' origin (phylogenetically in prehistory and ontogenetically in infancy) are shared by both music and words.

Conversely, words may enter music in several ways. To start at the other end, musical materiality may fuse with the sensuous force of words, and there are homologies between some musical and verbal forms. Music and other non-verbal modes can, thirdly, not be said to completely lack signification or even discursivity. Music may be efficient in expressing and creating feelings, through parameters like volume, beat and sound. But it is only some musical parameters that in some contexts induce 'semiotic' *jouissance*. Melodic, harmonic and formal elements in music often combine in discursive ways and semantically carry associations to extra-musical experiences or objects. Langer herself confesses that sign languages, pictorial languages and acoustic signals are discursive. But similar discursive traits are actually very common in images as well as in music; they are seldom purely presentational. Within the context of a specific genre, sounds and visual marks invite being read as sequences of reasonably separate motifs whose meaning contents are as relatively determined as in the case of the always polysemic but still intersubjectively fairly definable words. Discourses with pretty delimited meanings are often developed in music, most obviously in TV-signatures, mood and film music, as Philip Tagg (1979, 1982a and b, 1987, 1990a and b, 1994) has shown by dissecting how the meaningful units ('musemes') of which they consist combine into ideological discourses. To a certain extent even Bach's most abstract instrumental works mean something, by constructing sequences of meaningful units, using structural homologies with non-musical sounds, movements and sensations as well as references to musical styles with specific social connotations. It is more difficult to construct true propositional statements and arguments in music, but it certainly can contain chains of meaning. Against Roland Barthes, Susan McClary (1991, p. 102) argues that music is as socially organized and 'condemned to meaning' as is literature. 'Meaning is not inherent in music, but neither is it in language: both are activities that are kept afloat only because communities of people invest in them, agree collectively that their signs serve as valid currency' (p. 21).[52] It is true that music alone, 'in itself', possesses no meaning, but neither does a written word without its context, including its reader. All symbolic modes 'just' offer raw material for the construction of meaning in their use by human subjects.

The more diffuse meaning aspect of music thus differs more in degree than in kind from that of words. Music can therefore 'translate' or thematize literary narratives, form-relations or materialities. And like reflexive texts, musical pieces can also refer to music itself, by teasing our expectations, using musical genres ironically and directing the attention to their own constructedness by surprising montages. It is a romantic mistake to think of music as pure, meaning-less materiality and form. Music also has its formal rules that can be reflected upon and used rationally. Musical themes and motifs can also construct linear patterns where specific elements point towards intersubjectively shared extra-musical ideas.

The mutuality of the image/word relation is somewhat more obvious. Just as words can describe images, images can (like music) illustrate or translate words, but also (easier than can music) depict them.[53] Symbolic orders thus exist within as well as beside the verbal mode. Music and images are no diffuse flows that are given shape and meaning only by the presence of words. They also elaborate logical and meaningful structures, even though these differ from the verbal ones.

[52] While Blacking (1973, p. 21) refuses to see music as language and resists all analogies between verbal, visual and musical communication, Holland (1990), Shepherd (1991) and Bradley (1992) discuss tonality as musical signifier, discursive musical logics and music as language. Weber (1921/1958) is the classical analysis of musical rationalization. Middleton (1990) argues that music primarily signifies only structural relations (before/after, fast/slow, high/low, dissonance/consonance, mobile/static), while references to the external world are just secondary significations through conventional associations. But a similar argument is valid for all symbolic modes, including verbality. What Middleton terms primary signification are the internal form-relations, while real meaning is everywhere the result of contextually and historically situated, intersubjective interpretive practices.

[53] On pictorial semiotics and images in relation to words or music, see Barthes (1977), Hebdige (1991), Louis Marin (1991), Passeron (1991) and Sonesson (1992). Contrary to conventionalist models of 'visual literacy', Messaris argues that images are unique as a mode of communication in that 'they are not merely another form of arbitrary signification. Learning to understand images does not require the lengthy period of initiation characteristic of language learning, and permeability of cultural boundaries is much greater for images than it is for language' (1993, p. 290).

It is true that instrumental music sometimes strives away from the symbolic order associated with words, into the extra-verbal as the Other of language. This is particularly attempted by some avantgarde art and jazz musicians, where this search is very often tied to a movement away from the commercial 'vulgarity' of 'mass culture'.[54] This romantic critique of discursive rationality appears in varying shapes within most theoretical traditions – phenomenology, hermeneutics, psychoanalysis and (neo-)structuralism. The romantic anti-verbal ideology may, like aesthetic modernism in general, actually be more 'male' than 'female', in spite of its ideas of the verbal order as patriarchal. 'Female' literary genres and forms of expression may have retained more openings towards early forms of experience, enjoyment and closeness than the more control-oriented and system-dependent genres of writing dominated by men. While women may have retained an ability more freely to use both sides of speech and writing in diaries, poems or romance novels, some men may have suffered more of a tyranny of goal-oriented verbality and tried to escape to something totally other, in the form of 'free' instrumental music and abstract art. A strong logocentrism thus often hides in the romantic longing for the seemingly absolute freedom of wordless music. It is from a verbal prison that music appears as the immaculate Other.[55]

But rock or pop is subversive when it joins rhythms and sounds not only with the imagery of album covers, posters and stage shows, but first of all with sung verbal lyrics. Pure instrumental musics like most jazz have not in the same intense way had to wrestle with the relation between words and tones, with all its conventional connotations to cognition and emotion, mind and body, culture and nature, distance and proximity, meaning and sensuousness, reflexivity and devotion. The flight from words is therefore a futile strategy for reaching the depths of *jouissance*, since the discursive potentials of music itself easily transform the most self-consciously anti-discursive acts into the most feeble clichés. It is also an unnecessary strategy, since the pre-verbally rooted depth dimension is never absent in the materiality of the verbal order itself. The extra-verbal hides within the words, the presentational within the discursive.

Music thus can mean something, and even refer reflexively to itself. The verbal mode may have wider discursive and symbolic capacities than music or images, but wordless music is in a certain degree also 'textually' discursive, semantic and structured by conventional symbolicisms. Words conversely also contain 'musical' elements of iconicity, presentationality

---

[54] Pattison (1987) discusses romanticism within rock.

[55] It is as wrong to interpret verbality as male (through the dominant symbolic order in a patriarchal writing culture of institutions like school and state bureacracy) and the non-verbal as female (in style, fashion and design) as it is inversely to define images or music as male (metal, music video, comic strips, photo magazines, etc.) and verbality as female (diaries, book-reading, listening to rock lyrics, etc.). The symbolic modes are not gendered in such a crude way, even though certain genres are gender-biased.

and *jouissant* 'semioticity'.[56] In spite of their prolonged historical separation, music and words still have much in common. And if the 'protosymbolic' or the 'semiotic' are 'old' depth-levels of (all) symbolic or cultural phenomena, they cannot be identified with Langer's (particular) presentational symbol-systems. Presentational symbolic modes are only more open to these archaic aspects than the discursive ones. Both discursive/presentational and symbolic/semiotic are categories that actually distinguish not separate symbolic modes (as implied in the use of metaphors by Langer, Kristeva, Barthes and many others), but rather aspects or levels within each of them. Symbolic modes like writing/speech/images/music should not be conflated with symbol aspects like materiality/form/meaning.

Yet, there is a difference in degree. The meaning aspect is more predominant in verbal texts than in pure music, as literature and speech acts have developed our ability to form meaning in extremely elaborate ways. In Western societies, meaning and referentiality have therefore come to be associated with verbal language, while the pulses and sounds of materiality have been associated with the musical. The alternative symbolic modes of music or images cannot be understood other than in their tense relation to these verbal modes, to which they always with love–hatred turn. On the other hand, they also contain keys to understand aspects of verbal modes from which not even the most rationalized discursivity can escape.[57] However this dichotomy is deconstructed, it continues to function historically and discursively, before us, around us and within us. There is a whole spectrum of materiality/form/meaning in verbal modes as well as in music and images, but as a result of complicated historical processes, the word and music spectra have come to be hierarchically related to each other in the ways exemplified above, so that words tend to be reduced to cognitive and discursive significations while music has become used as metaphor for the 'Other' of meaning within language, namely its non-semantic, emotional or presentational materiality. In effect, they are parallel but separate and heterogeneous modes, each with their own meanings, forms and materialities. This romantic and ideological reduction is therefore misleading, even though it is almost unavoidable and contains a certain rational core.

No symbolic modes (or genres) are thus purely discursive or presentational, semantic or 'semiotic', but always mix these aspects to varying degrees and in varying ways. Discursivity, like meaning, is emphasized and highly

[56] 'On reflection, is seems clear that no language, not even the most arid of academic language, is completely and purely arbitrary, without any allusion or reference to sound's iconic potentials. All language, to be evocative, has rhythms and textural properties, the more so when it seems monotonous and flat. Equally, it seems clear that no music – not even the most rhythmic, the most textural on the one hand, or the most abstract, the most "syntactical," on the other – is without a range of meanings that have become conventional, traditional, and, to a certain degree, arbitrary in relation to the iconic potentials and possibilities of the sounds through which it receives articulation and life' (Shepherd 1993, p. 29).

[57] Cf. Todorov (1978/1983) or Lecercle (1992).

developed in verbal modes, but not confined to them. Presentationality, like materiality, is a basic aspect of all symbolic modes, but more obviously so in the non-verbal ones. The symbolic modes share basic characteristics but are still incomparable, since each of them combines materiality, form and meaning in a unique way. Outside of verbal modes, meaning-making is much more often one aspect among several rather than the ultimate key one: it exists there as well but is not necessarily in focus all the time. All these relative differences of degree become essential as they are accumulated and reinterpreted as absolute dichotomies that are in fact contextually constructed polarities.

Discursivity is thus a particular form of symbolicity that may evolve out of the presentational basis through the development of a distinct and discrete vocabulary with some linearity, abstraction, definability and translatability. Such discursivity pushes aside and marginalizes that which does not allow itself to be arranged in such strict forms, but it also makes possible a communicative rationality of argumentation and a self-thematizing reflexivity. If and when discursive forms within certain symbolic modes tend to close the doors to their origin and basis in the presentational aspects, they create needs for revitalization, dynamization, mobilization and flexibilization, which often turn to alternative symbolic modes that do not seem to be as subsumed under systemic goal-rationality and as dominated by the meaning aspect.

Symbols are thus born in the dialectical crossing of material force, relational form and semantic signification. Often only two of the three aspects are emphasized, as when Kristeva and others emphasize the materiality/meaning relation in terms of 'semiotic' versus 'symbolic'. Ricoeur's conceptual pair 'semiotic' (or semiological) versus semantic sign functions instead aims at the relation between formal structures and hermeneutic meaning.

> Opposing sign to sign is the *semiological* function; representing the real by signs is the *semantic* function, and the first is subordinate to the second. The first function serves the second; or, if one prefers, language is articulated for the purpose of the signifying or representative function. (Ricoeur 1969/1974, p. 252)

> Whereas the sign points back only to other signs immanently within a system, discourse is about things. Sign differs from sign, discourse refers to the world. Difference is semiotic, reference is semantic. (Ricoeur 1975/1986, p. 216)

Ricoeur's formulation that symbols are born in the crossing of force and form, or balance on the borderline between body and language, points to the third side of the conceptual triangle: materiality and form-relations.[58]

---

[58] Ricoeur (1976, pp. 45ff, 59 and 69). Blacking (1977, pp. 18ff) believes that the non-verbal communication of dance and music invalidates the dichotomy between body and soul. Jackson (1983) thinks that bodily communication precedes and supports verbal language. Johnson (1987) argues that propositional arguments can only be created on the basis of an underlying web of non-propositional, analogical and figurative image schemata deriving from basic bodily experiences. Yet, while being based on materiality, meaning crucially differs from it. Also, the symbolic modes of verbal language have developed particularly strong

All these different dichotomies can be interrelated with help of the three basic symbol aspects.

Material symbol aspects concern the bodily aspects of communication, but it is actually not all materiality that is 'semiotic' in Kristeva's sense or creates *jouissance* à la Barthes. Even the most discursively well-ordered expression has a materiality – body and sensuality are not absolutely contrary to the symbolic order of meanings. Only that materiality which is *not* subsumed under the form-relations and meaning-patterns of the prevailing symbolic order constitutes a rest, a potentially contradictory remainder of 'poetic' or 'semiotic' elements that may induce *jouissance* by opening sublime fractures and breaks in the syntactic and/or semantic levels of discourse, and thus create an innovative 'surplus of meaning'. All cultural texts rest on a sublimation that transforms, organizes and codes unconscious impulses according to social norms, but this established social logic can momentarily be shattered, either by an inner, subjective resistance of the id, or by an outer, objective resistance of the raw materiality of signs as things. Protosymbolic, semiotic or poetic *jouissance* thus has more to do with a particularly tense relation between the three symbol aspects than with materiality in itself: it exists as a subcurrent within the symbolic and presupposes form-relations and meaning as much as materiality.[59]

Music can never be reduced to meaningful messages or abstract form structures. There always remains a material corporality of sensuous vibrations. Music never only *says* something about something – it also *does* something, puts bodies in motion. But this is true for literature as well, and those theories that reduce words to carriers of meaning only, or to pure formal structures, are too reductionist long before they turn to the field of musics or visual images. The critique of logo- or verbocentrism is therefore relevant within the verbal mode itself as well, since speech and writing have accents, rhythm and materiality, in spite of the fact that we lack neutral terms and feel forced to use musical metaphors to describe these aspects.

Form-relations: composition, genre and style

In all symbolic modes, signifying and communicative practices create works, texts and discourses by cumulating symbols into aggregate totalities

potentials for discursivity and communicative rationality, giving it a unique position in human civilization.

[59] Middleton (1990, p. 288) argues that *jouissance* can arise not only from substructural materiality but also from form. I think this happens just when form structures contain unexpected openings which let materiality be more directly experienced, so that it is not really form itself but rather the form/materiality relation which is then the source. On the other hand, it should be noted that the 'semiotic rhythms' to which Kristeva refers also arise from form-relations (in music: temporal relations of repetition between notes).

where voices mingle in various ways. On the side of form-relations, these works have three important traits (cf. also Ricoeur 1981, pp. 136ff).

> By text I do not mean only or even mainly something written . . .; I mean principally the production of discourse as a work. With the work, as the word implies, new categories enter the field of discourse. Essentially these are pragmatic categories, categories of production and of labour. To begin with, discourse is the arena of a work of composition or arrangement, 'disposition' . . ., which makes of a poem or a novel a totality irreducible to a simple sum of sentences. Next, this 'disposition' obeys formal rules, a codification that belongs no longer to language but to discourse, and fashions from discourse what we have just called a poem or a novel. This code is the one of literary 'genres', that is, of genres that regulate the praxis of the text. Finally, this codified production ends in a particular work: this poem, that novel. Ultimately this third trait is the most important. It can be called style, where it is understood . . . as what makes the work a singular, individual thing. (Ricoeur 1975/1986, p. 219; cf. also Ricoeur 1976, p. 33)

Cultural phenomena ('texts') are webs of meaningful symbols, forming works as externalized units produced by human action or praxis. The work is a formally ordered *composition*, it follows the rules of some *genre*, and it has its own, individual *style*. Genres are institutionalized, intersubjective, stubborn but yet flexible sets of generic rules for cultural production and reception (as a production of meaning in the appropriation of texts). As ordering regulators of the work that creates singular texts and discourses, they are potentials for using symbolic modes to generate such works.[60]

A genre is a specific generic or generative set of symbolic codes for the production and use of texts (in the widest sense). The novel or heavy metal are such rule systems whose application creates a certain classification of literature or music. A style is a particular way of using such codes. Styles may be individual, but they may also refer to smaller or larger configurations than that. Toni Morrison writes novels in her own style, but a single book may also be said to be written in one specific style, and it is, on the other hand, possible to think of styles common to a group of works or writers. This makes the relation of styles to genres highly complicated. Sometimes the border is very fluid. Individual styles may be transformed into new genres, as when Dashiell Hammett's and Raymond Chandler's crime novels became models for the hard-boiled detective genre. Genres may, on the other hand, be used in certain styles, as when the hard-rock band Europe refers to classical music in their virtuoso guitar soli. Styles may be seen as particular instances within genres, but they frequently cross genres, as when the hard-boiled style can be found in novels, cartoons, films and television.

---

[60] Like 'genus' and 'gender', 'genre' is a term rooted in the Latin word for generating, engendering or creating. In French, it then came to indicate kind, manner or taste, mostly within the fine arts and their aesthetic conventions. For various theories of genre, cf. in literature Ricoeur (1976 and 1981) and Todorov (1978/1990), in popular music Fabbri (1982), in film and television Neale (1980), and in media studies Corner (1991).

It is sometimes stressed that a genre is (solely) defined through its relations to neighbour genres. These contextual relations of difference are indeed crucial, but the formulation is somewhat circular. The total set of genres is not an autonomous formal and abstract structure. First, generic rules also have a specific internal composition that can be described as such. Secondly, they are not only located among surrounding genres, but also connected to non-symbolic phenomena of a material, bodily, economic, political, social or psychological kind. Rock cannot be defined plainly as (culturally) different from other musical genres, but is also related to objective, social and subjective factors. If there were no determinations of materiality and meaning involved, no music-users would care to develop purely formal criteria to differentiate between genres at all.

Like symbolic modes and languages, genres are both static and dynamic structures. Compared to single works, they appear as relatively fixed systems. But, on the other hand, they continuously change and are redefined by new works that make use of them differently as well as by secondary (meta-)discourses that thematize them. A new genre does not abolish the old ones, but changes them subtly.[61]

The function of genres is basically more genetic and generic than taxonomic. If texts can be classified into genres, this is only because these various sets of generic rules have been put into motion. No such classification is complete, fixed or unanimous, since several conflicting ways of ordering genres coexist and are continuously redefined through a never-ending process of discursive and interpretive struggles.

Genres exist within all symbolic modes, art forms, and in fact all fields of activity. Branches of athletics may be thought of as genres as much as may types of literature. Sometimes they are obvious and well-noted, especially within the fields of popular culture. In avantgarde 'high' art, there is occasionally an ideology of individual uniqueness that tends to deny and repress genericity into an unconscious background pattern. It is perfectly possible to play with genre boundaries, and to move them, but they cannot be conjured away, and from the outside it is mostly very easy to discern clear genre rules that seem to govern even the most transgressive works.

Genres frequently overlap, but also exist on different levels that tend to be hierarchically ordered. Rock can, for example, be seen as a specific subgenre of popular music and also as a large and general supergenre including both rock'n'roll and thrash metal.

Styles are individual form patterns in singular works, located within various genre-rules. Common stylistic traits can be found between single works within a genre or several genres, by one author or a group of authors, from a limited period or across longer stretches of time, as marks

---

[61] This presentation is inspired the largely parallel ideas of Bakhtin (1963/1984 or 1986, pp. 60ff), Ricoeur (1976 and 1981), Todorov (1978/1983) and Kristeva (1980).

of the unique contextualized individuality of these authors.[62] Through stylization, individual (sets of) works, texts or discourses get their (cultural) identity. Neither genres nor styles are autonomous objectivized systems – they only exist as ordered patterns in human practices of creating cultural works by the use of symbolic modes. This is important to note against all tendencies to reify styles, in studies of art as well as of youth subcultures. Everyone has style – a lifestyle – as a result of the relative regularity by which one expresses oneself symbolically – in body and clothing, movements and language-use, music and consumer taste, daily habits and rituals. Individually and with the various groups with which an individual identifies him/herself, each person creates style by arranging cultural forms into combinatory patterns that follow prevailing aesthetic rules for stylization.

Each style has many unimportant and/or unconscious elements. The most central and widely recognized ones, around which a style is organized, are key symbols or style markers for that text, text-aggregate, individual, group, subculture, society or epoch.[63] Styles are partly actively chosen, developed and learned in exchanges with others, partly unintentional results of the social position and psychological deep structure of the individual or collective subjects (authors) who produce them. While the intended stylizations concern the teleology of the subject – its creation of new meanings and innovative praxis – the unconscious style traits point at the archaeology of the subject – its deep roots and extra-subjective sources. Style is shaped in the crossing between individual subjectivity (itself a product of preceding interactions) and intersubjective sociality. One cannot fully control one's own style (the style of one's works, whether written texts, body language or a form of life), but neither is it a pure result of biological determinations. With increased reflexivity, styles can be more intentionally cultivated, without ever becoming totally transparent. Styles are not only sets of technical tricks of representation, but include an unconscious, bodily habitus-aspect. Barthes (1953/1968, pp. 9–18) therefore distinguishes between, on one hand, language and style as, respectively, a horizontal and a vertical dimension of what appears to the subject as the blind force of an essentially biological order of nature, and, on the other hand, an intentionally chosen tone, ethos or mode of writing. In

---

[62] Cf. Ricoeur (1981, p. 137) and Gumbrecht and Pfeiffer (1986). The term probably derives from the Latin *stilus*, a slate-pencil for writing. It was early used for ways of writing, and transferred to denote regularities in various aesthetic expressions of individuals or groups. Simmel emphasizes the generalizing function of style: 'By virtue of style, the particularity of the individual work is subjugated to a general law of form that also applies to other works' (1908/1991, p. 64). His contrasting of the popular culture or handicraft stylization against the aesthetic individualization of true artist is no longer tenable. In later studies of self-presentation, everyday life and consumption, style is instead individualized configuration, opposed to fashion as general, genre-like rules and patterns, in line with my definitions (cf. Miller 1990, pp. 57ff and Ganetz 1992/1995).

[63] Cf. Ortner (1973) and Bjurström and Lilliestam (1994).

practice, this difference is hard to uphold, but it points at an important ambiguity of the style concept.

Genre and style are relative and context-bound concepts. There are innumerable styles that can be defined along varying and intersecting dimensions. At one end they border diffusely towards the unique form and composition of a single work, at the other end towards a likewise wide spectrum of sub- and supergenres as general generative principles and patterns within larger interpretive communities. Styles may be sited within specific genres, but also run across several of them, as when an author writes in his own way in many literary genres or when a macho style turns up in music as well as in clothing. Subgenres may in some contexts be perceived as styles (individual form patterns), while they may be understood as genres in relation to singular works. Thrash metal is a style within both the music video and the rock genre, but also a (sub)genre within which a particular band may form its personal style. Youth subcultures are subgenres within the supergenre of life forms, whereas youth and life styles are individual realizations within these genres. What is first an individual style may later be taken up by others and finally evolve into a new genre. Certain key style elements can become formative of a new genre, as when some instrumental idioms come to define a separate musical genre. Conversely, genre elements can become formative of an individual style, when, for example, a pop artist's paintings may be identified by their references to comic strips. Styles seem always to be more narrowly defined than genres, not only as individual instances but also as more autonomous aesthetic-symbolic patterns, whereas genres must be understood as inter-subjectively defined and therefore including certain social institutionaliz-ations. Genres relate to diachronic lines of collective kinship, history and tradition, while style is more about individually distinguishing synchronic markings. Fabbri (1982), for instance, thinks musical styles only concern patterns of sounds, while musical genres also include social relations around these sounds (the way performers behave, the organization of concerts, the visual forms of record covers, etc.). Even though a strict dichotomy is hard to uphold, genres tend to involve more aspects and variables than styles – especially more of the functional use context of the texts, including also the 'hardware' media forms through which they circulate (while styles tend to be defined mainly in relation to the 'software' artefacts or content of these media).

The concepts of style and genre apply not only to externalized aesthetic artefacts but also to individual and collective life forms, subcultures and cultural identities. Cultural practices create cultural identities: symbolic patterns or ordered sets of signs which interact both with subjectivities and with social communities. Neither social nor subjective identities can be directly observed. A person's collective belonging or inner self is not in itself clearly visible for another person. Only through signs and symbols can we show each other who we are and what we wish to be like, consciously or in secret. Cultural identities are specific structured units in our symbolic interaction with which we construct, designate or characterize collective (social) as well as individual (psychological) identities. Cultural identities thus mediate between the external and the internal, and between the objective, the social and the subjective. But they simultaneously form a arena of their own, a symbolic order with specific codes and processes.

Specific cultural identities are manifested as lifestyles. There is a wide spectrum from individual styles through specific group styles to wider subcultural styles. As symbolic constructs, they can be read as texts and analysed by semiotic and hermeneutic methods. While the concept of genre is often reserved for institutionalized fields of artistic creativity, the concept of style has been used more widely in subcultural studies. This has led to some confusion of their interrelations. Some think of genres as narrow aesthetical categories (e.g., musical genres) being part of styles (e.g., youth styles, including much wider social patterns). Others conversely think of (e.g., musical) styles as the narrow aesthetic core of (musical) genres that also include social aspects. This makes it hard to combine (youth) styles in the first sense with (musical) styles in the second sense. A solution is to add a missing link: the idea of youth or 'life' genres, on the same level as youth or lifestyles. One can then separate two interacting style/genre dialectics: a wide one of life forms and subcultures in general as meaningful textual structures, and a narrow one of specific aesthetic modes like music, literature or film.

Youth styles thus may be defined as particular patterns within youth cultural practices as a genre. They are age-specific parts of a wider set of specific lifestyles related to the genre of life forms. These styles are particular patterns in the formation of cultural identities which can be read as the extrovert languages of individual or collective identities in general. Lifestyles are styles of living, of which youth styles constitute a subgenre.

Meanings: interpretive directions

It is now time to concentrate upon the third symbol aspect, that of *meaning*. The meanings of symbols and texts are made and reconstructed in the meaning-making of discourses, through practices of interpretation where subjects encounter and use texts within contexts. 'Meaning is the effect of interaction between speaker and listener produced via the material of a particular sound complex' (Vološinov 1929/1986, pp. 102f). Meaning is more of a process than a fact, since a basically intersubjective act of interpretation is needed to reconstitute it by understanding it. It does not reside in the text as a given, material thing, but is produced by interpretive activities of human subjects in social interaction. Expressions like 'meaningful symbols' or 'the meaning of a text' are only simplified ways of referring to the capacity of interpretive communities to construct meanings in interplay with specific symbolic forms. Interpretation does not discover objectively given, pre-existing meanings, but neither does it arbitrarily invent subjective meanings out of empty nothingness – it is a socially and intertextually situated activity that clarifies the intersubjectively valid meanings of a specific text. Interpretation is a mediating act between subjects that transforms a given text to a form or symbolic mode that makes its meaning more comprehensible. Meanings are the intersubjectively agreed sets of references to objects to which a symbol or a text points.

Meaning is more than the materiality and the form-relations on which it necessarily builds. It concerns a pointing towards something else than what is present, in the minds of human beings as they confront material objects understood as symbols and texts. Understanding symbols is an act of interpretation, of deciphering, translating, rendering, explaining or making out their meanings, so that its pointing towards what is its significance for us is apprehended. This is done not only in all research, but in each moment of everyday life, however automatically and quickly.

Content is an ambiguous term that is sometimes used for meanings. Contents of texts and of media should, however, be kept apart. *Textual content* – as opposed to textual form – can mean textual meaning, but may also sometimes include textual materiality. *Media content* – as opposed to both media form, media materiality and media meaning – is generally understood as the media texts themselves, with all their material, form and meaning dimensions. These texts give media meaning, but media meaning is also the meaning of the medium itself as a text, which is something else. The materiality of radio consists of airwaves, frequencies and apparatuses. The form of radio concerns how this medium is put together. Radio's meaning is the significance we give it, which is certainly influenced by the content of radio, that is, the programmes as texts. These radio programmes in their turn have material aspects ('the grain of the voice' and other physical sound phenomena), form-relations (structural traits) and meanings. The content of these radio-texts is their meanings plus maybe their materiality.

Meanings are created by the use of symbols, and the meaning of a symbol can be determined as the ways in which it is used in intersubjective discourses or symbolic games. To understand a piece of text (a sentence, a picture, a tune), as the result of interpreting it, is to be able to use it in a relevant way, knowing under which conditions it is valid.[64] This validity has several dimensions: not only propositional truth but also normative rightness, symbolic well-formedness and personal honesty. These other aspects of validity – and especially the one concerning aesthetic form and taste – are certainly of high importance in the aesthetic discourses on works of art, which deal with human imagination and where direct cognitive truth

---

[64] This is a reformulation of a standard thesis on the understanding of an utterance in speech act theory (cf. Habermas 1981/1984–8), inspired by Wittgenstein's (1945/1976, e.g., p. 43) pragmatist ideas of that the meaning of a word is its use in language-games. Cf. also Vološinov (1929/1986). It is here extended beyond the verbal-discursive domain.

is therefore of less immediate concern. To understand a pop hit or a subcultural style is to know in which contexts and for whom they are aesthetically well-formed, subjectively expressive and/or normatively justifiable, not necessarily to like them or share these stylistic rules, personality traits or ethical norms. Conversely, to like something does not necessarily imply that one understands it. Understanding means judging on a secondary level, that is, deciding when, where and for whom something will get a favourable judgement of truth, rightness, aesthetic quality and/or authenticity.

Symbol theories analyse meanings in differing ways, in terms of sense, reference, signification, signified, denotation, connotation, etc.[65] There is a range of classifications of symbols into types, depending on the degree of (causal or habitual) closeness or similarity between sign and referent or whether the relation is conventional or in some way natural, sometimes using classical rhetorical terms like allegory, metaphor, metonymy and synecdoche. In the semiotics of Charles S. Peirce (1940/1955, pp. 74–119, 233–7 and 274–86), signs are triadic relations involving three fundamental phenomenological categories. Firstness is quality or autonomous existence, as in the primary sign or sign-vehicle, the monadic signifier or 'representamen' in itself, as materiality. Secondness is existence as relation or reaction to something first, as in the 'object' or reference that corresponds to meaning and for which the sign stands. Thirdness is existence as law, synthesis or mediation between something first and something second, as in the 'interpretant' or symbolic code of interpretation to whom or which the sign signifies in some particular respect or 'ground'.

> A sign, or *representamen*, is something which stands to somebody for something in some respect or capacity. It addresses somebody, that is, creates in the mind of that person an equivalent sign, or perhaps a more developed sign. That sign which it creates I call the *interpretant* of the first sign. The sign stands for something, its *object*. It stands for that object, not in all respects, but in reference to a sort of idea, which I have sometimes called the *ground* for the representamen. . . . A *Sign*, or *Representamen*, is a First which stands in such a genuine triadic relation to a Second, called its *Object*, as to be capable of determining a Third, called its *Interpretant*, to assume the same triadic relation to its Object in which it stands itself to the same Object. (Peirce 1940/1955, pp. 99f)

To Peirce, a symbol is a complete, triadic relation of sign, object and interpretant, where the meaning is conventional and thus explicitly dependent on the interpretant. He then subdivides signs according to three trichotomies, relating to the quality of the sign itself (qualisign, sinsign, legisign), the relation between sign and object (icon, index, symbol) and the character of the interpretant's representation of the sign (rheme, dicent sign, argument). Each of these three can either be primarily a monadic quality of firstness, a polar relation of secondness or a general law of

---

[65] Semiotic theory in particular; cf. Saussure (1916/1974), Peirce (1940/1955), Eco (1976), Kristeva (1981/1989) or Blonsky (1985).

thirdness. The most discussed triad is the second one. An icon is a monadic sign-relation of similarity or resemblance, as in images and diagrams, where some parallel quality connects sign and meaning. The icon simply shares this quality with what it is thought to refer to. An index is a dyadic sign with a physical proximity or connection to its object as its symptom. A symbol is a sign based on habit, a conventional rule or law which throws sign, object and interpretant together. 'The symbol is connected with its object by virtue of the idea of the symbol-using mind, without which no such connection would exist' (Peirce 1940/1955, p. 114).

All signs are in a sense actually full triadic symbols where there is always at least some degree of proximity and similarity involved, so that iconic and indexical traits are only more or less present.[66] The whole division is therefore more an issue of relative degree and of point of view than of absolute kind. There are no purely arbitrary signs, as little as there are pure icons or pure indices, but signs may be more or less symbolic, iconic or indexical. These classifications only turn our attention to how specific symbol-uses foreground specific aspects of meaning-making (likeness, proximity or convention) and hide other such aspects.

The signifying pointing towards something else is hierarchically stratified in an arc from the smallest units (phonemes, letters, numbers, morphemes, words, sounds, tones, gestures, colour-points, etc.), via an intermediate level of composite elements (utterances, sentences, motives, figures) up to larger dialogues and discourses (works, images). Structuralist semiotics tends to reduce this span to one unified chain from signs to discourses, seeing texts as more or less quantitative additions of micro-units according to rules of in principle one single kind. Against the 'semiotic monism' of Saussurian structuralism, Ricoeur advocates 'a dualism of semiotics and semantics, where the semantics of the sentence is built on principles distinct from all operations with respect to signs' (1975/1986, pp. 101ff). Meaning is shaped in discourses based on combinations of singular signs, but its semantics cannot be reduced to just this addition. Specific hermeneutic procedures are needed to interpret these qualitatively higher and more complex units. Formal semiotic-structural analysis is a useful distancing means to break with the primary, unreflected understanding and reach richer interpretations that encompass unconscious levels of signification. Semiotics is one of several such necessary distancing moves, but it is only useful to analyse those aspects of communication where a limited number of elements are successively joined into larger units according to a limited number of ordering rules. This is no good way to describe how meaning is shaped in larger texts. The hermeneutic search for meanings of works as based in the meaning-producing semantics of discourses is in principle different from the semiotic analysis of symbolic micro-structures

---

[66] Peirce (1940/1955, pp. 275f) emphasizes that the triadic production of the interpretant is essential to a sign. 'In practice, "music" is no more constituted exclusively through the "iconic" than is "language" through the "arbitrary"' (Shepherd 1993, p. 28).

based on the form-producing semiotics of signs. Within the verbal mode, the unit of semiotics is the singular sign, while the sentence is the basic unit of semantics. Words have a functional mediating position and a double nature as both parts of sentences and combinations of phonemes. 'With the sentence we leave the domain of language as a system of signs and enter into another universe, that of language as an instrument of communication, whose expression is discourse' (Benveniste 1966/1971, pp. 110f).

> To this unidimensional approach to language, for which signs are the only basic entities, I want to oppose a two-dimensional approach for which language relies on two irreducible entities, signs and sentences. . . . A sentence is a whole irreducible to the sum of its parts. It is made up of words, but it is not a derivative function of its words. A sentence is made up of signs, but is not itself a sign. There is therefore no linear progression from the phoneme to the lexeme and then on to the sentence and to linguistic wholes larger than the sentence. Each stage requires new structures and a new description. (Ricoeur 1976, pp. 6f)

The meanings of sentences or larger (spoken, literary, musical or pictorial) works cannot be understood as the sum of their constituents. Their juxtaposition can just as well reduce the signifying range of each element.

> Most of our words are polysemic; they have more than one meaning. But it is the contextual function of discourse to screen, so to speak, the polysemy of our words and to reduce the plurality of possible interpretations, the ambiguity of discourse resulting from the unscreened polysemy of the words. And it is the function of dialogue to initiate this screening function of the context. The contextual is the dialogical. It is in this precise sense that the contextual role of dialogue reduces the field of misunderstanding concerning the propositional content and partially succeeds in overcoming the non-communicability of experience. (Ricoeur 1976, p. 17)

The composition of signs into texts reduces the potential meaning span of each of the constituents, while at the same time also enriching their meanings by metaphorical creativity, montage and bricolage. The meaning of a tune or a lifestyle is created as much by the focusing of the meaning-potentials of a series of added symbols through their reduction by the context as by their addition. A septim chord can have a wide range of meanings, but within a twelve-bar blues on howling electric guitar at least some of the interpretations that would have been possible within the classical sonata form fall away. A baseball cap can mean many things, but with thick golden links and other hiphop attributes, associations to sportsmen become less plausible.

Texts are like montages, and all interpreters, like bricoleurs, constantly develop new meanings out of old ones. Such processes take place both vertically from micro- to macro-units, horizontally between elements on the same level within a larger text, and laterally across symbolic modes. When words are added to images, Barthes (1964/1985, p. 28) distinguishes between, on one hand, 'anchoring', where words select from the meaning-potentials of the image and thus semantically focus them, and, on the other hand, 'relaying', a supplementation where words add new meanings and thus semantically expand the image.

The raw materials of texts carry wide meaning-potentials that are used in unique ways within each context, when focused and enriched by the confrontation with each other. These earlier meanings do not disappear, but are modified. Traditionally 'female' style elements do not become non-gendered by being combined with conventionally 'male' ones, but such a montage may create a break in old patterns and open new interpretive possibilities that can transgress gendered stereotypes. Making meanings through textual work is an active and innovative process. By constructing metaphors that join fields of signification it makes us think in new ways about the texts, ourselves, each other and the world. Symbolic communication centres on such polysemic metaphors, whose meanings are what they do rather than something they possess a priori.[67] Each finished interpretation leaves a surplus of meaning in the text. If we decide that a picture depicts a certain house or a specific idea, there will always be shades that point in some other direction. Interpreting a poem, we will always find some elements that appear nonsensical or as pure rhythm. All these residual aspects of materiality and form-relations can contribute to further interpretation and become understood as meaningful anew. Semantics and ('semiotic', sublime, etc.) non-meaning are thus not two once and for all fixed blocs, but always relationally and contextually constructed and mutually open towards each other. Communication, dialogue, discourse and interpretation are processes in which meanings are remade out of such textual textures and structures.

Meanings are thus bound not only to the symbolic signs but also to the subject and context of interpretation, which implies that symbols are seldom unequivocal but have an open variety of meanings. Each text has an indefinite but confined range of potential meanings. Every type of living language has a degree of polysemy, in that each of its elements carries a partly open and historically dynamic meaning-potential. This does not mean that all meanings are illusions, only that there are always openings for new interpretations, in creative conflict with the old ones. No text implies only one meaning. No clever interpretation can produce one single and final meaning of a tune or a painting. There is always a spectrum of often contradictory interpretive possibilities, resulting from and in a never-ending 'conflict of interpretations' (Ricoeur 1969/1974).[68] Each interpretation is a provisional proposal and a searchlight directed at a text and ultimately at the world.

Discursive symbolic modes utilize limited sets of basic signs and formal operations, such as letters and grammar or musical scales and chord types. But this is seldom the whole truth. Even letters can be written in

---

[67] Cf. Ricoeur (1975/1986) and Madison (1988, pp.82ff, 148ff and 188f).

[68] Ricoeur's earlier works seem to imply the existence of an inherent meaning in each text, which the interpreter may find in a full interpretation. In later works, he much more clearly stresses the open and dynamic character of interpretation processes. Cf. Ricoeur (1985/1988, pp. 157ff) and Madison (1988, p. 176).

innumerable ways, which certainly do not change their basic meaning on
the semiotic sign level but subtly change their contextual meaning within
the semantic textual whole. As stated above, more 'presentational' modes
like music and images are often hard to decompose unambiguously into
basic units. Various genres tend to form and use discrete structures of
signs, fixed sets of standardized elements, formulas and clichés. But this
discursive formalization is not complete, and meaning on higher levels
cannot be determined this way alone. Words in living languages can never
quite fully be defined in any dictionary – each definition is just approximate. The meaning of each unit is open and context-dependent.

The polysemy in every symbolic order does not make meanings evapor-
ate. Contrary to the famous model of Saussure, the meanings of any
symbols are not even completely arbitrary. They carry open and historically variable meaning-potentials, but these are not *just* arbitarily conventional. 'Between the signifier and the signified, the connection is not
arbitrary; on the contrary, it is *necessary*', writes Benveniste (1966/1971,
p. 45). Ricoeur adds that an 'essential characteristic of the symbol is the
fact that it is never completely arbitrary. It is not empty; rather, there
always remains the trace of a natural relationship between the signifier and
the signified' (1969/1974, p. 319). And to Jakobson, the idea of 'verbal
signs as solely conventional, "arbitrary symbols" proves to be a misleading
oversimplification. Iconicity plays a vast and necessary, though evidently
subordinate part in the different levels of linguistic structure' (1968/1971,
p. 700): in simple signs as well as in complex textual works.

For symbols to be constituted and understood, some kind of likeness,
nearness or relatedness is needed between the material signifier and its
signified. After a while, symbols are absorbed in the play of the symbolic
mode, and such non-arbitrary relations can become very complex and well
hidden, as between letters and phonemes or between words and references. But even the most conventional symbol retains certain metaphoric
and metonymic roots that made people choose it instead of its, in principle,
infinite number of alternative competitors within the symbolic order. On
the other hand, since there are always several such possible root-relations
between signifier and signifieds, no sign is totally necessary or natural, but
always contains a conventional or rather intersubjective element. Symbols
are polysemic or polyvalent, but not in any totally arbitrary way.[69]

> Usage or use is at the intersection of language and speech. . . . Thus the word is,
> as it were, a trader between the system and the act, between the structure and
> the event. . . . Thus, heavy with a new use-value – as minute as this may be – it
> returns to the system. And, in returning to the system, it gives it history. . . .
> Thus is explained what one could call a regulated polysemy, which is the law of
> our language. Words have more than one meaning, but they do not have an
> infinity of meanings. (Ricoeur 1969/1974, pp. 92f; cf. also pp. 62–78)

[69] Vološinov (1929/1986, pp. 79ff) grounds the polysemantic multiaccentuality of the word
and the multiplicity of meanings in the fact that the meaning of a word is 'determined entirely
by its context', which is what 'makes it a living thing'.

It is sometimes possible to discern primary meanings, which are relatively more obvious in an interpretive community. Secondary meanings can then be created by metaphoric displacements, as in poetic creativity.

> [While] it is true that there is always more than one way of construing a text, it is not true that all interpretations are equal. The text presents a limited field of possible constructions. The logic of validation allows us to move between the two limits of dogmatism and scepticism. It is always possible to argue for or against an interpretation, to confront interpretations, to arbitrate between them and to seek agreement, even if this agreement remains beyond our immediate reach. (Ricoeur 1976, pp. 78f)

The connections between signifiers and signified may in late modernity have become even more complex, meandering and mediated through many links, but they are still not cut off. 'I don't agree with Baudrillard that representation is at an end because the cultural codes have become pluralized. I think we are in a period of the infinite multiplicity of codings, which is different. . . . Representation has become a more problematic process but it doesn't mean the end of representation' (Hall 1986b, p. 50). No symbolic order can liberate itself completely from the necessary, vitalizing remnants of earlier indexical and iconical bounds. Living metaphors renew signification by playing with tensions between words and old meanings, but when such new double or secondary meanings have been stabilized, metaphors 'die' or are transformed into clichés that can be fixated in ordinary dictionaries as polysemy.[70]

It is the context that decides the actual meaning of a symbol in a certain text. The specific discourse in which a symbol is used reduces the wide range of potential meanings to make it possible for the community of text-users to discern the meaning that is relevant in this particular case. This contextual narrowing or reduction of meaning is balanced by the widening or extension of meaning through the innovative use of metaphors that instead add new and unexpected meaning-layers to the old and familiar ones. In this way, the use of symbols in discourses not only chooses out of the stock of meanings offered by existing symbolic orders, but also creates new significations that make these symbolic orders evolve and change.[71]

Symbols acquire life by the tension between their formal logic and their pointing at something else. No symbolic mode is totally closed or autonomous. It is woven into the totality of human praxis, and its relative, systemic independence is a tendency and the goal of a process rather than its starting-point. Symbolic orders strive for autonomy against early protosymbolic-'semiotic' fields of association, without ever reaching it. What gives it its dynamics is its incomplete openness to something else.

---

[70] Ricoeur (1976, pp. 51f). Cf. Lorenzer (1970, 1972 and 1986) on protosymbols, Kristeva (1974/1984 and 1980) on semiotic vibrations. Cf. also Elias (1989/1991).

[71] Cf. Ricoeur (1975/1986) and Vigsø (1993, pp. 30 and 40).

There is certainly, as Saussure, Lacan and others have argued, a radical leap in the beginning of language, for humanity as well as for each child who enters the symbolic domain. Entering the dimension of meaning, of language, of symbols, of texts, of culture, of communication, means leaving an innocence that can never be regained. It is the start of a project that cannot be undone. But neither can it be fulfilled: its root-threads back to the real, pre-symbolic materiality remain.

Meanings also reach out of themselves, out of language and towards the world. They do not simply copy the real world, but construct ideas pointing towards it from a specific point of view. A symbol as a material thing is a part of reality which 'refracts another reality' (Vološinov 1929/1986, p. 10). This is true both of verbal language and of other symbolic modes.

> Language *re-produces* reality. This is to be understood in the most literal way: reality is produced anew by means of language. . . . Thus the situation inherent in the practice of language, namely that of exchange and dialogue, confers a double function on the act of discourse; for the speaker it represents reality, for the hearer it recreates that reality. This makes language the very instrument of intersubjective communication. (Benveniste 1966/1971, p. 22)

Discourse as a series of acts (symbolizations) extends in time, while each symbolic system forms a quasi-spatial structure (a symbolic order). Each discourse (text, utterance) refers not only (in a cultural direction) to other discourses, but also in a subjective direction to its author/speaker, in an objective direction to an external world, and in a social direction to other persons (e.g., the listeners/readers/watchers) (Ricoeur 1981). 'Language is no more a foundation than it is an object; it is mediation; it is the *medium*, the "milieu", in which and through which the subject posits himself and the world shows itself' (Ricoeur 1969/1974, p. 256).

> With the sentence, language is oriented beyond itself. It says something *about* something. This intending of a referent by discourse is completely contemporaneous with its event character and its dialogical functioning. . . . Language does not constitute a world for itself. It is not even a world. Because we are in the world and are affected by situations, we try to orient ourselves in them by means of understanding; we also have something to say, an experience to bring to language and to share. (Ricoeur 1976, pp. 20f or 1983/1984, p. 78)[72]

Poetic texts and all pointedly aesthetic products construct such references along very indirect routes, often by first negating and destructing the usual significations of the symbols used. This does not reduce symbols to

---

[72] In vol. 2 (1984/1985, pp. 159f) and vol. 3 (1985/1988, pp. 5f, 100f and 158f) of *Time and Narrative*, Ricoeur abandons the concept of reference for that of refiguration, in order to avoid any naïve concept of 'reality' and emphasize that imagination is always productive. Instead of the 'sense' of a text, 'referring' to the world, he now speaks about the 'configuration' of the text, transformed into 'refiguration' when subjects act inspired by reading it. Even if the vocabulary of reference is still used, it must be understood in this constructivist manner. A classic text on reference and sense is Frege (1892/1970). Cf. also Israel (1992, p. 24).

meaningless games. Instead, polysemy arises on the micro-level of words, ambiguity on the meso-level of sentences and polyphony on the level of texts and works. Bakhtin (1963/1984 and 1981) has studied this higher level of dialogic polyphony in speech and writing, where voices make separable utterances that succeed and overlap each other. Such polyphony can become so complex that discursivity is made impossible, giving room instead for presentational totalities with no discernible discrete units of meaning. But some degree of dialogicity inheres in all discourses, opening a sort of multi-discursivity where different chains of meaning can be discerned, rather than only a single and univocal one. Dialogic communication presupposes at least two interlacing voices that have a capability also to sometimes hold themselves back and be quiet, listening attentively to each other. The overlapping of two voices that make utterances or works with beginnings, extensions and endings will then enrich their meanings as much as it disturbs them.[73]

Reception, use, interpretation

Communication and culture are the making and *use* of meaningful texts in dialogically intersubjective discourses. As text-users, people use cultural phenomena in various ways. In capitalist societies, this use is often a *consumption* of products which have been produced and distributed in commodity form on a mass scale through media, splitting users into producers and consumers, who take up what is offered them by producers.[74] We consume the records we buy but not the bird-song we hear outside our windows. It is commodified culture that best fits the transmission-view of communication, since commodification institutes a clear separation of producer and consumer and makes texts into distinct commodities circulating in a market. Consumers of mass media are often called *audiences*, differentiated into listeners, watchers and readers listening to music, speech and radio, watching images, films, television and computer screens, reading books, papers and magazines.[75] *Reception* is the specific use of mediated cultural texts, including all that people care to do with them, while other things and products are used differently. To receive a text is to open oneself to the utterance of an Other, to let oneself be influenced by a symbolic work coming from someone else, as a first step towards communication. Receivers or recipients are not as passive as the word seems to imply, and reception researchers have been eager to show

---

[73] 'No text, no matter how "musicalized," is devoid of meaning or signification; on the contrary, musicalization pluralizes meanings' (Kristeva 1974/1984, p. 65).

[74] On consumption and everyday culture, see Lefebvre (1968/1984), de Certeau (1974/1988), Cohen and Taylor (1976/1992), Miller (1987), Ewen (1988), Fiske (1989a and b), *Culture and History* (1990), Willis (1990), Featherstone (1991), McRobbie (1991 and 1994), Ganetz (1992/1995) and Drotner (1994).

[75] The word 'audience' originally referred to listening, suggesting a uni-directional rather than dialogic flow of meaning, just as with the term 'reception'. Cf. Radway (1988, pp. 359f).

the creative activity involved, implying that communication is an intersubjective sharing which does not necessarily make people more alike in any other respect than just this gathering (discourse) around some meaningful text.[76] *Interpretation*, as the construction and reconstruction of meaning, is the core of reception, since what makes symbolic communication cultural is its production of meaning. All texts can be used for other things too, but it is as interpreters, creating and reconstructing meaning to reach understanding, that text-users are specifically making cultural practices.

Use, consumption, reception and interpretation are work and action. Each such set of textual or interpretive *practices* utilizes a number of *methods* or *techniques*. Strategies are goal-oriented practices that are often (but not necessarily) consciously calculated. Interpretive *strategies* are methods for interpretation seen as consistent sets of tools to achieve certain aims. By various short-range *tactics*, people handle texts in a more improvised fashion.[77] Interpretive *conventions* are socially and historically sedimented sets of habits concerning how to deal with generically bound texts, and text-users show their interpretive *competences* in how they manage to use interpretive strategies in relation to such genre-related conventions. Interpretive *repertoires* are sets of conventions and genre-knowledge that all text-users relate to, and sometimes interpreters gather in interpretive *communities* that share such repertoires, conventions and strategies to attribute characteristics to certain texts, thereby developing a shared *taste* for some genre. Each individual may take part in different communities and relate to distinct conventions and repertoires on various occasions.

Interactive media have always existed. 'Virtual reality' is no recent invention, but has forerunners in the engaged reader's 'disappearing act', in the alternative, imaginary worlds created by all narrative texts or performances, including the world turned upside-down of carnival.[78] In fact, all media are to some extent interactive, in that they allow an interpretive activity of their users. In late modernity, a range of new techniques have made media texts and apparatuses more open to modifications by users who become co-producers rather than mere receptive audiences. Just like all types of fan culture, such media problematize the

---

[76] Cf. Hall and Whannel (1964/1990), Hall (1973/1980), Prokop (1974 and 1981), Radway (1984), Lindlof (1987), Eskola and Vainikkala (1988), Højbjerg (1989), Baacke et al. (1990), Willis (1990), Ang (1991), Lisa A. Lewis (1992), Morley (1992), Bang and Lundby (1993), Buckingham (1993), Moores (1993), Drotner (1994), Reimer (1994), Silverstone (1994) and Zoonen (1994).

[77] 'Practice' has to do with acting or doing something. Military tactics are the methods used in actual combat situations, whereas strategies are the more general plans. The term 'strategy' originally means to lead an army, related to agency. 'Tactics' and 'techniques' go back to a Greek word for the art or means of arranging. Cf. de Certeau (1974/1988) on strategy/tactics, and Habermas (1981/1984) on strategic action.

[78] Tania Modleski (1982, pp. 35ff) describes women's identificatory reading of Harlequin romances as a disappearing act, where the reader loses herself in the narrated world. Cf. Bakhtin (1965/1984) on carnival and Ricoeur (1985/1988) on reading and narrativity.

relatively strict distinction between production and reception on which all transmission models of communication are based. The person who sings to a karaoke video consumes the tape but creates not only meanings but also sounds and gestures that are intrinsic parts of the realization of the tape (Fornäs 1994a). Interactive media and fan activities also tend to dissolve the strict line between amateurs and professionals. They thereby question the strict division made by Bourdieu (1993, pp. 39, 53, 115ff and 185ff) between 'the field of restricted production, in which the producers produce for other producers, and the field of large-scale production', which is 'symbolically excluded' and which 'produces cultural goods for non-producers of cultural goods', that is, for 'the public at large'. This model reformulates the high/low distinction between fine arts and industrialized popular or mass culture, and this very distinction is also continuously eroded by such interactive practices of interpretation and new self-organized production among the users of popular culture, forcing domi-nant social groups and institutions to just as continuously redefine and try to re-legitimize this dichotomy again.

Commodity production not only precedes consumption but also deter-mines it by forming nature and shaping human needs.[79] But even though consumption thus presupposes production, the same cannot be said of reception or interpretation. Both are productive acts that are primary in culture. There is music without musicians, but not without listeners. The wind in the trees may be perceived and understood as music, but a record that is never played is not. The work that creates works is double. It may create material structures, in which case it is a production of artefacts. But its core and minimum is the signifying practice of interpretation that produces meaning. To 'read' a natural object is an act that confers meaning on it and thus 'produces' it as such – that is, as meaningful – even if it is not produced as materiality or form. Reception is therefore more important to culture than is often imagined. Far from being a secondary processing of what cultural producers have created, it is the clue to symbolic work. Both producing senders and consuming receivers in communicative chains are active agents and creators of textual meanings. Production is still crucial, but it is the production of meaning rather than of artefacts that is the core of signifying processes.

Cultural processes of text-use, or the pragmatics of interactive dialogues that form discourses, always involve the communication of meanings, in several levels and ways. The pragmatic aspect of symbols can be differen-tiated into various series of sub-aspects, emphasizing different ways in which symbols are used and texts function. These various *aspects* of communicative acts cannot only be analytically separated, but also be developed and stressed differently in specific sets of practices, which may even be formally institutionalized. This makes it possible to think of these

---

[79] This is stressed by Marx (e.g., 1844/1975 or 1859/1969), who also acknowledges that consumption acts back on production.

aspects as giving rise also to different *types* of communicative acts, according to which aspects are mainly intended or effected in each specific case. Different pragmatic intentions and functions ordinarily coexist in every single symbolic expression, but each of them can sometimes be focused in a particular utterance or even a social institution, so that they may also be used to distinguish between such types of communication. Competing classifications have been suggested by information theory, speech act theory, semiotics and hermeneutics, and only some often recurring such aspects and types will be presented here.

First, media-use and other cultural processes involve a *transmission* of cultural artefacts or products from senders or producers (writers, speakers, actors, musicians, etc.) to receivers or consumers (readers, listeners, viewers, audiences, etc.). This objectively observable chain of transportation and transfer is often complex, and can be mediated by machines (media) and/or organized on a large scale (mass communication).

Another side is the *interpretation* each user (whether producer or recepient) makes of the textual symbols. What makes communication cultural is precisely that it requires this appropriation by someone who uses a text to produce meaning. A web of mutually conflicting interpretations is woven by different interpreters, in a process between texts and subjects joined in interpretive communities (studied by hermeneutics and reception theory).

By using and identifying with cultural artefacts and genres, people express their (real or wished for) identities and lifestyles to their sociocultural environment, setting limits and marking differences. This will here be called the *expositional* aspect of cultural phenomena and media use, since it is a matter of exposing one's taste to others, and of positioning oneself in a given, external sociocultural field. Cultural forms always have this function as taste markers of status positions in social hierarchies, by stressing identifications with, or distinctions and differences to others, as theorized by Pierre Bourdieu and explored in (sub)cultural studies by, for example, Paul Willis and John Fiske. But this is not their only function.

Another social use of cultural phenomena is for the users themselves, in their social *interaction*. Besides the extrovert lifestyle marking, there is a second social aspect, one of interaction within the interpretive community and the group or microculture itself. By using a text, people communicate with each other and shape (stable or temporary) mutual social relations and groups. These can often contain asymmetries in power and dominance, but they also have to include some aspects of mutuality in the sharing of belonging and meaning through collective interpretation, thus shaping communities. The social aspect of communication is always a constant play of both exposition and interaction, of difference and community.

A final communication aspect of culture relates to internal, subjective experiences and expressions. Each text-user (reader, listener, viewer, etc.) allows the text to start psychic processes that induce communication

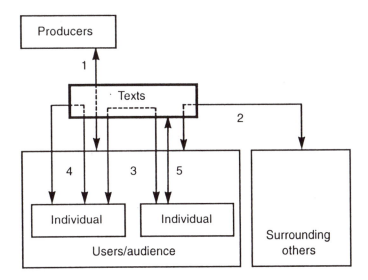

1 **Transmission:**
   objective mediations
2 **Exposition:**
   social style markings
3 **Interaction:**
   social group relations
4 **Impression:**
   subjective experiences
5 **Interpretation:**
   cultural meaning creation

Figure 4.2 *Communication aspects of cultural phenomena*

between various layers of the individual mind, for instance between the conscious and the unconscious.[80] Such processes of *impression*, of intra-subjective transformations of the psychic interiority, caused by impressions and experiences induced by cultural symbol formations, contribute to the development of personal identity and individual subjectivity (see Figure 4.2).

By listening to heavy metal with peers in a subway station, a young person can, for example, expose her identity, develop contacts with her peer mates and induce emotions. The objective transmission of the music makes possible its interpretation by its listeners, reconstructing meanings as a way of understanding what the music says, that is, what the musical symbols point at outside themselves. This in its turn strengthens what the music does by, on the one hand, enabling its users to expose their social position to others and interact in a mutual community, and, on the other

[80] A psychoanalytic understanding of inner life acknowledges the existence of different instances or levels within the psyche, which makes it relevant to talk about 'intra-subjective' communication between these. Hanna Segal for instance expresses the functions of symbols in 'internal communication . . . with unconscious phantasies' (1957, p. 396). However, this concept of internal communication within the individual is also meaningful in other theoretical traditions, e.g. symbolic interactionism.

hand, leaving deep inner impressions, inducing a restructuring of their subjectivities.[81]

In the use of texts, communication thus takes place in many different ways, all worth studying. Even though it can be useful to concentrate on one aspect at a time, no explanation should in principle reduce the polydimensional character of culture as communication. Unfortunately this is too often done, as when technologically or economically oriented media researchers only see the first aspect of production–consumption–transmission, or when cultural sociologists tend to exclude all other aspects than the marking of social position through the exhibiting of taste. No single model of communication alone suffices to cover all aspects – this is why it is important to appreciate that several different functions are involved.[82]

Types of communication

Semiotic literary theory has proposed several ways to classify aspects and types of communicative acts, by categories which have been used to distinguish between genres (of speech, literature, etc.) but are also functions within each genre. Roman Jakobson (1960) distinguishes between six functions of language, connected to different factors within the communicative chain. The *referential*, denotative or cognitive function of a (verbal) message is oriented towards the context (of referents): what it refers to in the outer world of objects. The *emotive* function expresses the addresser's (sender's or encoder's) attitude: the inner, subjective world of the one who speaks. The imperative or *conative* function focuses on the addressee (receiver or decoder), as, for example, in commands which direct attention to what the listener does or should do. The *phatic* function emphasizes the contact in the very act of communication, in expressions that seek to establish, prolong or break off communication, check if the channel works, attract attention or affirm the other. The *metalingual* or metalinguistic function occurs when messages are centred on the code, such as in the defining or clarification of the lexical meanings of the terms used. Finally, the *poetic* function focuses on the message at such: for example, the very sounds and rhythms of the words used. These distinctions are obviously based on a transmission–information model of communication.[83]

Stuart Hall's encoding/decoding model (1973/1980) was inspired by

---

[81] On the psychological functions of music, see Kohut and Levarie (1950), Kohut (1957), Noy (1966–7), Ruth-Gisela Klausmeier (1973), Rosolato (1974), Friedrich Klausmeier (1978), Fornäs et al. (1988/1995), Bradley (1992) and Moore (1993).

[82] Cf. Lee (1992, p. 414).

[83] Roland Barthes (1970/1975) distinguishes five voices and five codes in the process of reading/writing and its resulting texts: the empirical voice in the proairetic code of actions, the voice of the person in the semic code, the voice of knowledge in the cultural or referential code, the voice of truth in the hermeneutic code and the symbolic voice in the symbolic code of binary oppositions.

Jakobson and by Iser, Jauss and other literary reception theorists. It states that media and popular culture are based on codes that have been learned. First, certain meanings and ideologies are encoded into media texts, then they are decoded in the reception process, but there is no guarantee that this is done in the way the senders expected. There is an implied or preferred reading, which is obeyed as a 'dominant-hegemonic code' by some text-users. But many others only partly follow these norms and partly make their own interpretations, according to a 'negotiated code'. A third position is the openly 'oppositional code'.[84]

Hall's (e.g., 1986b, pp. 53ff) later articulation model of meaning, inspired by Laclau, tries to avoid the naturalistic, linear view of meaning-transmission implied in this earlier model and in Jakobson's formulations. A better model conceives of interpretation as involving constant struggles within specific social fields, a 'politics of signification' and 'struggle in discourse', which may be connected to the creative 'conflict of interpretations' already thematized by Paul Ricoeur (1969/1974).

Yet another model of communication aspects is offered by speech act theory.[85] Locutionary acts are saying, stating or expressing something, as in descriptions. Illocutionary acts make something by saying it, as in orders or promises. Perlocutionary acts have effects by influencing the listener, as a kind of strategic action. These are coexisting aspects of all speech acts, but can also ground a typology which may be extended to wider sets of symbolic acts.

In the formal pragmatics of Habermas (1981/1984), different types of symbolic expressions, texts or discourses focus upon different aspects of the world, relate to different objects (either the systems or one of the 'worlds' we phenomenologically inhabit), have different functions in intersubjective communication and are judged by a different criterion as to their validity. Here, the aspects of single symbolic acts are developed into larger categories of discursive argumentation. Because of some important inconsistencies and limitations in Habermas's model, I will here instead present my own modification of it, indicating the points of difference continuously (see Figure 4.3). This model makes some heuristic simplifications compared to some very detailed and complex formulations by Habermas, while avoiding some contradictions and shortcomings and generalizing the model to cover non-propositional and even non-verbal symbolic modes as well, keeping in mind that some aspects and functions are still most relevant for the verbal mode.[86]

---

[84] Morley (1992) and Steiner (1988) are two examples of how these concepts have been used in empirical studies of media reception. Morley studied the television audience, Steiner the readers of the women's magazine *Ms*.

[85] Austin (1962), Searle (1969) and Apel (1973/1980 and 1976/1982) are inspired by the later work of Wittgenstein (1945/1976), but there are also parallels with the concepts of dialogic speech performance and speech genres in Vološinov (1929/1986, pp. 19f and 83ff) and Bakhtin (1981 and 1986).

[86] The figure is a combination and reworking of several figures in Habermas (1981/1984).

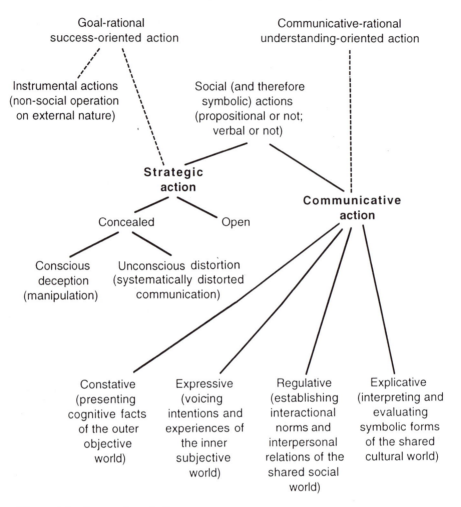

Figure 4.3 *Types of symbolic acts*

The basic distinction between strategic and communicative action which has been mentioned (in Chapter 2 above) can be further differentiated. *Strategic action* aims at success by efforts to influence others through coercion or manipulation related to social power. Strategic acts are systemically developed in market and state institutions, where they are meant to make profits and enforce decisions, and judged by criteria of effectivity. *Instrumental action* is non-social, technical operation on external nature.[87] Strategic and instrumental action are thus two different kinds of success-oriented or *goal-rational action*, primarily striving for

---

[87] Though instrumental action is as goal-rational as strategic action, Habermas sometimes puts it in the same box as cognitive-constative types of communicative action.

efficiency rather than understanding. The strategic/communicative polarity is the specifically social variant of a more general goal/understanding-oriented action.

Strategic action may in its turn be differentiated according to whether it is *openly* or *covertly* strategic, and, in the latter case, whether the deceit is the conscious result of *intentional manipulation* or the unconscious result of *systematically distorted communication*. A command is openly strategic, while a lie may exemplify covertly strategic but intentional manipulation. The psychoanalytical discovery of unconscious motives and the Marxist critique of ideology both exemplify systematical distortions of communication which are mostly concealed and unintentional, even though false ideologies may also involve open manipulation.

Communicative action co-ordinates actors by the development of shared understandings, in processes involving several subjects, a symbolic order (or language) and objects which are thematized by the intersubjective use of these symbolic forms. Its aim is thus to create mutual understanding: a shared knowing, trust, agreement and symbolism. To understand a symbolic utterance is to take part in such a process of understanding and to know under which conditions its 'validity claims' are acceptable, that is, when it is true, honest, righteous and well-formed. Communicative rationality is the ability to specify, criticize and defend such claims of validity in procedures of argumentation thematizing the relation to different worlds. Reason is thus a process where linguistic argumentation and concrete procedures are crucial. Within a modernizing lifeworld, actions are rationalized when they can become criticized and explicitly defended, making possible learning processes of cumulative knowing and historical improvement.

Communicative action may again be divided into subtypes, according to which aspect of communication is emphasized. Habermas mentions three of them, sometimes extending their number to four or even five. They are based on the distinction between the worlds we inhabit, but correspond to corresponding validity claims, ways of using language, classes of speech acts, attitudes one may have to the others in communication, and also to specialized institutional spheres where each of them is intensely elaborated.

Constative symbolizations present cognitive facts in the objective world in a true (or false) way. This aspect is related to Jakobson's referential function. It is always present – not only in every speech act but in non-verbal symbolic modes as well, which cannot avoid activating meanings pointing towards the external world, as has already been shown.[88] But the statements of conversational speech and writing put this propositional content and its corresponding validity criterion of cognitive truth in focus,

---

[88] Habermas's choice only to discuss verbal speech acts in propositional form can be defended for heuristic reasons, as words are a privileged mode for explicit argumentation. But it is untenable when it comes to constructing a general model for communication.

and are, moreover, particularly elaborated within the specialized sphere of science.

Expressive acts of dramaturgical self-representation relate to the subjective world in a (more or less) truthful, honest, authentic or veracious way. This pointing towards an inner world, related to the emotive function in Jakobson's model, is also ever-present in human communication. Not only verbal utterances but also songs, paintings and gestures can be interpreted as relating to intentions and experiences of inner subjectivity, particularly that of its author(s) or producer(s). But self-expression is central to certain dramaturgical types of symbolization, and these are most developed within the sphere of therapeutic care, including psychological institutions.[89]

Regulative acts use illocutionary acts to shape the interpersonal relationships and obligations of the social world in a (more or less) righteous way. Jakobson's conative function of imperatives which focuses on the addressee comes to mind here, but also to some extent his phatic function which emphasizes the contact in the very act of communication – these two are in fact hard to separate from each other. This establishment and thematization of norms for intersubjective interaction in society is again tendentially implicated whenever people communicate, whether in words or by other means, but sometimes more explicitly so, as in the sphere of the judicial system, where normative issues of right and wrong are institutionalized and channelled into the administrative state system.[90]

A fourth, explicative aspect and type of communicative action activates the capability of language and indeed of every symbolic mode to reflexively thematize itself: the symbolic dimension of the intersubjective world. This is developed either in aesthetically evaluative discourses on beauty, style and taste, related to Jakobson's poetic function, or in reflexively interpretive discourses on adequacy, semantic comprehensibility and syntactic well-formedness, close to the metalingual function. Both these two sub-aspects thematize the cultural dimension, as symbols here are used to reflect upon their own, symbolic order. They are in fact hard to separate from each other, since comprehensibility cannot be mechanically judged, but has to consider generic rules and preferences within the relevant interpretive communities. The institutions of art and of aesthetic theory are spheres where these dimensions are intensely cultivated, but just like the others, they are firmly rooted in everyday communication as well.

Outside of strategic action, there are thus at least four aspects and subtypes of communicative action: to convey knowledge of the external world, to express the subjectivity of the internal world, to establish norms of the intersubjectively shared social world or to interpret the symbolic forms of the likewise shared cultural dimension. Different pragmatic contexts, symbolic modes, textual genres, interpretive communities and

[89] As will soon be further discussed, Habermas instead often couples this communicative aspect with art works and art institutions.

[90] Cf. Benhabib (1992) and Habermas (1992b).

institutional spheres emphasize different combinations of these types and aspects.

Habermas has difficulties in placing aesthetics in his own models, as can be noticed in each of the four dimensions above.[91] This points at a problem with the understanding not only of art and the cultural sphere in a narrow sense, but also of symbolic communication and culture in the wide sense. He falls back on a pre-semiotic understanding of language (Dahlgren 1995), which needs to be corrected by ideas from Ricoeur's post-semiotic, critical and textual hermeneutics, so that the cultural-communicative turn can be carried through consequently and polydimensionally enough.

In the overview of lifeworld components (Habermas 1981/1988, pp. 140ff), culture is seen as a stock of knowledge and placed as an objective component, beside the (intersubjective) society and the (subjective) socialization and identity formation of the individual person. This idea of culture seems to fall back behind the semiotic-hermeneutic definitions which stress its fundamental character of symbolic-aesthetic practices and processes rather than only stored artefacts.

In most other places, however, aesthetics is not related to culture and not to the cognitive-objective dimension, but rather to the expressive-subjective one. When discussing which social spheres or institutions are related to the different worlds, Habermas connects science to the objective, external world, the judicial system to the social, intersubjectively shared world and art institutions to the subjective world. This subsumption of aesthetics under the subjective seems inspired by an outdated romantic model where art is conceived as a direct, authentic mirror of the unique, individual soul. While subjective authenticity is central in care and psychotherapy, only some aesthetic genres emphasize it, whereas other art genres stress realist truth or normative rightness instead – aesthetic well-formedness being always the most directly relevant criterion. Even though aesthetic works in various ways point towards a dimension of subjectivity (as well as towards the other dimensions), aesthetics cannot be fundamentally reduced to criteria of authenticity, but should rather be seen as a self-reflexive discourse within the intersubjective, cultural dimension, more closely related to explicative discourses of comprehensibility than to expressive ones of sincerity. The mistaken identification of the aesthetic and expressive modes neglects the specificity and fundamentally intersubjective character of aesthetic practices and discourses. Even the most expressive creativity is basically anchored within interpretive communities sharing genre-bound conventions and rules. The institutions related to the subjective world are rather those of the intimate sphere: the family and

[91] In Habermas's figure of types of argumentation (1981/1984, p. 23), expressive therapeutic critique is separated from both evaluative aesthetic criticism and explicative discourse. In his figure of aspects of rationality (1981/1984, p. 334), art works are connected to both therapeutic and aesthetic critique, and to dramaturgic action. Many formulations mention three main worlds or reality dimensions (objective, social, subjective), while other instances add language as a fourth dimension.

various psychological or therapeutic institutions, whereas the arts should instead be related to the cultural branch of the intersubjective world. Habermas (1985/1987, pp. 314 and 418, n. 18) sometimes hints at these problems, adding the criterion of 'aesthetic harmony' to those of propositional truth, normative rightness and subjective truthfulness, with a reference to Albrecht Wellmer (1984/1985), who has correctly shown that art values 'can by no means be reduced, without further ado, to authenticity or sincerity'.[92]

If the cultural-aesthetic should be more clearly distinguished from both the objective and the subjective worlds, its connections to the social world are never even mentioned by Habermas. Language on language as a communicative reflexivity is often placed as a special fourth box under the objective, social and subjective ones. To avoid this rigid polarity of either universal objectivity or subjective particularity, and instead fully adopt the intersubjective perspective on judgement deriving from both Peirce and the hermeneutic tradition, both language and art can be seen as a second, cultural subdimension of what is intersubjectively shared – closer to the social world of interaction, norms, groups and relations than to either external nature and science or inner subjectivities and psychology.

Within this fourth dimension, there arises yet another subdivision between aesthetics/art, on one hand, and culture/language/knowledge, on the other. Habermas seems not to appreciate their connections, since he separates aesthetics from comprehensibility and believes it possible to reach universal consensus about the well-formedness of propositions but not of aesthetic value, since it is too bound to unique personal experiences to be universalized. This is why he talks of theoretical, moral-practical and explicative 'discourses' but only of therapeutic and aesthetic 'critiques'. But the aesthetic and the explicative relate to the same reality domain (the symbols themselves), and the criteria of well-formedness and comprehensibility are in practice hard to separate, since correct symbol-use is bound to the rules of genres (whether of speech, writing or nonverbal modes) which regulate both grammatic-syntactical form-relations and semantic meaningfulness.

This fourth dimension differs from the other three by not being a separate world. Habermas and Ricoeur agree that culture and language constitute no world, but rather a medium for the processes whereby interacting subjects seek understanding and construct meaning by relating to the other worlds. However, culture is essentially intersubjectively shared and thus connected to the social world, and the late modern cultural

---

[92] A similar problematization is suggested by Stephen White: 'What constitutes art must always be related to some public, shared understanding of style and form' (1988, p. 151). Cf. also John B. Thompson (1981), Thompson and Held (1982), Bernstein (1985; particularly the texts by Wellmer, Jay and Habermas himself), Honneth and Joas (1986/1991; Seel, Alexander and Habermas), Honneth et al. (1989/1992; Apel, Arnason, Jay and Taylor), Steuerman (1989), Lee (1992) and Peters (1993). The concept of authenticity will be further analysed in the next chapter.

turn, including semiotic theory, has made it hard to think of the tools of symbolic communication as quite so transparent. The textual model of communication acknowledges the distanciation inherent in all symbol-use. The symbolic order is regulated by rules and patterns which are often unconscious to human subjects, and which are historically and socially embedded in interpretive communities. Because of their often hidden form-relations and polysemic meanings, symbols are never fully transparent. But it is true that neither do they constitute a totally separate world of their own, since interpretive work is capable of opening up language and culture to the other worlds. Habermas's unclear treatment of aesthetics seems to rest upon an iconoclastic reduction of cultural symbolization, falling back behind the semiotic challenges that caused Ricoeur to develop his critical-textual hermeneutics, where the full richness of language is taken seriously rather than reduced to abstract univocity.[93] It is to these late modern neo-hermeneutic ideas I will now turn, in order to develop some other aspects of meaning-making in symbol-use, besides those suggested by semiotics and speech act theory.

Hermeneutic dimensions

When interpreting a specific text in any of the symbolic modes, it is possible to search for its meanings along each of the points of the compass which are indicated by the model in Figure 4.4. Symbol formations point

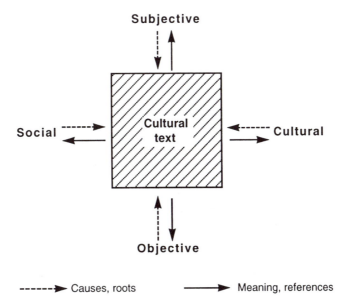

Figure 4.4 *Dimensions of interpretation*

---

[93] Cf. Peters (1993) and Kristensson-Uggla (1994, p. 178).

towards each of the four cardinal points that signifying acts may thematize, or each of the four world dimensions. Cultural texts (artefacts, styles, subcultures, etc.) not only thematize these world aspects – they also have causal sources and give rise to learning processes within each of them. These dimensions of interpretation are aspects of meaning production in daily life but also in research on such interpretation processes, that is, dimensions of cultural studies' (secondary) interpretations of everyday life's (primary) ones.

This model presupposes that all is not already symbolic. Everything cannot always and essentially be textual, even though texts and symbols are our only means of understanding the world. There are always things and aspects of materiality that we do not understand and which thus slide outside our conceptual horizon, outside of language and meaning, outside of the cultural world. It would be too narcissistically anthropocentric to declare that those non-symbolized areas do not exist: they affect us deeply and cannot be thought away, even though we have not found any means to think about them. Secondly, it cannot be true that reality is successively superimposed and annihilated by symbolic texts, even though we invent more and more symbolic forms that surround us in increasingly complex ways. There is more in reality than texts, and there has, on the other hand, never existed a time where objective nature was experienced in pure, direct fashion. If it is accepted that there are more worlds than that of culture itself, it is legitimate to study how cultural texts relate to these other worlds.

The multi-layered cultural processes of communication can be analysed in two main directions. On the one hand, there can be an 'archaeological' searching for roots and sources in explanations of the multi-layered patterns of causes and forces that govern a text. On the other hand, cultural analysis can make a 'teleological' tracing and (re)construction of the polydimensional webs and flows of meanings and consequences that the text creates: what texts say and do about material conditions, to subjects, to social relations and to other texts.[94]

Archaeologically, it is possible to trace sources and roots, origins and driving motive forces of a cultural phenomenon, and this can be done on different levels. Any text comes out of a set of productive forces, of specific demands and resources on each level. Some are objective or objectivized, material or institutional, like physical, economic or political forces and frames, as every text relates to resources and demands within the two systems and in the material world. Other aspects are the subjective needs, desires and competences in the only partly conscious mind of each single individual, to which texts answer, and which are studied by psychoanalysis. Still others are social, seated in the norms and group relations of

---

[94] Again, see Ricoeur (1965/1970). The concept of archaeology is also used by Foucault (1969/1972). The concept of teleology is here understood as free from theological implications: it is only meant to stress the meanings and effects shaped by an intending agency.

intersubjective interaction. Any text is finally also intertextually or culturally determined by or rooted in the stylistic rules and resources within its own genre and within other genres. Different forms of explanation need to be used to uncover the deeply hidden and historically produced determinants on these different levels.

On the other hand, texts also have (future) effects that can be studied teleologically. The meaning-aspect of symbols gives them the power to point in various directions by thematizing different things, moving along various routes. A media text – say, a pop song or a TV programme – is not only produced by a set of polydimensional forces, it also produces polydimensional meanings and effects when meeting its users. First, it points toward the objective world of material facts or objectivized institutions. Each text can be examined for what it says of matter, politics or economics, and it also produces material and institutional results. Secondly, it can be interpreted in relation to what it says about the inner world of subjectivity and desires, and how it helps to form it through learning processes of expressivity and reflexivity. The impression aspects of communication belong here. A third direction points towards the social world of intersubjective relations and interaction aspects of communication, as all texts express and shape such relations and norms. Finally, each text relates to, and affects, other cultural texts, that is, has a reflexive and intertextual relation to the cultural dimension itself. Culturally, it 'is about' other symbolic structures and enables aesthetic use and learning.

These aspects are always present, but of varying importance. Each piece of cultural analysis can focus one of the many possible lines, but no such analysis can pretend to say all there is to say about a cultural phenomenon. Each reductive 'nothing-but'-analysis provokes new counter-explanations and alternative interpretations, in an endlessly open play. It is fruitful and even necessary to reduce complexity by concentrating each analysis on some few chosen aspects. But such decisions are always provisional.

The interplay of archaeological and teleological directions in interpretation gives rise to a dialectics of explanation and understanding stretching a hermeneutical arc grounded in concrete lived experience but stretching from surface to depth interpretation via abstract theoretical models of explanation. The roots, sources and causes of phenomena are analysed by critical and analytical methods of explanation, while their polydimensional meanings bring forth synthesizing efforts to understand them. These two moves are not competing methods but fertilize each other in a necessary pendulum, circular or rather spiral movement. Interpretation is a narrative reconstruction of meaning, and it necessarily develops in spiral movements where interpretive guesses are continuously checked by critical validations, and where attempts to understand textual wholes are gradually enriched by detailed explanations using distancing tools and models. In this way, interpretation unites closeness and distance, understanding and explanation, fantasy and validation, creativity and critique in a unique arc stretched out from the first, superficial understanding, via a series of critical interrogations and distancing explanations, to a depth-hermeneutics that has a greater comprehension of what a text may mean, in various dimensions including indirect or second-order references that redescribe or refigure reality.[95]

Hermeneutics is a word which derives from the Greek *hermeneuein*, 'to bring to understanding', in three senses: to express, to translate and to interpret. It may be related to Hermes as the messenger of the gods, who mediates between two symbolic worlds by translating for the mortals and thus bringing understanding. A basic condition is that some distance has arisen; a lost immediacy or naïvety: the work of interpretation reveals an intention 'of overcoming distance and cultural differences and of matching the reader to a text which has become foreign' (Ricoeur 1969/1974, p. 4). Since all symbolic modes use external meaning-carriers, the cultural world is based on a mechanism of distanciation. The phenomenon of the text 'displays a fundamental characteristic of the very historicity of human experience, namely that it is communication in and through distance' (Ricoeur 1981, p. 131). Thus,

> distanciation is not the product of methodology and hence something superfluous and parasitical; rather it is constitutive of the phenomenon of the text as writing. At the same time, it is the condition of interpretation; *Verfremdung* is not only what understanding must overcome, but also what conditions it. We are thus prepared to discover a relation between *objectification* and *interpretation* which is much less dichotomous, and consequently much more complementary, than that established by the Romantic tradition. (Ricoeur 1981, pp. 139f)[96]

Face-to-face-interaction is therefore more similar to textualized mass communication than is often believed. The distanciation across time and space between author, utterance and interpreter, made possible and inevitable by writing, textual objectification and technological mediation, already exists in principle in every single interpersonal communicative act. Communication is always a fragile effort to bridge gaps between interacting subjects (between sending and receiving, uttering and understanding) by constructing shared meanings in interpretive communities.

While semantics is concerned with meanings of sentences or other smaller units, hermeneutics is the interpretation of meanings in texts or works, as larger units. There is no direct way to understand texts. They induce a preliminary surface-semantics of first understandings or 'prejudices' (intuitive judgements made before reflective analysis), but these guessings of primary and manifest meanings are often misleading.[97] In order to apprehend the ways texts point to meanings, an interpretation process is needed that utilizes explanatory detours in various directions,

---

[95] Ricoeur (1976, pp. 43f and 71–95; cf. also 1969/1974, 1978/1994 and 1981).

[96] The allusion is to Brecht's (1962) ideas of a deliberately produced aesthetic effect of distanciation or alienation, which makes aesthetic reception more similar to scientific analysis; cf. Benjamin (1966/1973). For a synthesizing comparison of hermeneutics and deconstruction, see Olsson (1987).

[97] Ricoeur's ideas of surface-semantics are inspired by Heidegger (1927/1978) and Gadamer (1960/1975).

systematically scrutinizing, criticizing and validating these first perceived meanings. Different types of 'decentring' methods of explanation (that disturb our first common-sense understanding of a phenomenon) are needed to study the materiality and form-relations of symbolic texts, which form a basis for their creation of meaning. Besides the detours through psychoanalysis and social theory, to uncover and reflect upon the subjective and social dimensions of texts, it is also necessary to reconstruct the texts themselves as formal structures, for example with semiotic tools.

Such methods of distancing and decentring explanations are used with the aim of making possible an enriched interpretation of textual meanings, a critical understanding of what texts say – objectively about the outside world, subjectively about our inner worlds, socially about our mutual relations and reflexively about themselves. The goal is to reach a depth-semantics that catches hidden second-degree meanings of the text.

All this happens in everyday life, when people try to understand better what they hear or see by making analytical explanations of its causes. And cultural analysis must start in a closeness to its objects, but has to make detours using distancing and structuring theoretical models, to again reach down to a deeper apprehension of the phenomenon studied. Explanations searching for archaeological determinations and deep form-relational structures of texts are necessary roads to a richer understanding of their meanings. These explanatory moves may include the critique of ideology, psychoanalysis, structuralist semiotics or cultural sociology. This process is in principle infinite, since competing interpretations may always be suggested. That final truths can never be reached should not prevent us from throwing ourselves into this whirlpool of struggling interpretations.

Intertextuality and aesthetics

Cultural identities and patterns of meaning make various forms of intertextual or intercultural references to each other, within and across works and genres in time and space, constructing a pointing within the cultural dimension itself, which forms complex nets of relations on all levels, from singular signs to overarching supergenres. This level of reflexive, intertextual and aesthetic relations of the cultural dimension itself is central here in two ways. First, all human praxis evolves around the intersubjective and communicative use of symbols, and all insights are based on text-use as well. Symbols are tools both of interaction and of research, including this book itself. Secondly, its explicit theme is culture rather than economic, social or psychological phenomena. This makes the cultural aspect doubly privileged here.

Inspired by Bakhtin's work on dialogicity, Kristeva formulated the influential concept of intertextuality in 1969.[98] While Bakhtin's dialogism is

---

[98] In a text reprinted as 'Word, Dialogue, and Novel' in Kristeva (1980, pp. 64ff). Kristeva defines intertextuality as the 'transposition of one (or several) sign system(s) into another' (1974/1984, pp. 59f). The following quotations are, however, from an interview with Kristeva by Margaret Waller in O'Donell and Davis (1989, p. 281).

about how voices intersecting in discourse combine semantic meanings, intertextuality is an 'intervention of external plurality at different levels – not only at the level of meaning but at the level of syntax and phonetics, too'. Intertextuality is a 'plurality of phonic, syntactic and semantic participation', that is, it involves aspects of both materiality, form-relations and meaning. It also exists on all levels, from single symbols via textual works to larger genres. One example is when metaphors are transposed from one symbolic mode to another, as in expressions like 'tone-colour' or 'colour-tone'. Another is when a book explicitly or implicitly refers to an earlier one, or when a whole genre is constituted in relation to another. Intertextualities can be explicit and perceptible to various degrees, from the aura or discursive space of genres and earlier texts that surrounds each particular text, to an explicit presence of other texts in form of quotations and obvious references.[99]

A more detailed taxonomy is offered by Gérard Genette (1982).[100] All literature is basically 'transtextual', 'second-degree' constructs connected to other texts. But only some texts are explicitly 'intertextual', making another text effectively copresent by means of quotation, plagiarism or allusion. 'Paratextuality' refers to the relation between a work and all accessory messages and commentaries which surround it (prefaces, illustrations, jacket cover, etc.). 'Metatextuality' includes the commentaries one text makes to another without necessarily explicitly citing it. 'Architextuality' relates to the hierarchy of taxonomies invoked, for instance, by the title of a text, which somehow positions it within a genre order. 'Hypertextuality' is finally the relation of a ('hyper-')text to anterior ('hypo-')text, which it transforms or elaborates. While this distinction between ideal types of transtextuality is instructive, it is in practice often difficult to distinguish them neatly from each other, particularly the first, third and fifth ones. It seems unavoidable to retain the more vague concept of intertextuality as including the whole range from implicit to explicit transtextual references.

Aesthetics can be defined as the self-reflection of culture.[101] The concept is rooted in the old Greek term for the sensuous perceiving that is at the basis of all cultural practices. It was long used to denote doctrines on sensations, but has from the sixteenth century come to primarily concern definitions of beauty in nature and the arts. Aesthetic practices are those cultural practices which reflect upon the cultural field itself, and everyday

---

[99] Cf. Collins (1989, pp. 44ff), who argues that while Culler, Barthes and Macherey tend towards the first, wide and diffuse definition, Bloom and Kristeva herself use the second, more narrow one.

[100] Cf. also Stam (1985/1992, pp. 22ff) and, in a more critical tone, O'Donell and Davis (1989, pp. 266ff).

[101] This definition is rooted in classical philosophical models such as those of Kant and Hegel: 'Aesthetic judgement is thus the reflexion or self-presentation of the faculty of presentation' (Roberts 1994, p. 177).

aesthetics is that sector of everyday culture which concerns formal taste patterns and evaluations. Aesthetics is thus culture reflected on its own terms, while cultural sociology, for example, relates symbolic forms to social relations. Asking for the aesthetics of a cultural phenomenon means interrogating which form patterns and criteria are valid there, that is, which doctrine of well-formedness is implicated.

Judgements of taste are only one part of aesthetics, but a crucial one. As reflections on the social dimension, ethics and sociology cannot be reduced to normative regulations, and likewise aesthetics, as a discourse searching to understand how symbols work, has more facets than the making of evaluations. But aesthetics certainly includes the reflection on cultural forms in discourses of taste about the validity of symbolic forms, judged and evaluated according to criteria of well-formedness, comprehensibility, beauty and textual richness. In aesthetic practices in the narrow sense, that is, in artistic contexts where the cultural dimension is explicitly focused upon, those are the most important criteria. Arguments of strategic effectivity, cognitive truth, normative rightness or expressive truthfulness may also be relevant, and they are even emphasized within certain genres, subcultures or interpretive communities. But the relative autonomy of the cultural field ensures that these criteria are mostly of secondary importance, compared to the genuinely aesthetic ones.

Definitions of taste and distaste are organized in intersubjective patterns of style, anchored in interpretive communities and based upon deeply felt distinctions between noise and order, deposited in objectivized institutions, social rituals and status hierarchies, as well as in socialization practices and mental structures.[102] Contrary to the misrecognition of some influential social groups and institutions, there is no single and universally valid such taste/distaste definition. Different discourses define good and bad taste very differently. Cultural producers, audiences, subcultures, mediators, critics, media people, academics and politicians tend to stress different aspects of cultural phenomena as valuable or objectionable. They also use different sorts of criteria, talking about good and bad, right and wrong, good and evil, progressive and reactionary, useful and meaningless, or using other terms that often relate aesthetic value to ethical, political, economic, social or psychological factors. Some taste patterns concentrate on evaluating the way texts and genres are produced (commercial/authentic, etc.), others judge their effects in reception (immoral/uplifting, etc.), still others focus on the symbolic products themselves (conventional/inventive, etc.). Tastes emphasize different symbolic modes (e.g., judging musical performances mostly by their sounds, lyrics or visual expressions) or even parameters within each mode (e.g., melody, rhythm or form structures).[103] Some criteria may be consciously and explicitly used, others

---

[102] Cf. Douglas (1966/1984) on pollution/purity, Attali (1977/1985, including the afterword by McClary, p. 156) on noise/order, and Kristeva (1980/1982) on the abject.

[103] Frith (1994) analyses music tastes: which criteria are used, and by whom.

remain implicit, hidden in the discourses around culture. And all such evaluative codes are formulated in relation to each other. Conflicts of interpretation and critiques of others' judgements arise when conscious taste patterns collide. Vague antipathies may result from such unconscious collisions. Tensions between conscious and unconscious criteria within one single group or individual give rise either to misrecognition, double standard and inner conflict, or to reflexivity, critical self-recognition and learning processes.

Aesthetics often is normatively prescriptive, particularly when tied to the traditional dichotomy between high élite and low mass culture, as in most discussions of media and popular culture. This is of course true of explicit defences of classical or avantgarde art against the alleged debasement of media and popular culture, but there are also more indirect versions. During early and high modernity, popular culture was mostly criticized in academic discourses, as the dichotomy between high and low was felt as rather stable, and the aesthetic hierarchy was consolidated by rather clearly separated social and economic circuits, institutions and public spheres.

The late modern dynamization and partial erosion of older, more rigid high/low distinctions has also affected cultural theory, where more voices have been raised to defend popular culture against its monocular enemies. Such defences are often forced into normative counter-positions, reproducing the same underlying figure, only turned upside-down. When Jean Baudrillard (1983 and 1988, pp. 207ff) argues that postmodern media simulations implode the social and end history, he reproduces outdated ideas of the flatness and manipulatory power of mass culture and the homogeneity and passivity of its audiences, only with a cynical twist that reformulates this as a new form of resistance.[104] When Roland Barthes (1970/1975) contrasts '*readerly*' or closed and '*writerly*' or open texts, or (1973/1975) *plaisir* and *jouissance*, he also reproduces the universalizing evaluative norms inherent in the conventional dichotomy between mass culture and modernist avantgarde. And when Fiske (1989a, pp. 50f and 103ff; 1989b, pp. 62f and 115ff) tries to use both these dichotomies in his reversed defence of popular culture (including the use of media culture), collecting all the good in a progressive 'bloc of the people' against the 'power bloc' of élite culture (including high art as well as the commercial producers of media culture), he is stuck in a similarly normative and naturalizing hierarchical mode of thinking. No such aesthetic dichotomy of formal criteria can classify a high and a low sphere of culture, since both concepts invariably can be found on both sides of each side of such divisions. Aesthetic values are genuinely intersubjective – they are formed in public discourses and thematize relations between texts and subjects who are situated within specific contexts. Such values are therefore only

---

[104] In a feminist critique of Baudrillard, Fiske and Chambers, Morris (1990) argues that they reproduce a view of mass culture as banal and vulgar. Cf. also Modleski (1986a).

valid within these specific contexts, genres and interpretive communities, and do not apply between them.[105]

To think of one's own taste as universal and natural is a 'misrecognition' that in some epochs and some social strata is shared by many.[106] This misrecognition is, however, partly balanced by the late modern growth of reflexivity. It is true that some groups consider their taste for music or fashion as pure and simple, but there are also large groups today that are readily prepared to associate different genres with social status positions.[107] Only certain strata within the élite seem still to be blind to the sociocultural basis and thus intersubjective relativity of aesthetic taste. And structures of misrecognition are not quite rigid givens, but are continuously modified by learning processes of recognition (of the self, of others, of the world and of the symbolic processes themselves), through which subjects (both in everyday life and in research) reach at least partial understanding of their society and culture.

Instead of trying to rebuild those rigid hierarchies that are now being partly eroded, cultural studies should strive to avoid the normativizing trap and accept that issues of taste as well as of norms are always intersubjective and particular constructions. Ethics and aesthetics comprise more than issues of morality and taste. They contain some universalizable pragmatic rules – for interethnic conflict resolvement and for general quality judgement, respectively – but both also contain large and necessarily particular areas where judgements of good relations and norms or pleasurable works and genres cannot be shared by all except for within specific interpretive communities. What can be shared by communicative and interpretive practices is only an understanding of how such rule-systems are constructed and how they can be locally motivated by those who prefer them. In both ethics and aesthetics, late modern individualization and reflexivity processes have offered us the possibility of developing an ability to live with and endure differences, in life as well as in theory – in spite of the strong fundamentalist countercurrents that flourish in both cases.

Aesthetic judgements may be discussed and motivated by more or less well-founded arguments. Such aesthetic discourses make a kind of aesthetic rationality possible.[108] But even though in principle a universal consensus may thus be reached concerning which works are considered well-formed within a particular genre, this does not make everyone prefer

---

[105] Adorno (1973/1984) and Marcuse (1977/1978) offer classical, fascinating and radical but problematic defences for autonomy aesthetics. In media research, Gripsrud (1989) has tried to reinstitute value hierarchies that transgress genre boundaries and may be determined by well-informed experts. Schrøder (1992) instead defends individual needs as the only and irreducible criterion of quality. Wolff (1983) discusses aesthetic values in modernity.

[106] The term is used by Bourdieu (1979/1984) as a sociological critique both of Kant's absolutizing philosophical theory of aesthetic judgement and of the taste patterns and self-understanding of the dominating élites in general.

[107] Cf. de Certeau (1974/1988, pp. 50ff).

[108] Seel (1985, particularly pp. 32ff, 127 and 197f) theorizes aesthetic rationality.

or even appreciate them. A reflecting metal fan may be convinced that the Pet Shop Boys make fine pop, but that conclusion does not force her to like it. And the same is true also for simple comprehensibility. Works or propositions may be judged as logically and grammatically well-formed and understandable, according to formal criteria, but there will always be some aspects open to intersubjective variance. A sentence that first seemed utterly complicated can within the context of a certain genre (e.g., experimental poetry or philosophical theory) turn out to catch complex experiences and make them comprehensible. Different scientific disciplines and traditions have different criteria, as have different forms, genres and currents of art as well as different arenas and groups in everyday life. An aesthetic discourse can open dialogues between such spheres and search for rational arguments for each value judgement that will then become comprehensible for all participants, without necessarily being shared as such by them. The metal fan will know what is good pop but it will still not be her favourite taste.

Reflexivity and mediatization

There is in late modernity a generally increasing *reflexivity* in individuals, society and culture. Institutions, patterns of social interaction and the media demand continuous self-definitions and offer increasingly more resources for such self-referentiality. Reflexivity can cause a difficulty in experiencing devotion and presence, which creates needs for moments of decreased self-observation. But it also offers symbolic tools for presenting authentic self-images to others and to oneself. It induces an increasing general awareness of the cultural aspects of identity, and is thus associated with the process of *culturalization* or *aestheticization* of everyday life that has influenced the turn in our century among theorists to cultural analysis of meaning production, linguistic discourses and textual processes, within academic disciplines such as history, sociology, anthropology and psychology. Both reflexivity and aestheticization are further related to the growing media presence in identity constructions which has been termed *mediatization*. Not only are the media becoming increasingly culturalized: culture is also more and more dependent on communication media. One can mirror or relate to one's identity through other means than the media as well, for instance by talking, dancing or dressing, but the expanding media system is a crucial tool and factor in the growth of reflexivity.

The concept of reflexivity primarily indicates a phenomenon of pictorial visuality. Mirror-images are seen rather than heard, and it is true that people often mirror their identities in concrete images, both in front of the bathroom-mirror and by reading or watching mass media. But reflections may also be aural or use any symbolic mode. Verbal writing implies a potentially discursive fixation on paper and a distanciation towards the text that fits conscious (and critical) reflection particularly well. But the ear also assists in self-mirroring, already when parents talk and sing to the infant to answer and identify it, and when the infant listens as its own screaming or playful voice and movements resound.[109]

'Reflexivity' derives from the Latin *reflectĕre*: fold back. In cultural contexts, what is being folded back is thought, consciousness or symbolizations.[110] A general concept of (late modern societal) reflexivity comprises at least four important sub-aspects. First, there are two main types of object of reflection. On one hand, individual subjects or social groups mirror their own identities in various ways, using physical mirrors or symbolic expressions. What is reflecting itself in this *self-reflexivity* is basically a subject position. On the other hand, *textual reflexivity* relates to the likewise increasing self-thematization of cultural texts. Utterances, books, songs, films and radio or television programmes often point towards themselves by making more or less ironic and intertextual comments on their own styles and structures, putting themselves within quotation marks and inviting their recipients to become more aware of the codes and rules of the genre.

Secondly, the mirroring can take place in various contents or genres. One is the increasing self-awareness of science, a *theoretical reflexivity* where the research process mirrors itself, as discussed in Chapter 1. Another is *daily life reflexivity*, where everyday interaction within the lifeworld contains such mirroring acts. Yet another is *media reflexivity*, which can be seen as a special type of textual mirroring but which may also contain moments of self-reflexivity.

All these forms are generally mixed in complex ways. For example, theoretical reflexivity is a mixture of self- and textual reflexivity within the field of research: on one hand, researchers become more self-aware and self-critical; on the other hand, the texts they produce also openly thematize themselves. Media (and other) texts increasingly often thematize people mirroring themselves, showing subjects who have problems with their identities talking about who they are or creating open, unstable or complex self-images. Here, media contents show examples of self-reflexivity, making it a cultural theme, so that the self-reflexivity of the subjects appearing in these texts makes us think of these texts themselves as reflexive, even when they perhaps are actually not textually reflexive in

---

[109] Cf. Goody (1986, p. 129) or Lowe (1982, pp. 6f), but also Giddens (1990, pp. 36ff). Freud and Lacan associate the ego and the self-image either with the mirror and the glance (of oneself or the Other), or with verbal word-presentations deriving from the symbolic order. Implications of reflexivity for subjectivity will be discussed in the next chapter.

[110] Frank (1991) discusses the complicated relation between self-consciousness and self-knowledge. Ricoeur (1965/1970 and 1990/1992), Kristeva (1983/1987) and Laplanche (1987/1989) analyse the necessity for subjectivity to develop by detours through externalized symbolic forms, which does not reduce the subject to a mere illusory effect of the game of sign systems. Some followers of Lacan (1966/1977) have not managed to avoid that pitfall. Discussions of reflexivity and self-referentiality are found in Hutcheon (1980/1984), *Semiotica* (1980), Stam (1985/1992), Beck (1986/1992), Ziehe (1991 and 1993), Habermas (1992a), Fornäs (1994b and c; 1995a and b); Lash and Urry (1994) and Robinson and Rundell (1994).

the sense defined above. On the other hand, people mostly use symbolic forms like words or media images to mirror themselves, particularly those texts that also offer representations of people mirroring themselves. A highly confusing whirl of mirrorings thus results from repeated combinations of the two main simple forms described above as self- and textual reflexivity, making it hard to keep the basic forms strictly apart. Whereas the next chapter will concentrate upon the subjective dimension of self-reflexivity and study how it affects subject formulation, this section will emphasize its cultural dimension and discuss the role of symbols in various mirroring processes, whether of subjects or of texts.

Conscious reflection is a special case of general self-mirroring processes of physical, psychic, social or cultural reflexivity. Reflexivity is not necessarily a conscious intellectual reflection. Self-mirroring can also take place by other means, as when you use certain style elements to explicitly express your position, or media texts to confirm your identity. Theoretical concepts are only one possible type of tool for reflexivity, and hardly the most common one.

Neither is reflexivity always 'positive'. On one hand, it can imply a painful fixation to one's own person, a subjectivization that intrudes upon the ability to enter into real dialogues with others. On the other hand, it can be connected to a societal colonization, a compulsory expropriation of the self by dominant symbolic systems, especially in connection with media and institutions that are under heavy pressure from the demands of the economic and political systems. In such instances, reflexivity might need to be counteracted, but it can also be a useful resource for communication and identity work. All depends on how it is used; it is highly ambivalent.

When identities – individual or collective, psychic, social or cultural – are mobilized and problematized, the ability and need to define oneself both increase. Reflexivity is intense in the life phase of adolescence and youth, where childhood is to be reworked into adulthood. It is also intensified among sub- or microcultures, cultivating styles and forms of expression. And when epochal shifts are taking place, societal reflexivity is generally increased. In late modern youth culture, these focal points coincide.

Reflexivity is a cultural process of communicative (inter)actions relating human subjects to symbolic texts, thus connecting spheres, symbols and subjects. As cultural and communicative, it takes place in and through symbolic texts that involve communities and spheres for public interaction as well as acting and mirroring subjects. Aesthetic judgements and critical self-reflexivity presuppose not only thinking and acting subjects but also public spheres that offer both communicative tools of symbolic modes and spaces of social interaction with and against others (cf. Rundell 1994, pp. 106ff). Reflexivity turns out to be a key concept that connects this chapter to the preceding and following ones. While its subjective sides will be discussed more in the next chapter, some of its more general aspects in relation to symbolic forms and communication media will conclude this one.

Sources of reflexivity appear on different levels. There are objective, material, technical or institutional frameworks such as technology or the political and economic systems of state and market. Media technologies, cultural commodities and social institutions present tools for mirroring identities and they force each of us to use them. Other roots dig down to the subjective level of inner driving forces within each person's psychic constitution. New socialization patterns give rise to a widened narcissistic potential – a growing ability and need for reflecting one's self.

There are, thirdly, also intersubjective mechanisms in group relations and symbolic languages. On a social level, a greater mobility and fluidity of social groups increase our collective self-awareness of positions, norms and lifestyles, caused by increasing communications and modern individualiz- ation tendencies. Factors within the cultural level itself finally add yet other pushes towards reflexivity. Late modern aesthetic trends have cultivated reflexive themes, and new artistic techniques for intertextual references have been developed.[111]

These sources present demands as well as resources. Cultural phenom- ena have not only causes and motives but also meanings in all these dimensions. In people's talk, styles, songs or media-uses, one can search not only archaeologically for the forces that shaped them, but also teleologically for the meanings they shape. And these meanings point at objective institutions, at subjective selves, at social relations as well as – intertextually – towards other stylistic formations. There is an objectivizing reflexivity, thematizing external life conditions, when people define them- selves in terms of class, gender or ethnic belonging to what are perceived as fixed categories or frameworks, or in relation to system-dependent insti- tutions like school or work. Another common reflexivity form is the subjectivizing one: an inner-directed reflexivity defining identities in terms of individual development through the life stages. Thirdly, a normative reflexivity points in a social direction, towards norms, group relations and concrete interaction. In the cultural direction, expressions of aesthetic reflexivity finally relate to other texts within the symbolic field itself, to musical, visual or literary styles and genres.

Late modernity increases reflexivity of all these types. This gives mass media an increasing role in the production of objective, subjective, social and cultural identities. New media and new sociocultural tendencies facilitate and demand that their own identity gets explicit attention.

The explicitly reflexive texts produced in various symbolic modes today have given rise to large discussions on 'postmodern' aesthetics, intertextu- ality, pastiche and irony within architecture, art, literature, theatre, television, dance and music. It is true that experiments to explode and

---

[111] A rising general mirroring preparedness, caused by expanding media or other cultural trends, can give rise to more intense narcissistic tendencies in many individuals, as well as the other way around. Hutcheon (1980/1984) uses the concept of narcissism for metafictional narrative text types, which are preferably called reflexive so as not to interfere with the specific psychoanalytical theory of narcissism, discussed in the Chapter 5.

fragment traditional narratives have been popular, but reflexivity need not mark the end of narrativity, nor of the author or the subject. Narrative and non-narrative forms are always present as textual possibilities. In some times and contexts the narrative modes are actualized and activated, in other cases the non-narrative ones are sought for. One has to differentiate carefully between different genres and works and between different individuals and groups. It was never the case, for instance, that MTV was wholly a postmodern revolt against meaningful narrativity.[112] The allegedly new, reflexive, aesthetic traits can be shown to have obvious forerunners, in folk and popular culture as well as within modernist avantgardes. And it is easy to observe that traditional narrativity persists in all media forms. What happens is not that subject positions disappear or fragment totally, but rather that they are more often relativized and consciously thematized by certain reflexive techniques that correspond to similar reflexive potentials among and within the subjects that use these media texts.

To measure the weight of culture or aesthetics in a society or an epoch is of course very hard. Statistics offer some indices, but one should not draw too quick conclusions. Taste and style may, for example, in a given period become more important to certain strata, but not to others, and television news may deal with more cultural issues while other news genres change in the opposite direction. There is a danger in underestimating the different forms of cultural activity earlier in history, but the very fact that cultural aspects are so much discussed today indicates that aestheticization is a late modern trend.

In cultural practices, young people are prominent. They use a large amount and plurality of media and cultural resources (concerts, theatre, libraries), and are also more diligent producers of cultural expressions (music, dance, video, writing, etc.) than other population groups. They are also particularly style-conscious, being interested in and aware of bodily aesthetics and subcultural signs as a way to formulate actual and wished identities. They are also often pioneers in the use of new media forms. Video, walkman, CD and computer games were all early tested by teenagers, before adults in some cases managed to surpass them. All these cultural activities seem additionally to have increased for many decades now, among young people as well as among their parents.[113]

Several causes for this development may be proposed. The colonizing growth of the market and state systems is one of them. The demands of schools and work-places for goal-oriented self-control create compensatory

---

[112] Cf. Goodwin (1993) and Frith et al. (1993) for critiques of earlier postmodern readings of MTV.

[113] Forms and causes of aestheticization of late modern (youth) life are discussed by Fornäs (1987), Fornäs et al. (1988/1995), Drotner (1991a and b) and Ziehe (1991 and 1994).

needs for escape and freedom, and aesthetic forms of expression then offer a welcome alternative zone of free play, autonomy and self-determination.

But aesthetic activities also presuppose surplus time and resources beyond what is needed to satisfy primary needs of survival. Welfare creates time, space and raw material for cultural practice, and a growing welfare in certain social strata has made it possible for some people to put more energy into 'post-material' needs and interests.[114] Young people in the post-war decades got more money, space and leisure time to spend and control, which formed the basis for a youth-oriented supply of the cultural industries and for everyday amateur creativity.

Spare time may also be caused by marginalization and a lack of productive functions. Young people with few productive tasks other than their own socialization and qualification may let aesthetic projects fill this void. In modern society, youth has a functional deficit that creates a wish to leave marks and gain importance and visibility instead through leisure-based style production. Young people are separated into a category of being adolescent – 'not-yet-adults' in a state of tiresome waiting and moratorium.[115] They are simultaneously brought together in peer groups offering plenty of opportunities for self-identifying style experiments.

If certain groups are threatened by unemployment or other forms of direct marginalization, the needs to work and to form a social identity can be directed towards aesthetic fields. It would be paradoxical to argue that both welfare and impoverishment increase the weight of culture, but some social marginalization within the general frames of a welfare state can give such results, as long as it does not lead all the way to isolation and destitution, in which case the importance of style and culture again may diminish, as seems to have happened in many neoliberal ex-welfare countries.

But the main reason for the increased centrality of culture among young people as well as adults is probably the problematization and intensification of identity work. The needs to formulate one's personal and social identity grow, as identity constructions are denaturalized, and it is through cultural discourses that relations and positions are negotiated. Young people have a relatively high amount of physical, mental and social flexibility, which make them more active in creating cultural texts which formulate subjective and social identifications.

Identities are often mirrored spontaneously without much verbal and rational formulating; at other times, however, they are concentrated in conscious reflections. Meeting an 'other' in face-to-face interaction lets you know more about yourself through the other's reactions as well as through the perceived similarities and differences between you. Intersubjective dialogues give you an opportunity jointly to formulate who you are. But the soft- and hardware of the media and the cultural industries offer great

---

[114] The concept derives from Inglehart (1977).
[115] Youth as a moratorium is analysed by Erikson (1968).

resources for reflexivity, self-mirroring and subject production. The media-explosion of the so-called 'post-industrial' 'information society' is not only an expansion of an economic sector, but also implies a mediatization of everyday life.

Everyday life is increasingly permeated with media. Cultural practices and expressions are incorporated, disseminated and transformed by mass media, whose presence in daily life is continuously intensified. Mediated texts are more and more central to individual and collective identity constructions as well as to how people relate to each other and know the world around them. Surrounded by musical sounds, posters or television-flows your self is unconsciously measured and positioned. Watching a film or reading a novel about people like yourself can also give you impulses to think over your own identity and life choices. You can compare your own body with the pictures in magazines and decide how you look and whether you accept certain ideals or not.

The media expansion thus leads to a mediatization of culture. Cultural phenomena that were first primarily based on face-to-face interaction are continuously being included and reshaped by various media forms. And as the speed and range of such micro-processes of mediatization increase, the result is a longer historical process of general cultural mediatization on a macro-level, whereby media become relatively more important in all cultural phenomena of late modern society. Processes of micro-mediatization add up to a macro-mediatization which in its turn makes micro-mediatizations more common and more focal to identity formations and everyday life.

Within youth culture, the 'bedroom culture' and fashion tastes of best girlfriends are mirrored by the weekly magazines they read, in a complex spiral movement: girls form their identities aided by reading magazines writing about girls' friendship activities. Similarly, peer group amateur pop-playing is mirrored by MTV, which in turn offers bands patterns for visual images and gestures. Media refer and relate to young people's experiences, needs and wishes, but they also form them by formulating and disseminating certain styles and genres across geographic and social borders. Generational as well as ethnic discourses are both generated and reproduced in media. Identities are mirrored by media texts, but media texts are also used as raw materials and tools in the creation of identities. When people define themselves as young, men or women, with specific class, geographic and ethnic positions, they appear to use more and more mediated images and concepts. People often define their cultural positions by expressing taste values for and against different media channels and genres, reflected as related to social, gender and ethnic positions. This reflexivity works against a traditional misrecognition of taste patterns. Local microcultures are again and again absorbed by cultural industries and disseminated by broadcasting or phonogram as medially constructed subcultural styles. On the other hand, each microculture is from its start imbued with mediated ingredients rather than any pure product of non-mediated experiences and relations. New media such as music videos increasingly influence local cultural practices.

A colonization of the lifeworld occurs when bureaucratization and commercialization let power and money supersede symbolic communication in areas where this is dysfunctional for the development of knowledge, norms and identities. Mediatization refers to the (increasing) use of media in identity constructions. Reflexivity occurs when intersubjective images, symbols and discourses affect the same identity production. Colonization is only the negative side of the other two – their positive side is a growing symbolization and communicative competence that actually increases communicative rationality and the power of the lifeworld to resist colonization. Mediatization can be one important tool for a growing reflexivity, adding to direct face-to-face interaction. Getting exposed to media may increase reflexivity, but growing reflexive needs in everyday life may also induce the spread of media.

Media and youth have both become scapegoats for fears of modernization problems that they are actually only a limited part or a symptom of. New media forms or genres tend to attract suspicion and hostility from conservative camps, as do the activities of younger generations. Regular patterns of panic reactions arise, where often marginal and pretty harmless youth and/or media phenomena provoke fear and disgust among certain influential groups that react in interplay with various authorities, media and youth groups, thus inducing a specific accelerating spiral movement with certain recurrent characteristics, before the whole issue fades away again. The converging moral panics or meeting of scapegoats in discourses on young people's media-uses often formulate real ethical problems caused by modernization, and should therefore not be dismissed as repetitions of just the same old panic reaction. But such scapegoating panic makes it hard to understand the causes and possible remedies of such problems.

Like all other cultural phenomena, moral panics have roots and meanings in several directions. Objectively, they thematize and are caused by economically based class conflicts and demands from institutions that aim at socializing the young and upholding social order. Subjectively, they thematize the formation of individual personality and express deep psychological conflicts between order and chaos, fear of dirt and disgust of the 'abject', as can be seen in the strong emotional language which they use, as the scapegoat is depicted as dirty, excessive, promiscuous, etc. Socially, they relate to the validation of ethic norms and to the interaction between people within various contexts (family, school, peer group etc.). Culturally they thematize relations between genres and media forms, for example, by writing articles that attack video and defend books.

Media panics often presuppose a pure transmission model of communication as direct copying or imprint of messages in receiving subjects. They argue that what people see or hear is what they then do, which is certainly not correct in any such direct sense, and would never be thought of the high art audiences. Young people attending death metal concerts are feared to become satanist murderers, whereas educated adults attending a performance of *Macbeth* are never supposed to imitate these bloody actions.

There is an amount of continuity in how moral panics develop, but there is also a tendency for them to change. The golden age of moral panics may be over, as consensual normality has been denaturalized and traditional values demystified. Individualization, pluralization and reflexivity has caused a heterogenization of interest groups that makes it harder to achieve the closed circles of fear and condemnation that could earlier be seen. Some groups will of course always try to get moral panics started again, but the differentiation of the schools, the media and the family makes it hard to reproduce as all-embracing panic reactions as before. When some voices gather to ban displeasing cultural phenomena, counter-voices tend to argue against them in a much more heterogeneous public debate than was the case up to the 1970s. Panics tend to become more localized in specific fundamentalist groups, rather than spread throughout society, where the larger public sphere often contains as many counter-voices directed against these panics. The public sphere has always contained such heterological and antilogical dialogues, but now more than ever.

Mediatization is often seen as just a threat to an original authenticity.[116] It is true that the process has negative aspects, by confronting us with a flow of symbolic expressions of ideals and wishes, that can be hard to recast into one's own, personal life. But, first, the concept of a non-mediated origin is a myth: media and socially formed images have for hundreds or even thousands of years affected our identity constructions. Before disks and modems, tales and pictures provided the symbols that helped people define themselves.

Secondly, mediatization also has positive sides, for example, the opening up of the world geographically and socially to offer insights into cultures and life areas formerly unknown to most young people, to give access to various symbolic forms of expression, to offer mirroring tools for one's identity development, and to give richer possibilities for pleasure and expand our needs. An increasing media-use need not diminish direct, non-mediated, cultural activity – statistics, on the contrary, tell us that an increase in music-listening through media has, for example, been paralleled by a rise in concert-going as well as in music-making.[117] Media can be used in combination with other activities, which makes a rise in media-use possible without a similar decline in other activities. Mediatization might have made us more aware of the fact that lived cultures and identities are always shaped through symbolic interaction, with or without machines. Image and reality need not necessarily stand in inverse proportion to each

---

[116] Cf. Morin (1962), Joli Jensen (1990), Lipsitz (1990) and Krenzlin (1992) for critical analyses of anti-modern critiques of media culture.

[117] See Feilitzen et al. (1989) and Roe & Carlsson (1990).

other: more mediated images do not equal less 'real' reality. Even authenticity itself is constructed by cultural representations and media techniques, which makes it an intersubjective discourse but therefore no illusion.

Media constitute an economic–political machinery, but at the same time also a production of meaning by their active users. Media are a battle-field for the conflict between communication and production of meaning in the lifeworld, on one hand, and demands from the economic and political systems, on the other. These systems have a threatening tendency to colonize everyday life with their instrumental, goal-oriented rationality and demands for profit, effectivity and control. But these macrostructural frames do not totally annihilate the meaningful communicative actions of the lifeworld. In spite of the threats from state and market, power and profit, late modern media also contain communicative aspects, in production as well as in reception. Media constitute an ambivalent arena between the systems and the lifeworld (Habermas 1981/1988). They have authoritarian as well as emancipatory potentials, as they combine the intrusion of systemic demands into everyday life with the developing of communicative competence to produce knowledge, test social norms and express personal feelings.[118]

Popular media culture is crucially colonized by the market system in the form of commercial cultural industries aiming for expanding economic profits. As Marx and later critical theory have shown, commodification creates tensions between use values and exchange values, leading to various forms of alienation (towards products, nature, other human beings and the totality of humanity). However, this has often been misconstrued as if the commodity form would let use values be replaced with exchange values, meanings with money, human needs with profits. It is true that economic valorization affects use values: the concrete shapes of products and the specific needs and uses to which they relate are not left untouched by the processes of commercialization. But use values can never disappear: all capitalist commodity production presupposes and reproduces needs and use values, otherwise no economic exchange value would exist.

A variant of this misunderstanding is when it is argued that besides exchange values and real use values, late capitalism creates new symbolic values related to the stylish packaging of commodities. The images of commodity aesthetics and advertisements are thought to form a particular

---

[118] Habermas (1992a) explains how these ambivalences contradict his earlier (1962/1989) ideas, which were much closer to the cultural pessimism of Adorno and Horkheimer (1944): 'At the time, I was too pessimistic about the resisting power and above all the critical potential of a pluralistic, internally much differentiated mass public whose cultural usages have begun to shake off the constraints of class. In conjunction with the ambivalent relaxation of the distinction between high and low culture, and the no less ambiguous "new intimacy between culture and politics", which is more complex than a mere assimilation of information to entertainment, the standards of evaluation themselves have also changed' (pp. 438f). Cf. also Arato and Cohen (1988, p. 51).

kind of illusory value which seduces consumers into forgetting the real and original functions of products.[119] This theory conceals a realist assumption and builds on an overly narrow conception of use value. Symbolic and fantasy-related aspects have always been crucial elements of use values, and are not at all excluded from the commodity theory of Marx.[120] In popular culture it is impossible to think of symbolic fascination as something that exceeds ordinary use value – this is instead the main function of these products. Human needs are also of aesthetic kinds, and what appeals to our emotions or our sense of beauty and stylistic perfection is a fundamental part of use values rather than something additional, artificial, superfluous or illusory. Only an ascetic puritan can believe that people once satisfied their needs in a world without aesthetic surfaces. Signs and images belong to the material 'reality' as well. The relation between needs and use values is historically and intersubjectively defined, rather than naturally given. This has always been true, but has only become more evident as a result of late modern aestheticization of everyday life. The popular cultural industries expand more than they destroy use values and human needs, while they distribute the means to satisfy those needs in an uneven way. The increasing number of differentiated needs makes life richer and increases people's life expectations, even if not all needs are indisputable. Symbols and aesthetics are more than simple effects of commodification and more than a secondary aura above a firm material basis.

Mediatization does not necessarily standardize, homogenize or delete direct personal experiences. Cultural modernization of and through media binds people together by globally transgressing traditional geographic, ethnic and social borders, while at the same time producing new differences between subcultures and lifestyles.[121] Modernization may in a first stage lead to homogenization, but then again shapes new heterogeneities and pluralities in a way rarely seen by its early protagonists and antagonists.

Media and popular culture can counteract as well as reinforce sexism and racism. Mediated expressions that are oppositional in one aspect (i.e., class) can be reactionary in another aspect (i.e., gender or race). Cultural

[119] See, e.g., Haug (1971/1986), Hall (1982, p. 68) or Baudrillard (1988).

[120] Marx (1858/1986, pp. 187, 250, 335f and 451f; 1867/1976, Chapter 1) shows that exchange values always presuppose use values, based on any human needs, whether arising in the stomach or in fantasy, and that it is a civilisatory tendency of capitalism to expand and differentiate the human sphere of needs. Cf. also Heller (1974/1976) and Schanz (1981). A main critique of the concept of need is that needs should not be seen as essences that pre-date their fulfilment in social action, but are themselves discursively formed. Still, it seems hard to refute that social life and socialization create lacks, demands, interests and expectations in subjects and groups, which then collide with either means of satisfaction or frustrating denials. Cf. how Elliot (1974) problematizes the theory of 'uses and gratification' in media research.

[121] Fuglesang (1994) describes how television and video contribute to the appearance of a young hiphop microculture and changing modes of femininity in a village in eastern Kenya.

phenomena cannot unambiguously be divided into 'good' and 'bad' – media culture is, like modernity itself, ambivalent.

Crossing cultural streams

This chapter has elaborated upon the core dimension of cultural theory, and suggested a series of important concepts to analyse how symbolic practices construct and interpret textual compounds in a multidimensional way. The three symbolic aspects of materiality, form-relations and meaning were introduced, extended by a fourth one: use or pragmatics.

The material aspect gave rise to a lengthy discussion of symbolic modes and a series of debated conceptual polarities like oral/literate, discursive/ presentational and symbolic/semiotic. The formal aspect then inspired a scrutinization of concepts like genre and style. Finally, the aspects of meaning and use motivated a clarification of concepts like reception and interpretation, and the presentation of a series of ways to distinguish between types of communicative symbol-use and dimensions of meaning-making.

After a general discussion of intertextuality and aesthetics as the self-reflexivity of the cultural dimension, the concluding discussion of mediatization and reflexivity points towards the one remaining analytical direction which has yet to be clarified, that of subjectivity.

5
Subjects

Subjects swim in symbolic streams, but are also pervaded by them. Cultural flows fill and constitute our bodies and minds, in processes of socially organized subject formation through socializing identity work. Humans move on and in these cultural waters, diving into those interconnected gushing inner springs from which symbolic texts flow. Subjects are formed by symbols in discourses, whose intersecting movements they simultaneously propel by moving in time and space, constructing and inhabiting social spheres and infusing life into the symbolic resources for communication simply by using them in more or less inventive and creative ways.

This chapter will navigate some of these depths within the navigating agents. It will pay particular attention to how subjects mirror themselves in texts, and what late modern historical changes can be discerned in these processes. It will visit the mirror of the water where identity is recognized, and the pool in which Narcissus, son of a water-nymph and a river-god, tried to mirror himself, deaf to the yearning voice of Echo.

Subjectivities and identities are no simple, singular entities, but always split, fragmented and polydimensional. Again, it is necessary to carefully separate dimensions of identity, in order to be able to see how they are interrelated and superimposed. Becoming a subject is a difficult process of separation and connection, in individual development as well as in the history of the human race. Subject formation takes place in a network of crossing and crossed aspects of identity, associated with a series of biological, social and cultural categories like age, gender, ethnicity and class. All the objective, subjective, social and cultural dimensions thus turn up here again, now in the form of identity-aspects.

The inner constitution of subjectivity cannot simply be reduced to an illusory effect of language or interaction, even though it cannot exist without them. Like spheres and symbols, subjects deserve to be treated as a separate dimension of cultural theory. Subjects are capable of learning and remembering, and this accumulation of experience develops a particular inner structure, with its own specific laws, demanding specific tools of understanding which can neither be reduced to nor completely detached from sociology and discourse theory. This is where psychological and psychoanalytical theories are indispensable. There is still some suspicion towards psychoanalytical models among many sociologists and anthropologists inside as well as outside of cultural studies. A political reason for this may be that psychologists and therapists have been thought to divert people's attention from real social problems and construct them as inner, developmental issues in a way that pathologizes the individual and affirms a repressive society. While this has certainly often been true, psychoanalysis also contains strong counter-currents of critical thinking which thematize the connections between subjects and society, including its power, class and gender orders.

A related problematic point has been the universalism of many psychological explanations, where historical, ethnic and social variations seem to be neglected. There is a surprising lack of ethno-psychoanalysis or historical studies of subject formation, and many basic concepts and models are formulated in essentialist and naturalizing ways. Again, however, this is not a necessary implication of psychological theory, either in psychoanalysis (and its offsprings in ego psychology, self psychology, object relations theory and Lacanianism) or in other traditions (e.g., cognitive psychology). As with theories on the other levels (social and aesthetic ones), subject theories may well be reread with historicizing and contextualizing glasses, so that their subtle explanations of inner structures and processes can be integrated in a more dynamic and multifocal framework.[1]

Modernization certainly affects subject formation very deeply. One may well argue that it is capitalist development in early modernity that creates those socialization patterns which are crucial to our understanding of human subjectivity and individual identity. This model of identity work has successively spread to various regions and strata, taking varying forms dependent on which social categories are involved. In this century, a long theoretical discussion has scrutinized recent general changes in these socialization patterns, resulting in subtly different subjectivity forms. As important patterns for family life, schools, media and other general conditions of everyday life, identity definitions, norms and relations are transformed, subject theories have tried to understand what this means for the development of selves, desires, needs and competences.

The fact that subjects are individually unique makes it particularly difficult to construct general models here. Each concrete subject can only be understood if its specificity is strictly respected, rather than subsumed under some abstract category. All talk about modern identity forms and the like is therefore intrinsically problematic. What is valid for one person misses what is most important for another – more so here than when discussing social or cultural phenomena that are at least intersubjective rather than subjective. Still, theory cannot do without abstractions, but they should be understood more as guiding searchlights than as accurate descriptions.

With these reservations, it is plausible to look for late modern transformations also on this level of subjectivity, as well as within social spheres or

---

[1] For ethno-psychoanalysis, see Parin (1978) and Erdheim (1982 and 1988).

symbolic forms. There are many elements to such an analysis, and as the discussion of narcissistic personality traits as part of a late modern form of individuality and identity will be focused upon here, it should be remembered that this is only one particular tendency among many others. Late modern subjectivity is characterized by fragmentation and differentiation into many contradictory options, rather than by the growth of one particular new model of normal development. The catchword of narcissism hints at some important displacements that have been much discussed in psychoanalysis, and that connects to my interest in the role of media and culture. This discussion is fruitful, both in its unique focus on adolescence in relation to the early childhood experiences which are otherwise most studied, and in its crucial historicization and dynamicization of psychoanalytical thinking.[2] Biologist, essentialist and normative assumptions of an ideal and linear identity development are invalidated when it is recognized that not only have genders, classes, ethnic groups and subcultures differing 'normal' socialization forms, but that these are also transformed over time. The deepest psychic structures are drawn into the historical process of modernization. Subjects are as historically produced as are social spheres and symbolic modes, though some structures of identity may be very stubborn.

Subjectivity and identity

Subject and subjectivity are extremely complicated terms to define, particularly in their polar relation to object and objectivity.[3] In Latin, an object is a thing that is 'thrown towards or against', while a subject is what is 'thrown under'. To object against something is to go against it, and an object may be conceived as a thing which we as subjects or human agents confront. The objective world is all that which opposes us as 'real' and external to ourselves – that which exists in and for itself, independent of our activities and of our understanding of it, and which is thrown before our senses and minds as objects of perception.

A subject of state power is someone who is cast under its dominion. The subject of a study, a text, a talk or a picture is the (subject-)matter, substance, theme or topic on which it works and which is therefore thrown

---

[2] Though the unconscious does not in itself know of any time dimension, it is far from ahistorically given. According to Laplanche (1987/1989), Freud is in total agreement with Margaret Mead concerning the assertion that the pair masculinity–femininity is a complex, relatively late arisen and accidental result, where the sociological factor plays a decisive role. The psychoanalytical discussion of late modern changes in individual identity development, including Keniston (1970), Kohut (1971) and Ziehe (1975), is a useful contrast to the ahistorical, socio-, andro- and ethnocentric tendencies within ego-psychology, cognitive psychology, Lacanianism and certainly the highly problematic idea of archetypes suggested by Jung. Historians of mentality like Ariès (1960/1962) have historicized subjectivity in a longer perspective.

[3] Cf. Williams (1976/1988, pp. 308ff).

under its operation. Such an aura of domination and subjection still rings in critical understandings of subjectivity as something which is produced and dominated by social or cultural systems, for example, the symbolic order of texts.[4] In grammar, logic and classical Enlightenment philosophy, however, an almost contrary sense gradually developed, where the subject of a sentence or an operation is the agency who acts, thinks, feels and wants, while its object is that which is other than this active mind and on which it operates. This transformation is deeply related to modernity and its denaturalizing disenchantment of nature, religion and tradition. While subjects were once under the dominion of a higher and pre-determined cosmic order, the human self was now seen as self-defining and to some degree autonomous.[5] Today, the subject is mostly conceived as this thinking and acting self, and the subjective is understood as its unique point-of-view. However, the opposite conception has resounded like a return of the repressed as this free individual subject has repeatedly been questioned, by psychoanalysis, structuralism, feminism and theories of ethnicity.

Both aspects are in fact needed. Subjects are born and constituted in an irreversible way, so that one cannot doubt their existence. But their self-identity is not given – neither for themselves nor for the surrounding others. We know that we are, but not who or how we are. To understand our identities is a task that forces us to reflect on what we do, to interpret the texts we produce. Subjectivity is therefore both a starting-point and a project. It is, on one hand, the combined result of processes of individual socialization and historical modernization, which constitute our individual existence with all its potentials; and on the other hand, the goal of an indeterminate process or project, where each subject strives to become full and to find or reconstitute itself through acts of self-realization. The first, primary subjectivity is highly ambivalent, broken and split. Its character of a self-propelling project derives from its initial and fundamental lack of self-sufficiency. The subject is an indissoluble union of mind and body in a specific context (Schulze 1992, pp. 35 and 47). This thinking–acting mind–body is always and necessarily incomplete. It is an individual agent but also subjected to opaque external forces. Its potential self-consciousness is only partial and it therefore also has to some extent an object-status. All the critiques of this subject are in a way right. The subject is much less given, autonomous, individual, self-controlled and free than it may think. The subject may be a sociocultural construction, but even as such, it exists. It may be deeply split and incomplete, but the becoming-more-subject can nevertheless be a crucial goal of its identity work. Subjects do not exist as fully developed totalities, but more as germs and potentialities, as subjects-

[4] Cf. Lacan, Foucault and others.

[5] Taylor (1989, e.g., p. 188) depicts the historical development of this (early) modern view of the subject as separate from (and opposed to) the object, which induces both a subjectivism and an objectivism, and is connected to the fixing of a clear boundary between the psychic and the physical. Cf. also Taylor (1975, pp. 6ff).

in-process.[6] They are neither full wholes nor empty holes, but complex projects. Subjective identity is more of a creative project of identity work than either a completed given or an empty illusion. The analysis of texts not only points towards objective forces, but also – through the intersubjective codes and relations – towards the agency of interacting human subjects, without which no meanings would ever be formed.

These 'subjects-in-process' (Kristeva 1980, p. 135) develop through their texts, and these texts are the only channel to understand them. One can only reflect upon oneself and upon others by interpreting textual and symbolic discourses of various kinds, and these texts express subjects as heterogeneous and split into necessarily unconscious fragments. While asserting the agency of subjects, therefore, cultural theory needs also to decentre and deconstruct them by reading the traces of the unconscious: those aspects of the subject of which it has itself no full knowledge.

Psychoanalytical theory is a method to interpret forms of subjectivity by studying the interplay between consciousness and the unconscious in the various symbols that subjects create.[7] It offers clues to the inner, psychic determinants of cultural phenomena, of their basis in desires formed by the individual history of each subject and touched by the text which this subject meets. Psychoanalytically oriented media studies have tried to discover how texts transform subjective identities of their users, through learning processes and mechanisms of identification, projection, transference and reflexivity that can be related to the impression aspect of communication. By recognizing the work of unconscious impulses in the mind–body, the individual subject is decentred and problematized. Consciousness can no longer be thought of as a unitary and transparent essence, but is always coupled to unconscious motives and structures of various kinds, which can only be reached indirectly, through the interpretation of its traces in what the subject makes. The unconscious appears in the mistakes and unintended acts people make, in the rifts and lacunae of conscious subjectivity, and it can only be studied by indirect reconstructions. To discover unconscious aspects of cultural phenomena, one has to search widely on many levels and through many channels to find the places where silences, voids, inner tensions and hidden logics systematically operate.[8]

Symbols thus give clues to the subject positions which determine them. But they also have effects on subjects – indirectly through imperceptible

---

[6] Kristeva (1974/1984) develops a rich theory of the subject-in-process; cf. also Ricoeur (1965/1970), Laplanche (1970/1985 and 1987/1989), Kristeva (1973/1986), Döbert et al. (1980) and Frank et al. (1988).

[7] See Fairbairn (1938), Kris (1952), Hanna Segal (1952), Kohut (1964), Ricoeur (1965/1970), Lorenzer (1970 and 1986), Winnicott (1971), Kristeva (1974/1984), Coward and Ellis (1977), Rose (1980), Erdheim (1982), Kraft (1984), Wirth (1984), Solomon (1985), Spitz (1985) and Donald (1991) on psychoanalytical symbol theory.

[8] 'Conscious' literally means to 'know together', but usually indicates a state of awareness in thinking beings. Freud's psychoanalysis explains how the unconscious self interacts with consciousness. Williams (1976/1988, pp. 320ff) traces the history of these concepts.

processes of impression; openly through the explicit and reflexive thematization of identity in cultural texts. The relations between cultural texts and human subjects run in both directions: texts emanate from interacting subjects who are themselves continuously transformed by using texts.

This model might invite to a spatial thinking in terms of surface and depth, where the unconscious is understood as a deep layer below consciousness, as in the common term 'subconscious'. This is clear in Freud's topological model of the psyche, structured into the it, the I and the above-I – or, in the problematically reifying English translation of Freud's terms: the id, the ego and the super-ego (cf. Bettelheim 1983/1991). A romantic interpretation of this model sees the unconscious as an underground parallel world under the surface of the conscious self. Some want to repress, extinguish or enlighten it through goal-rational ego-control, others launch primitivist expeditions into its tempting jungle.

This model of the self as containing an essential hidden depth has later been attacked from various directions, both within and outside of psycho-analysis. In Lacanian as well as in object relations theory, the unconscious is conceived in not so spatial terms, more like a misrecognized logic within the self than an alternative sub-self. Foucault (1974/1979) shows how the idea of the self as containing a 'depth' has historically been used as an instrument of institutional control and power. But the useful critique against simple surface/depth models cannot make them superfluous, as admitted by Foucault himself in a more humble tone: 'I wanted not to exclude the problem of the subject, but to define the positions and functions that the subject could occupy in the diversity of discourse' (1969/1972, p. 200). His critical investigation of old categories (including the subject and its unconscious) is only a temporary questioning that is meant to 'show that they are not self-evident, that they are always the result of a construction' (p. 32), and does not forbid the use of these older categories but only 'demands that they are theoretically elaborated' (p. 62). Such a demand for critical reflection on conceptual categories is widely shared among theorists, as the result of a growing late modern reflexivity. It was not even alien to Freud's own ideas. Psychoanalysis, structuralism and poststructuralism have all questioned the unity of the thinking subject by showing its deep inner splits and fractures, and by positioning it in the context of social and cultural structures. Its unconscious aspects can only be known indirectly, interpreted through signs and traces in its conscious acts. While the existence of the subject cannot be doubted, its identity can only be constructed through the intersubjective work of interpretation. There is no immediate or intuitive road to understanding one's subjectivity, even though the teleological goal of each subject is to become a conscious self, which is only possible through a hermeneutics of suspicion that casts doubt on the subject's first self-understanding.

Ricoeur (1965/1970) has clarified how subjectivity can be studied through cultural texts, in two opposing directions. Symbols may, on one hand, be deciphered as traces of repressed drives or pre-symbolic impulses of the kind that Julia Kristeva (1974/1984) has described as 'semiotic'. In language-use and cultural works unconscious aspects of subjectivity can be traced which expose the differentiated working and contradictory tensions in the core of the subject. Psychoanalysis explores the archaeology of the subject – the way subjects are formed and developed in all their hetero-geneity, through processes of socialization and subject formation. This method is a critical hermeneutics of suspicion and distanciation that goes against the immediate self-understanding of everyday life and searches for formative structures by means of systematizing explanations.

Subjectivity is thus a construct, but nevertheless it exists, or rather, it works, and can thus be approached teleologically, by interpreting the intended meanings of its symbolic works, to try to understand how human beings shape symbolic orders and texts of consciousness, full of signifi-cance. This method is a hermeneutics of understanding which traces what subjects signify and searches for their created meanings. Subject theory needs to understand both the historical determinations of subject forma-tion and the activity of subjects that creates the future. If subject archaeology focuses on unconscious drives, effects of impression and moments of regression in psychological development, subject teleology instead illuminates the conscious self and its strivings for expression, learning and progression. The union of these two perspectives opens up a dynamic perspective on subjectivity, based not on a peaceful and harmonic coexistence of the two sides, but on a dramatic series of painful confron-tations between them in human life as well as in cultural expressions. It is the contrast between the conscious self and the unconscious drives which propels the subject to develop in interaction with others and with the world. Ricoeur (1965/1970) emphasizes the necessary duality of psycho-analysis as 'energetics' and 'hermeneutics', conceptualizing the duality of the subject as both a dynamic play of forces and a creator of meaning.

> Thus, reflection must be doubly indirect: first, because existence is evinced only in the documents of life, but also because consciousness is first of all false consciousness, and it is always necessary to rise by means of a corrective critique from misunderstanding to understanding . . . . In this way, a teleology of the subject opposes an archaeology of the subject. But what is important for our intention is that this teleology, just like Freudian archaeology, is constituted only in the movement of interpretation, which understands one figure through another figure. (Ricoeur 1969/1974, pp. 18 and 22)

Both symbols and subjects are formed by a collective process where people interact, and they are from the beginning intrinsically interwoven. 'It is the text, with its universal power of world disclosure, which gives a self to the ego' (Ricoeur 1976, p. 95). Still, subject and culture cannot be collapsed into one single dimension. It is as problematic to regard cultural phenom-ena as pure and direct expressions of inner subjectivities as it is conversely to view the subject as a pure and direct effect of language.

Subjects have non-symbolic sides but yet are simultaneously formed by cultural processes, with language as a focal symbolic mode. Subjects become reflexively aware of themselves only through the detour through the interpretation of the embodied meanings of their produced objects: 'we understand ourselves in the mirror of the word. The relation between the text and the mirror – *liber et speculum* – is basic to hermeneutics' (Ricoeur 1969/1974, p. 386). Ricoeur's hermeneutic–phenomenological method of 'concrete reflection' is concerned with reconstructing 'the acts, operations, and productions in which the self-consciousness of humanity is constituted', and 'it attains to subjectivity only by the long detour of the signs that subjectivity has produced from itself in the works of culture . . . – the detour through the texts of a culture in which the self is documented' (pp. 473f). Each subject must lose and retrieve itself by interpreting its cultural expressions, and a theory of subject formation therefore has to use the same avenue, that is, via cultural analysis. All understanding of subjectivity is a combination of self-understanding and interpretation of others, or of the Other. All self-reflection is mediated by texts. By narrating itself in the works, texts and discourses of symbolic modes, the subject reconstructs itself in intelligible form. Subjective experience becomes meaningful when it can be narrated or 'emplotted' – given a temporal structure with direction, beginning and end.[9] We develop subjectivity by investing our selves with meaning, and we begin to understand who we are by creating biographies, that is, narrative life (hi)stories. Subjectivity is related to culture and communication through reflexivity – the competence for self-thematizing communicative action which formulates the identity of a subject, making it meaningful and comprehensible:

> . . . *reflection is not intuition*; or, in positive terms: reflection is the effort to recomprehend the *ego* of the *ego cogito* in the mirror of its objects, its works, and ultimately its acts. . . . A reflective philosophy is precisely the opposite of a philosophy of the immediate. The first truth – *I think, I am* – remains as abstract and empty as it is unassailable. It must be 'mediated' by representations, actions, works, institutions, and monuments which objectify it; it is in these objects, in the largest sense of the word, that the *ego* must both lose itself and find itself. We can say that a philosophy of reflection is not a philosophy of consciousness if, by consciousness, we mean immediate self-consciousness. . . . The concept of appropriation signifies that the original situation from which reflection proceeds is 'forgetfulness'; I am lost, 'astray' among the objects of the world, separated from the center of my own existence, just as I am separated from others and the enemy of all. Whatever may be the secret of this separation, this *diaspora*, it signifies that I do not originally possess that which I am. . . . This is why reflection is a task – an *Aufgabe* – the task of equating my concrete experience with the affirmation: *I am*. . . . We can now say: the positing of the self is not a given, it is a *task . . . reflection is the appropriation of our effort to exist and our desire to be by means of works which testify to this effort and this desire*. (Ricoeur 1969/1974, p. 327ff)

---

[9] Ricoeur (1983–5/1984-8) shows how historical narratives and fictional literature create temporal structures by 'emplotment'. Cf. Ricoeur (1965/1970, pp. 514ff; 1975/1986), Burgos (1988), Madison (1988, pp. 92ff, 98f, 164, 183f), Vigsø (1993, pp. 50ff) or Kristensson-Uggla (1994). Ricoeur (1981, pp. 197ff) and Madison (1988, p. 97) think of meaningful action as a text.

That all knowledge and self-knowledge is symbolically mediated does not imply that all *is* language. Not even the intersubjective world can be reduced to nothing but symbolic games. The subject is not an effect created by language. So called 'shifters' in language are clues to subjectivity, since words like 'I', 'you', 'here', 'now' and 'that' are only meaningful in relation to the interacting subjects who use them. Language offers to us the word 'I' as an empty sign that is given semantic meaning only in its use by real, living subjects:

> . . . the expression *I* as little creates the postulate *I* as the demonstrative pronoun *this* creates the spectacle of this world toward which the deictic indicator points. The subject posits itself, just as the world shows itself. . . . Language is no more a foundation than it is an object; it is mediation; it is the *medium*, the 'milieu', in which and through which the subject posits himself and the world shows itself. (Ricoeur 1969/1974, p. 256)

> Nothing could be more dangerous, in fact, than to extrapolate the conclusions of a semiology and to say: everything is sign, everything is language. (p. 265)

> We can retain . . . the statement that the unconscious is structured like a language; but the word 'like' must receive no less emphasis than the word 'language.' . . . The mechanisms of the unconscious are not so much particular linguistic phenomena as they are paralinguistic distortions of ordinary language. (Ricoeur 1965/1970, p. 404)

Kristeva also warns against 'stressing the inherence of language in the human state, by overestimating the subject's having been the slave of language since before his birth' (1980/1982, pp. 62f). Jean Laplanche (1987/1989) likewise criticizes Jacques Lacan and others for tending to reduce the subject to a linguistic illusion, reifying symbolic orders and forgetting that they always depend on non-symbolic, non-verbal and non-linguistic forces (inner, unconscious drives and external materialities). Historically, there are pre-verbal stages in the infancy of each individual, and structurally, all symbolic modes rely on a drive-related substrate. Laplanche (1987/1989), Frank (1983/1989, 1988 and 1991) and Taylor (1989) all argue that there is a kind of pre-symbolic presence in the world, a primary, perceptive and non-verbal bodily consciousness long before any languages are learned. If no such pre-symbolic self-awareness existed, it would be impossible to recognize oneself in words or mirrors. How could anyone know that it is oneself that a mirror-image or the word 'I' refers to, if there were not at least a rudimentary primary self-experience? How could one understand another being as an 'I' or a subject if one was not already familiar with the state of being a subject? Still, it is through symbols and interpretation that we have to pass in order to develop our individual identity as a unique, separate and singular person. What lies in the primary existence of subjectivity, as a general potential for self-awareness in relation to the objective world, is precisely this task rather than a fully achieved and unitary self-identity. The need and potential for subjectivity may come before language, but its realization and full development depends on the use of symbols in social confrontations with other subjects. Neither intersubjectivity nor subjectivity can be put 'first' (onto- or genealogically). They must exist together: without the intersubjective confrontations of plural subjects and symbolic texts no subject can exist, but the reverse is also true – there can be no social or cultural intersubjectivity without subjects. They are mutually dependent, and the one cannot be reduced to the other, as little as any of them can replace or be reduced to the objective world of external reality.

Subjects and symbols are distinct but interconnected spheres. The one can only be studied through the other, but their connections are mediated in many steps. Kristeva (1990), for example, relates the fluid openness of some novels to that psychodynamic openness of adolescence which has already been discussed above. She therefore speaks of an adolescent literature. But such structural homologies should not be reduced to oversimple causal equations. It may, but need not, be the most psychologically 'open' individuals who make or prefer the most 'open' works. An open-minded person will perhaps create and like open-ended texts better than a very rigid one. But it might conversely turn out that a particularly flexible person instead needs and searches for sociocultural stability and strict traditions, while a certain inner rigidity might foster needs for opening avantgarde experiments with forms and styles.[10] Cultural phenomena are certainly related to subject-structures, but their social and aesthetic determinations force us to reconstruct such interdependencies with the utmost care for the mediations and contexts involved in each concrete case.

Specific uses of texts offer a set of different entrances for the subject. A young woman may, for example, relate her subjectivity to a certain pop tune through many different types of identification. First, she can identify with various figures in the song lyrics, marked by shifters like 'I'/'we', you or 'she'/'he'/'they'. A text containing an 'I', a 'you' and a 'she' may offer a range of complementary potential subject-positions for identification processes in its reading. Secondly, she can relate to the (explicit or implicit) narrator in the text, either positively through identification or negatively as its (listening) other in a dialogic communication act. Thirdly, there is the origin of the singing in either the voice, the media-constructed artist image (persona) or the (real or assumed) personal identity of the singer. Fourthly, identification can be with or against the origin of the song in producer, composer and/or author, and then again as artistic positions and/ or as psychological individuals. A fifth possibility is to identify with the real or assumed audience of the performance, or with a dispersed community of fans. These various options may be combined in complicated ways, and there are strong interferences between them, as can be seen in careful interpretations of such contextually situated texts, where there are always fascinating transferences between, for example, the 'I' of the lyrics, the singer's voice and persona, and the collective author of the band/composer/ writer behind her or him. This gives rise to interwoven networks of

[10] Cf. Bakhtin (1981), Kristeva (1974/1984), Eco (1979) and Boëthius (1992/1995).

contemporaneous identification processes, with transferences and counter-transferences running between all participants in such communicative processes. This is all the more true for ensembles of works (stars, styles, genres, etc.), giving rise to rich possibilities of analysing the subjective dimensions of each cultural phenomenon.

With Richards (1989, p. 2), a *self* can be defined as 'the psychic totality of an individual', that is, a subject, of which 'the object of self-awareness', or self-image, is only one part.[11] The germ of subjectivity is born with the germ of intersubjective sociality, but the development of all identities, including the most personal, inner or psychological ones, takes shape through intersubjective acts, and can only appear to us in communicative–symbolic form. Subjectivity is *identity* of one particular kind: inner, personal and individual. Identity, as originating in the Latin *idem* (the same), indicates some sort of permanence and continuity that is crucial to being a subject but also applies to certain collective (intersubjective) unities which are furnished with self-awareness and an ability to develop and learn. A series of interlocking concepts have already been used here to separate various types of identity: individual and collective, internal and external, subjective and objective, psychic and social. Their mutual relations are extremely complicated. For example, an individual has both a body and a mind, and both have psychic as well as social aspects. The result is a multidimensional model of identity, even before it is filled with any specific content related to dimensions like gender, age, ethnicity or class.

If identity implies that something is identical or rather similar to something else, there must be two fundamental aspects of it: time and space. On one hand, identity is temporal continuity. The identity of an individual or a group is something that can be recognized in them for a longer period, as a somewhat stable characteristic. But there is also a spatial aspect: personal identities bind various parts of the individual together through structural patterns of consistency, and collective ident-ities concern similarities between people as something they share though they are separate.

It is important not to conceive of identity too narrowly. First, if identity is understood too strictly, it completely disappears. Nothing is *exactly* the *same* as something *else*. We have to accept more vague criteria of family likeness as either approximate similarity or partial identity (which is in fact much the same thing). As for individual or subjective identity, I am never totally identical with the one I was a year ago, but we might be pretty similar, or there are some important aspects of me that remain fairly constant over time and between the various spheres and contexts in which I live. As for collective or social identity, two persons are never totally identical, but they may have sufficiently much in common in some aspect to be found to share an identity.

---

[11] George H. Mead (1934) contrasts the 'I' as an acting and thinking subject or consciousness to the 'me' as its self-image or self-consciousness.

Neither should identity be reduced to (for example) only the social or only the psychic aspect. *Collective* or *social identity* concerns groups, positions and patterns of norms and interpersonal relations within society, while *individual* or *subjective identity* is inner subjectivity with both mental and bodily aspects. A third identity form can be named *cultural identity*, constituted by meaningful symbols and texts. Subjective and social identities can only be seen and formulated through cultural identities, since all communication depends on symbolic formulations. Just as individuals shape their personal and inner identities or selves through self-thematizing texts, so groups, subcultures or other communities share texts to create collective identities, which can be read as narratives about these constructed communities. This third level is not simply an effect of (one or both of) the others.

The process of formulating or symbolizing identity positions is not completely transparent. It obeys certain generic codes and rules which both enable and distort. Conceiving identity in a symbolic mode involves a distanciation from it: the identity becomes to a certain extent reified, objectivized and separate, whereas in actual social life it might be much more fluid and interactive. Without any such distanciation, however, it cannot even be experienced as an identity. Any identity formula also has to follow some more specific genre rules which delimit what it is possible to contain. Expressing identity in words gives rise to narratives, stories which imply a beginning and an end, even where real social or subjective identities are unfinished and open-ended. But there is no telling of identity without such symbolic codes, so, again, symbolization simultaneously enables and restricts identity formation.

Each subject elaborates and occupies several different but interlocking identities which are often deeply split and contradictory.[12] An individual's identity is what connects her life-course through the double mechanisms that connect her to some or all others while distinguishing her from somebody or everyone else. Identities express subject-positions in relation to the different 'other', created by processes of identification and discrimination:

> . . . we find in consciousness itself a fundamental hostility towards every other consciousness; the subject can be posed only in being opposed – he sets himself up as the essential, as opposed to the other, the inessential, the object. But the other consciousness, the other ego, sets up a reciprocal claim. (de Beauvoir 1949/ 1988, p. 17)

Neither individuals nor collectives are homogeneous units. They are split in various aspects of identity, of which some are unconscious. Identities are not only plural, split and fragmented, but also fluid and dynamic, in spite of the constancy that defines them. The aspects that remain the same and

[12] Cf. Richards (1989), Rutherford (1990), Adams et al. (1992, pp. 1, 123 and 138ff).

make it possible to discern an identity as such are always mingled with aspects that develop continously. These processes may be so intense and extensive that virtually all the characteristics of a subject or community are changed. As with family likeness in general, what holds an identity together may be only an unbroken chain of events and experiences which mediate between one state or another, but where the start otherwise has nothing in common with the end-point, except for the general status of being a subject (or a collective agent consisting of joint subjects).

Haraway (1989) problematizes the double distinction that traditionally defines subjects in relation to something other, non-subjective. One dichotomy is between humans and animals, the other between humans and machines. Genetic engineering, artificial intelligence and cyborgs in science fiction and in real science have problematized them both, but in contradictory ways. Questioning the difference between subjects and animals underlines the biological, bodily similarities that anchor us in nature. Blurring the line between subjects and machines instead empha-sizes mind functions and considers us as cultural constructions or texts. That both these borders are today scrutinized may imply a useful human reflexivity, but the tensions between the two make it hard to believe that they should or could ever be completely erased. Subjects are both animals and machines, nature and culture, bodies and minds, tools and actors: their specificity is precisely to be both at the same time – which also makes them unique. Reducing them to either of these sides means forgetting this defining inner tension. Only human beings can be made answerable to both animals, plants and machines, which is why they as responsible, self-reflecting subjects are organisms, creatures and even a kind of machines, but yet more than that.

Identity work and identity orders

Subjects are formed in productive processes of *socialization* and practices of *identity work*, shaping the subjective identity of each individual. It is interactions in society that develop the individualities of human beings. Socialization is an intersubjective process of learning and impression, by which human infants are made into fully social beings as well as mature individual subjects and where the subjectivity-germ of a physical individual is developed into the adult subjectivity of a social and psychological person. Its primary phase appears in the close interaction between the child and its parents, within the family, while secondary socialization includes a wide range of other institutions, like the educational system. The process never ends – it continues through all phases of life and engages all possible areas of activity. On one hand, it gradually introduces the individual into various sets of intersubjective and societal relations through successive patterns of interaction and identification. On the other hand, it also leads to a stepwise separation from the mother and the parental family, and to an individuation where a unique, synthesizing individuality and continuous self-autonomy is attained. This dialectical process of separation–individuation from carepersons and relating–integration into society characterizes all identity formation: it is simultaneously a socialization into social positions as well as an individuation into adult identity and a separation into autonomy. And the socialization process is life-long, even though it takes particularly long steps in certain phases, of which early childhood and adolescence are two of the most important.[13]

Socialization has both enabling and repressive sides, just as society and intersubjective sociality have. It develops individual capabilities for inter-action, but also enforces social norms and rules, of which some are highly problematic or even unjust, oppressive and destructive. Some critical theorists have tended to base their social criticism in a nature/culture polarity, in which polarities like body/mind and individual/society have been collapsed. There are tendencies by, for instance, Wilhelm Reich, Herbert Marcuse and Oskar Negt to 'anthropologize' social resistance by reducing it to a supposed 'emancipatory minimum' as the natural basis or limit to all oppression. It is important to remember that the capability of individual resistance to collective and institutional socializing powers is also historically and communicatively developed, even though it might make use of bodily and biological resources. Socialization and identity work produces subjects in both senses of the word: subjected to dominating rules but also, as individual agencies, capable of reflecting on and opposing these rules.[14]

If cultural praxis is the process whereby interacting subjects form texts, then identity work is the process whereby social and cultural practices form subjects through manifold learning-processes where competences are achieved and experiential traces are deposited in the individual mind–body. Such learning relates to all the worlds we inhabit: nature, society, symbols and selves. We learn facts and modes of thought, norms and relations, genre-rules and symbolization, expressivity and reflexivity.

Identity formation is a work done by the subject in co-operation with other subjects (parents, teachers, friends and fellow-beings). Identity itself is therefore also a work, just as the art work is the product of creative practices. But unlike many art works, identities are not in any way completed or closed products. Their intrinsic openness implies not only that their meanings can always be reinterpreted in new ways, but also that their very materiality and form-relations are never finished. In spite of their partial fixity, identities can and do change continuously. They are

[13] Cf. Mahler et al. (1975) and Chodorow (1989) on individuation, separation and relation; Blos (1962) and Kaplan (1984) on adolescence as a second individuation phase; Lorenzer (1972), Ziehe (1975) and Ziehe and Stubenrauch (1982) on identity work; Marx (1858/1986), Mead (1934) and Habermas (1988/1992) on the necessary interplay between individuation and socialization; Bakhtin (1963/1984) and Ricoeur (1990/1992) on how the inner human being only appears in the dialogic interchanges with other beings.

[14] Apel and Heidorn (1977) criticize Negt on similar grounds. Cf. also Ricoeur: 'Critique is also a tradition' (1981, p. 99).

actions and processes as much as they are products or works. This is true both of the individual or inner identities of subjectivity, and of the collective or social identities of groups and communities. Identity work is thus production only in a wide sense of the word: it is no strategic or goal-oriented labour, but a creative, communicative praxis. Only death finishes the identity work of a human life, after which the reinterpretation process of what this particular identity means becomes more similar to that of artistic works. A living subject is in this respect more like a living city than a painting: it is an unfinished product whose production is a continuous work and which therefore can only be provisionally 'frozen' in an instant and regarded as a temporary totality. In daily interaction we often reify our own and other people's identities into delimited wholes with a certain inertia, continuity and consistency. We search our identity, and even sometimes think we find it. But we cannot escape having to look for it again, as we and our surrounding others develop further. Like the dynamic city, identity is not a fixed thing but an unfinished construction where the old and the new coexist side by side in any identity, where experiences and memories are accumulated, and where goal-oriented projects are carried out while sudden steps forward or backward often surprise us (Benjamin 1983). To become adult is never to complete one's identity work and become a finished person, even though that is what people often may believe until they learn differently the hard way. Late modernity has generally demystified adulthood and identity by making it more obvious that they both are open works under construction rather than given by nature or finished by schooling. Since this is in fact true also of many material and cultural works (like cities, genres or, to some extent, theatre plays), it seems useful to continue discussing subject formation as identity work, bearing in mind both the metaphoric character of the expression and the communicative, non-instrumental character of the work involved.

Identity work flows in dialectical movements of intense *progression* of creative acquisition of new competences and temporary *regression* to earlier positions. The psychoanalytical concept of regression has three aspects.

> Applied to a psychical process having a determinate course or evolution, 'regression' means a return from a point already reached to an earlier one. *Topographically* speaking, regression occurs, according to Freud, along a series of psychical systems through which excitation normally runs in a set direction. In *temporal* terms, regression implies the existence of a genetic succession and denotes the subject's reversion to past phases of his development . . . .. In the *formal* sense, regression means the transition to modes of expression that are on a lower level as regards complexity, structure and differentiation. (Laplanche and Pontalis 1967/1988, pp. 38f)[15]

Topographical regression activates the unconscious psychical system in dreams, hallucination and memories. In temporal regresssion, subjects

---

[15] Cf. also Ricoeur (1965/1970, pp. 91, 105 and 440ff).

return to former positions concerning object relations, libido or ego development. Formal regression is a transition to those primary processes that belong to the id and the little infant, a destructuration of those differentiated identity forms that have been created by ego development. The three are not separate phenomena but aspects of the same return to an earlier achieved but then abandoned position.

Options for regression are offered in cultural practices, but of various kinds, depending on the depth to which it reaches. The longest step back and down is to the early pre-symbolic stadium and depth-level that with Lacan may be named the 'real', experienced only indirectly as an ultimate bodily limit and basis for human life. The following level of regression goes back to the pre-verbal and pre-narcissistic impulses of the id, touched again in 'semiotic' (Kristeva) moments of merging, *jouissant* involvement. The next level is the imaginary order of mirroring play where the ego finds its first pleasures in re-enactments of primary separation. Then comes the long series of successive development phases through Oedipal conflicts and adolescence up to adulthood. All these positions or options for momentary regression appear in contrast to a symbolic order constituted by society.

However, regression is not pathological if it does not become compulsory or permanent. An interplay between progression and regression is in fact necessary to creative learning and life. Regression, therefore, mostly implies no dysfunctional aberration into a childish past that should have been abandoned long since, but often rather a revitalization of the subject by a reconnection to deeply seated forms of experience which have normally been succeeded by other modes in ordinary adult life but have not completely disappeared.

These concepts are controversial, in their implication of a specific linear direction of subject development and a problematic normativity in evaluation of ways of functioning. It is certainly tempting to think of progression as a victory and regression as a defeat, and in the very thought of subject formation as a development with early and late phases lies an automatic normativity: progression becomes the norm while regressions are deemed to become deplorable deviations. A critical deconstruction of such thinking is useful, in order to avoid an over-emphasis on adaption and integration, but it should not make it impossible to speak about subjective processes as having a specific direction, organized by memory and learning. Progression, the partly irreversible development of identity, preserves traces of its past in memories, competences and psychological deep structures. The ability to use a wider mental register therefore belongs to progression itself: a mature individual retains the capability to play and temporarily abandon herself in bodily *jouissance*.

The past always remains within us, with paradoxical results. On one hand, it gives an irreversible direction to both individual and collective history – a time arrow that continuously adds new experiences and competences to the old ones. On the other hand, it also means that we have access to the past, which can be temporarily 'revisited' (as concerns contents) through the recalling of memories or (as concerns psychical modes of functioning) through moments of regression. We pass through events, learning processes and socialization stages which cannot be erased or turned around, and our subjectivity is to some extent an ordered structure, even if it also is open to the flux of sudden or continuous change. We should, however, avoid totalizing this partial linearity, and recognize that it does not encompass all of subjectivity. In some aspects, we shift permanently between different modes of functioning and experiencing which cannot be classified as higher or lower, adult or childlike. And even though some capacities are developed through learning processes, it is mostly quite normal – even necessary and productive – to keep earlier stages and deeper psychical levels open and accessible instead of closing them off. To be adult is then to be creative enough to dare to use this whole spectrum of levels. The entrance to the symbolic order of language is to some extent irreversible, while it is also true that the pre-verbal inner currents of 'semioticity' still flow as a vitalizing force to keep language-use creative.[16] The past history lives on in the present, in innumerable ways, giving it direction, richness and meaning.

' "Regression" and "progression" would be not so much two diametrically opposed processes as two aspects of the same creativity . . . "regressive progression" ' (Ricoeur 1969/1974, p. 141). Kris (1952) introduced the influential concept of 'regression in the service of the ego', which, in spite of its functionalistic–rationalistic bias, catches something of the same interdependence of the two sides.[17] To take the unconscious seriously is to understand the subject as split and multi-layered, so that older and newer strata coexist. But if identity work and cultural creativity demand a delicate balance of progressive and regressive moves, of controlling, distancing differentiation and opening, merging dissolution, the two sides do not disappear in one single movement: they are mixed and mediated, but can still be analytically separated as two different processes, just as id and ego or primary and secondary processes mix but still are different.

The productive interplay of progression and regression is particularly obvious in adolescence, sometimes seen as a 'second birth' (Blos 1962). Actually, it is more of a 'fifth birth', after conception, delivery and the two-step entrance into the symbolic order from the partial separation from the mother and acquisition of language (around the age of one year) up to the resolution of the Oedipal crisis a couple of years later. These series of 'births' are intense phases of identity development where crucial and in principle irreversible steps are taken. All of them contain moments of repetition and regressions to the earlier ones, but in new conditions which make each such transition different. It is true that adolescence repeats

[16] Cf. Langer, Lorenzer and Kristeva as discussed in Chapter 4 above.
[17] Cf. also Ricoeur (1965/1970, pp. 91ff, 161, 175f, 440ff, 491ff, 522 and 539), Lorenzer (1972), Kristeva (1974/1984), Ziehe (1975 and 1991) and Ziehe and Stubenrauch (1982).

some early childhood conflicts in a new setting, but it also takes some important new steps that have been too little studied by psychoanalysts.[18]

In education and pedagogy, progression and regression interests coexist (Ziehe and Stubenrauch 1982). Pedagogic progression is to learn new things, transgress one's limits and meet the strange or foreign, while regression includes consolidating and feeling safe in what has already been achieved. If progression interests dominate, one is chiefly afraid of standing still, feeling suffocated and becoming stuck in introversion. If regression interests dominate, one is primarily scared of being hurt, exposed or left alone with responsibilities that are too heavy to carry. One-sided regression is as devastating as progression running wild, in pedagogy as in the psyche. School always contains both sides: the forward march through books and performance-demands is mixed with the sometimes infantilizing routines and rituals. Dominant educational ideologies tend to forget the needs for partial regressions, which are therefore relegated into the hidden curriculum of the educational unconscious, together with the reproduction of class, gender, ethnicity and other power structures, also made invisible by most idealizing and legitimizing educational programmes. Informal and different youth cultural learning processes outside of school often mix progression and regression interests in more dynamic ways. In music-making or media-use, people both learn new things, establish what they already are and re-enact earlier states of mind, by encountering and exploring new texts and by letting loose and forgetting oneself in experiencing the familiar.[19]

In each historical and societal context there are on all levels of identity specific patterns and rules of varying tenacity. These organizing principles form sets of dominating *identity orders*, such as those of age, gender, ethnicity or class. They are often named 'systems', but in contrast to the market and state systems, such identity orders (like the structure of language) are not differentiated out of the lifeworld, in which they instead lie deeply embedded. If systems are autonomously self-reproducing structures, 'identity orders' is a better term for these rule-bound models for how people form identities in their mutual, everyday and communicative production of relations and meaning.

Identity orders will exist on all levels (social, cultural, subjective) and in several dimensions (age, gender, ethnicity, class, etc.), as long as these

[18] Erdheim (1982) and Wirth (1984) emphasize the innovative potentials of adolescence, which is not only a rehearsal of the early childhood constitution of subjective identity. Gilligan et al. (1990) criticize the traditionally masculinist view of adolescence.

[19] These subjective aspects could be added to the social ones discussed in Willis's (1978) analysis of bike-boys and hippies. The bike-boys' striving for physical self-control and musical conservatism might express not only a working-class habitus but also a regression-oriented security principle, balanced by the attachment anxiety that leads to progression-oriented bodily mobility. The hippies' expansion of the senses and musical openness not only reproduces middle-class norms but also exemplifies how progression interests of the risk principle are counteracted by a separation anxiety which makes them search for warmth and closeness in drugs and relations (regression interests).

levels and directions are of any importance for subjectivity. Since sex and
gender are crucial to human life, they are always invested with important
norms and meanings, and therefore also organized by intersubjective
patterns of some firmness. Various versions of masculinity and femininity
are possible positions open to subjects within the gender order. Its social
facet concerns gender norms, roles and relations, its cultural aspect gender
images and discourses, and the psychological side is about gendered inner
subjectivity. There are always power relations in these identity orders, but
they need not necessarily be simple one-dimensional hierarchies of
domination. The gender order may involve more or less mutuality, in that
gendered power structures may be more or less reciprocally balanced. How
a society organizes its identity orders is an empirical issue, and the degree
of dominance in these orders varies.[20]

Subjective identities are subject formations – the individual selves or
subjects made up of bodies and minds and with conscious and unconscious
elements. Social identities concern how people in real interaction form
patterns and rules for relations and self-awareness. These 'roles' are not as
in a theatre superficial fake identities that real people can hide behind, but
rather prescribed or conventionalized positions for human intercourse.
They are not rigid masks that can easily be donned or abandoned, but,
rather, fluid habits that are laboriously learned, upheld and developed
through various more or less institutionalized practices. Cultural identities
are symbolic positions composed by textual (verbal, visual or aural)
identity images. They are needed because neither the social nor the
psychological aspects are in themselves observable. Only through symbolic
forms can we show who we are and who we want to be, consciously or
unconsciously. Cultural identities thus mediate between the external and
the internal worlds, but also possess their own logic as a symbolic order.

These aspects of identity are interconnected but seldom completely
coincident. People do not totally identify with their social or cultural
position, and this in turn makes them, on one hand, suffer from frustration
and lack and, on the other hand, capable of transforming themselves on
the basis of an inner motivation for change.

A play of affinity and difference lies behind all identities. Subjects and
communities are formed by belongings and separations, identities by

---

[20] Gemzöe et al. (1989) argue against defining the gender order as a priori misogynistic,
patriarchal and/or androcentric. Cf. Elliott (1992), Fraser (1992b) and Lash and Friedman
(1992) for critiques of Lacan's (1966/1977) problematic universalization of our historically
determined gender order as 'phallocentric'. If each symbolic order must be phallocentric, and
if the phallus has anything whatsoever to do with the male, male dominance cannot be
transgressed. Lacan wavers between either interpreting the biological penis as a symbol of the
phallus of social power, or conversely regarding the phallus of the symbolic order as a signifier
for the male penis. In the first version, the phallus in principle becomes non-gendered, and
could as well have other signifiers, e.g., the female breast – but then why call it 'phallus' at all?
The latter version leads to biologism by letting physical gender cement and legitimate the
existing androcentric order.

contrastive mirrorings against the Other – that which is not I or we. In symbolic interactionism, George Herbert Mead (1934) defines 'the generalized other' as the 'organized community or social group which gives to the individual his unity of self' (p. 154). 'Selves can only exist in definite relationships to other selves' (p. 164), and Mead distinguishes between 'I' as 'the response of the organism to the attitudes of the others' and 'me' as 'the organized set of attitudes of others which one himself assumes' (p. 175). But the concept of the Other has old philosophical roots, leading up to Hegel, Kierkegaard, Lévinas, Beauvoir and Sartre. In the ethics of Emmanuel Lévinas (1947/1987 and 1961/1979), the face of the Other is the ultimate non-reciprocal alterity that demands of each subject a total responsibility, and he sees gender as the most absolute difference (1947/ 1987, p. 84–90). These ideas were developed by Simone de Beauvoir in a forceful formulation of otherness in gender:

> Thus humanity is male and man defines woman not in herself but as relative to him; she is not regarded as an autonomous being. . . . For him she is sex – absolute sex, no less. She is defined and differentiated with reference to man and not he with reference to her; she is incidental, the inessential as opposed to the essential. He is the Subject, he is the Absolute – she is the Other. (1949/1988, p. 16)

These themes reoccur in the psychoanalytical work of Lacan and in recent feminist literature. Like the object relationists, Kristeva connects the intersubjective relation to the other with the development of the subject:

> The subject exists only inasmuch as it identifies with an ideal other who is the speaking other, the other insofar as he speaks. . . . The subject's identification with the symbolic Other, with its Ego Ideal, goes through a narcissistic absorption of the mother as object of need, an absorption that sets up the Ideal Ego. . . . The subject exists because it belongs to the Other . . . . (Kristeva 1983/ 1987, pp. 35f)

The first difference recognized by an individual subject is that between the self and its surrounding, represented by the mother. Breaking up the diffuse, boundless symbiosis of the mother/child dyad creates a primitive differentiation of I/you, self/other or subject/object which contains the germ of two important social differentiations – those of age (young/old) and for the male child also of gender. While mother and child mostly share class, ethnic and other crucial identities, they always differ in age. The age dimension – related to the experience of time passages – is therefore the deepest one in the construction of subjectivity. There appears a strong asymmetry in the adult/infant practices of feeding, protecting, etc., beside the symmetrical dialogicity which they also contain.

The second experienced difference is that of gender – if not already in the mother/boy dyad, then at least later in the Oedipal mother/father/child triangle, where the third pole of the father may be either real or imaginary. Here, a masculine position enters the process of identity formation, either directly or through the desires and ideas of the mother. This secondary

gender dimension becomes closely knit to the primary self/other difference. Age and gender tend to be dimensions appearing in most social
groups in which individuals live, not least in the family, but while ages are
continually changing, so that the young will be old in the future, it is much
harder to radically switch one's gender. Gender therefore becomes a basic
model for difference in general, for the most unavoidable difference in
human life. Gender enters into the core of subjectivity, through a
secondary reworking of the originally non-gendered subject/object differentiation. This is true both of each individual's ontogenetic development
and of the phylogenetic history of humanity, where gender orders seem to
have always existed as a permanent second or third life condition, beside
the age succession and the relations to external nature, while ethnic and
class differences have changed much more quickly.

In the formation of collective or social identities, ethnicity then becomes
of the utmost importance. As a family, clan or local community defines
itself in contradiction to others, ethnic discourses immediately appear, and
where age and gender groups live closely together, ethnic differences seem
easier to absolutize in that nobody has either to become (as in age) or to
interact closely with (as in gender) the (paradigmatically ethnic) other.
Ethnic differences, therefore, are often regrettably frozen and rigid, so
that if an old man wants to depict women or the young as totally alien, he
would use ethnic concepts like 'a foreign tribe'.

The different identity orders and self/other dimensions interplay in a
complex way. The passage through age makes clear that identities change
continually. Gender is markedly relational. Ethnicity is explicitly about
making connections that integrate individuals in communities and
traditions. Class and status stratification are most obviously connected.
Each dimension of identity puts a different aspect in focus, but all of them
actually have both dynamic, relational, identificatory and stratifying
functions.

All polarities of centre and periphery, power and resistance, First and
Other, are asymmetrical. There might be a centrifugal tendency that
produces some homgeneity in the pole of dominance, but to totalize the
marginalized Other is always a great mistake. This often happens, as when
several differing dominated positions are lumped together under one single
notion or when identity dichotomies are constructed as binary lists of traits
said to characterize the two poles in question (young/old, male/female,
black/white, high/low, etc.). Often one such polarity is supposed to be the
most important one, thus hiding the others. This leads to much confusion.
Oppositional, alternative or rebellious traits of some cultural form (such as
some rock music) are sometimes classified as (late or post)modern in
contrast to earlier traditions, sometimes inversely designated as pre-
capitalist remnants of an older, alternative carnival culture, sometimes
interpreted as based in black, African roots in contrast to a white,
European cultural sphere, sometimes regarded as deriving from working-
class culture, sometimes traced back to youthfulness or to a repressed

femininity. Most such dualisms contain a grain of truth, but they can obviously not all at once and separately offer exhaustive explanations for a certain phenomenon.

Important traits distinguish different Others from each other. To accept the logic of power and formulate its Other as unitary is to violate the specificity of this Other. All identity orders are dimensions in which power is effective, but what is dominated along one dimension need not be identical with what is dominated along another one. It is also interesting to discuss why certain parallels between such different identity dimensions exist. The dominance relations as such may give rise to certain experiences and identity traits, so that youths, women, workers, immigrants, precisely by being relatively marginalized in society, share these characteristics and competences.[21] The fact that some groups are not allowed to take part in dominating legitimate culture may invest them with other experiences of concrete work and communicative action instead of abstract profit-orientation and goal-rationality. This may induce parallels between different identity orders and different Others, but it would be wrong to turn any of them into the primary Other and define these shared traits as deriving from one specific identity order rather than from power relations as such. It would also be as wrong to see women, blacks, etc., as just 'Other', that is, to reduce them to their position in relation to power structures. All identities have aspects of power but can never be reduced only to these.

The transient age of youth

Among the ages of a life-course, youth seems to be the one which in our society and culture is most riddled with ambivalences. Like all other categories, youth is no undifferentiated unity, but intersected by all the other identity orders and filled contradictions. Still, there are things that young people have in common, related to their specific age-position in between childhood and adulthood, and reinforced by a series of societal institutions (family, school, leisure provisions, law, labour-market, cultural industries and mass media) which keeps them within this category of youth.

The fact that all people pass through some sort of a youth stage before they become and count as adult makes youth a very flexible category. It is inhabited by everyone for a span of time, and therefore by different individuals in each moment, in a succession of different generations that continuously add new shades to the meaning of youth.

Actually, age and generation are not one but two identity orders, although both are temporally defined and closely related to each other. In a way, they are each other's opposite, since among all the main identity orders, an age is the only one nobody can belong to for long, while a

---

[21] Cf. Hegel's master/slave dialectics, which Marx elaborated for class relations and Reeder (1990) for the gender interplay.

generation is the one which each person is necessarily tied to forever. Everyone has to climb continually up the age ladder, but it is virtually impossible to move between generations.

Since everyone can at least for some time be young, youth implies a certain equality. Youth is, however, unevenly distributed and differently shaped among genders, classes and ethnicities. Also, a certain social power is exercised over young people as such, which provokes the development of resistance in youth culture. While childhood is sometimes conceived of as a semi-autonomous state in itself (though totally dependent on adult care-takers), youth is mostly defined as clearly subsumed under adulthood, as in the very term 'adolescence': the young are in the state of becoming-adult, they are not yet fully grown up citizens, but only on their way to reaching maturity. Society does not offer adolescents full human rights and responsibilities, but forces them to prepare for adult life in particular institutions, foremost schools, organized according to dominating social norms. These patterns of domination induce characteristic germs of resistance which, however, develop very differently depending both on the spatio-temporal conditions and on the series of other identity orders in which young people are also positioned.

The flexibility and mobility of youth lie deeply in modern society. Youth is in most epochs and classes a rapidly changing life phase and a category that is particularly sensitive to social transformations. This does not make all teenagers more radical or even flexible, politically, socially or even stylistically. Many of them in fact try to counter the instability of youth and modernity with efforts to erect rigid and stable walls around identity constructs which they clutch tightly. They can be reactionary convention-alists, but it is no coincidence that they form radical avantgardes of many kinds in a more visible way than most other age-groups. Even then, they continue to live in a state of inner and outer flux, of rapid transformations not only of the kind that we all experience in modern times and other periods of transition, but also in their very bodies and minds as well as in their social conditions, where there is, in spite of all boredom and routinization, a particular density of changes in activities and status, through the classes and stages of school as well as in the succession of steps into work and the formation of a new family.

The definition of youth is necessarily polydimensional. It is biologically delimited as a stage in the physical growth of the body, starting with sexual maturation in puberty and finishing with all physical functions in place. This objective aspect of youth closely interacts with the subjective one of adolescence as a phase of psychological development, a phase marked by identity work through temporary regressions in the service of a secondary individuation and separation from one's family of origin. Neither of these two aspects is totally autonomous, but they interact with a series of social, political–juridical and economic demarcations, often organized through rites of passage associated with rights and duties acquired at specific chronological ages defined by each society. These social definitions of youth as an age category can then again finally be connected and contrasted with youthfulness as a set of cultural or practices of (life)style-production. These physical, psychological, social and cultural determinations of youth overlap and interact, but they are not identical, either in meaning, function or extension. While physical youth may last for some teenage years, late modern psychological youth is often stretched out far longer. While some try to adopt an adult lifestyle before even moving out from the parents' home or getting a job, others may be culturally youthful long after having become socially adult, by continuing to adhere to youth-cultural tastes while living and working as a grown-up. All this makes it impossible to pinpoint one definition of youth as universally valid, or even as valid in a certain time and group.[22]

This confusion need not force us to abandon the concept as illusory, only to recognize and separate its interacting dimensions. Youth exists as a discursive formation as well as a social category, related to stages of mind–body development. The widespread idea that youth emerged in high modernity is false. In some ways it has always existed, but modernity has led to the growth of a series of institutions that frame and redefine youth in a generalized way – particularly schools, cultural industries and voluntary organizations. This gradual process was partly stratified, so that different groups had more or less of a youth period in different phases.[23]

Social modernization affects young people particularly intensely, since they lack the well-worn adult habits and routines and are not as strictly positioned in the world of family and school as are smaller children. The many self-chosen (sub)cultural styles and life forms among young people can be read as a tentative experimentation with new norms, relations and lifestyles in response not only to adolescence but also to modernization. Young people move rapidly between family, school and public spaces, and they are eager to explore alternative ideals and norms found in communication through media or peers. Their raids into the public arena are balanced by a fierce protection of their private territories, the agents of which are the peer group as well as the individual, in individuating preparation for adult personal autonomy.

The relation between childhood, youth and adulthood changes in complex ways. While identities have always been reworked during youth, in the passage from childhood to adult maturity, late modernity has made identities more open and insecure also for many grown-ups, raising the demands for continuous identity development, with stylistic forms as an important tool. Therefore, young people's activities and qualifications for flexibility have become highly estimated competences, increasing the cultural status of youth, while the social power of young people has remained weak.

[22] Cf. Blos (1962), Erikson (1968), Kaplan (1984), Zinnecker (1985) and Ziehe (1991).
[23] Cf. Gillis (1981 and 1993), Nitschke (1985) and Mitterauer (1986/1992 and 1992). Even the term 'teenager' is in fact much older than is often believed – its Swedish counterpart goes back at least to the early nineteenth century (Hellquist 1922/1989, p. 1203).

There are interesting interferences between youth and modernity.[24] Real interrelations exist in the fact that youth is unusually open to the modern, and modernity particularly concerned with the young. But there are also influential imaginary vibrations between them. Dynamic modernity resonates with transient and transgressive youth in recurrent metaphoric discourses that connect them. Whatever the real modernity of youth and youthfulness of modernity may be, strong ideas tend to forge their union. While childhood is reminiscent of the lost innocence of pre-modernity, youth, with its flexibility and fast changes, has often become a metaphorical symbol for modernity and the new, ambivalently regarded as either an ideal or a threat. As the intensified and secondary modernization of late modernity makes modernization itself problematic, youth, with its more 'naïve' thrust towards continuous change, is increasingly seen as an innocent utopia. The recurrent nostalgias for the 1950s, 1960s, 1970s and 1980s seem to long back to the times not of pre-modernity but of an unproblematized modernity, while childhood sometimes has become more threatening in its stubborn otherness. And the recurrent pastiche reconstructions of the past seem to contain a certain ambiguity: they promise a release from the present quest for distanced reflexivity, but at the same time they increase this same ironic self-distance. The contradiction between naïve self-abandonment and distancing reflexivity seems to have become a central cultural theme of late modernity, associated with images of youth as both reflexively ego-centric and self-forgettingly intense.

The whole age-identity order is generally bound to the time-dimension and therefore to temporal change, associated with the flexibility of identity-shifts. If this is so, then the age of youth is particularly temporal, transient and transgressive. Of the temporal stages of life, youth most directly points at the passage of time and the possibility to transform identities that each person experiences at least in age-shifts, however fixed all other identity aspects may be.

Great and problematic generational shifts have often been thematized as the most important effect of modernity on youth. Much youth research has found its main impetus in this question of whether young people differ from their parents or if they instead will eventually become pretty much like them. While some have argued that youth research has its legitimacy in the alleged fact that young people now completely differ from earlier generations, others have instead emphasized the continuities caused by the integration aspect of socialization. However, this debate has now partly become irrelevant, for both internal and external reasons. As the study of youth has become a more established research area, so it becomes less important to underline how different young people are – although it does seem clear that their lives are sufficiently different to motivate a study of it. And as late modernity has disclosed, through the intensified individualization and reflexivity of adult identities, generational shifts have become

[24] Cf. Fornäs (1984), Kristeva (1990), Ziehe (1991) and Drotner (1991c).

less epochal: people have got used to them and parents or teachers can more often recognize the quest for separation in youth rebellions than when older generations expected continuity.

It is certainly interesting to study whether conflicts between generations increase or decrease, and which habits and attitudes are taken over by teenagers and which are renounced. But such generational relations are only partially related to modernization. On one hand, age conflicts are as often caused by other types of change, like accidental events or reversible cyclical processes. Not all traits of the new generations may be interpreted as signalling epochal shifts – some are more related to the need for distinguishing oneself against the preceding age-group or even a reproduction of the value-patterns of the upcoming parental generation. And, on the other hand, while it is certainly true that phases of rapid modernization tend to increase the distance between age-groups, since the younger then get a very different socialization than the older had before and therefore acquire qualitatively other experiences, modern changes still also often strongly affect older generations as well, at least in certain strata of the population. A change of adult roles that makes them more similar to young ones and thus diminishes generation gaps may therefore sometimes be the result of cultural modernization, even though the opposite seems to be the more general pattern. There are good reasons to study and interpret phenomena of youth culture without always discussing if they really only apply to youth. A rich image of what youth means cannot restrict itself to what is unique to it – it is the specific combination of traits, each of which is shared with many other ages, that defines youth, rather than any exclusive essence. And it is also important to remember that age and generation are different things: what is specific to an age-group may be reproduced from generation to generation, while traits bound to a generation may follow it through its growing ages.

The dichotomy between deviant subcultures and 'ordinary mainstream youth' also has to be deconstructed and de-dramatized, as has already been argued. Youth culture is about cultural forms belonging to any young people, and if the necessary insight that the young generation is internally differentiated is fully understood, then one must also see that youth-specific styles and identities take on many shades, of which only some are clearly subcultural while the mainstream hardly exists at all, other than as an imaginary construction that legitimizes one's own position in relation to such a generalized other.

Relational gender

When young people or other ages, blacks or other ethnicities, workers or other classes are studied, their male representatives are mostly focused on, but this fact is seldom made explicit as a gender dimension. However, when women and cultural phenomena connected to females are thematized, gender is almost always seen as a crucial aspect. Women seem always to be furnished with a definite gender, while men are treated as general human beings. This creates problematic and mutually amplifying identifications of man≈human being and woman≈gender. Since research on class, ethnicity or generation has so often been focused on men, the question of women tends directly to be coupled with the fresh curiosity of gender aspects, and the fact that gender studies tend to put the differences of women in focus tends paradoxically to reinforce masculinity as a neutral norm.

Gender is a polar order with masculinity and femininity as interdependent opposites. Male and female identities are no homogeneous essences but complex and varied positions offering many possibilities for intermediate identities. The androgynous as a 'third gender' can be constructed as either non-gendered, one who avoids choosing between male or female traits, or as double-gendered, one who combines them both into a polymorphous montage. In times where the male/female polarity is more problematized, such alternative images are important as experiments staked in an ongoing struggle of renegotiation of the gender contracts.

Gender is the most explicitly relational identity order, and it is sometimes seen as a key model for the relational aspect of all identities and social relations. Only in very special circumstances (such as monasteries) do men and women live in totally separate spheres – otherwise they meet and interact in daily life, if not at work or school, then at least at home. Genders interact everywhere in society, but the intimate familial sphere is where they come closest to each other and also where they unite to produce new, gendered subjects through sexual intercourse and primary socialization. It is also normally there that the infant first experiences gender difference and obtains a gender identity, choosing between the many male, female and androgynous elements that are offered by its surroundings.

Beside friendship and peer groups, family is the most informal and non-systemic social institution. Yet, while it is deeply embedded in the core of the lifeworld, it is also framed by a set of juridical and economic rules. The modern Western family is a privileged unit of consumption as well as of the physical and psychological reproduction of subjectivity. Interacting with public spheres, it is also a place for the exercise and development of communicative rationality. In family, infants receive their first cognitive insights in the external world, which later becomes more of a matter for the educational school system. The development of norms and ethics is also importantly based in familial interaction, as is the testing of aesthetic values. The communicative aspect most cultivated in this sphere is that of subjective expressivity, where sexuality has a central function.

Gender and sexuality are closely related, as indicated by the fact that 'sex' as being male, female or hermaphrodite can imply both erotic sexuality, propagation and the biological, bodily aspect of gender. Gender is first of all a grammatical classification of objects corresponding to the two sexes plus sexlessness, but has also come to be used to denote any symbolic aspects of male/female, while sex then tends to be reduced to biological aspects. Like the word 'genus' (kind, class, order or tribe), 'gender' goes back to Greek and Sanskrit words for breeding and birth, which also turn up in concepts like generation and genre. To avoid some confusion, gender will here be used as a general term for all male/female dimensions (distinguishing between social, cultural, biological and psychological gender), while sex will be reserved for sexuality as the tense combination of erotic desire and reproduction of the species.

As usual, sociocultural and psychobiological gender is only partially coextensive: separate yet interrelated. A strong anti-essentialist discourse in feminist theory has destabilized all naturalizing ways of conceiving gender, arguing for a constructivist definition where the biology of the body tends to disappear, by being reduced to a derivative effect of a linguistic or symbolic play of signifiers that defines gender as an almost purely conventional symbolic or textual phenomenon. Others have warned against such a neostructuralist dissolution of the body and its sexuality into language and tried to find ways to retain biology in a more complex model of gender. To Jane Gallop (1989, p. 37), feminist studies have historicized motherhood, reproduction and female biology so much that biology no longer threatens to exist outside history. The insistence on the intersubjective constructedness of gender (as social and cultural) has had results, and it might be time to reformulate the tensions between inner, shared and external aspects again, avoiding any total split between body and language or sex and gender (i.e., biological and sociocultural gender). It also seems important not to reduce the psychological dimension either to sociocultural intersubjectivity or to objective biology. Instead, all the dimensions of gender are needed as separate yet interacting.

Sexuality is connected to gender, since sexuality is crucially gendered and gender is always associated with (among other things) sexuality. It is crucial to avoid essentialism here: it is an empirical question how male and female sexuality works, and it cannot be assumed that they are automatically directed at the other gender just because that seems to be what reproduction demands. The existence of homosexuality warns us not to take the man/woman relation for an evident and natural gender order. Psychoanalysis situates sexuality as a core of psychological gender identity. Sexual drives and desires are based upon partly inherited biological instincts, but not reducible to them. Early interaction with the mother (or whoever is the primary caretaker) causes a specifically human break in subject-development, through which sexual drives appear in and as a separate, psychological level rather than as purely instinctual. Laplanche (1970/1985 and 1987/1989) argues that sexuality (the drives) is uniquely human in that it 'anaclitically' 'leans on', ties to, links up to or connects on to the physiological body functions (the instincts), but simultaneously breaks with them and thus constitutes the psychological as a separate dimension. Sexual drives do not evolve from biological reproduction instincts, but are only tied to them in later, genital development of the sexual desires. All of the mental or psychic sphere of subjectivity connects to biological life-processes, but is as much rooted in fantasies, desires and symbolic patterns deriving from the inner and sociocultural world of the parents. The care for the infant transmits certain eroticized charges and meanings into the world of the child, giving rise to inner tinglings that organize the body into erogenous zones which then become crystallization points of new fantasies and desires. It is the adult care of the infant which, like a seduction in good faith, awakens it to a sexuality that is only after the fact (*nachträglich*) anaclitically connected to the physical body organs as such. The bodily functions exist in embryonic form before the psychological, but when subjective drives and desires have been developed through intersubjective transferences, they are retrospectively awarded a sexual dimension, which is in its turn for most people strongly correlated with gender relations.

The dimension of gender invites a discussion of power that connects abstract macro-political structures to the most intimate practices of everyday life. Gender identification occurs through processes of dichotomization where men and women use each other as mirroring Others to constitute themselves against and reflect their selves in. As was stated earlier, this relation is asymmetrical: in favour of maleness. A series of historical processes have put men closer to various power-centres, but power is not intrinsic to some male essence, as little as any other identity traits can be understood in such an essentialist way.

Gender identities are not innate or cultural universals, but are shaped in interaction between subjects in sociocultural settings. Women's identities cannot be reduced only to the Other of men, however much this function is an inescapable condition of life in present society. Likewise, male characteristics are mostly the result of complex socialization processes determined by much more than biological gender as such. Being goal-rational is the result of experiences in social positions where such behaviour is needed and expected, positions which men more often occupy, rather than any fundamental trait of men. Female care- and relation-orientation can likewise not be explained as an expression of an essential femininity, but is created by the positions in which female subjects are often placed.

Each construction of dichotomies where personality traits like instrumental goal- versus relation-orientation are more or less univocally classified as male or female is highly problematic and in the end normative, since men or women who do not conform to such schemata appear as abnormal. Nancy Chodorow (1979) and Carol Gilligan (1982) have constructed interesting theories of how male and female identities come to differ. In our society, female mothering in early socialization is the rule. As soon as a child experiences gender differences, boys will find it easier to separate themselves from the mother, whereas girls will have a more ambivalent relation of both separateness and belonging. This reproduces the social pattern of men being more separate, concentrating on individualistic projects, while women are more oriented towards care, relations and connectedness with others. This model is certainly useful to explain the roots of gender difference in the early mother–child dyad, but like all other binary models it can be interpreted in too definite a way. Much against its own intention to avoid biologism, it has been accused of essentialism by other feminists, who lean on French Lacanian theory.[25]

It is not quite obvious that the whole French tradition can be classified as anti-essentialist. Lacan (1966/1977) argued that women, as a result of pre-Oedipal development, are more open to the deep, pre-verbal levels of 'the real' that can be experienced in the total, orgasmic *jouissance*, outside of any conscious control by the ego, in opposition to the more partial, controlled and conventional pleasure or *plaisir* of the ego. In spite of all efforts to think gender as positions in language, Lacan and Barthes (1973/1975 and 1977), who has taken up these concepts in aesthetic theory, both share a mystifying absolutization of women as this *jouissant* Other, outside of the symbolic order and open instead to the real order of the pre-symbolic body. But neither women nor femininity can be reduced to the Other, that which resides outside of the symbolic order of dominating phallocracy. Kristeva (1974/1984 and 1980) has reworked these concepts in a more positional way, questioning the male Lacanian mystification of Woman.[26] While the male/female dichotomy resonates with those of symbolic/semiotic, *plaisir/jouissance*, separation/symbiosis, reason/emotion and language/body, they are not identical. A reduction of dimensions onto each other only reinforces prejudiced clichés and prescribes (even if critically) gender identities that are too homogeneous. Genders are not defined as either bound to the symbolic order or to semiotic *jouissance*, but rather concern how these two are experienced and connected. Female positions may offer other routes to *jouissance* or to the Other than do male ones, but ego-abandonment is no essentially female privilege. Binary logics do function in social life and cultural genres, but specific female or male identities cannot be reduced just to them.

Essentialism (whether biologistic or not) also makes it impossible to relate such polarities to other dimensions such as class or ethnicity, where similar combinations of characteristics may appear, but with different explanations. Such interdisciplinary, interdiscursive dialogues are much more fruitful if each identity order is seen in a more constructivist way, so that no property is designed as basically male (or essentially belonging to any particular position in any other identity order), only particularly

---

[25] Cf. Fahlgren (1988). Moi (1985), Harding (1986, pp. 163ff) and Lauretis (1987) also argue for a relational or positional feminism.

[26] Cf. also Lechte (1990) and Elliott (1992). Fraser thinks Kristeva is not altogether successful in this, but is stuck with a 'quasi-biologistic, essentializing identification of women's femininity with maternity' that 'dehistoricizes and psychologizes motherhood' and erects an 'essentialist stereotype of femininity' (1992b, pp. 66f). Huntington (1995, pp. 44ff) argues that though Kristeva is best among the French poststructuralists at acknowledging the agency of the 'subject in process', she still misses a 'positive dialectic of autonomy' allowing for intentionality, responsibility, learning and self-determination.

accessible to men (and/or to other categories) because of social and cultural forces of various kinds. Instead of destructive collisions between perspectives proclaiming that a certain property is essentially nothing but male, middle-class or Western–white, it will then be possible to continue dialogues where it can be shown how such multiple identity determinations interact and mutually reinforce or contradict each other, due to the position each individual occupies in the various identity dimensions in question. Instead of the unproductive debates between feminist gender perspectives, Marxist class explanations and arguments about the ultimate importance of ethnicity for the establishment of social hierarchies or cultural practices, it can then be seen how these different identity orders mix and interplay. They can only be weighed against each other in relation to clearly specified factors, while in a general sense they are basically equally important.

Like all other identity orders, gender also has aspects belonging to the outer, the shared and the inner world. Gender is, on one hand, a biological fact of innate but modifiable bodily organization. It is also institutionalized by systemic rules in market and state, developed under the pressure of social forces which codify gender as a set of interactional relations and norms in all parts of society, and chisel out how men and women relate to each other and distribute duties in everyday life. This social gender in its turn interplays with cultural gender – sets of symbols and images which signify the male and the female to different interpretive communities. And each man and woman has through complex socialization processes shaped an inner, psychological or subjective gender that connects to the objective, external world of material facts and systemic institutions as well as to the intersubjective world of social norms and cultural symbols but still is a unique subject formation emanating out of particular personal experiences and learning processes.

Traditional gender relations have been deeply problematized by modernization, leading to phases where social and cultural gender develop in asynchronic ways. Sometimes changes in the labour market or the law clash with stubborn traditions and self-images; in other phases or aspects there is instead a gap between high expectations among women for equal chances and a reality of unequal resources. In both cases, tensions and conflicts arise between (some) men and (some) women. From the 1970s, such themes have received increasing attention among anthropologists, sociologists and psychologists. Combining Chodorow's theory of gendered socialization with the modernity theories of Berman and Ziehe, Bjerrum Nielsen and Rudberg (1994) see parallels between the experience of modernity and the excessive autonomy of male identity in what they regard as the gender polarizing phase of nineteenth- and early twentieth-century modernity. The individualized bourgeois male presupposed an intimate familial sphere as his basis, that is, that women reproduced the home as a place of rest and contrast to public life and waged labour. The separation and autonomy of male identity thus presupposed the relation-orientation and dependence of women. In a new phase, signalled by the new women's movement from the 1960s onwards, women's demands for career opportunities and individual autonomy have grown, as is evident both in politics and in media images. The resultant crisis of the gender order has enforced a renegotiation of gender contracts and a restructuring of male identities as well. Gender differences change, but do not disappear, since women's autonomization develops when the back-sides of modernity have become more generally visible and when, on one hand, women can make use of the earlier male experiences in the public domain, while, on the other, they lack the support that men have had from those women who then upheld the intimate sphere of the home. Individualization processes have gradually and partially released individual identities from predefined collective categories.[27] They affect inner individuation processes (leading to the experience of oneself as a separate and unique person) in both men and women, but differently.

Empirical studies of young Western women have testified to a raised level of expectation, a widespread wish to make use of all the aspects of individual development that schools and media promise: career, pleasure, man and children. Bjerrum Nielsen and Rudberg argue that 'for the girl of today, yielding to body and love is no longer opposed to using your head', that 'sexuality is no longer shameful and taboo, and being in love and being an active individual are no longer a contradiction in terms', so that 'gender is less a matter of destiny', and 'family and career will be no longer the dominant opposites, but two aspects of the good life, just as they have been to men' (1994, pp. 62ff). Holstein-Beck (1991/1995) describes how young women dream of their future life as fulfilling a series of needs: exciting travel, good education and a glamorous career, but also a safe family, wonderful children and a perfect husband.[28] The kids may well be many and the young women plan to stay at home with them for some years, before continuing their careers. These huge wishes are revised with growing age. The large commercial investigation *Future Woman* (1991) studied the attitudes of thousands of women, of between 20 and 35 years of age, in over 26 European countries. These women showed similar tendencies, but with a larger amount of realism, not least in their relation to men, which was much more specified and problematized than among their younger Swedish sisters. They wanted their men to unite the best of both traditional masculinity and the 'new man', but if they could not find such a man, they were prepared to live alone as single mothers rather than accept second-best. While thus prepared for a mother–child family, they were filled with optimistic hope for their personal future. Achieving balance between spheres of life, controlling one's own life and having a job was self-evident: the traditional housewife was dead. And as one of the

[27] Cf. Ziehe and Stubenrauch (1982) and Ziehe (1991).

[28] That young women of today expect more of both family, sex and career is also shown by the ethnologist Åström (1986) and the psychologist Bengtsson (1991b).

main results of a large Swedish empirical study of media-use and lifestyle patterns, Reimer concludes that the years around 1990 constitute

> a time period in which the everyday life practices of men and women, especially of young men and women, are becoming more similar. Young women increasingly turn to everyday life practices traditionally associated with men. Instead of spending their time in the private sphere carrying out 'female' practices, young women are becoming increasingly visible in the public sphere. (1994, p. 204)

As for young men, many studies show a tendency towards 'feminization' of the cultural male role in ads, styles and consumption habits. Bjerrum Nielsen and Rudberg argue that 'for the boy, paternal authority tends to represent less a live reality than a vague longing', resulting in 'a new model of masculinity, which advocates the importance of coming in from the cold without becoming suffocated by cosiness' (1994, pp. 62f). In a study of Swedish and Italian magazines, Holmqvist (1990) has shown that advertisement images in the 1980s changed mostly in how men were depicted. While women were constantly shown in a traditional way as young, passive and beautiful objects, the function of men gradually evolved from an active, confident career role to a self-mirroring aesthetic body. The growing male importance of bodily looks is also confirmed in various studies of sports and of consumption: Czaplicka and Ekerwald (1986) showed that one of the largest differences in young people's consumption habits between 1977 and 1985 was that men had started to buy almost as many make-up, hair- and body-care products as women. As Åström (1990) indicates, a certain convergence between male and female identity patterns appears also as a result of this 'feminization' of masculinity. Men have become a little bit more interested in close relations and child-care, in spite of the backlash that such trends regularly provoke, in the form of revived traditionalist macho ideals. While women change most in political attitudes, social behaviour and expectations of work and status related to individualization, men probably display more new aspects in the cultural field of subjectivizing self-images and aesthetic pleasures. To look and dress 'male' has long been possible as part of womanliness as a masquerade, but to act male in work or public arenas is a more recent possibility for women, whereas male images which are interpreted as 'female' may be more provocative to traditional gender values.[29]

Women are in some respects a vanguard of cultural modernization, just as some peripheral regions and social groups sometimes run ahead of the centres of the world system. Dominating norms just tend to value the male, Western and white areas higher than the others. Popular culture is, for example, often associated with femininity in high modernist discourses where a feminized mass culture is feared as the Other of intellectual rationality.[30] This also applies to other aspects of youth culture than the

---

[29] Cf. also Bjurström (1990) and Bengtsson (1991a) on new trends in masculinity, Riviere (1929/1986) and Straayer (1990) on femininity as a masquerade.

[30] Cf. Huyssen (1986) and Modleski (1986a).

ones related to violent gangs, for example adolescent insecurity and search for identity, idol worship or narcissist body fixation. Youth and popular culture are often feared as the Other and thereby associated with femininity. Late modern discourses on youth and popular culture are ambivalent, and a closer look at them makes it hard to uphold the simple dichotomizing identifications that they first seem to invite.

The genders have not become one, but there has been a period of interchange between them in a complicated interplay. Counter-tendencies always arise among those groups who feel threatened by such changes. The result is no uniform equality, but a breaking up of the relatively unitary 'normality' of high modern gender positions into a series of parallel, contradictory identity forms, making predictions of future developments extremely difficult.

Traditional and new traits are very often mixed. On one hand, many adolescent women still form dyads of best friends (developed out of the mother/daughter relation), extended to triangles through ambivalent relations to horses, teachers, idols and finally boys (successively entering the Oedipal position originally filled by the father), while young men more often form larger and more hierarchical, pyramid-like peer groups or gangs. On the other hand, more girls seem to enter larger (all-female or mixed) peer groups in various public arenas, and the rigid hierarchies of gangs in late modernity frequently tend to dissolve into more diffuse microcultures which function as mutually protective 'social wombs' more than status battle-fields.[31] It has already been mentioned how the conventional correlation between private/public and female/male should not be taken quite for granted. The effects of certain socialization patterns are often ambivalent or contradictory, as when the close mother/daughter dyad may make many women more capable of handling intimate relations and caring for others, but simultaneously creates in others a strong wish to escape the bonds and control that this closeness implies, resulting in a greater mobility, while men may avoid relational responsibility but have not so much to lose in staying close to the old home. If girls are more protected than boys, they may become more home-bound, but some instead experience a stronger sense of revulsion against the confinement of close dyadic relations which threaten the separate identity for which they have to struggle so hard. If boys are more centrally positioned in institutions and activities geared towards progression and control (work, politics, sports, etc.), they might often also develop a particularly strong need for escape into regressive behaviours (in drugs, violence or just letting go and having fun) to get away from this external and internalized pressure to achieve. In some aspects men have been a vanguard for modernity, but in other aspects women are the first to explore modern

---

[31] Cf. Deutsch (1944), Ziehe (1975), McRobbie and Nava (1984), Ganetz and Lövgren (1991), McRobbie (1991 and 1994), Kleven (1992), Sørensen (1992), Drotner and Rudberg (1993) and Bjerrum Nielsen and Rudberg (1994).

possibilities (including mobility and so-called 'post-materialist values'). Old and new patterns exist side by side, and none should be absolutized into the only essential gender norm.

The connections between youth and gender are also complex. Public images of adolescent rebellion, gangs, subcultures and hardcore music are strongly male-biased, so that it might seem that women have hardly any youth culture at all.[32] But other aspects of the dominant image of youth have clearly female traits. When puberty is discussed in terms of instability and a search for identity, idols, acne and body stylization in front of the mirror, the typical teenager is as much a woman. Like popular culture in general, youth culture is often associated with the Other, and denounced as feminine.[33] All these ambivalences problematize all clear dichotomizations – particularly in the intense flux of late modernity.

The gender perspective thus teaches us both to see and to transgress boundaries: to separate dimensions in order to reunite them. Gender is positionally constructed out of polar relations of mirroring and distinction which create hierarchical dominance patterns and are connected to other identity orders through patterns of self/other identification.

Connecting ethnicity, stratifying class

Other identity orders, like ethnicity and class, share many of the general characteristics of age and gender, such as being both transient, positional and relational. In some important aspects, however, they differ, both in basic constitution and in the ideological figures that surround them. There are finally also plenty of interrelations between these orders.

In Western societies, there have been two particularly strong discursive traditions of the ethnic Other: Orientalism and Africanism. Orientalism is structured in an East/West polarity which stereotypes the East as the Other, from the old Greek polarity of Dionysus/Apollo up to more recent ideas of Islam as a fascinating or threatening alien to Western civilization. Orientalism may idealize or stigmatize the Oriental Other, but it always, on one hand, forgets the differences between Muslims, Jews, Hinduists, Buddhists and Confucians, North Africa, Turkey, the Middle East, Arabia, India, Southeast Asia, China and Japan, and all the internal shades within these many cultures, and, on the other hand, also neglects the differences between various aspects and parts of Europe and North America. The result is a stereotyped dichotomization which reduces many dimensions and subsumes them under an imaginary polarity that is metaphysically connected to fundamental categories of good/evil or modern/traditional (cf. Said 1978/1991 and Hall 1992a). This polarity is

[32] Hudson (1984) argues that this bias in public discourses makes it hard for girls to combine youth cultural activities with the development of an adult female identity.

[33] Huyssen (1986) shows that high cultural modernists have associated mass culture with the woman and strived to attack both in a fear and disgust of the Other. Similar tendencies are found in various moral panics.

mainly culturally formulated, but may also contain racist undertones of anti-semitism or a white/yellow distinction.

Africanism goes back to a North/South division, but has since the slave trade been transposed into a mostly racist white/black polarity of Euro-Americans versus Afro-Americans (cf. Hall 1990 and 1992b; Gilroy 1993a and b). These two Us/Them discourses are influential in popular culture, as two meta-patterns that repeatedly resonate within various concrete discourses around the vast plurality of heterogeneous ethnic differences. There is an immense multiplicity of struggling ethnicities in human life forms, as well as certain common features that unite people, but there are also dominant imaginary stereotypes such as these two, which tend to interfere with and organize other ethnic relations. They get their often murderous force through deep resonances with fundamental self/other experiences rooted in early infancy, where the child expels with utmost disgust the object (e.g., mother's empty breast) or self-object (e.g., excrement), making it an 'abject' in the primary process of self-formation against the non-I (cf. Kristeva 1980/1982 and 1988/1991).

Ethnic discourses explicitly focus connections which bind individuals in space and in time, to communities and to traditions. As dimensions of identification, age, gender and class also have such unifying powers of course, but here this is a clearly emphasized aspect. Ethnic belongings are seldom self-chosen, mostly inherited or innate: people are born within ethnic communities that are almost as hard to switch between as it is to change gender, even though one can choose between many individual lifestyles within this frame. However, the fact that some ethnic groups differ only in social habits (and not at all in genetic or bodily constitution), and that some people move between ethnic communities (through exile, migration, adoption, etc.), confirms that they are basically sociocultural formations. The reductions of tradition to ethnicity and of ethnicity to race are imaginary ideological processes that serve to hide this and legitimate dominance forms.

Ethnicity often stands symbolically for those traditional roots that still survive. Ethnicity, race and tradition are by no means identical, but they resonate strongly with each other in various everyday discourses.[34] While youth evokes the temporal dimension, immigration actualizes the spatial dimension of geographical movements. Ethnicity often signifies spatial and social differences and diversity, and appears as the Other of modernity, grounded in (often imaginary) backgrounds and roots back to pre-modern traditions, sometimes even to assumedly biological differences of race. Such symbolizations are in many ways false, but they have an impact on our everyday lifeworld which makes the combination of youth and ethnicity highly complex. If the young are quick to respond to modernization and its demands and resources for individualization and reflexivity,

---

[34] Cf. Hall (1986a, 1990, 1992a and b), Ehn et al. (1990), Palmgren et al. (1992) and Gilroy (1993a and b).

immigrants sometimes also form innovative avantgardes, experimenting with new ways of life included in the spectrum of youth cultures, but in other cases uphold traditional forms of life that oppose cultural modernity. Sometimes youth cultural markers are therefore seen almost as opposite to ethnic ones, as when modern urban youthfulness or commercial media culture is opposed to traditional roots; at other times ethnicities are actively constructed precisely by young people and seen as an integrated part of the culture of the younger generation, as in hiphop.

Essentialist fundamentalisms can be of a biologist (racist) or a culturalist kind. Biologists bind ethnicity to race, culturalists to structural constants in sociocultural traditions. As for the social class order, it no longer allows biological legitimation, but is still sometimes interpreted in an essentialist way as an inherent necessity in each society and a semi-natural result of traditional life forms. Class distinctions are related to the organization of labour and wealth in society, and are most explicitly associated with stratification, status and power.[35] While age and gender appear as most bound to biological factors, ethnicity and, even more, class are much more obviously intersubjectively constructed categories, and therefore also usually less visible. A person's gender and approximate age can normally be pretty easily determined, but ethnic and class affiliation often have to be exhibited via consciously exhibited styles in order to be decipherable by others.

The more hidden orders (particularly class) are neither of greater nor of less importance than the more visible ones. Visibility and importance are, again, separate dimensions that should not be confused. Just because class might be forgotten in everyday interaction more easily than gender, theoretical reflection should not make the opposite mistake and reduce gender to class. Each identity order is to be respected in its unique specificity, and they simply have varying importance in different contexts. There is no way to grade their general weight in any hierarchical order. Instead of analysing these orders in greater detail, another aspect of identity formation will now be investigated: the function of reflexivity in the constitution of the subject.

The mirrored self

Modernization on the subjective level consists of transformation of individual identity forms and psychic structures. They are caused 'from above' by new social and cultural contexts which place subjects in new contexts with different demands on them, as well as 'from below' by changing socialization forms all the way down to early infancy, producing subjective identities differently than before. Some such shifts have been mentioned in Chapter 2 above. Here, only that late modern tendency towards heightened 'narcissistic' reflexivity will be discussed, which has

---

[35] See Chapter 3 above, and cf. also Peter A. Berger (1987), Bocock and Thompson (1992) and Frow (1993).

been suggested by historicizing developments within psychoanalysis and social psychology. This has been related to shifts in symbolic forms of narrative and aesthetics as well as in social forms of norms, relations and groups, particularly among the younger generations. Such cultural and social trends have been used as indicators of a more evasive subjective modernization, which in its turn has been used as one possible explanation for those discernible tendencies. To the methodological, social and cultural aspects of reflexivity discussed earlier will now be added its psychological facets. First, the concept of narcissism in myth and psychoanalysis will be presented, drawing attention to Echo as the (female, aural and verbal) mirror of Narcissus. After a general discussion of mirroring and transgression the chapter will end by relating reflexivity to authenticity. Age and gender are the identity orders chosen as a focus, but the reader is invited to consider how other aspects could be introduced.

Echoes of narcissism

Some cultural phenomena are characterized as narcissistic, particularly those involving ecstatic experiences, sex, drugs, rock, dance, individual body culture or collective group involvement, which enable and actualize states of unbounded merging or self-mirroring, rooted in early infancy, before the acquisition of language. Such narcissistic traits are associated both with the necessary adolescent regression to preverbal developmental stages and with more generalized late modern cultural tendencies related to changing forms of socialization, mediatization and the erosion of traditions. But narcissism can mean many things. It can refer to psychological stages of development, pathological character disorders, general late modern changes in normal personality traits or new cultural tendencies. It is important to distinguish between narcissism as an early phase of life and as a particular form of experience in all ages, just as it is crucial to separate between narcissism as a pathological disturbance and as a general late modern tendency within 'normal' subject formations. One way to uncover these aspects of narcissism is to start with Narcissus himself.

The myth of Narcissus, son of the water-nymph Liriope and the river-god Cephissus, starts with his birth.[36] The mother asked the blind seer Tiresias if the child would live and reach old age, getting the answer: 'If he shall himself not know.' By the age of 16, the boy was so beautiful that everyone loved him, both men and women, but was so hard and arrogantly proud that he didn't care for anyone else.

When the great god Jove (Jupiter) was once frolicking with some mountain-nymphs, the nymph Echo had protected them by distracting his wife Juno with entertaining conversation until the nymphs had had time to escape. This made Juno very angry, and as she uncovered Echo's deceit,

---

[36] The most important literary formulation of this myth is by Ovid in his *Metamorphoses* (c. AD 8), which is here referred to in an English translation (Ovid 8/1986). Ovid's version of the myth is of course a cultural text that only indirectly, through metaphorical interpretation, tells something about inner, psychological processes.

she made her lose the freedom of her voice, so that this 'strange-voiced nymph' could only repeat the last words of other people's utterances.

'Echo was still a body, not a voice', and as Narcissus hunted deer in a forest, she saw him and fell in love. He searched for his hunting friends, and called: 'Anyone here?' She used this opportunity to answer 'Here!' He looked around and called again: 'Come this way!' and 'Join me here!', but she was only able to resound these words again. She ran out of the woods and approached him to embrace him, but he shunned her with the words: 'Keep your arms from me! Be off! I'll die before I yield to you.' 'I yield to you' was her echo, as she, ashamed and rejected, fled into the woods again and hid in lonely caves, where she pined away from incurable yearning. She disappeared, her bones turned to stone, and only her voice remained, 'for all to hear, alive, but just a sound.'

Among the young men who loved Narcissus in vain there was one who, frustrated, prayed to the gods: 'So may *he* love – and never win his love!' His prayer was heard by Nemesis, the goddess of revenge.

The next time Narcissus hunted deep into the woods, he got thirsty and caught a glimpse of his own mirror-image in a quiet pool. While slaking his first thirst, another thirst awakened: the love for his own image. This 'hope unreal' made him spellbound, and he lay 'like a marble statue staring down', gazing into his own eyes. 'All he admires that all admire in him, himself he longs for'; 'desiring is desired'. He tried to kiss and touch his own face in the pool, but in vain. 'Not knowing what he sees, he adores the sight', only seeing 'a phantom of a mirrored shape; nothing itself'. He wondered why this beautiful boy could not be reached: 'your sweet lips appear to move in speech, though to my ears your answer cannot reach'.

Suddenly he understood: 'I am he! Oh, now I know for sure the image is my own; it's for myself I burn with love; I fan the flames I feel.' And: 'Would I might leave my body! I could wish (strange lover's wish!) my love were not so near!' From sorrow he pined away by the pool: 'But now we two – one soul – one death will die.' He cried bitter tears that dropped into the pool, making the image disperse, which made him cry: 'stay! Oh cruelty to leave your lover so! Let me but gaze on what I may not touch'. He tore his robe and beat his fists on his white, naked breast, so that it turned partly red.

Echo was still angry, but grieved for the boy she loved, repeating his words 'alas! the boy I loved in vain!' and 'farewell'. In death, he still gazed at his own image, now mirrored in the underworld pool of Styx, while his Naiad sisters and the Dryads wailed, echoed again by Echo. On earth, his body had disappeared, 'and in its stead they found a flower – behold, white petals clustered round a cup of gold!' With this image of the narcissus flower, the sad story ends.[37]

---

[37] The narcissus 'grows from itself' and 'needs no cross-fertilization': 'no more than its mythical originator does it know the intervention of another either as a person or in death' (Mitchell 1974/1975, p. 40).

This myth was first used within psychoanalysis in 1898 and 1899 by Havelock Ellis and Paul Näcke, to describe a certain type of perversion. Texts by Sigmund Freud from 1910 to 1915 – most importantly, 'On Narcissism' (1914/1957) – related narcissism to a phase of the normal development of the child.[38] This is a stadium between autoeroticism and object love, associated with the formation of the ego and crucial to identity formation. The narcissistic desire is necessary for the constitution of the I, but has to be reduced if one is not to get stuck in a vicious circle, like Narcissus was. The means to break the circle is the development of the ego ideal, which may form the positive parts of the superego, complemented by the negative, prohibitory ones. Instead of desiring what one is (or has been), one should search for that which one wants to be.

In 'Mourning and Melancholia' (1915/1957), Freud related narcissism to sorrow and melancholy. The depressed melancholic mourns a loss but cannot give up the lost object (the mother) and transfer her or his libido onto other objects. Instead, libido is again bound to the I, which is identified with the lost object. In real mourning, one takes farewell of the lost beloved, but in melancholia this process is blocked, the loss is hidden by the narcissistic identification and the feeling of sadness therefore becomes vague and undirected, with no clear source in sight.

Kristeva (1987/1989) has developed this line of thought and analysed melancholy as an incapacity to overcome the sorrow caused by the separation from the (early, archaic) mother inevitably resulting from the entrance into the symbolic order of language and the formation of a tendentially autonomous ego-identity.[39] The melancholic is not able to transfer her or his desire from the maternal body onto language (or other symbolic forms), which therefore closes itself and becomes dead. One has to accept that symbolic mediations are necessary for communication with others, and experience that symbolic forms may offer consolation and even enjoyment, in spite of the fact that they also cut off the immediate, archaic contact with the material–maternal world. Only the reinvestment of libido in symbols, in symbolic interaction with others, makes it possible to retain a mediated contact with the deep streams of pre-narcissistic presence in the world, with what Lacan has called the 'real' and Kristeva the 'semiotic' (related to the unconscious primary processes). Instead of just effecting a loss of immediacy and presence, the symbolic order (of form-structures and meanings related to the conscious secondary processes of the ego in its interaction with others within a social order) then may open channels to love and communication with others.

This connects to what was said about symbols in the preceding chapter. Ricoeur's (1965/1970 and 1969/1974) ideas of living versus dead metaphors, or Lorenzer's (1972) thoughts on full symbols versus clichés, might well be connected to how Kristeva thinks of poetic works and artistic practices as

---

[38] Cf. also Laplanche and Pontalis (1967/1988, pp. 255–7).
[39] Cf. also Kristeva (1980/1982, 1983/1987, 1990) and Lechte (1990).

giving new life to language by revitalizing the contrast between its semiotic and symbolic sides, in a 'semiotization of the symbolic', or a 'flow of jouissance into language' (1974/1984, p. 79). In all these models, symbolic texts are renewed and made vital by reconnections to subterranean streams of drive-related primary processes, instead of crystallizing into closed, formal structures.

Kristeva understands the semiotic as 'pre-thetic, preceding the positing of the subject. Previous to the ego thinking within a proposition, no Meaning exists, but there *do* exist articulations heterogeneous to signification and to the sign: the semiotic *chora*' (1974/1984, p. 36). The speaking subject is a subject in process, developing through the use of texts (p. 37). 'The subject never *is*. The *subject* is only the *signifying process* and he appears only as a *signifying practice*' (p. 215). This subject is a differentiated unity of semiotic, symbolic and signifying processes, just as Freud saw it as split in unconscious drives and conscious thought and action. Its symbolic side is constituted in a 'thetic' phase, by a break that cuts off immediacy and forces the subject to jump into the symbolic order of positions and of meanings (Kristeva 1974/1984, p. 43).

This thetic phase occurs at two developmental points, first in 'the mirror stage' and then with the 'discovery' of castration (Kristeva 1974/1984, p. 46). The first of these is most relevant for reflexivity and narcissism. In Lacan's analysis of the mirror phase, the infant has no ego but is undifferentiated, distinguishing neither between self and surrounding nor between conscious and unconscious. By between 6 and 18 months of age, it discovers itself as a separate unit in some mirror-image, which need not be a physical mirroring glass but can as well be the interactional mirror offered by the parents as they affirm and name the child, giving it a language through which it can view itself 'from the outside'. The child then starts shaping its identity by mirroring itself in others and in symbolic forms. This constitutes the ego but also a deep split within the subject, between the 'I' as an acting agent and the 'me' as a socioculturally mediated self-image.[40] This subject, split both in unconscious id versus conscious ego and I versus me, is no mere illusion, only deeply intersubjectively dependent upon others. It is constituted by viewing itself as distinct from others (particularly from the mother) but also in or with the eyes of the others – separate and yet connected, united and yet differentiated.

Narcissism is already in the myth associated with the origin of the ego, of language and of difference (particularly of gender).[41] Narcissus first does not understand that the image in the pool is himself, until he finally discovers this in an unsuccessful 'mirror stage'. Both he and Echo fail to use words to make contact with their respective love-object, and in many

---

[40] Cf. Lacan (1966/1977, pp. 1ff and 292ff) and Mead (1934).

[41] Cf. Laplanche (1970/1985, p. 68) and Mitchell: 'The subject is constituted as the opposition between presence and absence, its foundation is dependent upon the discovery of difference' (1974/1975, p. 386).

variants a (lack of) difference both of self/other and of man/woman is the key factor in this complex narrative. Echo is punished for betraying a woman to protect a man, Narcissus is androgynous in being loved by men and women alike, and the ways in which their mutual relation contains gender aspects will soon be further discussed.

The mirror phase starts a process whereby self and world are separated, as the child discovers its symbolically formed self-image, shown to it by the mother and the adult world. In the beginning of this phase, before the ego-formation is completed, one may find what has been defined as a primary narcissism: 'Inside and outside are not precisely differentiated here, nor is language an active practice or the subject separated from the other' (Kristeva 1980/1982, p. 60). These narcissistic experiences are not confined to infancy only, but reappear more or less in all stages of life, not only in narcissistic disorders but also in 'normal' conditions. They are particularly strong in the 'second thetic phase' of Oedipal crisis, but also in the 'fifth birth' of adolescence. There is a set of 'narcissistic' cultural practices and textual forms which actualizes such experiences, by dissolving fixed boundaries and offering confusing mirrors to the self. These experiences involve a paradoxical mixture of merging and mirroring: on one hand, a transgressive merging with others in music, reading or love, on the other hand, a self-mirroring in others, such as idols, friends or beloveds. To mirror oneself is to identify oneself by 'merging' with one's image. Affirming one's identity in the 'social womb' of a peer group allows one to feel as one with the group. Dissolving rigid ego boundaries by strong volume, beat and sound experiences in rock listening allows for a deep-reaching mirroring of inner feelings in these musical forms.

But the connection of symbiotic merging and reflexive mirroring in narcissism is also paradoxical, since mirroring presupposes that the subject who mirrors herself is and recognizes herself as separate from the surrounding world and from the mirror itself. Identification with an image or a group is only possible if one is first separate rather than limitlessly united with everything else. Narcissus would not have been able to enter the reflexive process and later discover that the image was his own if he had not already had at least some rudimentary experience of himself as to some extent separate from the lake and the figures he encountered (including the surrounding others as well as his own image).

The merging of symbiosis and self-dissolution is only a liminal reconstruction, built on memory-traces of earliest infancy before the first mirroring in the Other, but never possible to fully attain again, once the ego has emerged. It is this self-forgetting abandon that is connected to the *jouissance* of total, orgasmic pleasure, and in the early phase of subject history is contrasted with what Kristeva (1980/1982) calls *abjection* and the abject: a similarly unconditional feeling of nausea and disgust which is an essential impetus for the first separation of self from other. In abjecting the (mother-)object, the child marks the first boundaries around its self, much the same way as Narcissus rejects Echo: 'Keep your arms from me! Be off!

I'll die before I yield to you!' In terms of this psychoanalytical reading of the myth, he has already left the primary, archaic symbiosis which is in itself pre-narcissistic rather than narcissistic, but important as a tragically absent aim for narcissism. It is this total merging with the mother, in the limitless water-flow, to which he longs back and which drives him to fixate his own image. Mirroring does not give him this symbiosis back, but locks him into the normally transient experience of narcissism. He has been stuck at the mirroring moment that ought to lead him out of pre-narcissistic symbiosis and into the intersubjective symbolic order of language, culture and communication. Like the melancholic, he is not able to invest or discover delight in symbols; he refuses to speak to Echo and is deaf to her words, as he, closed within himself, balances on the cold mirroring surface.

The merging and mirroring aspects of narcissism can be related to two different ways in which Freud explained original or primary narcissism, as opposed to the secondary narcissism which appears whenever a fully developed ego mirrors its identity.[42] In his later works, from c. 1920 onwards, the infant is seen almost as a closed monad, suddenly opened to the surrounding world as a result of inner drive pressures and a 'primitive hallucination'. The origin then tends to be seen as a closed biological system, and primary narcissism as an 'anobjectal' state of an infant with no psychological relations to the external world. According to Laplanche, this view can be interpreted as a myth or *Urfantasie* of a return to the maternal womb, rather than a truthful description. It makes it hard to understand how the leap into mirroring and ego-formation can ever be taken. And in such an interpretation of narcissism, the whole mirroring moment of the Narcissus theme is lost.

The other version can be found in Freud's earlier writings, from around 1914–15. Here, narcissism is no originary state but rather emerges in parallel to the ego, as a result of the parents projecting their own narcissistic self-love onto the infant. Narcissism is not the origin of the whole individual subject with its needs, but rather of the ego with its sexuality and desire, as an inner instance distinct from both the id and the external world. The origin of sexuality and the ego is later than that of the individual subject and its perceptive–motorial interaction with the surrounding world. A non-sexual bodily relation to the world (and the mother) exists from the beginning, as self-mirroring narcissism develops out of earlier autoerotic drives, and is only afterwards interpreted as an originary state. If narcissism is defined as love directed towards one's self-image, as an introjection of how others 'mirror' oneself, not even primary narcissism can appear until an ego ('I') with a self-image ('me') exists; I cannot love myself before 'I' and 'me' are born. Narcissism, ego and self-image emerge at the same moment.

---

[42] Cf. Laplanche and Pontalis (1967/1988, pp. 255–7) and Laplanche (1970/1985 and 1987/1989). Like Klein, Laplanche is critical of concepts like symbiosis and mother/infant dyad: intersubjective relations are primary to (or contemporaneous with) autonomous subjects.

Narcissistic forms of experience in childhood, adolescence and adult life always contain both a mirroring and a balancing on the border of transgressive symbiosis, as they re-enact the moment where ego and world are first experienced as separate unities. The merging aspect in itself is a projection of fantasies pointing back towards the first and second births, that is, to a reunion with the maternal womb. The mirroring aspect can appear on its own, without the self-dissolving merging moments, in other types of later reflexive phenomena. It is their specific combination that defines the narcissistic form of reflexivity. Narcissism thus unites oceanic feelings of oneness with the universe with an intriguing self-mirroring.

Tiresias' strange reversal of the famous oracular utterance of the Delphic Apollo, 'if he shall himself not know' instead of 'know thyself', is as paradoxical as is the fate of Narcissus. Narcissus first does not know what he sees – he does not know himself, and therefore falls in love with his own image and cannot live. It is often believed that he knows and loves himself too much, but this is not quite true. He suffers from a lack of self-insight, an incapability to recognize his own self-image as identical and yet separate. In fact, in the pool he sees his image, not himself. In both myth and psychoanalysis, the narcissist loves a self-image that does not give the subject a satisfying self. This is important for the discussions of increasingly narcissistic traits in late modern socialization and culture, particularly among young people. Late modern adolescence may be more dependent upon finding useful self-mirrors, but this is not because young people love themselves more than anything else, but rather because they cannot love themselves enough. They are doubtful as to who they are, since identities have become increasingly problematic. Like Narcissus, they need to mirror themselves – in each other, in stars, media and music – because cultural release and individualization has made identities more open, and because reflexivity makes self-definition more demanding. Narcissus gets stuck by the pool because he wonders who he (the self-image) is, and late modern youth may reflect much in the same way. Changes in early socialization have been combined with sociocultural transformations in the present to problematize identity formation, giving momentary mirrorings and mergings greater use value to increase the feeling of self-presence.

An extensive discourse has evolved around the question of allegedly increasing narcissistic tendencies in late modernity. This central aspect of recent modernization on a subjective level was brought up by many different theorists. In America, there were psychoanalysts like Heinz Kohut (1971) as well as sociologists and cultural critics like Richard Sennett (1977/1986) and Christopher Lasch (1979). A very interesting discussion developed in West German socialization theory, particularly with Thomas Ziehe (1975), inspiring a series of Scandinavian studies of narcissism in youth culture.[43] One source of these ideas has been clinical

---

[43] Cf. Frimodt (1983), Fornäs et al. (1984/1994 and 1988/1995), Fornäs (1987), Layton and Schapiro (1986) and Alvesson (1989).

observations of new types of disturbances, assessing that borderline cases and narcissistic pathologies tend to grow at the cost of earlier, hysterical and neurotic symptoms. This has led critics either to use these observations to pathologize the young generations of late modernity, or to denounce the whole idea, since obviously most people do not seem to be seriously mentally ill. It is very important to avoid all such pathologization of personality traits which are in fact 'normal', so that all new tendencies are not branded as sick. Changes of normality are always first compared with the earlier norm and interpreted as disturbances or disorders, and it tends to be easier to note changes first in the most deviant and problematic cases. This was true for psychoanalysis in its early stages, developing a model of the 'normal' psyche through observations of suffering clients, and it was also true for subcultural studies, understanding style formations through studying extremely visible and oppositional groups rather than common culture. The troubles with such methods do not make them invalid: changes in abnormality may indeed tell a lot about changes in the normal, since identities are always defined in relation to others, and the borders between normal and pathological, straight and deviant, are only relative constructions.

In wider streams of Western youth and popular culture as well, thematizations of regressive, narcissistic modes – of unstable identities, evasive floating or gliding 'oceanic' feelings, etc. – seem to have increased from the 1960s onwards.[44] New socialization patterns in family, daycare and school joined a general sociocultural erosion or de-naturalization of traditional identities to increase the urge for narcissistic experiences, both by adults and even more by adolescents. Youth cultural 'sex, drugs and rock'n'roll' developed from deep-rooted carnivalesque hedonism to an emphasized regression into temporary ego-dissolution and mirroring–merging. A common basis for many drugs, sexual *jouissance* and musical power can be found in deep psychological experiences of momentary and self-chosen regression to narcissistic states, needed to affirm and develop subjective identity in late modern contexts. Such juvenile, temporary regressions are radically different from the permanent ones of either infantile life or pathological misdevelopments. Narcissism opens certain doors to regression, but its juvenilization of culture is no infantilization. It is youthfulness more than childishness that has become attractive also to adults who no longer want to get stuck in static identities. Young people's search for intense expressions and presence in music, dance and style goes long back in history, but seems to have been radicalized and generalized in late modernity to include most social strata and extend downwards and upwards through the ages. This development may be interpreted as efforts to transgress the limitations and the rigidity of the strategic forms of

---

[44] 'Oceanic feelings' were discussed by Freud (1930/1961) in connection with regressive aspects of religious experiences. The water symbolism fits well among the metaphors around primary narcissism.

interaction consolidated in the latency period, supported by the school institution, where the written and goal-oriented word is favoured.

Both Sennett (1977/1986) and Lasch (1979) tend to pathologize late modern narcissism. To Sennett, the rise of narcissist character disorders is related to a collapse of public life, giving the private self tasks that it cannot manage. Narcissism is interpreted as a constantly frustrated search for self-identity, blocking any truly interactive relations with others. Lasch echoes similar pessimistic denouncements of late modern mass society as super-ficial and egocentric.[45] Thomas Ziehe's (1975) development of Kohut's ideas is much more rich and ambivalent. In his account, narcissistic traits combine unstable identifications and structural flexibility with a weak ego and a high-flying but dependent ego-ideal (pp. 106–9), as part of a severe but immature super-ego (p. 159). An early quasi-symbiotic mother-bonding results in a narcissistic adherence to the stage in which the mother was not yet experienced as a distinct object, but rather as diffusely omnipotent, so that the inner representation of the archaic mother is conserved in the infant's unconscious instead of being reworked into traditional ego and super-ego formations through an Oedipal crisis (pp. 120f). The absence or weakness of the father (or the paternal authority position in socialization) prevents the Oedipal conflict from developing as before (pp. 127ff). The basic problematics of the narcissist constellation consists of a double inversion of the internal and the external: an external disappointment with the parents and an internal fixation on the introjected archaic mother imago, which is then turned into a longing for 'symbiotic' external object relationships. Primary narcissism is thus separated from a continued formation of psychical structures (Ziehe and Stubenrauch 1982, p. 93). This constitutes a new normality, causing new mental disorders but in itself neither more nor less healthy or deviant than formerly normal socialization patterns.[46]

Increasing late modern reflexivity is closely related to this narcissistic tendencies. On one hand, 'from below', reflexivity in parents and teachers induces the new forms of primary socialization in infancy and early childhood which later make adolescents and adults show more narcissistic traits. On the other hand, 'from above', transformations of culture support narcissistic needs in the present, youth or adult everyday life.[47]

The negative aspect of this development is a growth of new types of diffuse self-disturbances, where narcissism becomes so strong that it

[45] For further criticisms, see Fornäs et al. (1984/1994) and Giddens (1991, pp. 169ff). Cf. Giddens's (1992, p. 166) use of Marcuse (1955/1970) to formulate a 'positive' (and insufficiently ambivalent) account of narcissism as an 'alternative reality', revealing a 'potential for transcendence'.

[46] Ziehe (1975, pp. 238ff). Cf. Nielsen (1977/1984) and Fornäs et al. (1988/1995, 1990a and b) for analyses of narcissistic traits in rock music and peer groups.

[47] Narcissism 'from below' and 'from above' is discussed by Ziehe and Stubenrauch (1982, pp. 88f). Cf. Simonsen and Illeris (1989, pp. 84–7) and Holstein-Beck (1991/1995) for feminist critiques.

distorts social relations, and is hard to treat with conventional therapies. The psychological 'de-Oedipalization' process is related to social tendencies of fathers to be more absent in family life and authority figures to be devalued in public culture. This 'pre-Oedipal turn' is definitely not only a liberation from traditional restraints but also creates great dangers. Part of the recent problems with violence and paranoid xenophobia towards the Other may have been escalated by these subjective trends.

Its positive aspect is, according to Kohut and Ziehe, a greater empathic openness to others, creativity, ego-flexibility and self-reflection. 'Normal' late modern narcissism implies a need and an ability to enter the floating state that resembles the origin of the ego, of language and of differences, in which new experiences and cultural expressions are born, as these liminal experiences confront the dominant symbolic order. Kristeva has formulated strikingly similar ideas:

> As to the mythical Narcissus, he is a modern character much closer to us. He breaks with the ancient world because he turns sight into origin and seeks the other opposite himself, as product of his own sight. He then discovers that the reflection is no other but represents himself, that the other is the presentation of the self. Thus, in his own way, Narcissus discovers in sorrow and death the alienation that is the constituent of his own image. Deprived of the One, he has no salvation; otherness has opened up within himself. . . . What analysands are henceforth suffering from is *the abolition of psychic space*. Narcissus in want of light as much as of a spring allowing him to capture his true image, Narcissus drowning in a cascade of false images (from social roles to the *media*), hence deprived of substance or place: these contemporary characters are witnesses to our being unable today to elaborate primary narcissism. (1983/1987, pp. 121 and 373f)[48]

In another text, Kristeva relates the open psychic structure of adolescence to the open aesthetic structure of the polyphonic novel and, again, to cultural modernization:

> [The] adolescent structure opens itself to the repressed at the same time that it initiates a psychic reorganization of the individual – thanks to a tremendous loosening of the superego. . . . The evolution of the modern family and the ambiguity of sexual and parental roles within it, the bending or weakening of religious and moral taboos, are among the factors that make for these subjects *not* structuring themselves around a fixed pole of the forbidden, or of the law. The frontiers between differences of sex or identity, reality and fantasy, act and discourse, etc., are easily traversed without one being able to speak of perversion or borderline – and perhaps this would only be because these 'open structures' find themselves immediately echoing the fluidity, i.e., the inconsistency, of a mass media society. The adolescent is found to represent *naturally* this structure that can be called a 'crisis' structure only through the eyes of a stable, ideal law. (1990, pp. 8f)[49]

An 'adolescent text' is open and in crisis, just as is adolescent identity. This convergence of youth, modernity and cultural openness is parallel to

---

[48] Cf. also Lévinas (1947/1987), Kristeva (1983/1987, pp. 103ff and 1985/1987) and Witt-Brattström (1984) on the dialectics of narcissism, love and identity.

[49] Cf. also Kristeva (1987/1989, pp. 12f).

Blos's, Kohut's and Ziehe's theories of adolescence as a 'second chance' to restructure subjective identity, by means of what has been called a narcissistic 'regression in the service of the ego' (Kris 1952). The narcissism in younger generations does not signal a new type of social character or personality. The partial dissolution of old, neurotogenic patterns of socialization does not create one uniform subject form, but rather opens up a wide spectrum of possible subject positions, in which narcissism may be more central, but where openness seems more relevant than narcissism as a general characteristic of late modern subjectivity as a whole. And these new traits of course spread unevenly among individuals, groups, classes and genders.

Like Laplanche, Kristeva argues that primary narcissism, before the mirror phase, is no originary, undifferentiated state: 'one is not born a Narcissus (one is born autoerotic), and one becomes Narcissus only following the impact of a paternal identification subsequently producing the Ego Ideal' (1983/1987, p. 126). This primary narcissism already contains what could be called a triadic 'protorelation' between the infant as emergent subject, the mother as Other and proto-object, and a third part, a potential ideal outside of the mother–child dyad (p. 13). This third part is 'an archaic disposition of the paternal function, preceding the Name, the Symbolic, but also preceding the "mirror stage" . . . a disposition that one might call that of the Imaginary Father' (p. 22). Narcissism has to do with the deep structure of the love relation, where I love the Other as I encounter a positive image of myself in him/her, mediated through an archaic third part between me and my mother. Freud calls this a primary identification with 'the father of individual prehistory', which Kristeva sees as the zero point of the subject. This imaginary father is actually a mixture of both parents, as the infant cannot yet distinguish between male and female. The third pole may refer to the mother's work, her desire for someone else (like a man) or some social instance, but is identified with the paternal position to indicate its crucial difference from the intimate mother–child dyad. 'Identity, in the sense of a stable and solid image of the self where the autonomy of the subject will be established, emerges only at the end of this process when narcissistic shimmering draws to a close in a jubilatory assumption that is the work of the Third Party' (Kristeva 1987/ 1989, p. 257).[50] The very early, archaic or primary narcissist mother/father function develops into elaborated gender positions later in socialization, as ideological, social and cultural gender orders enter to reinterpret this mother/father dichotomy as one of male/female identity, thus binding women to motherhood and masculinity to the dominant symbolic order or the 'Law of the Father'.

Socialization in late modernity, influenced by cultural individualization and reflexivity, through media, school and family patterns, seems to make the gender identities that are shaped by the Oedipal conflict less stable.

---

[50] Cf. also Kristeva (1983/1987, pp. 26 and 202) and Witt-Brattström (1984, p. 51).

Ziehe (1975, p. 131) explains that the son finds it more difficult to identify with the weakened father, the daughter with the Oedipal (post-archaic, 'real') mother. Instead, they both retain the narcissist mother-bond. Ziehe concludes that this explains why the convergence between gender roles is so often interpreted as 'feminization', while in fact it is rather the result of a regression to an archaic, narcissist developmental stage.

In the myth, the young woman (Echo) is likewise, in her relation to the young man (Narcissus), placed in a mirroring and waiting position reminiscent of the mother (Juno). As the son of a water-nymph and a river-god, Narcissus is born of a water element to which he looks back (the pool) and to which he returns in death (Styx). He finds it hard to rise above and separate from the archaic, pre-Oedipal and unconscious maternal flows, and it is no coincidence that the pool is described by Ovid in a way that alludes to the mysterious maternal opening which once gave him life.[51] 'If it be true that in Narcissus' universe there is no other, one might nevertheless think of the *spring* as his partner. A symbol of the maternal body . . .' (Kristeva 1983/1987, p. 113). This archaic mother figure is from the view of the infant a body without a voice (without language, symbols, meaning), while Echo instead of dying becomes a fettered voice without body, doomed to repeat the speech of man.

> He Loves, he loves Himself – active and passive, subject *and* object. Actually, Narcissus is not completely without object. *The object of Narcissus is psychic space; it is representation itself, fantasy.* But he does not know it, and he dies. If he knew it he would be an intellectual, a creator of speculative fictions, an artist, psychologist, psychoanalyst. (Kristeva 1983/1987, p. 116)

A similar possible development of narcissism to aesthetic and intellectual creativity by working it through and completing reflection by interaction with others was also thematized by Kohut, Lorenzer and Ziehe. It is exactly what happens in much youth culture, dance and rock practice, where narcissist regressions develop learning processes that revitalize the signifying and symbolizing creativity of the subject.

The unconscious in itself has no gender, as is implied by the psychoanalytical term id (or rather It). It goes back to the less differentiated infantile psyche, but emerges as a separate instance parallel to the ego, as the mirror phase dissolves primary narcissism. Psychological forms emerge from a biological origin but create a new ground, where the id, the 'mechanical', that which is in 'third person', in the form of 'it', is deepest in the human subject without having been there from the beginning.[52] The unconscious lacks both time, negations and gender difference. In the narcissist experiences of infancy or adolescence, the maternal has not yet become definitely

---

[51] 'There was a pool, limpid and silvery . . .; grass grew around it, by the water fed, and trees to shield it from the warming sun' (Ovid 8/1986, p. 63). 'This pool is not only as glassy as a mirror; its shadiness, secrecy, mysterious coolness and inaccessibility to anyone but Narcissus surely designate it as the entrance/exit of the mother's genital' (Naomi Segal 1989, pp. 170f). More aquatic symbolism is mentioned by Donen (1983, p. 105).

[52] Cf. Ricoeur (1965/1970, p. 154) and Laplanche (1987/1989).

gendered. The narcissist mirroring in the mother-object is therefore a relation that has only started to constitute gender. It is after the fact, or from the view of adult parents, that the gender polarity is fixated and the mother identified as female. In narcissist forms of experience, the archaic mother is as little a woman as the subject has any clear gender. The archaic mother-object and the pre-Oedipal protosubject both are undifferentiated ('semiotic'). The first object-relations of overwhelming and omnipotent *jouissance* or paralysing and disgusting abjection inhabit the land of dawn where ego, symbols and gender are about to be born.[53]

This may explain the difficulties in simply identifying Echo as female and Narcissus as male, since they are mythical representations of positions rooted beyond the gender difference.[54] Narcissus is loved by women and men, and his vain and egocentric self-attachment combines conventionally male and female traits. Echo's restless talk and responsiveness is likewise androgynous. Still, they are woman and man, and it is something of a pity that both the myth and later discussions tend to reduce the woman to an unindependent Other that only mirrors the male hero as his opposite echo. Both search for the Other in vain. Mirroring in the Other is necessary to develop their subjective identities, but this route is blocked for them. To Echo, Narcissus is the aim of her love, but he only desires his own image and abjects her. She is impossible to be attached to, as she has lost the agency of her own voice and thus cannot express her identity as the Other for Narcissus. The borrowed words are correct in content but lack the authentic voice of subjectivity needed to hear them as meaningful utterances. Echo's predicament is reminiscent of a melancholic, who, according to Kristeva (1987/1989), lacks the ability to find pleasure in language. To the melancholic Echo, words are dead and do not mean anything, and she cannot express what she feels to anyone. The words are felt as foreign or lifeless, just as cultural expropriation through the media makes symbolic images empty and useless if they are not assimilated into one's own voice.

None of them is able to transform the double mirroring (in water and echoes) into fully communicative interaction. While Narcissus' problems centre on the body, the gaze and the eye, Echo's mode is that of the word, the voice and the ear. His visual mirror-image cannot hear and answer his loving voice, while her acoustic mirror of him makes herself invisible. In both versions of mirroring – male and female, pictorial and verbal, visual and aural, of the self and of the other – intersubjective encounter is avoided. What would have happened if Echo instead had been a visual mirror, or if Narcissus had become attached to her words as they echoed his own? Then maybe some interaction could have opened, breaking the vicious circles.

A crucial way through adolescence to adulthood involves finding and giving love. The cold game of narcissistic self-mirroring can only be broken

[53] Cf. Widerberg (1990, p. 68). 'Narcissus rules. . . . Rock's sexual effect is not just on the construction of femininity and masculinity: Rock also contributes to the more diffuse process of the sexualisation of leisure' (Frith and McRobbie 1978, p. 19).

[54] Ovid seems to have been the first to link the myth of Echo with that of Narcissus.

by the true meeting with a different Other, someone who can love and be loved, in a relation both of reciprocity and of difference – that is, in communication. This Other may be anyone, including a sexual partner or a child. The advent of such a seemingly 'magical' encounter or communication prevents self-mirroring from turning into a self-dissolving spiral, and instead opens a development of growth.

Echo's duty to mirror the man and try to fulfil his desires points at an asymmetrical power aspect in gender relations. Her knowledge and desire is silenced and isolated as she is doomed to be the acoustic mirror of man. The glance in which she in vain tries to mirror herself is unfortunately that of Narcissus, who is unable to go beyond his own self-image (Naomi Segal 1989, p. 171). 'Female narcissism revolves around surface phenomena – poses in mirrors, clothing, make-up. It is meant to create ever more elaborate surfaces for the male gaze to penetrate' (p. 183).[55] Or, in the words of the art critic John Berger: 'A woman must continually watch herself. She is almost continually accompanied by her own image of herself. . . . *men act* and *women appear*. Men look at women. Women watch themselves being looked at' (1972, p. 46–7). The psychoanalytical film theorist Laura Mulvey (1975/1989) analysed the male gaze on images of women as a sign of domination. In her analysis of Harlequin romances, Tania Modleski adds: 'women are supposed to be unconscious of themselves if they are not to incur the charge of narcissism, and yet they are continually forced to look at themselves being looked at' (1982, pp. 111f) – in art, films, soap operas and books. Echo is the subordinated who is surveilled, who talks, mirrors and supports.[56]

As women thus tend to be placed in an object-position in the gender order, a puristic counter-strategy can be to avoid mirroring in men and instead develop their own ideals, independent of the male gaze. But one has to be mirrored in the Other in order to find oneself, and it is impossible to demand full control over such mirrorings, since one has to be open to unpredictable dialogues with these Others. What can be demanded is rather a minimal amount of communicative mutuality in such dialogues, and a critical reflection on its mechanisms. And more recent feminist theories have tried to avoid the almost fatalistic conclusions of the dichotomizing model of the actively observing male versus the passively observed female. Mary Ann Doane (1987), Jackie Stacey (1994) and others have analysed female spectatorship as more dynamic and variable in terms of identification. Kaja Silverman (1988) has studied the female voice and the psychological mechanisms involved in hearing sounds, in an analysis of 'the acoustic mirror' which avoids the bias toward visuality inherent in focusing only on Narcissus and forgetting Echo. There is a traditional social tendency towards agency defined as male and women as

---

[55] Cf. Riviere (1929/1986), Burgin et al. (1986), Modleski (1986b), Doane (1987), Ganetz (1992/1995) and Zoonen (1994) on fantasy, masquerade and femininity.

[56] Chodorow (1979), Gilligan (1982) and Bjerrum Nielsen and Rudberg (1994) see female rationality as oriented towards care and relations.

objectified, but this tendency is no total or uniform law. Even in dominant genres of popular culture like the classical Hollywood films there are at least some important ambivalences and openings to other types of identifications, both in viewing and in listening. Simplistic and totalizing dichotomies are again misleading.

If men are still traditionally more like Narcissus in identifying with the position of the self-centred One, and women are more like Echo in occupying a marginalized and relationally supportive position of the Other (while reminiscent of Narcissus in his self-watching), then a general late modern development in 'narcissistic' direction will have different implications for the two genders. For many men, one result may be an increasing sexualization ('femininization') of the bodily self-image and a heightened dependence on affirmation by others, while an increasing self-centredness among many women may instead appear as a new degree of self-sufficient autonomy. Even if we thus assume that there exists a general late modern tendency in subjectivity formation, it must be analysed as gender- (age-, ethnically, regionally and class-)specific, since its effects will vary according to the conditions on which it operates.

Regressions to pre-narcissistic stages of oceanic experiences have a non-gendered side in that these stages know of no gender difference. But their functions depend upon secondary transformations which separate genders since this difference is constituted in the narcissistic moment of self-mirroring in the Other. Later regressions are always tinted by the way the identification with a female or male position relates to the vague memory of an archaic mother who gradually becomes increasingly gendered.

For men, regression often is associated with a suppressed 'female' side. Young men jump into transgressive experiences in rock and rave cultures, where aggressive masculinity is often dissolved into androgynous hybridity. The merging in close bounds with an other is often thought of as female, which may threaten a man's gender identity but may also offer a welcome loosening of its overly rigid demands. In traditional contexts, such regression is often covered by secondary ideological or religious rationalizations. Closeness and ego-dissolution has been associated with mystical revelations, and the archaic maternal has been sublimated into various god-figures, often converted into omnipotent patriarchal idealizations, in order to keep the threatening, strong internalized mother at a distance.[57] For women, by contrast, regression to symbiotic experiences affirms conventional gender identity by reuniting with the inner mother representation, but its androgynously omnipotent aspects can then instead be used to explore a new-won individual autonomy. Regression differs depending not only on the stage to which it goes back, but also on the position from which it starts.

The same is true for another important theme in cultural practices, that of border transgressions. They also appear on different levels. Socially,

[57] Cf. Kristeva (1983/1987 and 1985/1987), Lorenzer (1986) and Ziehe (1991).

some individuals cross conventional borders between genders or classes by developing interaction with others or experimenting with opposite roles and breaking taboos. Culturally, they may also transcend limits between genres and styles in hybrid bricolages. There are also subjective transgressions where inner boundaries are violated, as in the narcissistic play with the I/you and inside/outside borders.[58] These different types of transgression are often not co-ordinated. A strict marking of social borders might, for instance, create the feeling of security that allows for cultural and/or psychological transgressions, and vice versa. Again, dimensions have to be kept apart in order to see how they interrelate in each context.

Reflexive authenticity

The thematization of how texts point towards the subjective dimension gives rise to the complicated issue of authenticity. The word 'authenticity' has its origin in Greek, denoting that someone is doing something by him/ herself and is therefore the real and responsible origin of this work. Authentic is that which is genuine or supported by a reliable authority from which it emerges. An authentic text emanates from the authorial origin which it claims to have, and expresses what he/she honestly means, so that it corresponds in some way to his/her subjectivity. Authenticity as a characteristic of symbolic works or genres concerns how the textual structures are constructed to present themselves as related to the subjects that created them. Communication involves two categories of subjects – creators and appropriators – but both are active users and (re)constructors of meaning. Through various markers, symbolic expressions present themselves as honest and genuine, implying a continuity or homology between a textual form (style and message) and an authorial subject position (intention and desire). Aesthetic judgements of truthfulness or honesty are used to evaluate this relation. While truth concerns the relation of symbolic expressions to the external or objective world, righteousness to the shared, social world and aesthetic well-formedness to the likewise shared, cultural world, authenticity concerns their relationship to the internal or subjective world. Just as truth relates to the external world but can only be validated in intersubjective dialogues, the internal claims for authenticity, honesty or credibility are constructed and evaluated in interpretive communities.

Even a false and illegitimate proposition can be honest, since it only becomes a lie if the speaker him/herself doesn't believe in it. And conversely, even a cognitive truth can be inauthentic if it does not touch the speaker's heart. Since subjects are internally split into conscious and unconscious sides, it is more difficult to decide whether expressions are honest or not. Texts convey meanings of which their authors have no (conscious) insight. This gives rise to a range of possible text/subject

---

[58] Cf. Winnicott (1971) on play and transitional phenomena.

relations. The simplest case is when the manifest content of a text connects to the conscious ego of its author, who then thinks of the text as an honest self-expression. But sometimes a depth-interpretation of a text may reveal hidden aspects which either make a virtual lie more true than it first seemed or instead show that something seemingly honest covers a deep inauthenticity.

Only a reflecting subject can be made 'respons-ible' for what she says and does, by alone being capable of answering 'I did it' and motivating her words and actions by arguments.[59] Individual subjectivity and authenticity is anchored in communicative acts and intersubjective dialogues. That is also why authentic expressions may use any accessible symbolic mode, genre and form – not only those which have roots back to the subject's origin. What was there from the beginning need not be the foundation of what presently exists: historical genesis and synchronic validity are two different things. An adult individual can form authentic expression with more sophisticated means than cries and screams, in other languages than the mother-tongue and in more genres than those inherited from childhood. The appropriation of foreign tongues and styles is often a crucial means to express deep inner states better than is possible with the tools inherited from childhood or the parental culture.[60] Secondary socialization is not only an outward progression to widening competences, but also a striving to integrate and develop the contradictory unconscious sides of one's subjectivity. Its tools may well be extremely modern and artificially constructed, as long as they manage to connect to the inner subjectivity in question. Contrary to many ideological discourses, authenticity and artificiality are no opposites, and authenticity is not exactly the same as pure originality or naïve naturalness.

Particularly in aesthetic discourses, the realist demand for truth can become too narrow and one-dimensional, denouncing all indirect and mediated symbolic presentations. In a similar way, the demand for absolute honesty may also be exaggerated in a dysfunctional way, particularly when it is understood as a unitary conformity to naturalized origins. But subjectivity is a product of both nature and intersubjective identity work, and credibility is constructed through complex cultural practices which use both illusions and technology.[61] A seemingly artificial text may also be an authentic expression of true life experiences in an artificial society. Since there are always many and split facets of identity, there are several ways to make authentic symbolizations.

Authenticity is constructed with textual markers that imply a close relation between the text and its author, that is, that the expression of a subject is honestly meant. It also invites a close identification between a text and its users, by its capability to convince and move them and to offer

[59] Cf. Madison (1988, p. 27), Peter Kemp (1991/1992) and Heller (1994, p. 53).
[60] Cf. Lorenzer (1972), Ziehe (1975), Erdheim (1982) and Wirth (1984).
[61] Cf. Grieves (1983), Frith (1986 and 1988), Mercer (1987) and Connor (1987).

a full experience of emotive involvement, affective presence and acceptance of what the text expresses. These sides can sometimes diverge: a song that dresses itself up as authentic can be cynically produced and be seen through as such by its audience; an honest artist's intention might fail in the ears of a listener; or an explicitly artificial song can still carry an impression of authenticity from a conscious artist to a similarly well-informed fan.

All cultural products have some authentic aspects, as they cannot but express something of their authors' identities. One cannot totally avoid putting a personal stylistic mark into one's voice. But the different aspects of authenticity may be more or less emphasized, within cultural forms as well as in discourses around them. Discourses on authenticity are not always important, but can always be re-emphasized. Authorship is sometimes less relevant and often problematic, but, contrary to what Barthes and Foucault may have thought, the (issue of the) author is obviously not 'dead'.

Grossberg (1993, pp. 202f) distinguishes three forms of authenticity in rock discourses. The most common is associated with hard rock and folk rock, and builds on the romantic ideology of rock as a construction by and expression of a magically dense community. In more dance-oriented and black genres authenticity is instead localized in the construction of a rhythmical and sexual body. A third form appears in postmodernist self-conscious pop and avantgarde rock, which plays with styles, well understanding that they are always artificially constructed, but through this very cynical self-knowledge shows a kind of realistic honesty.

I propose a generalized modification of this model. A first form can be named *social authenticity*, since it uses criteria taken from the level of collective group interaction. Here, the judgement of genuineness is based on the norms that are legitimate within a certain (real or imagined) social (interpretive) community. The next form might be called *subjective authenticity*, since it focuses on the individual's mind and body, as a state of presence. The third form could be defined as *cultural or meta-authenticity*, since it moves within (and derives legitimacy from) the level of the symbolic expressions (texts) themselves: the well-formedness of cultural works related to historically determined aesthetic genre rules. This third form is strongest when it works through (because of, rather than in spite of) obviously lacking social and/or subjective authenticity. The more 'synthetic' texts are, the more convincing would a shown meta-reflexivity of their authors be of their honesty and consciousness.

This last type has become more and more important in late modern popular culture (music, films, novels, fashion, etc.). The two first forms have not been eroded, but an increased demand for reflexivity has forced older and more naïve conceptions of authenticity to develop meta-authentic traits. It seems increasingly difficult to forget all intermediary links of social and cultural constructions between subjects and texts, between human feelings and stylistic manifestations. Artists and audiences can continue to strive for experiences of spontaneous community or bodily presence, but it has become hard to repress the insight that this takes place through a complicated play of gestures, signs and strategies, so that social and subjective authenticity is also in fact filtered through cultural authenticity. One may now have the best chance to attain social and subjective authenticity if the symbolic contexts are made conscious.

All three forms can be found in both conservative and progressive variants. The striving for community in social authenticity can long regressively for a pre-modern local deep-rootedness, but it can also be an effort to produce a late modern collectivity of choice (as in the rave party where everyone mingles with others for one night). The striving for individual bodily presence in subjective authenticity can take the form of an anti-intellectual biologism that avoids all reflexivity in a mythologizing return to pure nature, or it can enjoy the heterological interplay of body and language in the praxis of dance or stylization. The striving for reflexive self-consciousness in cultural authenticity can be locked up in an authoritarian submission to the burden of convention, in a regressive obedience to pre-determined traditions. But it can also be a free play with newly created self-presentations which draw on historical references and reconstruct genealogical trees to subvert established power relations and search for roots as a defence against oblivion.

Late modern reflexivity has problematized earlier, naïve and romantic views on authenticity, but not obliterated the relevance of this concept itself. It is in fact through reflexivity that authenticity becomes a possible issue, and reflexivity is only interesting if the mirror shows something that can be recognized as 'I' or 'we'.[62]

The symbolic mirroring of identities can be a conscious verbal and intellectual reflection, but is more often a very bodily and non-conceptual praxis using real mirrors, stylistic signs or other people as tools for defining and confirming oneself. Reflexivity may or may not have the narrative and discursive form of an explicit self-referentiality. Narcissism is only one possible limit form of reflexivity, when mirroring coincides with a merging self-dissolution. Mass media are increasingly important to reflexive practices. Reflexivity can be practised through lyrics as well as musical structures, and through externalized visual images as well as social interaction. In fact, self-mirroring always uses other people as well as cultural symbols, even though one of these *relational* and *symbolic* sides may sometimes be more apparent than the other. In the choice of textual genres, people mirror and confirm their identities, through various perceived homologies between these identities and symbolic aspects. This choice seems to have become more and more conscious and debated in late modernity, through a cultural release from naturalizing traditions and a growth in the stock of available stylistic tools.

Just as authenticity might be grounded (legitimized) in three principal ways, reflexivity can also point in at least three different directions. *Social*

---

[62] Cf. Fornäs (1995b) on expressions of reflexivity in youthful song texts.

reflexivity defines one's identity in terms of social groups, communities or categories, for example in terms of class or ethnicity. Here, reflexive use of genres anchors them and, by identification, oneself in social collectives. *Subjective reflexivity* defines identities in terms of individual development through life stages. In this form, symbolic tools are used to mirror more or less unique personal experiences through memories and various encodings of affective states. *Cultural reflexivity* is, finally, when certain works are intertextually related to and identified with other texts or genres.

Neither authenticity nor reflexivity must, however, be seen only as positive values. A partly oppressive side of reflexivity is what Foucault (1974/1979) or Elias (1969/1978) would perhaps call 'autosurveillance': an intense self-observation that shields off unwanted drives and desires in conformation with societal norms. But there is also an emancipatory side, in the potential access that self-knowledge offers to self-determination and textual self-expression. There can be good reasons not to be so authentic/ reflexive all the time, that is, to hold back the demands for honesty and self-observation. In some spaces and occasions it can be good to find relief from these pressing demands – to express oneself without immediately observing one's own performance. But this can no more be done completely or for long – it soon becomes necessary and attractive to reflect upon the created work and relate it to one's subjectivity.

A crucial way to adult subjecthood involves finding and giving love. If the game of narcissistic self-mirroring is not to turn into a self-dissolving spiral, but instead to open a development of growth, it must include an encounter with a different Other, someone who can love and be loved, in a relation both of mutual, dialogic, reflexive reciprocity and of asymmetric difference – that is, in communication.

This loving affirmation of the self in the mirror of the Other, does not make self-reflection or even narcissism superfluous, however. When the subject sees not only itself but also the Other in or behind the mirror, then a deeper self-understanding in relation to others can be reached. Reflexivity then expands rather than imprisons or destroys the self, and in at least three ways. First, when I disclose hidden depths in me for myself and for others, I am enlarged with formerly concealed or unconscious aspects. If I openly show bad sides of myself, at least I add a certain richness and complexity to my self-image. Secondly, the distancing involved in self-observation lets me transgress what I was before by integrating this very self-observing position itself in me. Even self-criticism can widen my identity by showing me as capable of being otherwise than I have hitherto been. If I confess that I know of weaknesses in my way of writing this text, we can perhaps agree that this self-insight somewhat increases my credibility. Thirdly and most importantly, the symbolic forms used in all self-mirroring introduce elements of the Other, of other people's eyes and ears, and of the symbolic order that enters me from my social and historical context, thus letting me incorporate more of this Other and thus again letting me grow rather than being reduced.

In a process of widening circles of self-mirroring outside of the family and the local community, one can get sight both of oneself and of the world. Then, the subject will continue to be open, flexible and in process, but not more alone in front of echoing screens. Interactive communication may then evolve out of mirroring pleasures, helping us see each other and experiment with our identities, rather than get stuck in them.

Most theorists agree that late modern culture is increasingly reflexive, filled with demands and opportunities for self-mirroring and symbolic self-definition. Sometimes this is interpreted as an irreversible loss of all authentic subjectivity. If the genuine voice is understood as something originally given, natural and spontaneous, then certainly all efforts to actively reconstruct it or reflect (upon) it can be felt as irreparable degradings.

However, this is a mistaken conclusion. In fact, reflexivity is not possible without a certain amount of authenticity. If you hide behind a 'false' voice/style, it is not *your* voice that you hear. And even if we accept that voices and subjects are in a continuous process of development, interfering with other subjects and voices, with the external world and with a range of symbolic systems, we need not abandon this constructed subject-in-process as an illusion. The conflict or oscillation between a striving for intense, close, symbiotic devotion and a distancing reflexivity seems to have become a main cultural theme in late modernity, not least in media-use.

Communicating selves

It is thus important to separate different aspects: age, gender, ethnicity and class; narcissism, reflexivity, mediatization, cultural expropriation and lifeworld colonization; psychological, social and cultural aspects; regression from different positions and to various stages; permanent and temporary regression; normality and pathologies; merging and mirroring; traditional patterns and late modern tendencies . . . Once again, distinctions are necessary for making useful connections – just as Narcissus would have needed to accept the distance from his own self-image in order to be able to love himself and join the Other, or as Echo would have to liberate herself from the slavish bounds to the male voice in order to express herself and be heard by her beloved. To meet the Other, one has to be reconciled to the insight that all human beings are irreversibly separated yet unavoidably intertwined, and that symbolic texts, while never substituting completely for the self, the world or the Other, are the only means to connect to them, through winding processes of interpretation. Then it becomes possible to discern not only oneself but also each other (unlike Narcissus) in the murmuring spring-water of cultural interactions, while (unlike Echo) revitalizing both the polyphonic voice and one's own acting, moving body.

Complex temporal processes of modernization have opened up the dimensions structuring this book. It first showed how spheres of power are cut through by resistant but conflicting social agencies. The central passage then analysed the crossing cultural streams of symbols, texts and discourses that are the core of cultural theory. This last chapter was devoted to the communicating selves which inhabit these temporal processes, social spaces and symbolic flows, as well as jointly create them by interactive practices. The long navigation along late modern cultural dimensions has thus mapped a communicative cultural theory which wants to be used and transformed by such interacting reading and writing subjects: *you*.

References

Where two dates are given, the first is the original publication date and the second is the date of the edition/translation for which the bibliographical details are supplied.

Adams, Gerald R., Thomas P. Gullotta and Raymond Montemayor (eds) (1992) *Adolescent Identity Formation*. Newbury Park, CA: Sage.

Adorno, Theodor W. (1973/1984) *Aesthetic Theory*. London: Routledge and Kegan Paul.

Adorno, Theodor W. and Max Horkheimer (1944) *Dialectic of Enlightenment*. New York: Social Studies Association.

Adorno, Theodor W., Else Frenkel-Brunswik, Daniel J. Levinson and R. Nevitt Sanford (1950/1969) *The Authoritarian Personality*. New York: Norton.

Aggleton, Peter J. and Geoff Whitty (1985) 'Rebels Without a Cause? Socialization and Subcultural Style among the Children of the New Middle Classes', *Sociology of Education*, 58 (January).

Althusser, Louis (1965/1966) *For Marx*. London: Verso.

Althusser, Louis and Étienne Balibar (1968/1970) *Reading Capital*. London: New Left Books.

Alvesson, Mats (1989) *Sociala störningar av självet: Om den narcissistiska karaktärsstörningens utbredning*. Lund: Studentlitteratur.

Anderson, Benedict (1983/1991) *Imagined Communities: Reflections on the Origin and Spread of Nationalism*. 2nd edition. London: Verso.

Ang, Ien (1991) *Desperately Seeking the Audience*. London: Routledge.

Apel, Hartmut and Joachim Heidorn (1977) 'Subjektivität und Öffentlichkeit: Kritik der theoretischen Positionen Oskar Negts', *Prokla*, 29.

Apel, Karl-Otto (1973/1980) *Towards a Transformation of Philosophy*. London: Routledge and Kegan Paul.

Apel, Karl-Otto (ed.) (1976/1982) *Sprachpragmatik und Philosophie*. Frankfurt am Main: Suhrkamp.

Arato, Andrew and Jean Cohen (1988) 'Civil Society and Social Theory', *Thesis Eleven*, 21.

Arendt, Hannah (1958) *The Human Condition*. Chicago: University of Chicago Press.

Ariès, Philippe (1960/1962) *Centuries of Childhood: A Social History of Family Life*. New York: Vintage/Random House.

Åström, Lissie (1986) *I kvinnoled: Om kvinnors liv genom tre generationer*. Malmö: Liber Förlag.

Åström, Lissie (1990) *Fäder och söner: Bland svenska män i tre generationer*. Stockholm: Carlssons.

Attali, Jacques (1977/1985) *Noise: The Political Economy of Music*. Manchester: Manchester University Press.

Austin, J.L. (1962) *How to do Things with Words*. Oxford: Oxford University Press.

Baacke, Dieter (1968) *Beat – die sprachlose Opposition*. Munich: Juventa.

Baacke, Dieter, Günter Frank, Martin Radde and Manfred Schnittke (1989) *Jugendliche im Sog der Medien: Medienwelten Jugendlicher und Gesellschaft*. Opladen: Leske + Budrich.

Baacke, Dieter, Uwe Sander and Ralf Vollbrecht (1990) *Lebenswelten Jugendlicher*. 2 volumes. Opladen: Leske + Budrich.

Bakhtin, Mikhail (1963/1984) *Problems of Dostoevsky's Poetics*. Manchester: Manchester University Press.

Bakhtin, Mikhail (1965/1984) *Rabelais and his World*. Cambridge, MA: MIT Press.

Bakhtin, Mikhail (1981) *The Dialogic Imagination*. Austin: University of Texas Press.

Bakhtin, Mikhail (1986) *Speech Genres and Other Late Essays*. Austin: University of Texas Press.

Balet, Leo and E. Gerhard (1973) *Die Verbürgerlichung der deutschen Kunst, Literatur und Musik im 18. Jahrhundert*. Frankfurt am Main/Berlin/Vienna: Ullstein.

Bang, Jørgen and Knut Lundby (eds) (1993) *Media Reception. PROFF Papers*. Oslo: Department of Media and Communication, University of Oslo (Report no. 9).

Baron, Stephen W. (1989) 'Resistance and its Consequences: The Street Culture of Punks', *Youth and Society*, 21:2.

Barry, Kevin (1987) *Language, Music and the Sign: A Study in Aesthetics, Poetics and Poetic Practice from Collins to Coleridge*. Cambridge: Cambridge University Press.

Barthes, Roland (1953/1968) *Writing Degree Zero*. New York: Hill and Wang.

Barthes, Roland (1964/1985) 'Rhetoric of the Image', in *The Responsibility of Forms: Critical Essays on Music, Art, and Representation*. New York: Hill and Wang.

Barthes, Roland (1970/1975) *S/Z*. London: Cape.

Barthes, Roland (1973/1975) *The Pleasure of the Text*. London: Jonathan Cape.

Barthes, Roland (1977) *Image, Music, Text*. London: Fontana Press.

Baudrillard, Jean (1983) 'The Ecstasy of Communication', in Foster 1983/1985.

Baudrillard, Jean (1988) *Selected Writings*. Cambridge: Polity Press.

Beauvoir, Simone de (1949/1988) *The Second Sex*. London: Picador.

Beck, Ulrich (1986/1992) *Risk Society: Towards a New Modernity*. London: Sage.

Beck, Ulrich (1991) *Politik in der Risikogesellschaft*. Frankfurt am Main: Suhrkamp.

Beck, Ulrich, Anthony Giddens and Scott Lash (1994) *Reflexive Modernization: Politics, Tradition and Aesthetics in the Modern Social Order*. Cambridge: Polity Press.

Bender, John and David E. Wellbery (eds) (1991) *Chronotypes: The Construction of Time*. Stanford, CA: Stanford University Press.

Bengtsson, Margot (1991a) 'Den dekonstruerade maskuliniteten', in Johan Fornäs, Ulf Boëthius and Sabina Cwejman (eds), *Kön och identitet i förändring: FUS-rapport 3*. Stockholm/Stehag: Symposion.

Bengtsson, Margot (1991b) 'Från oidipal rivalitet till att bygga självet: Om könssocialisation och social förändring från 1950-tal, till 1970/80-tal', in Anders Löfgren and Margareta Norell (eds), *Att förstå ungdom: Identitet och mening i en föränderlig värld*. Stockholm/Stehag: Symposion.

Benhabib, Seyla (1992) *Situating the Self: Gender, Community and Postmodernism in Contemporary Ethics*. Cambridge: Polity Press.

Benjamin, Walter (1966/1973) *Understanding Brecht*. London: New Left Books.

Benjamin, Walter (1968) *Illuminations*. New York: Harcourt Brace.

Benjamin, Walter (1983) *Das Passagen-Werk*. Frankfurt am Main: Suhrkamp.

Bennett, H. Stith (1980) *On Becoming a Rock Musician*. Amherst: University of Massachusetts Press.

Bennett, Tony, Colin Mercer and Janet Woollacott (eds) (1986) *Popular Culture and Social Relations*. Milton Keynes: Open University Press.

Benveniste, Émile (1966/1971) *Problems in General Linguistics*. Coral Gables: University of Miami Press.

Berg, Axel van den (1990) 'Habermas and Modernity: A Critique of the Theory of Communicative Action', *Current Perspectives in Social Theory*, 10.

Berger, John (1972) *Ways of Seeing*. Harmondsworth: BBC/Penguin.

Berger, Peter A. (1987) 'Klassen und Klassifikationen: Zur "neuen Unübersichtlichkeit" in der soziologischen Ungleichheitsdiskussion', *Kölner Zeitschrift für Soziologie und Sozialpsychologie*, 39.

Berger, Peter L. and Thomas Luckmann (1966/1984) *The Social Construction of Reality: A Treatise in the Sociology of Knowledge*. Harmondsworth: Pelican.

Berkaak, Odd Are and Even Ruud (1992) *Den påbegynte virkelighet: Studier i samtidskultur*. Oslo: Universitetsforlaget.

Berman, Marshall (1982) *All That is Solid Melts into Air: The Experience of Modernity*. New York: Simon and Schuster.

Bernstein, Richard J. (1983) *Beyond Objectivism and Relativism: Science, Hermeneutics and Praxis*. Philadelphia: University of Pennsylvania Press.

Bernstein, Richard J. (ed.) (1985) *Habermas and Modernity*. Oxford: Basil Blackwell.

Bettelheim, Bruno (1983/1991) *Freud and Man's Soul*. Harmondsworth: Penguin.

Bjerrum Nielsen, Harriet and Monica Rudberg (1993) 'Gender, Body and Beauty in Adolescence', *Young: Nordic Journal of Youth Research*, 1:2.

Bjerrum Nielsen, Harriet and Monica Rudberg (1994) *Psychological Gender and Modernity*. Oslo: Scandinavian University Press.

Björnberg, Alf (1991) 'Sign of the Times? Om musikvideo och populärmusikens semiotik', *Svensk tidskrift för musikforskning*, 72 (1990).

Bjurström, Erling (1990) 'Raggare: En tolkning av en stils uppkomst och utveckling', in Peter Dahlén and Margareta Rönnberg (eds), *Spelrum: Om lek, stil och flyt i ungdomskulturen*. Uppsala: Filmförlaget.

Bjurström, Erling and Johan Fornäs (1988) 'Ungdomskultur i Sverige', in Ulf Himmelstrand and Göran Svensson (eds), *Sverige – vardag och struktur*. Stockholm: Norstedts.

Bjurström, Erling and Lars Lilliestam (1994) 'Stilens markörer', in Johan Fornäs, Ulf Boëthius, Michael Forsman, Hillevi Ganetz and Bo Reimer (eds), *Ungdomskultur i Sverige: FUS-rapport 6*. Stockholm/Stehag: Symposion.

Blacking, John (1973) *How Musical is Man?* Seattle/London: University of Washington Press.

Blacking, John (ed.) (1977) *The Anthropology of the Body*. London/New York/San Francisco: Academic Press.

Blix, Jacqueline (1992) 'A Place to Resist: Reevaluating Women's Magazines', *Journal of Communication Inquiry*, 16:1.

Bloch, Ernst (1935/1991) *Heritage of Our Times*. Oxford: Polity Press.

Bloch, Ernst (1959/1986) *The Principle of Hope*. Cambridge, MA: MIT Press.

Blonsky, Marshall (ed.) (1985) *On Signs: A Semiotics Reader*. Oxford: Basil Blackwell.

Bloomfield, Terry (1991) 'It's Sooner Than You Think, or Where are We in the History of Rock Music?', *New Left Review*, 190.

Blos, Peter (1962) *On Adolescence: A Psychoanalytic Interpretation*. New York: Free Press.

Bocock, Robert and Kenneth Thompson (eds) (1992) *Social and Cultural Forms of Modernity: Understanding Modern Societies: An Introduction. Book 3*. Cambridge/Milton Keynes: Polity Press/Open University.

Boëthius, Ulf (1990/1995) 'The History of High and Low Culture', in Johan Fornäs and Göran Bolin (eds), *Youth Culture in Late Modernity*. London: Sage.

Boëthius, Ulf (1992/1995) 'Controlled Pleasures: Youth and Literary Texts', in Johan Fornäs and Göran Bolin (eds), *Youth Culture in Late Modernity*. London: Sage.

Boëthius, Ulf (1993/1995) 'Youth, the Media and Moral Panics', in Johan Fornäs and Göran Bolin (eds), *Youth Culture in Late Modernity*. London: Sage.

Bois-Reymond, Manuela du and Mechtild Oechsle (eds) (1990) *Neue Jugendbiographie? Zum Strukturwandel der Jugendphase*. Opladen: Leske + Budrich.

Bordo, Susan (1993) ' "Material Girl": The Effacements of Postmodern Culture', in Cathy Schwichtenberg (ed.), *The Madonna Connection: Representational Politics, Subcultural Identities, and Cultural Theory*. Boulder, CO/San Francisco/Oxford: Westview Press.

Born, Georgina (1993) 'Afterword: Music Policy, Aesthetic and Social Difference', in Tony Bennett, Simon Frith, Lawrence Grossberg, John Shepherd and Graeme Turner (eds), *Rock and Popular Music: Politics, Policies, Institutions*. London/New York: Routledge.

Bourdieu, Pierre (1972/1977) *Outline of a Theory of Practice*. Cambridge: Cambridge University Press.

Bourdieu, Pierre (1979/1984) *Distinction: A Social Critique of the Judgement of Taste*. London/New York: Routledge and Kegan Paul.

Bourdieu, Pierre (1980/1993) *Sociology in Question*. London: Sage.

Bourdieu, Pierre (1987/1990) *In Other Words: Essays Towards a Reflexive Sociology.* London: Routledge.

Bourdieu, Pierre (1990) 'La domination masculine', *Actes de la recherche en sciences sociales*, 84.

Bourdieu, Pierre (1992) *Les règles de l'art: Genèse et structure du champ littéraire.* Paris: Seuil.

Bourdieu, Pierre (1993) *The Field of Cultural Production: Essays on Art and Literature.* Cambridge: Polity Press.

Bradley, Dick (1992) *Understanding Rock'n'roll: Popular Music in Britain 1955–1964.* Buckingham: Open University Press.

Brake, Mike (1985) *Comparative Youth Culture: The Sociology of Youth Cultures and Youth Subcultures in America, Britain and Canada.* London: Routledge and Kegan Paul.

Brantlinger, Patrick (1983) *Bread and Circuses: Theories of Mass Culture as Social Decay.* New York: Cornell University Press.

Brantlinger, Patrick (1990) *Crusoe's Footprints: Cultural Studies in Britain and America.* New York/London: Routledge.

Brecht, Bertolt (1962) *Brecht: A Collection of Critical Essays.* Englewood Cliffs, NJ: Spectrum.

Broady, Donald (ed.) (1986) *Kultur och utbildning: Om Pierre Bourdieus sociologi.* Stockholm: UHÄ.

Broady, Donald (1991) *Sociologi och epistemologi: Om Pierre Bourdieus författarskap och den historiska epistemologin.* Stockholm: HLS.

Brückner, Peter, Gerhard Bott, Eberhard Knödler-Bunte, Oskar Negt, Peter v. Oertzen, Michael Vester and Thomas Ziehe (1981) 'Industrialisierung der inneren Natur: Kapitalismus und bürgerliche Gesellschaft', in Eberhard Knödler-Bunte (ed.), *Was ist heute noch links?* Berlin: Ästhetik und Kommunikation.

Buckingham, David (ed.) (1993) *Reading Audiences: Young People and the Media.* Manchester: Manchester University Press.

Budd, Mike, Robert M. Entman and Clay Steinman (1990) 'The Affirmative Character of US Cultural Studies', *Critical Studies in Mass Communication*, 7:2.

Bürger, Christa, Peter Bürger and Jochen Schulte-Sasse (eds) (1982) *Zur Dichotomisierung von hoher und niederer Literatur.* Frankfurt am Main: Suhrkamp.

Burgin, Victor, James Donald and Cora Kaplan (eds) (1986) *Formations of Fantasy.* London/ New York: Methuen.

Burgos, Martine (1988) *Life Stories, Narrativity, and the Search for the Self.* Jyväskylä: Research Unit for Contemporary Culture.

Burke, Peter (1978) *Popular Culture in Early Modern Europe.* New York: Harper and Row.

Cahoone, Lawrence E. (1988) *The Dilemma of Modernity: Philosophy, Culture, and Anti-Culture.* New York: State University of New York Press.

Calhoun, Craig (ed.) (1992) *Habermas and the Public Sphere.* Cambridge, MA: MIT Press.

Carey, James W. (1989/1992) *Communication as Culture: Essays on Media and Society.* New York/London: Routledge.

Carle, Jan and Abby Peterson (eds) (1992) *Social Movements and Social Change.* Gothenburg: Sociologiska institutionen.

Carlsson, Ulla (ed.) (1987) *Forskning om populärkultur.* Gothenburg: Nordicom-Sverige.

Carragee, Kevin M. (1990) 'Interpretive Media Study and Interpretive Social Science', *Critical Studies in Mass Communication*, 7:2.

Castoriadis, Cornelius (1989/1992) 'Power, Politics, Autonomy', in Honneth et al. 1989/1992.

Certeau, Michel de (1974/1988) *The Practice of Everyday Life.* Berkeley/Los Angeles: University of California Press.

Certeau, Michel de (1985) *Heterologies: Discourse on the Other.* Minneapolis: University of Minnesota Press.

Chambers, Iain (1986) *Popular Culture: The Metropolitan Experience.* London: Methuen.

Chambers, Iain (1990) *Border Dialogues: Journeys in Postmodernity.* London: Routledge.

Chartier, Roger (1988) 'Texts, Printing, Readings', in Lynn Hunt (ed.), *The New Cultural History.* Berkeley: University of California Press.

Chodorow, Nancy (1979) *The Reproduction of Mothering: Psychoanalysis and the Sociology of Gender*. Berkeley/Los Angeles/London: University of California Press.

Chodorow, Nancy J. (1989) *Feminism and Psychoanalytic Theory*. New Haven/London: Yale University Press.

Clarke, Gary (1981/1990) 'Defending Ski-Jumpers: A Critique of Theories of Youth Subcultures', in Frith and Goodwin 1990.

Clarke, John (1976) 'Style', in Hall and Jefferson 1975/1976.

Classen, Constance (1993) *Worlds of Sense: Exploring the Senses in History and across Cultures*. London/New York: Routledge.

Clifford, James and George E. Marcus (eds) (1986) *Writing Culture: The Poetics and Politics of Ethnography*. Berkeley/Los Angeles/London: University of California Press.

Clüver, Claus (1993) 'Interartiella studier: En inledning', in Lagerroth et al. 1993.

Cohen, Anthony P. (1985) *The Symbolic Construction of Community*. Chichester/London: Ellis Horwood/Tavistock.

Cohen, Jean and Andrew Arato (1989/1992) 'Politics and the Reconstruction of the Concept of Civil Society', in Honneth et al. 1989/1992.

Cohen, Jean and Andrew Arato (1992) *Civil Society and Political Theory*. Cambridge, MA: MIT Press.

Cohen, Phil (1972/1980) 'Subcultural Conflict and Working-Class Community', in Hall et al. 1980.

Cohen, Philip (1986a) 'Historical Perspectives on the Youth Question Especially in Britain', in Dowe 1986.

Cohen, Philip (1986b) *Rethinking the Youth Question*. London: Institute of Education (Post Sixteen Education Centre Working Paper 3).

Cohen, Phil and David Robins (1978) *Knuckle Sandwich: Growing Up in the Working-Class City*. Harmondsworth: Penguin.

Cohen, Stanley (1972/1980) *Folk Devils and Moral Panics: The Creation of the Mods and Rockers*. Oxford: Basil Blackwell.

Cohen, Stanley and Laurie Taylor (1976/1992) *Escape Attempts: The Theory and Practice of Resistance to Everyday Life*. 2nd edition. London: Routledge.

Coleman, James S. (1961) *The Adolescent Society: The Social Life of the Teenager and its Impact on Education*. New York: Free Press.

Collins, Jim (1989) *Uncommon Cultures: Popular Culture and Post-Modernism*. New York/London: Routledge.

Connor, Steve (1987) 'The Flag on the Road: Bruce Springsteen and the Live', *New Formations*, 3.

Corner, John (1991) 'Meaning, Genre and Context: The Problematics of "Public Knowledge" in the New Audience Studies', in James Curran and Michael Gurevitch (eds) *Mass Media and Society*. London: Edward Arnold.

Coward, Rosalind and John Ellis (1977) *Language and Materialism: Developments in Semiology and the Theory of the Subject*. London: Routledge and Kegan Paul.

Crane, Diana (1992) *The Production of Culture: Media and the Urban Arts*. Newbury Park, CA: Sage.

Crespi, Franco (1987) 'Social Action and the Ambivalence of Communication: A Critique of Habermas's Theory', *European Journal of Communication*, 2:2.

Crisell, Andrew (1986) *Understanding Radio*. London/New York: Routledge.

Crook, Stephen, Jan Pakulski and Malcolm Waters (1992) *Postmodernization: Change in Advanced Society*. London: Sage.

Culture and History (1990), 7.

Czaplicka, Magdalena (1987) *Tonåringar och fritid: Hur skolungdomar använder sin tid*. Stockholm: Konsumentverket.

Czaplicka, Magdalena and Hedvig Ekerwald (1986) *Ungdomars konsumtion -85*. Stockholm: Statens ungdomsråd/Konsumentverket.

Dahl, Göran (1987) 'Ludwig möter Jacques: Kring språkspelsteori och psykoanalytisk förståelse av språkliga symboler', *Res publica*, 7.

Dahlgren, Peter (1995) *Television and the Public Sphere: Democracy, Citizens, and the Media.* London: Sage.

Dahmer, Helmut (1973) *Libido und Gesellschaft.* Frankfurt am Main: Suhrkamp.

Deleuze, Gilles (1988/1994) 'Foldings, or the Inside of Thought (Subjectivation)', in Kelly 1994.

Denselow, Robin (1989) *When the Music's Over: The Story of Political Pop.* London/Boston: Faber and Faber.

Denzin, Norman K. and Yvonna S. Lincoln (eds) (1994) *Handbook of Qualitative Research.* Thousand Oaks, CA: Sage.

Derrida, Jacques (1967/1973) *Speech and Phenomena.* Evanston, IL: Northwestern University Press.

Derrida, Jacques (1967/1976) *Of Grammatology.* Baltimore/London: Johns Hopkins University Press.

Derrida, Jacques (1967/1978) *Writing and Difference.* London: Routledge and Kegan Paul.

Deutsch, Helene (1944) *The Psychology of Women: A Psychoanalytic Interpretation.* New York: Grune and Straton.

DiMaggio, Paul and Paul Hirsch (1976) 'Production Organization in the Arts', *American Behavioral Scientist*, 19.

Doane, Mary Ann (1987) *The Desire to Desire: The Woman's Film of the 1940's.* Bloomington/Indianapolis: Indiana University Press.

Döbert, Rainer, Jürgen Habermas and Gertrud Nunner-Winkler (eds) (1980) *Entwicklung des Ichs.* (2nd edition). Königstein: Verlagsgruppe Athenäum, Hain, Scriptor, Hanstein.

Donald, James (ed.) (1991) *Psychoanalysis and Cultural Theory: Thresholds.* London: Macmillan/ICA.

Donen, Jack (1983) 'Narcissus-myten', *Psyke og Logos*, 1/1983.

Douglas, Mary (1966/1984) *Purity and Danger: An Analysis of the Concepts of Pollution and Taboo.* London: Ark.

Dowe, Dieter (ed.) (1986) *Jugendprotest und Generationenkonflikt in Europa im 20. Jahrhundert: Deutschland, England, Frankreich und Italien im Vergleich.* Bonn: Verlag Neue Gesellschaft.

Drotner, Kirsten (1991a) 'Kulturellt kön och modern ungdom', in Johan Fornäs, Ulf Boëthius and Sabina Cwejman (eds), *Kön och identitet i förändring: FUS-rapport 3.* Stockholm/Stehag: Symposion.

Drotner, Kirsten (1991b) *At skabe sig – selv: Ungdom, æstetik, pædagogik.* Copenhagen: Gyldendal.

Drotner, Kirsten (1991c) 'Intensities of Feeling: Modernity, Melodrama and Adolescence', *Theory, Culture and Society*, 8:1.

Drotner, Kirsten (1992) 'Modernity and Media Panics', in Michael Skovmand and Kim Christian Schrøder (eds), *Media Cultures: Reappraising Transnational Media.* London/New York: Routledge.

Drotner, Kirsten (1994) 'Ethnographic Enigmas: "The Everyday" in Recent Media Studies', *Cultural Studies*, 8:2.

Drotner, Kirsten and Monica Rudberg (eds) (1993) *Dobbeltblikk på det moderne.* Oslo: Universitetsforlaget.

Durkheim, Émile (1912/1976) *The Elementary Forms of the Religious Life.* London: George Allen and Unwin.

Eco, Umberto (1967/1987) 'Towards a Semiological Guerrilla Warfare', in *Travels in Hyperreality.* London: Picador.

Eco, Umberto (1976) *A Theory of Semiotics.* Bloomington: Indiana University Press.

Eco, Umberto (1979) *The Role of the Reader: Explorations in the Semiotics of Texts.* Bloomington: Indiana University Press.

Eco, Umberto (1979/1987) 'Language, Power, Force', in *Travels in Hyperreality.* London: Picador.

Ehn, Billy, Barbro Klein, Owe Ronström and Annick Sjögren (1990) *The Organization of Diversity in Sweden.* Stockholm: Invandrarminnes-arkivet.

Elias, Norbert (1969/1978) *The Civilizing Process.* 2 volumes. Oxford: Basil Blackwell.

Elias, Norbert (1989/1991) *The Symbol Theory.* London: Sage.

Elliot, Philip (1974) 'Uses and Gratifications Research: A Critique and a Sociological Alternative', in Jay G. Blumler and Elihu Katz (eds), *The Uses of Mass Communications.* London: Sage.

Elliott, Anthony (1992) *Social Theory and Psychoanalysis in Transition: Self and Society from Freud to Kristeva.* Oxford/Cambridge, MA: Basil Blackwell.

Ellis, John (1982) *Visible Fictions. Cinema : Television : Video.* London: Routledge.

Erdheim, Mario (1982) *Die gesellschaftliche Produktion von Unbewußtheit: Eine Einführung in den ethnopsychoanalytischen Prozeß.* Frankfurt am Main: Suhrkamp.

Erdheim, Mario (1988) *Psychoanalyse und Unbewußtheit in der Kultur: Aufsätze 1980–1987.* Frankfurt am Main: Suhrkamp.

Ericson, Staffan (1991) *Kulturindustrins fiktioner. Skandinavisk forskning om populärfiktion: Översikt och kommenterad bibliografi.* Stockholm: JMK.

Eriksen, Trond Berg (1987/1989) *Budbärarens övertag: Om orden som medium.* Stockholm: Rabén & Sjögren.

Erikson, Erik Homburger (1968) *Identity, Youth and Crisis.* New York: Norton & Co.

Eskola, Katarina and Erkki Vainikkala (eds) (1988) *The Production and Reception of Literature: A Seminar Report.* Jyväskylä: Research Unit for Contemporary Culture.

Evans, William A. (1990) 'The Interpretive Turn in Media Research: Innovation, Iteration, or Illusion?', *Critical Studies in Mass Communication,* 7:2.

Ewen, Stuart (1988) *All Consuming Images: The Politics of Style in Contemporary Culture.* New York: Basic Books.

Eyerman, Ron (1987) 'Modernitet och sociala rörelser', in Ulla Bergryd (ed.), *Den sociologiska fantasin: Teorier om samhället.* Stockholm: Rabén and Sjögren.

Eyerman, Ron and Andrew Jamison (1991) *Social Movements: A Cognitive Approach.* Cambridge: Polity Press.

Fabb, Nigel, Derek Attridge, Alan Durant and Colin MacCabe (eds) (1987) *The Linguistics of Writing: Arguments between Language and Literature.* Manchester: Manchester University Press.

Fabbri, Franco (1982) 'A Theory of Musical Genres: Two Applications', in David Horn and Philip Tagg (eds), *Popular Music Perspectives.* Gothenburg/Exeter: IASPM.

Fahlgren, Margaretha (1988) 'Drömmen om den allomfattande moderligheten', in *Häften för kritiska studier,* 21:1.

Fairbairn, W.R.D. (1938) 'The Ultimate Basis of Aesthetic Experience', *British Journal of Psychology,* 29, part 2.

Featherstone, Mike (1988) 'In Pursuit of the Postmodern: An Introduction', *Theory, Culture and Society,* 5:2–3.

Featherstone, Mike (ed.) (1990) *Global Culture: Nationalism, Globalization and Modernity.* London: Sage.

Featherstone, Mike (1991) *Consumer Culture and Postmodernism.* London: Sage.

Feilitzen, Cecilia von, Leni Filipson, Ingegerd Rydin and Ingela Schyller (1989) *Barn och unga i medieåldern: Fakta i ord och siffror.* Stockholm: Rabén & Sjögren.

Filipson, Leni and Jan Nordberg (1992) 'Barns och ungdomars medie- och kulturvanor', in Johan Fornäs, Ulf Boëthius, Hillevi Ganetz and Bo Reimer (eds), *Unga stilar och uttrycksformer: FUS-rapport 4.* Stockholm/Stehag: Symposion.

Finnegan, Ruth (1989) *The Hidden Musicians: Music-Making in an English Town.* Cambridge: Cambridge University Press.

Fischer, Ernst (1959/1978) *The Necessity of Art.* Harmondsworth: Penguin.

Fish, Stanley (1980) *Is There a Text in this Class? The Authority of Interpretive Communities.* Cambridge, MA: Harvard University Press.

Fiske, John (1989a) *Understanding Popular Culture.* Boston: Unwin Hyman.

Fiske, John (1989b) *Reading the Popular.* Boston: Unwin Hyman.

Fiske, John (1992) 'The Cultural Economy of Fandom', in Lewis 1992.

Fiske, John (1993) *Power Plays, Power Works.* London/New York: Verso.

Fornäs, Johan (1979) *Musikrörelsen – en motoffentlighet?* Gothenburg: Röda Bokförlaget.

Fornäs, Johan (1982) 'Rockmusikens kraft', *Krut*, 26.

Fornäs, Johan (1984) 'Framtiden i det som hittills varit', in *Tvärspel – trettioen artiklar om musik*. Gothenburg: Musikvetenskapliga institutionen.

Fornäs, Johan (1987) ' "Identity is the Crisis": En bakgrund till kulturella uttrycksformers funktioner för ungdomar i senmoderniteten', in Carlsson 1987.

Fornäs, Johan (1990a): 'Popular Music and Youth Culture in Late Modernity', in Roe and Carlsson 1990.

Fornäs, Johan (1990b) 'Moving Rock: Youth and Pop in Late Modernity', *Popular Music*, 9:3.

Fornäs, Johan (1991) 'Thinking about More than One Thing at a Time', in Jari Ehrnrooth and Lasse Siurala (eds), *Construction of Youth*. Helsinki: VAPK-Publishing/Finnish Youth Research Society.

Fornäs, Johan (1993) ' "Play it Yourself": Swedish Music in Movement', *Social Science Information*, 32:1.

Fornäs, Johan (1994a) 'Karaoke: Subjectivity, Play and Interactive Media', *Nordicom-Review*, 1/1994.

Fornäs, Johan (1994b) 'Mirroring Meetings, Mirroring Media: The Microphysics of Reflexivity', *Cultural Studies*, 8:2.

Fornäs, Johan (1994c) 'Listen to Your Voice! Authenticity and Reflexivity in Rock, Rap and Techno Music', *New Formations*, 24.

Fornäs, Johan (1995a) 'The Future of Rock: Discourses that Struggle to Define a Genre', *Popular Music*, 14:1.

Fornäs, Johan (1995b) 'Do You See Yourself? Reflected Subjectivities in Youthful Song Texts', *Young: Nordic Journal of Youth Research*, 3:2.

Fornäs, Johan and Göran Bolin (eds) (1992) *Moves in Modernity*. Stockholm: Almqvist and Wiksell International.

Fornäs, Johan, Ulf Lindberg and Ove Sernhede (1984/1994) *Ungdomskultur: identitet och motstånd*. 4th edition. Stockholm/Stehag: Symposion.

Fornäs, Johan, Ulf Lindberg and Ove Sernhede (1988/1995) *In Garageland: Rock, Youth and Modernity*. London: Routledge.

Fornäs, Johan, Ulf Lindberg and Ove Sernhede (1990a) *Speglad ungdom: Forskningsreception i tre rockband*. Stockholm/Stehag: Symposion.

Fornäs, Johan, Ulf Lindberg and Ove Sernhede (1990b) 'Under the Surface of Rock: Youth Culture and Late Modernity', *Popular Music and Society*, 14:3.

Foster, Hal (ed.) (1983/1985) *Postmodern Culture*. London: Pluto Press.

Foucault, Michel (1969/1972) *The Archaeology of Knowledge*. London: Tavistock.

Foucault, Michel (1974/1979) *Discipline and Punish*. New York: Random House.

Foucault, Michel (1976/1990) *The History of Sexuality. Vol. I: An Introduction*. London: Penguin.

Foucault, Michel (1982) 'Afterword: The Subject and Power', in Hubert L. Dreyfus and Paul Rabinow, *Michel Foucault: Beyond Structuralism and Hermeneutics*. Chicago: University of Chicago Press.

Foucault, Michel (1983/1984) 'What is Enlightenment?', in Paul Rabinow (ed.), *The Foucault Reader*. New York: Pantheon Books (also as 'The Art of Telling the Truth' in Kelly 1994).

Foucault, Michel (1983/1994) 'Critical Theory/Intellectual History', in Kelly 1994.

Fowler, Bridget (1994) 'The Hegemonic Work of Art in the Age of Electronic Reproduction: An Assessment of Pierre Bourdieu', *Theory, Culture and Society*, 11:1.

Frank, Manfred (1983/1989) *What is Neostructuralism?* Minneapolis: University of Minnesota Press.

Frank, Manfred (1988) *Die Grenzen der Verständigung: Ein Geistergespräch zwischen Lyotard und Habermas*. Frankfurt am Main: Suhrkamp.

Frank, Manfred (1991) *Selbstbewußtsein und Selbsterkenntnis*. Stuttgart: Reclam.

Frank, Manfred, Gérard Raulet and Willem van Reijen (eds) (1988) *Die Frage nach dem Subjekt*. Frankfurt am Main: Suhrkamp.

Frankenberg, Ruth and Lata Mani (1993) 'Crosscurrents, Crosstalk: Race, "Postcoloniality" and the Politics of Location', *Cultural Studies*, 7:2.

Franklin, Sarah, Celia Lury and Jackie Stacey (1991) 'Feminism and Cultural Studies: Pasts, Presents, Futures', *Media, Culture and Society*, 13:2.

Fraser, Nancy (1987) 'What's Critical about Critical Theory? The Case of Habermas and Gender', in Sheyla Benhabib and Drucilla Cornell (eds), *Feminism as Critique: Essays on the Politics of Gender in Late-Capitalist Societies*. Cambridge: Polity Press.

Fraser, Nancy (1992a) 'Rethinking the Public Sphere: A Contribution to the Critique of Actually Existing Democracy', in Calhoun 1992.

Fraser, Nancy (1992b) 'The Uses and Abuses of French Discourse Theories for Feminist Politics', *Theory, Culture and Society*, 9:1.

Frege, Gottlob (1892/1993) 'On Sense and Reference', in A.W. Moore (ed.), *Meaning and Reference*. Oxford: Oxford University Press.

Freud, Sigmund (1901/1966) *The Psychopathology of Everyday Life*, in *The Standard Edition of the Complete Psychological Works of Sigmund Freud, Vol. VI*. London: Hogarth Press.

Freud, Sigmund (1914/1957) 'On Narcissism: An Introduction', in *The Standard Edition of the Complete Psychological Works of Sigmund Freud, Vol XIV*. London: Hogarth Press.

Freud, Sigmund (1915/1957) 'Mourning and Melancholia', in *The Standard Edition of the Complete Psychological Works of Sigmund Freud, Vol. XIV*. London: Hogarth Press.

Freud, Sigmund (1930/1961) *Civilization and its Discontents*, in *The Standard Edition of the Complete Psychological Works of Sigmund Freud, Vol. XXI*. London: Hogarth Press.

Friberg, Mats and Johan Galtung (eds) (1984) *Rörelserna*. Stockholm: Akademilitteratur.

Friedman, Jonathan (1990a) 'The Political Economy of Elegance', *Culture and History*, 7.

Friedman, Jonathan (1990b) 'Being in the World: Globalization and Localization', in Featherstone 1990.

Frimodt, Jens (1983) *Narcissisme: Freud, Kohut, Ziehe*. Copenhagen: Unge Pædagoger.

Frith, Simon (1981) *Sound Effects: Youth, Leisure, and the Politics of Rock'n'roll*. New York: Pantheon Books.

Frith, Simon (1986) 'Art versus Technology: The Strange Case of Popular Music', *Media, Culture and Society*, 8:3.

Frith, Simon (1988) *Music for Pleasure: Essays in the Sociology of Pop*. Cambridge: Polity Press.

Frith, Simon (ed.) (1989) *Facing the Music*. New York: Pantheon Books.

Frith, Simon (1994) 'What is Bad Music?', in Simon Frith, Kate Augestad, Robert Burnett, Hroar Klempe and Roger Wallis, *We're only in it for the Money: Ungdomskultur, pengar och makt i populärmusiken*. Stockholm: Kungl. Musikaliska akademien (Musiken år 2002: Rapport 11).

Frith, Simon and Andrew Goodwin (eds) (1990) *On Record: Rock, Pop, and the Written Word*. New York: Pantheon Books.

Frith, Simon and Angela McRobbie (1978) 'Rock and Sexuality', *Screen Education*, 29.

Frith, Simon, Andrew Goodwin and Lawrence Grossberg (eds) (1993) *Sound and Vision: The Music Video Reader*. London/New York: Routledge.

Frow, John (1987) 'Accounting for Tastes: Some Problems in Bourdieu's Sociology of Culture', *Cultural Studies*, 1:1.

Frow, John (1992) 'The Concept of the Popular', *New Formations*, 18.

Frow, John (1993) 'Knowledge and Class', *Cultural Studies*, 7:2.

Fuglesang, Minou (1994) *Veils and Videos: Female Youth Culture on the Kenyan Coast*. Stockholm: Stockholm Studies in Social Anthropology.

Fukuyama, Francis (1992) *The End of History and the Last Man*. London: Hamish Hamilton.

Future Woman (1991), Paris: BBDO Europe.

Gadamer, Hans-Georg (1960/1975) *Truth and Method*. London: Sheed and Ward.

Gallop, Jane (1989) 'Moving Backwards or Forwards', in Teresa Brennan (ed.), *Between Feminism and Psychoanalysis*. London/New York: Routledge.

Ganetz, Hillevi (1992/1995) 'The Shop, the Home and Femininity as a Masquerade', in Johan Fornäs and Göran Bolin (eds), *Youth Culture in Late Modernity*. London: Sage.

Ganetz, Hillevi and Karin Lövgren (eds) (1991) *Om unga kvinnor: Identitet, kultur och livsvillkor*. Lund: Studentlitteratur.

Gans, Herbert J. (1974) *Popular Culture and High Culture: An Analysis and Evaluation of Taste*. New York: Basic Books.

Garnham, Nicholas (1979) 'Contributions to a Political Economy of Mass Communications', *Media, Culture and Society*, 1:2.

Garofalo, Reebee (1987) 'How Autonomous is Relative: Popular Music, the Social Formation and Cultural Struggle', *Popular Music*, 6:1.

Garofalo, Reebee (ed.) (1992) *Rockin' the Boat: Mass Music and Music Movements*. Boston, MA: South End Press.

Geertz, Clifford (1973) *The Interpretation of Cultures*. New York: Basic Books.

Gemzöe, Lena, Tove Holmquist, Don Kulick, Britt-Marie Thurén and Prudence Woodford-Berger (1989) 'Sex, genus och makt i antropologiskt perspektiv', *Kvinnovetenskaplig tidskrift*, 10:1.

Genette, Gérard (1982) *Palimpsestes: La littérature au second degré*. Paris: Seuil.

Gesser, Bengt (1987) 'En sociologisk visionär: Anteckningar kring Pierre Bourdieu', *Res publica*, 9.

Giddens, Anthony (1990) *The Consequences of Modernity*. Cambridge: Polity Press.

Giddens, Anthony (1991) *Modernity and Self-Identity: Self and Society in the Late Modern Age*. Cambridge: Polity Press.

Giddens, Anthony (1992) *The Transformation of Intimacy: Sexuality, Love and Eroticism in Modern Societies*. Cambridge: Polity Press.

Gilligan, Carol (1982) *In a Different Voice*. Cambridge, MA: Harvard University Press.

Gilligan, Carol, Nona P. Lyons and Trudy J. Hanmer (eds) (1990) *Making Connections: The Relational Worlds of Adolescent Girls at Emma Willard School*. Cambridge, MA: Harvard University Press.

Gillis, John (1981) *Youth and History*. New York/London: Academic Press.

Gillis, John (1993) 'Vanishing Youth: The Uncertain Place of the Young in a Global Age', *Young: Nordic Journal of Youth Research*, 1:1.

Gilroy, Paul (1987) *There Ain't No Black in the Union Jack: The Cultural Politics of Race and Nation*. London: Hutchinson.

Gilroy, Paul (1993a) *Small Acts: Thoughts on the Politics of Black Cultures*. London: Serpent's Tail.

Gilroy, Paul (1993b) *The Black Atlantic: Modernity and Double Consciousness*. London/New York: Verso.

Gilroy, Paul (1993c) 'Between Afro-Centri and Euro-Centrism: Youth Culture and the Problem of Hybridity' *Young: Nordic Journal of Youth Research*, 1:2.

Goffman, Erving (1959) *The Presentation of Self in Everyday Life*. New York: Doubleday.

Goffman, Erving (1969) *Strategic Interaction*. Philadelphia: University of Pennsylvania Press.

Goodman, Nelson (1976) *Languages of Art: An Approach to a Theory of Symbols*. Indianapolis: Hackett.

Goodwin, Andrew (1993) *Dancing in the Distraction Factory: Music Television and Popular Culture*. Minneapolis: University of Minnesota Press.

Goody, Jack (1986) *The Logic of Writing and the Organization of Society*. Cambridge: Cambridge University Press.

Goody, Jack (1987) *The Interface between the Written and the Oral*. Cambridge: Cambridge University Press.

Gramsci, Antonio (1971) *Selections from the Prison Notebooks*. New York: International Publishers.

Grieves, Jim (1983) 'Style as Metaphor for Symbolic Action: Teddy Boys, Authenticity and Identity', *Theory, Culture and Society*, 1:2.

Grignon, Claude and Jean-Claude Passeron (1985) *À propos des cultures populaires*. Marseilles: EHESS (Cahiers du Cercom, 1).

Gripsrud, Jostein (1989) ' "High Culture" Revisited', *Cultural Studies*, 3:2.

Gripsrud, Jostein (1995) *The Dynasty Years: Hollywood Television and Critical Media Studies*. London: Routledge.

Grossberg, Lawrence (1988) 'It's a Sin: Politics, Post-Modernity and the Popular', in Lawrence Grossberg, Tony Fry, Ann Curthoys and Paul Patton, *It's a Sin: Essays on Postmodernism, Politics and Culture*. Sydney: Power Publications.

Grossberg, Lawrence (1989) 'Putting the Pop Back into Postmodernism', in Andrew Ross (ed.), *Universal Abandon? The Politics of Postmodernism*. Edinburgh: Edinburgh University Press.

Grossberg, Lawrence (1992) *We Gotta Get Out of This Place: Popular Conservatism and Postmodern Culture*. New York/London: Routledge.

Grossberg, Lawrence (1993) 'The Media Economy of Rock Culture: Cinema, Postmodernity and Authenticity', in Frith et al. 1993.

Grossberg, Lawrence, Cary Nelson and Paula A. Treichler (eds) (1992) *Cultural Studies*. New York/London: Routledge.

Gudmundsson, Gestur (1984) *Let's Rock this Town: Subkulturel produktion af subjektivitet*. Copenhagen: Sociologisk institut.

Gudmundsson, Gestur (1992) *Ungdomskultur – som overgang til lønarbejde*. Copenhagen: Forlaget Sociologi.

Gumbrecht, Hans Ulrich and K. Ludwig Pfeiffer (eds) (1986) *Stil: Geschichten und Funktionen eines kulturwissenschaftlichen Diskurselements*. Frankfurt am Main: Suhrkamp.

Gurevitch, Michael, Tony Bennett, James Curran and Janet Woollacott (eds) (1982) *Culture, Society and the Media*. London: Methuen.

Haavind, Hanne (1985) 'Förändringar i förhållandet mellan kvinnor och män', *Kvinnovetenskaplig tidskrift*, 6:3.

Habermas, Jürgen (1962/1989) *The Structural Transformation of the Public Sphere: An Inquiry into a Category of Bourgeois Society*. Cambridge, MA: MIT Press.

Habermas, Jürgen (1976/1979) 'What is Universal Pragmatics?', in *Communication and Evolution of Society*. London: Heinemann.

Habermas, Jürgen (1979) 'Consciousness-Raising or Redemptive Criticism', *New German Critique* (Spring).

Habermas, Jürgen (1981/1984–8) *The Theory of Communicative Action*, 2 volumes. Cambridge: Polity Press.

Habermas, Jürgen (1983/1990) *Moral Consciousness and Communicative Action*. Cambridge: Polity Press.

Habermas, Jürgen (1984/1989) 'Taking Aim at the Heart of the Present: On Foucault's Lecture on Kant's *What is Enlightenment?*', in *The New Conservatism: Cultural Criticism and the Historians' Debate*. Cambridge: Polity Press (also in Kelly 1994).

Habermas, Jürgen (1985) *Die neue Unübersichtlichkeit*. Frankfurt am Main: Suhrkamp.

Habermas, Jürgen (1985/1987) *The Philosophical Discourse of Modernity: Twelve Lectures*. Cambridge: Polity Press.

Habermas, Jürgen (1988/1992) *Postmetaphysical Thinking: Philosophical Essays*. Cambridge, MA: MIT Press.

Habermas, Jürgen (1992a) 'Further Reflections on the Public Sphere', in Calhoun 1992.

Habermas, Jürgen (1992b) *Faktizität und Geltung: Beiträge zur Diskurstheorie des Rechts und des demokratischen Rechtsstaats*. Frankfurt am Main: Suhrkamp (forthcoming as *Facticity and Validity*. Cambridge, MA: MIT Press).

Hall, Stuart (1973/1980) 'Encoding/Decoding', in Hall et al. 1980.

Hall, Stuart (1980) 'Cultural Studies: Two Paradigms', *Media, Culture and Society*, 2:1 (also in Tony Bennett, Graham Martin, Colin Mercer and Janet Woollacott (eds) *Culture, Ideology and Social Process: A Reader*. London: Open University Press, 1981).

Hall, Stuart (1981) 'Notes on Deconstructing "the Popular" ', in Raphael Samuel (ed.), *People's History and Socialist Theory*. London: Routledge and Kegan Paul.

Hall, Stuart (1982) 'The Rediscovery of "Ideology": Return of the Repressed in Media Studies', in Gurevitch et al. 1982.

Hall, Stuart (1986a) 'Gramsci's Relevance for the Study of Race and Ethnicity', *Journal of Communication Inquiry*, 10:2.

Hall, Stuart (1986b) 'On Postmodernism and Articulation: An Interview with Stuart Hall (edited by Lawrence Grossberg)', *Journal of Communication Inquiry*, 10:2.

Hall, Stuart (1990) 'Cultural Identity and Diaspora', in Rutherford 1990.

Hall, Stuart (1992a) 'The West and the Rest: Discourse and Power', in Stuart Hall and Bram Gieben (eds), *Formations of Modernity. Understanding Modern Societies: An Introduction. Book 1*. Cambridge/Milton Keynes: Polity Press/Open University Press.

Hall, Stuart (1992b) 'The Question of Cultural Identity', in Stuart Hall, David Held and Tony McGrew (eds), *Modernity and its Futures. Understanding Modern Societies: An Introduction. Book 4*. Cambridge/Milton Keynes: Polity Press/Open University Press.

Hall, Stuart (1992c) 'What is This "Black" in Black Popular Culture?', in Gina Dent (ed.), *Black Popular Culture*. Seattle: Bay Press.

Hall, Stuart and Tony Jefferson (eds) (1975/1976) *Resistance Through Rituals: Youth Subcultures in Post-War Britain*. London/Birmingham: Hutchinson/CCCS.

Hall, Stuart and Paddy Whannel (1964/1990) 'The Young Audience', in Frith and Goodwin 1990.

Hall, Stuart, Chas Critcher, Tony Jefferson, John Clarke and Brian Roberts (eds) (1978) *Policing the Crisis: Mugging, the State, and Law and Order*. London: Macmillan.

Hall, Stuart, Dorothy Hobson, Andrew Lowe and Paul Willis (eds) (1980) *Culture, Media, Language*. London: Hutchinson.

Halonen, Irma Kaarina (1991) 'Kvinnor och offentlighet', in Ulla Carlsson (ed.), *Medier, människor, samhälle: 14 artiklar om nordisk masskommunikationsforskning*. Gothenburg: Nordicom-Sverige.

Hannerz, Ulf (1992a) *Cultural Complexity: Studies in the Social Organization of Meaning*. New York: Columbia University Press.

Hannerz, Ulf (1992b) 'Stockholm: Doubly Creolizing', in Åke Daun, Billy Ehn and Barbro Klein (eds), *To Make the World Safe for Diversity*. Stockholm: The Swedish Immigration Institute and Museum/The Ethnology Institute.

Haraway, Donna (1989) 'A Manifesto for Cyborgs: Science, Technology, and Socialist Feminism in the 1980s', in Linda Nicholson (ed.), *Feminism/Postmodernism*. London: Routledge.

Harding, Sandra (1986) *The Science Question in Feminism*. Milton Keynes: Open University Press.

Harris, David (1992) *From Class Struggle to the Politics of Pleasure: The Effects of Gramscianism on Cultural Studies*. London/New York: Routledge.

Hartwig, Helmut (1980) *Jugendkultur: Ästhetische Praxis in der Pubertät*. Reinbek bei Hamburg: Rowohlt.

Harvey, David (1990) *The Condition of Postmodernity*. Cambridge, MA/Oxford: Basil Blackwell.

Hassan, Ihab (1985) 'Postmodern Culture', *Theory, Culture and Society*, 2:3.

Haug, Wolfgang Fritz (1971/1986) *Critique of Commodity Aesthetics: Appearance, Sexuality and Advertising in Capitalist Society*. New York: International General.

Hauge, Hans and Henrik Horstbøll (eds) (1988) *Kulturbegrebets kulturhistorie*. Århus: Aarhus Universitetsforlag.

Hauser, Arnold (1951/1962) *The Social History of Art*. London: Routledge and Kegan Paul.

Hebdige, Dick (1979) *Subculture: The Meaning of Style*. London/New York: Methuen.

Hebdige, Dick (1988) *Hiding in the Light: On Images and Things*. London/New York: Routledge.

Hebdige, Dick (1990) 'Fax to the Future', *Marxism Today*, 1/1990.

Hebdige, Dick (1991) 'What is "Soul"?', in Pam Olson (ed.), *Video: Icons and Values*. New York: State University of New York Press.

Hegel, Georg Wilhelm Friedrich (1812/1969): *Science of Logic*. London: Allen & Unwin.

Hegel, Georg Wilhelm Friedrich (1842/1975) *Aesthetics: Lectures on Fine Art, Volume II*. Oxford: Oxford University Press.

Heidegger, Martin (1927/1978) *Being and Time*. Oxford: Basil Blackwell.

Heller, Agnes (1974/1976) *The Theory of Need in Marx*. London: Allison and Busby.

Heller, Agnes (1994) 'The Elementary Ethics of Everyday Life', in Robinson and Rundell 1994.

Hellesnes, Jon (1988/1991) *Hermeneutik och kultur: Filosofiska fragment*. Gothenburg: Daidalos.

Hellquist, Elof (1922/1989) *Svensk etymologisk ordbok*. 3rd edition. Malmö Liber.

Hermansen, Klaus (1990) *Zum Einfluß der Kulturindustrie auf das Bewußtsein Jugendlicher*. Pfaffenweiler: Centaurus.

Hill, Leslie (1990) 'Julia Kristeva: Theorizing the Avant-Garde?', in John Fletcher and Andrew Benjamin (eds), *Abjection, Melancholia and Love: The Work of Julia Kristeva*. London: Routledge.

Hirdman, Yvonne (1988) 'Genussystemet: Reflexioner kring kvinnors sociala underordning', *Kvinnovetenskaplig tidskrift*, 9:3.

Hobsbawm, Eric and Terence Ranger (eds) (1983) *The Invention of Tradition*. Cambridge: Cambridge University Press.

Hobson, Dorothy (1982) *Crossroads: The Drama of a Soap Opera*. London: Methuen.

Hodge, Robert and Gunther Kress (1988) *Social Semiotics*. Cambridge: Polity Press.

Højbjerg, Lennard (ed.) (1989) *Reception af levende billeder*. Odense: Akademisk Forlag.

Højrup, Thomas (1983) 'The Concept of Life-Mode: A Form-Specifying Model of Analysis Applied to Contemporary Western Europe', *Ethnologia Scandinavica*, 13.

Holland, Dietmar (1990) 'Musik als Sprache', in Hans Werner Henze (ed.), *Die Chiffren: Musik und Sprache*. Frankfurt am Main: Fischer.

Hollingshead, A.B. (1949) *Elmstown's Youth*. New York: John Wiley.

Holmqvist, Tove (1990) *Carmen och Romeo: Om femininitet och maskulinitet i damtidnings-reklam 1980 och 1988*. Stockholm: Konsumentverket.

Holstein-Beck, Sabina (1991/1995) 'Constancy and Change in the Life-World of Young Women', in Johan Fornäs and Göran Bolin (eds), *Youth Culture in Late Modernity*. London: Sage.

Honneth, Axel and Hans Joas (eds) (1986/1991) *Communicative Action*. Cambridge: Polity Press.

Honneth, Axel, Thomas McCarthy, Claus Offe and Albrecht Wellmer (eds) (1989/1992) *Cultural-Political Interventions in the Unfinished Project of Enlightenment*. Cambridge, MA: MIT Press.

Hosokawa, Shuhei (1984) 'The Walkman Effect', *Popular Music*, 4.

Hoy, David Couzens and Thomas McCarthy (1994) *Critical Theory*. Oxford/Cambridge, MA: Basil Blackwell.

Hudson, Barbara (1984) 'Femininity and Adolescence', in McRobbie and Nava 1984.

Hunt, Lynn (ed.) (1988) *The New Cultural History*. Berkeley: University of California Press.

Huntington, Patricia (1995) 'Toward a Dialectical Concept of Autonomy: Revisiting the Feminist Alliance with Poststructuralism', *Philosophy and Social Criticism*, 21:1.

Huspek, Michael (1993) 'Dueling Structures: The Theory of Resistance in Discourse', *Communication Theory*, 3:1.

Hutcheon, Linda (1980/1984) *Narcissistic Narrative: The Metafictional Paradox*. New York/London: Methuen.

Huyssen, Andreas (1986) *After the Great Divide: Modernism, Mass Culture and Postmodernism*. London: Macmillan.

Inglehart, Ronald (1977) *The Silent Revolution: Changing Values and Political Styles among Western Publics*. Princeton, NJ: Princeton University Press.

Israel, Joachim (1992) *Språk och kunskap*. Gothenburg: Daidalos.

Jackson, Michael (1983) 'Knowledge of the Body', *Man*, 18.

Jakobson, Roman (1960) 'Closing Statement: Linguistics and Poetics', in Thomas A. Sebeok (ed.), *Style in Language*. Cambridge, MA: MIT Press.

Jakobson, Roman (1968/1971) 'Language in Relation to other Communication Systems', in *Selected Writings II: Word and Language*. The Hague/Paris: Mouton.

Jameson, Fredric (1971) *Marxism and Form: Twentieth-Century Dialectical Theories of Literature*. Princeton, NJ: Princeton University Press.

Jameson, Fredric (1981) *The Political Unconscious*. Ithaca, NY: Cornell University Press.

Jameson, Fredric (1988a) *The Ideologies of Theory. Essays 1971–1986. Volume 1: Situations of Theory*. London: Routledge.

Jameson, Fredric (1988b) *The Ideologies of Theory. Essays 1971–1986. Volume 2: The Syntax of History*. London: Routledge.

Jameson, Fredric (1991) *Postmodernism, or, the Cultural Logic of Late Capitalism*. Durham, NC: Duke University Press.

Jencks, Charles (1986/1989) *What is Post-Modernism?* 3rd edition. London/New York: Academy Editions/St Martin's Press.

Jenkins, Richard (1992) *Pierre Bourdieu*. London/New York: Routledge.

Jenks, Chris (1993) *Culture*. London/New York: Routledge.

Jensen, Joli (1990) *Redeeming Modernity: Contradictions in Media Criticism*. Newbury Park, CA: Sage.

Jensen, Klaus Bruhn and Nicholas W. Jankowski (eds) (1991) *A Handbook of Qualitative Methodologies for Mass Communication Research*. London/New York: Routledge.

Johansen, Anders (1994) 'Soul for Sale', *Cultural Studies*, 8:2.

Johansson, Thomas and Fredrik Miegel (1992) *Do the Right Thing: Lifestyle and Identity in Contemporary Youth Culture*. Stockholm: Almqvist and Wiksell International.

Johnson, Mark (1987) *The Body in the Mind: The Bodily Basis of Meaning, Imagination, and Reason*. Chicago/London: University of Chicago Press.

Kant, Immanuel (1784/1963) 'What is Enlightenment?', in *Kant on History*, Indianapolis/New York: Bobbs-Merrill (also in Kant: *Political Writings*. 2nd edition. Cambridge: Cambridge University Press, 1991).

Kaplan, Louise J. (1984) *Adolescence: The Farewell to Childhood*. New York: Simon and Schuster.

Kausch, Michael (1988) *Kulturindustrie und Populärkultur*. Frankfurt am Main: Fischer.

Kearney, Richard (1988) *The Wake of Imagination*. London: Hutchinson.

Kellner, Douglas (1995) *Media Culture: Cultural Studies, Identity and Politics between the Modern and the Postmodern*. London/New York: Routledge.

Kelly, Michael (ed.) (1994) *Critique and Power: Recasting the Foucault/Habermas Debate*. Cambridge, MA: MIT Press.

Kemp, Peter (1981/1990) *Döden och maskinen: En introduktion till Jacques Derrida*. Stockholm/Stehag: Symposion.

Kemp, Peter (1991/1992) *Das Unersätzliche: Eine Technologie-Ethik*. Berlin: Wichern-Verlag.

Kemp, Sandra (1992) 'Conflicting Choreographies: Derrida and Dance', *New Formations*, 16.

Keniston, Kenneth (1968) *Young Radicals: Notes on Committed Youth*. New York: Harcourt, Brace and World.

Keniston, Kenneth (1970) 'Youth: A "New" Stage of Life', *American Scholar*, 39.

Keppler, Agneta and Martin Seel (1991) 'Zwischen Vereinnahmung und Distanzierung: Vier Fallstudien zur Massenkultur', *Merkur*, 510/511.

Kirshenblatt-Gimblett, Barbara (1992) 'Performing Diversity', in Åke Daun, Billy Ehn and Barbro Klein (eds), *To Make the World Safe for Diversity*. The Swedish Immigration Institute and Museum/The Ethnology Institute.

Klausmeier, Friedrich (1978) *Die Lust, sich musikalisch auszudrücken*. Reinbek bei Hamburg: Rowohlt.

Klausmeier, Ruth-Gisela (1973) 'Pubertät und Beatmusik', *Psyche*, 27.

Kleven, Kari Vik (1992) *Jentekultur som kyskhetsbelte*. Oslo: Universitetsforlaget.

Kohut, Heinz (1957) 'Observations on the Psychological Functions of Music', *Journal of the American Psychoanalytical Association*, 5.

Kohut, Heinz (1964) 'Some Problems of a Metapsychological Formulation of Fantasy', *International Journal of Psychoanalysis*, 45.

Kohut, Heinz (1971) *The Analysis of the Self: A Systematic Approach to the Psychoanalytic Treatment of Narcissistic Personality Disorders*. New York: International University Press.

Kohut, Heinz (1977) *The Restoration of the Self*. New York: International University Press.

Kohut, Heinz and Siegmund Levarie (1950) 'On the Enjoyment of Listening to Music', *Psychoanalytic Quarterly*, 19.

Koselleck, Reinhart (1979/1985) *Futures Past: On the Semantics of Historical Time*. Cambridge, MA: MIT Press.

Kosík, Karel (1963/1976) *Dialectics of the Concrete: A Study on Problems of Man and World*. Boston: Reidel.

Kraft, Hartmut (ed.) (1984) *Psychoanalyse, Kunst und Kreativität heute: Die Entwicklung der analytischen Kunstpsychologie seit Freud*. Cologne: DuMont.

Krenzlin, Norbert (ed.) (1992) *Zwischen Angstmetapher und Terminus: Theorien der Massenkultur seit Nietzsche*. Berlin: Akademie Verlag.

Kris, Ernst (1952) *Psychoanalytic Explorations in Art*. New York: International Universities Press.

Kristensson-Uggla, Bengt (1994) *Kommunikation på bristningsgränsen: En studie i Paul Ricoeurs projekt*. Stockholm/Stehag: Symposion.

Kristeva, Julia (1973/1986) 'The System and the Speaking Subject', in Toril Moi (ed.), *The Kristeva Reader*. Oxford: Basil Blackwell.

Kristeva, Julia (1974/1984) *Revolution in Poetic Language*. New York: Columbia University Press.

Kristeva, Julia (1974/1986) 'About Chinese Women', in Toril Moi (ed.), *The Kristeva Reader*. Oxford: Basil Blackwell.

Kristeva, Julia (1980) *Desire in Language: A Semiotic Approach to Literature and Art*. New York: Columbia University Press.

Kristeva, Julia (1980/1982) *Powers of Horror: An Essay on Abjection*. New York: Columbia University Press.

Kristeva, Julia (1981/1989) *Language – the Unknown: An Initiation into Linguistics*. Hemel Hempstead: Harvester Wheatsheaf.

Kristeva, Julia (1983/1987) *Tales of Love*. New York: Columbia University Press.

Kristeva, Julia (1985/1987) *In the Beginning was Love: Psychoanalysis and Faith*. New York: Columbia University Press.

Kristeva, Julia (1987/1989) *Black Sun: Depression and Melancholia*. New York: Columbia University Press.

Kristeva, Julia (1988/1991) *Strangers to Ourselves*. New York: Harvester.

Kristeva, Julia (1990) 'The Adolescent Novel', in John Fletcher and Andrew Benjamin (eds), *Abjection, Melancholia and Love: The Work of Julia Kristeva*. London: Routledge.

Kroeber, A.L. and Clyde Kluckhohn (1952/1963) *Culture: A Critical Review of Concepts and Definitions*. New York: Vintage Books.

Kroeber, A.L. and Talcott Parsons (1958) 'The Concepts of Culture and of Social System', *American Sociological Review*, 23:5.

Krogstad, Anne (1990) 'Punkare och symbolförändring: Från yttre provokation till inre moralism', in Peter Dahlén and Margareta Rönnberg (eds), *Spelrum: Om lek, stil och flyt i ungdomskulturen*. Uppsala: Filmförlaget.

Lacan, Jacques (1966/1977) *Écrits: A Selection*. London: Tavistock.

Laclau, Ernesto (1990) *New Reflections on the Revolution of our Time*. London: Verso.

Laclau, Ernesto and Chantal Mouffe (1985) *Hegemony and Social Strategy: Towards a Radical Democratic Politics*. London: Verso.

Laermans, Rudi (1992) 'The Relative Rightness of Pierre Bourdieu: Some Sociological Comments on the Legitimacy of Postmodern Art, Literature and Culture', *Cultural Studies*, 6:2.

Lagerroth, Ulla Britta, Hans Lund, Peter Luthersson and Anders Mortenson (eds) (1993) *I musernas tjänst: Studier i konstarternas interrelationer*. Stockholm/Stehag: Symposion.

Laing, Dave (1978) *The Marxist Theory of Art: An Introductory Survey*. Brighton: Harvester Press.

Laing, Dave (1985) *One Chord Wonders: Power and Meaning in Punk Rock.* Milton Keynes: Open University Press.

Landes, Joan B. (1991) 'Women and the Public Sphere Revisited: Considerations for Contemporary Feminist Theory', in Anne-Marie Berggren, Ebba Witt-Brattström, Mona Eliasson, Anita Göransson and Anna Jónasdóttir, *Könsrelationernas betydelse som vetenskaplig kategori.* Stockholm: JÄMFO.

Landow, George P. (1992) *Hypertext: The Convergence of Contemporary Critical Theory and Technology.* Baltimore, MD/London: Johns Hopkins University Press.

Langer, Susanne K. (1942) *Philosophy in a New Key.* Cambridge, MA: Harvard University Press.

Laplanche, Jean (1970/1985) *Life and Death in Psychoanalysis.* Baltimore, MD: Johns Hopkins University Press.

Laplanche, Jean (1987/1989) *New Foundations for Psychoanalysis.* Oxford: Basil Blackwell.

Laplanche, Jean and Jean-Bertrand Pontalis (1967/1988) *The Language of Psychoanalysis.* London: Hogarth Press.

Larson, Reed and Robert Kubey (1983) 'Television and Music: Contrasting Media in Adolescent Life', *Youth and Society*, 15:1.

Lasch, Christopher (1979) *The Culture of Narcissism.* New York: Warner.

Lash, Scott (1990) *Sociology of Postmodernism.* London: Routledge.

Lash, Scott and Jonathan Friedman (eds) (1992) *Modernity and Identity.* Oxford: Basil Blackwell.

Lash, Scott and John Urry (1994) *Economies of Signs and Space.* London: Sage.

Lauretis, Teresa de (1987) *Technologies of Gender: Essays on Theory, Film, and Fiction.* Bloomington/Indianapolis: Indiana University Press.

Layton, Lynne and Barbara Ann Schapiro (1986) (eds) *Narcissism and the Text: Studies in Literature and the Psychology of Self.* New York: New York University Press.

Lecercle, Jean-Jacques (1992) 'To Do or Not to Do Without the Word: Ecstasy and Discourse in the Cinema', *New Formations*, 16.

Lechte, John (1990) 'Art, Love, and Melancholy in the Work of Julia Kristeva', in John Fletcher and Andrew Benjamin (eds), *Abjection, Melancholia and Love: The Work of Julia Kristeva.* London: Routledge.

Lee, Benjamin (1992) 'Textuality, Mediation, and Public Discourse', in Calhoun 1992.

Lefebvre, Henri (1968/1984) *Everyday Life in the Modern World.* New Brunswick: Transaction Publishers.

Lembo, Ronald and Kenneth H. Tucker Jr (1990) 'Culture, Television, and Opposition: Rethinking Cultural Studies', *Critical Studies in Mass Communication*, 7:2.

Lenz, Karl (1986) *Alltagswelten von Jugendlichen: Eine empirische Studie über jugendliche Handlungstypen.* Frankfurt am Main: Campus.

Lévi-Strauss, Claude (1958/1963) *Structural Anthropology.* London: Penguin.

Lévi-Strauss, Claude (1962/1966) *The Savage Mind.* London: Weidenfeld and Nicholson.

Lévinas, Emmanuel (1947/1987) *Time and the Other.* Pittsburgh, PA: Duquesne University Press.

Lévinas, Emmanuel (1961/1979) *Totality and Infinity.* The Hague: M. Nijhoff.

Levy, Jette Lundbo (1991) 'Indirekt dialog om begärets, givmildhetens och offrets moral', *Res publica*, 18.

Lewin, Kurt (1951) *Field Theory in Social Science.* New York: Harper and Brothers.

Lewis, George H. (1978) *The Sociology of Popular Culture.* London: Sage (*Current Sociology*, 26:3).

Lewis, Lisa A. (ed.) (1992) *The Adoring Audience: Fan Culture and Popular Media.* New York/London: Routledge.

Lilliestam, Lars (1988) *Musikalisk ackulturation – från blues till rock: En studie kring låten Hound Dog.* Gothenburg: Musikvetenskapliga institutionen.

Lindlof, Thomas R. (ed.) (1987) *Natural Audiences: Qualitative Research of Media Uses and Effects*, Norwood, NJ: Ablex.

Lipsitz, Georg (1990) *Time Passages: Collective Memory and American Popular Culture*. Minneapolis: University of Minnesota Press.

Lorenzer, Alfred (1970) *Kritik des psychoanalytischen Symbolbegriffs*. Frankfurt am Main: Suhrkamp.

Lorenzer, Alfred (1972) *Zur Begründung einer materialistischen Sozialisationstheorie*. Frankfurt am Main: Suhrkamp.

Lorenzer, Alfred (ed.) (1986) *Kultur-Analysen*. Frankfurt am Main: Fischer.

Lowe, Donald M. (1982) *History of Bourgeois Perception*. Chicago: University of Chicago Press.

Lundström, Jan-Erik and Berit Sahlström (eds) (1992) *Talspråk, skriftspråk, bildspråk*. Linköping: Tema Kommunikation.

Lury, Celia (1992) 'Popular Culture and the Mass Media', in Bocock and Thompson 1992.

Luthersson, Peter (1986) *Modernism och individualitet: En studie i den litterära modernismens kvalitativa egenart*. Stockholm/Lund: Symposion.

Lyotard, Jean-François (1979/1984) *The Postmodern Condition: A Report on Knowledge*. Manchester: Manchester University Press.

MacCabe, Colin (ed.) (1986) *High Theory/Low Culture: Analysing Popular Television and Film*. Manchester: Manchester University Press.

McClary, Susan (1991) *Feminine Endings: Music, Gender, and Sexuality*. Minnesota/Oxford: University of Minnesota Press.

McGuigan, Jim (1992) *Cultural Populism*. London/New York: Routledge.

McLaughlin, Lisa (1993) 'Feminism, the Public Sphere, Media and Democracy', *Media, Culture and Society*, 15:4

McLuhan, Marshall (1962) *The Gutenberg Galaxy*. Toronto: Toronto University Press.

McLuhan, Marshall (1964) *Understanding Media: The Extensions of Man*. London: Routledge and Kegan Paul.

McRobbie, Angela and Mica Nava (eds) (1984) *Gender and Generation*. London: Macmillan.

McRobbie, Angela (1991) *Feminism and Youth Culture: From* Jackie *to* Just Seventeen. London: Macmillan.

McRobbie, Angela (1994) *Postmodernism and Popular Culture*. London/New York: Routledge.

Madison, Gary Brent (1988) *The Hermeneutics of Postmodernity: Figures and Themes*. Bloomington/Indianapolis: Indiana University Press.

Mahler, Margaret S., Fred Pine and Anni Bergman (1975) *The Psychological Birth of the Human Infant: Symbiosis and Individuation*. London: Hutchinson.

Malmgren, Gun (1992) *Gymnasiekulturer: Lärare och elever om svenska och kultur*. Lund: Didaktikseminariet.

Mandel, Ernest (1972/1975) *Late Capitalism*. London: New Left Books.

Mander, Mary S. (1987) 'Bourdieu, the Sociology of Culture and Cultural Studies: A Critique', *European Journal of Communication*, 2:4.

Marcus, George E. and Michael M.J. Fischer (1986) *Anthropology as Cultural Critique: An Experimental Moment in the Human Sciences*. Chicago/London: University of Chicago Press.

Marcuse, Herbert (1955/1970) *Eros and Civilization*. London: Allen Lane.

Marcuse, Herbert (1977/1978) *The Aesthetic Dimension: Toward a Critique of Marxist Aesthetics*. London: Macmillan.

Marin, Cristobal (1994) 'Modernity in the Periphery: The Latin American Case', *Cultural Studies from Birmingham*, 3.

Marin, Louis (1991) 'Opacity and Transparence in Pictorial Representation', in Karin Gundersen and Ståle Wikshåland (eds), *Est I: Grunnlagsproblemer i estetisk forskning*. Oslo: NAVF.

Márothy, János (1974) *Music and the Bourgeois, Music and the Proletarian*. Budapest: Akadémiai Kiadó.

Marshall, Barbara L. (1994) *Engendering Modernity: Feminism, Social Theory and Social Change*. Cambridge: Polity Press.

Martin, Bernice (1981) *A Sociology of Contemporary Cultural Change*. Oxford: Basil Blackwell.

Marx, Karl (1844/1975) 'Economic and Philosophical Manuscripts of 1844', in Karl Marx and Friedrich Engels, *Collected Works. Vol. 3*. London: Lawrence and Wishart.

Marx, Karl (1858/1986) 'Economic Manuscripts of 1857–58' [*Grundrisse*], in Karl Marx and Friedrich Engels, *Collected Works. Vol. 28*. London: Lawrence and Wishart.

Marx, Karl (1859/1969) 'Preface to *A Contribution to the Critique of Political Economy*', in Karl Marx and Friedrich Engels, *Selected Works in Three Volumes. Vol. 1*. Moscow: Progress Publishers.

Marx, Karl (1867/1976) *Capital. Vol. 1*. Harmondsworth: Penguin.

Marx, Karl (1933/1969) *Resultate des unmittelbaren Produktionsprozesses*. Frankfurt am Main: Verlag Neue Kritik.

Marx, Karl and Friedrich Engels (1846/1970) *The German Ideology*. London: Lawrence and Wishart.

Marx, Karl and Friedrich Engels (1848/1965) *Manifesto of the Communist Party*. Peking: Foreign Languages Press.

Mathiesen, Thomas (1982) *Makt och motmakt*. Gothenburg: Bokförlaget Korpen.

Mead, George H. (1934) *Mind, Self and Society*. Chicago: University of Chicago Press.

Melucci, Alberto (1989) *Nomads of the Present: Social Movements and Individual Needs in Contemporary Society*. London: Hutchinson Radius.

Menne, Klaus, Max Looser, Astrid Osterland, Karola Brede and Emma Moersch (1976) *Sprache, Handlung und Unbewußtes*. Kronberg: Athenäum Verlag.

Mercer, Kobena (1987) 'Black Hair/Style Politics', *New Formations*, 3.

Messaris, Paul (1993) 'Visual "Literacy": A Theoretical Synthesis', *Communication Theory*, 3:4

Meyrowitz, Joshua (1985) *No Sense of Place: The Impact of Electronic Media on Social Behavior*. New York: Oxford University Press.

Middleton, Richard (1990) *Studying Popular Music*. Milton Keynes: Open University Press.

Miller, Daniel (1987) *Material Culture and Mass Consumption*. Oxford: Basil Blackwell.

Miller, Daniel (1990) 'Fashion and Ontology in Trinidad', *Culture and History*, 7.

Millot, Benoît (1988) 'Symbol, Desire and Power', *Theory, Culture and Society*, 5:4.

Milner, Andrew (1994) 'Cultural Materialism, Culturalism and Post-Culturalism: The Legacy of Raymond Williams', *Theory, Culture and Society*, 11:1.

Mitchell, Juliet (1974/1975) *Psychoanalysis and Feminism*. Harmondsworth: Penguin.

Mitterauer, Michael (1986/1992) *A History of Youth*. Oxford: Blackwell.

Mitterauer, Michael (1992) 'Youth Groups in Transformation', in Fornäs and Bolin 1992.

Modleski, Tania (1982) *Loving with a Vengeance: Mass-Produced Fantasies for Women*. New York/London: Methuen.

Modleski, Tania (ed.) (1986a) *Studies in Entertainment: Critical Approaches to Mass Culture*. Bloomington: Indiana University Press.

Modleski, Tania (1986b) 'Femininity as Mas(s)querade: A Feminist Approach to Mass Culture', in MacCabe 1986.

Moi, Toril (1985) *Sexual/Textual Politics: Feminist Literary Theory*. London/New York: Methuen.

Moi, Toril (1991) 'Appropriating Bourdieu: Feminist Theory and Pierre Bourdieu's Sociology of Culture', *New Literary History*, 22.

Moore, Allan F. (1993) *Rock: The Primary Text. Developing a Musicology of Rock*. Buckingham/Philadelphia: Open University Press.

Moores, Shaun (1993) *Interpreting Audiences: The Ethnography of Media Consumption*. London: Sage.

Morin, Edgar (1962) *L'esprit du temps*. Paris: Éditions Bernard Grasset.

Morley, David (1992) *Television, Audiences and Cultural Studies*. London/New York: Routledge.

Morris, Meaghan (1990) 'Banality in Cultural Studies', in Patricia Mellencamp (ed.), *Logics of Television*. Bloomington and Indianapolis/London: Indiana University Press/British Film Institute.

Müller, Gisela (1992) 'Der Massencharakter des Lebens und das ratlose Ich: Eine Lesart zu Simmels Moderne-Bild', in Krenzlin 1992.

Müller, Rudolf Wolfgang (1977) *Geld und Geist: Zur Entstehungsgeschichte von Identitätsbewußtsein und Rationalität seit der Antike*. Frankfurt am Main: Campus.

Mulvey, Laura (1975/1989) 'Visual Pleasure and Narrative Cinema', in *Visual and Other Pleasures*. Bloomington/Indianapolis: Indiana University Press.

Murdock, Graham (1993) 'Communications and the Constitution of Modernity', *Media, Culture and Society*, 15:4

Murdock, Graham and Peter Golding (1977) 'Capitalism, Communication and Class Relations', in James Curran, Michael Gurevitch and Janet Woollacott (eds), *Mass Communication and Society*. London: Edward Arnold/Open University Press.

Mylov, Peer (1988) 'Lorenzer, Freud og Habermas', in Hans Jørn Nielsen (ed.), *Kultur, identitet og kommunikation*. Aalborg: Aalborg Universitetsforlag.

Nakayama, Thomas K. and Lisa N. Peñaloza (1993) 'Madonna T/races: Music Videos Through the Prism of Color', in Cathy Schwichtenberg (ed.), *The Madonna Connection: Representational Politics, Subcultural Identities, and Cultural Theory*. Boulder, CO/San Francisco/Oxford: Westview Press.

Naremore, James and Patrick Brantlinger (eds) (1991) *Modernity and Mass Culture*. Bloomington/Indianapolis: Indiana University Press.

Nattiez, Jean-Jacques (1987/1990) *Music and Discourse: Toward a Semiology of Music*. Princeton, NJ: Princeton University Press.

Neale, Stephen (1980) *Genre*. London: British Film Institute.

Negt, Oskar and Alexander Kluge (1972/1993) *The Public Sphere and Experience*. Minneapolis: University of Minnesota Press.

Nelson, Cary and Lawrence Grossberg (eds) (1988) *Marxism and the Interpretation of Culture*. Urbana/Chicago: University of Illinois Press.

Nielsen, Elo (1977/1984) 'Narcissism och rockmusik', in Fornäs et al. 1984/1994.

Nielsen, Henrik Kaare (1991) *Demokrati i bevægelse: Sammenlignende studier i politisk kultur og nye sociale bevægelser i Vesttyskland og Danmark*. Århus: Aarhus Universitetsforlag.

Nitschke, August (1985) *Junge Rebellen. Mittelalter, Neuzeit, Gegenwart: Kinder verändern die Welt*. Munich: Kösel-Verlag.

Nørager, Troels (1987) *System og livsverden: Habermas' konstruktion af det Moderne*. Århus: Forlaget Anis.

Noy, Pinchas (1966–7) 'The Psychodynamic Meaning of Music', *Journal of Music Therapy*, 3:4–4:4.

O'Donell, Patrick and Robert Con Davis (eds) (1989) *Intertextuality and Contemporary American Fiction*. Baltimore, MD/London: Johns Hopkins University Press.

Oldfield, Paul (1989) 'After Subversion: Pop Culture and Power', in Angela McRobbie (ed.), *Zoot Suits and Second-Hand Dresses: An Anthology of Fashion and Music*. London: Macmillan.

Olsson, Anders (1987) *Den okända texten: En essä om tolkningsteori från kyrkofäderna till Derrida*. Stockholm: Bonniers.

Ong, Walter J. (1982) *Orality and Literacy: The Technologization of the Word*. London: Methuen.

Ortner, Sherry B. (1973) 'On Key Symbols', *American Anthropologist*, 75:5.

Ovid (8/1986) *Metamorphoses*. Oxford/New York: Oxford University Press.

Palm, Anders (1985) *Möten mellan konstarter: Studier av dikt, dans, musik, bild, drama och film*. Stockholm: Norstedts.

Palmgren, Cecilia, Göran Bolin and Karin Lövgren (eds) (1992) *Ethnicity in Youth Culture*. Stockholm: JMK.

Parin, Paul (1978) *Der Widerspruch im Subjekt: Ethnopsychoanalytische Studien*. Frankfurt am Main: Syndikat.

Parsons, Talcott (1951/1964) *The Social System*. New York: Free Press.

Parsons, Talcott (1961) *Essays in Sociological Theory*. New York: Free Press.

Passeron, Jean-Claude (1991) 'Ögat och dess herrar: Fabel om måleriets njutningar och kunskaper', *Ord & Bild*, 100:1.

Pattison, Robert (1982) *On Literacy: The Politics of the Word from Homer to the Age of Rock*. New York/Oxford: Oxford University Press.

Pattison, Robert (1987) *The Triumph of Vulgarity: Rock Music in the Mirror of Romanticism*. New York/Oxford: Oxford University Press.

Peirce, Charles S. (1940/1955) *Philosophical Writings of Peirce*. New York: Dover Publications.

Peters, John Durham (1993) 'Distrust of Representation: Habermas on the Public Sphere', *Media, Culture and Society*, 15:4.

Peters, John Durham (1994) 'The Gaps of Which Communication is Made', *Critical Studies in Mass Communication*, 11:2.

Peterson, Richard (ed.) (1976) *The Production of Culture*. Beverly Hills, CA: Sage.

Pike, Kenneth L. (1967) *Language in Relation to a Unified Theory of the Structure of Human Behaviour*. The Hague: Mouton.

Pochat, Götz (1983) *Der Symbolbegriff in der Ästhetik und Kunstwissenschaft*. Cologne: DuMont.

Poster, Mark (1989) *Critical Theory and Poststructuralism: In Search of a Context*. Ithaca/London: Cornell University Press.

Prokop, Dieter (1974) *Massenkultur und Spontaneität: Zur veränderten Warenform der Massenkommunikation im Spatkapitalismus*. Frankfurt am Main: Suhrkamp.

Prokop, Dieter (1979) *Faszination und Langeweile: Die populären Medien*. Stuttgart: Deutscher Taschenbuch Verlag.

Prokop, Dieter (1981) *Medien-Wirkungen*. Frankfurt am Main: Suhrkamp.

Punter, David (ed.) (1986) *Introduction to Contemporary Cultural Studies*. London: Longman.

Radway, Janice (1984) *Reading the Romance: Women, Patriarchy, and Popular Literature*. Chapel Hill/London: University of North Carolina Press.

Radway, Janice (1988) 'Reception Study: Ethnography and the Problems of Dispersed Audiences and Nomadic Subjects', *Cultural Studies*, 2:3.

Radway, Janice (1989) 'Ethnography among Elites: Comparing Discourses of Power', *Journal of Communication Inquiry*, 13:2.

Radway, Janice (1992) 'Mail-Order Culture and its Critics: The Book-of-the-Month Club, Commodification and Consumption, and the Problem of Cultural Authority', in Grossberg et al. 1992.

Rasmussen, Tove Arendt (1989/1990) 'Actionfilm och killkultur', in Peter Dahlén and Margareta Rönnberg (eds), *Spelrum: Om lek, stil och flyt i ungdomskulturen*. Uppsala: Filmförlaget.

Redhead, Steve (1990) *The End-of-the-Century Party: Youth and Pop towards 2000*. Manchester: Manchester University Press.

Reeder, Jurgen (1990) *Begär och etik: Om kön och kärlek i den fallocentriska ordningen*. Stockholm/Stehag: Symposion.

Reimer, Bo (1992/1995) 'Youth and Modern Lifestyles', in Johan Fornäs and Göran Bolin (eds), *Youth Culture in Late Modernity*. London: Sage.

Reimer, Bo (1993/1995) 'The Media in Public and Private Spheres', in Johan Fornäs and Göran Bolin (eds), *Youth Culture in Late Modernity*. London: Sage.

Reimer, Bo (1994) *The Most Common of Practices: On Mass Media Use in Late Modernity*. Stockholm: Almqvist and Wiksell International.

Reyher, Ulrich (1975) 'Massmedia och subversiv längtan', in Robin Cheesman and Carsten Kyhn (eds), *Masskommunikation och medvetandeproduktion*. Copenhagen: Nordisk Sommeruniversitet.

Richards, Barry (ed.) (1989) *Crises of the Self: Further Essays on Psychoanalysis and Politics*. London: Free Association Books.

Richters, Annemiek (1988) 'Modernity–Postmodernity Controversies: Habermas and Foucault', *Theory, Culture and Society*, 5:4.

Ricoeur, Paul (1965/1970) *Freud and Philosophy: An Essay on Interpretation*. New Haven/London: Yale University Press.

Ricoeur, Paul (1969/1974) *The Conflict of Interpretations: Essays in Hermeneutics*. Evanston, IL: Northwestern University Press.

Ricoeur, Paul (1975/1986) *The Rule of Metaphor: Multi-disciplinary Studies of the Creation of Meaning in Language*. London: Routledge and Kegan Paul.

Ricoeur, Paul (1976) *Interpretation Theory: Discourse and the Surplus of Meaning*. Fort Worth: Texas Christian University Press.

Ricoeur, Paul (1978/1994) 'Imagination in Discourse and in Action', in Robinson and Rundell 1994.

Ricoeur, Paul (1981) *Hermeneutics and the Human Sciences: Essays on Language, Action and Interpretation*. Cambridge: Cambridge University Press.

Ricoeur, Paul (1983–5/1984–8) *Time and Narrative*. 3 volumes, Chicago/London: University of Chicago Press.

Ricoeur, Paul (1986) *Lectures on Ideology and Utopia*. New York: Columbia University Press.

Ricoeur, Paul (1990/1992) *Oneself as Another*. Chicago/London: University of Chicago Press.

Rigby, Brian (1991) *Popular Culture in Modern France: A Study of Cultural Discourse*. London: Routledge.

Riviere, Joan (1929/1986) 'Womanliness as a Masquerade', in Burgin et al. 1986.

Roberts, David (1994) 'Sublime Theories: Reason and Imagination in Modernity', in Robinson and Rundell 1994.

Robinson, Gillian and John Rundell (eds) (1994) *Rethinking Imagination: Culture and Creativity*. London/New York: Routledge.

Roe, Keith (1983) *Mass Media and Adolescent Schooling: Conflict or Co-existence?* Stockholm: Almqvist and Wiksell International.

Roe, Keith (1985) 'The Swedish Moral Panic over Video 1980–1984', *Nordicom-information*, 2–3/1985.

Roe, Keith (1987) 'Culture, Media and the Intellectual: A Review of the Work of Pierre Bourdieu', in Carlsson 1987.

Roe, Keith (1992) 'Different Destinies – Different Melodies: School Achievement, Anticipated Status and Adolescents' Music Taste', *European Journal of Communication*, 7:3.

Roe, Keith and Ulla Carlsson (eds) (1990) *Popular Music Research*. Gothenburg: Nordicom-Sweden.

Rose, Gilbert J. (1980) *The Power of Form: A Psychoanalytic Approach to Aesthetic Form*. Madison: International Universities Press.

Rosolato, Guy (1974) 'La voix: entre corps et langage', *Revue française de psychanalyse*, 38:1.

Ross, Andrew (1989) *No Respect: Intellectuals and Popular Culture*. New York/London: Routledge.

Roszak, Theodore (1968/1970) *The Making of a Counter Culture: Reflections on the Technocratic Society and its Youthful Opposition*. London: Faber and Faber.

Rundell, John (1994) 'Creativity and Judgement: Kant on Reason and Imagination', in Robinson and Rundell 1994.

Rutherford, Jonathan (ed.) (1990) *Identity: Community, Culture, Difference*. London: Lawrence and Wishart.

Ryan, Jenny (1994) 'Women, Modernity and the City', *Theory, Culture and Society*, 11:4.

Ryan, Michael (1982) *Marxism and Deconstruction: A Critical Articulation*. Baltimore, MD/London: Johns Hopkins University Press.

Said, Edward W. (1978/1991) *Orientalism: Western Conceptions of the Orient*. London: Penguin.

Sapir, Edward (1932) 'Cultural Anthropology and Psychiatry', *Journal of Abnormal and Social Psychology*, 27.

Sartre, Jean-Paul (1960/1982) *Critique of Dialectical Reason*. London: Verso.

Saussure, Ferdinand de (1916/1974) *Course in General Linguistics*. London: Fontana/Collins.
Schanz, Hans-Jørgen (1981) *Træk af behovsproblematikkens idehistorie med særligt henblik på Marx og Engels*. Århus: Modtryk.
Schrøder, Kim Christian (1992) 'Cultural Quality: Search for a Phantom? A Reception Perspective on Judgements of Cultural Value', in Michael Skovmand and Kim Christian Schrøder (eds), *Media Cultures: Reappraising Transnational Media*. London/New York: Routledge.
Schulze, Gerhard H. (1992) *Die Erlebnisgesellschaft: Kultursoziologie der Gegenwart*. Frankfurt am Main: Campus.
Schulze, Laurie, Anne Barton White and Jane D. Brown (1993) ' "A Sacred Monster in her Prime": Audience Construction of Madonna as Low-Other', in Cathy Schwichtenberg, (ed.), *The Madonna Connection: Representational Politics, Subcultural Identities, and Cultural Theory*. Boulder, CO/San Francisco/Oxford: Westview Press.
Searle, John R. (1969) *Speech Acts*. Cambridge: Cambridge University Press.
Seel, Martin (1985) *Die Kunst der Entzweiung: Zum Begriff der ästhetischen Rationalität*. Frankfurt am Main: Suhrkamp.
Segal, Hanna (1952) 'A Psycho-analytical Approach to Aesthetics', *International Journal of Psychoanalysis*, 37.
Segal, Hanna (1957) 'Notes on Symbol Formation', *International Journal of Psychoanalysis*, 37.
Segal, Naomi (1989) 'Echo and Narcissus', in Teresa Brennan (ed.), *Between Feminism and Psychoanalysis*. London/New York: Routledge.
Seguin, Eve (1994) 'A Modest Reason', *Theory, Culture and Society*, 11:3.
Semiotica (1980) 30:1/2 (theme: 'Signs about Signs: The Semiotics of Self-reference').
Sennett, Richard (1977/1986) *The Fall of Public Man*. London: Faber and Faber.
Shepherd, John (1991) *Music as Social Text*. Cambridge: Polity Press.
Shepherd, John (1993) 'Popular Music Studies: Challenges to Musicology', *Stanford Humanities Review*, 3:2.
Shiach, Morag (1989) *Discourse on Popular Culture: Class, Gender and History in Cultural Analysis, 1730 to the Present*. Cambridge: Polity Press.
Sholle, David J. (1988) 'Critical Studies: From the Theory of Ideology to Power/Knowledge', *Critical Studies in Mass Communication*, 5:1.
Silverman, Kaja (1988) *The Acoustic Mirror: The Female Voice in Psychoanalysis and Cinema*. Bloomington/Indianapolis: Indiana University Press.
Silverstone, Roger (1994) *Television and Everyday Life*. London: Routledge.
Silverstone, Roger, Eric Hirsch and David Morley (1991) 'Listening to a Long Conversation: An Ethnographic Approach to the Study of Information and Communication Technologies in the Home', *Cultural Studies*, 5:2.
Simmel, Georg (1900/1990) *The Philosophy of Money*. 2nd edition. London: Routledge.
Simmel, Georg (1908/1991) 'The Problem of Style', *Theory, Culture and Society*, 8:3.
Simmel, Georg (1908/1992) *Soziologie*. Frankfurt am Main: Suhrkamp.
Simmel, Georg (1909/1994) 'Bridge and Door', *Theory, Culture and Society*, 11:1.
Simmel, Georg (1911/1983) *Philosophische Kultur*. Berlin: Wagenbach.
Simonsen, Birgitte and Knud Illeris (1989) *De skæve køn*. 2 volumes. Copenhagen: Unge Pædagoger.
Skogerbø, Eli (1990) 'The Concept of the Public Sphere in a Historical Perspective: An Anachronism or a Relevant Political Concept?', *Nordicom-information*, 4/1990.
Skovmand, Michael (1988) 'Bourdieu og medie/kulturforskningen', *Mediekultur*, 7.
Small, Christopher (1987) *Music of the Common Tongue: Survival and Celebration in Afro-American Music*. London/New York: John Calder/Riverrun Press.
Sohn-Rethel, Alfred (1970/1978) *Intellectual and Manual Labour: A Critique of Epistemology*. London: Macmillan.
Solomon, Robert (1985) 'Creativity and Normal Narcissism', *Journal of Creative Behavior*, 19:1.

Sonesson, Göran (1992) *Bildbetydelser: inledning till bildsemiotiken som vetenskap*. Lund: Studentlitteratur.

Sørensen, Anne Scott (1992) *Kønnets kultur: Om unge og ungdom*. Århus: BUKS.

Spitz, Ellen Handler (1985) *Art and Psyche: A Study in Psychoanalysis and Aesthetics*. New Haven, CT/London: Yale University Press.

Stacey, Jackie (1994) *Star Gazing: Hollywood Cinema and Female Spectatorship*. London: Routledge.

Stam, Robert (1985/1992) *Reflexivity in Film and Literature: From Don Quixote to Jean-Luc Godard*. New York: Columbia University Press (Morningside Edition).

Stauth, Georg and Bryan S. Turner (1988) 'Nostalgia, Postmodernism and the Critique of Mass Culture', *Theory, Culture and Society*, 5:2–3.

Steiner, Linda (1988) 'Oppositional Decoding as an Act of Resistance', *Critical Studies in Mass Communication*, 5:1.

Steuerman, Emilia (1989) 'Habermas vs Lyotard: Modernity vs Postmodernity?', *New Formations*, 7.

Storey, John (1993) *An Introductory Guide to Cultural Theory and Popular Culture*. New York/Hemel Hempstead: Harvester Wheatsheaf.

Straayer, Chris (1990) 'The She-Man: Postmodern Bi-sexed Performance in Film and Video', *Screen*, 31:3.

Street, John (1986) *Rebel Rock: The Politics of Popular Music*. Oxford: Basil Blackwell.

Tagg, Philip (1979) *Kojak – 50 Seconds of Television Music: Toward the Analysis of Affect in Popular Music*. Gothenburg: Musikvetenskapliga institutionen.

Tagg, Philip (1982a) 'Analysing Popular Music: Theory, Method and Practice', *Popular Music*, 2.

Tagg, Philip (1982b) *Nature as a Musical Mood Cathegory*. Gothenburg: IASPM-Norden.

Tagg, Philip (1987) *Musicology and the Semiotics of Popular Music*. Gothenburg: IASPM-Norden.

Tagg, Philip (1990a) 'Music in Mass Media Studies: Reading Sounds for Example', in Roe and Carlsson 1990.

Tagg, Philip (1990b) 'An Anthropology of Stereotypes in TV Music', *Svensk tidskrift för musikforskning*, 71 (1989).

Tagg, Philip (1994) 'Subjectivity and Soundscape, Motorbikes and Music', in Helmi Järviluoma (ed.), *Soundscapes: Essays on Vroom and Moo*. Tampere/Seinäjoki: Department of Folk Tradition/Institute of Rhythm Music.

Taylor, Charles (1975) *Hegel*. Cambridge: Cambridge University Press.

Taylor, Charles (1989) *Sources of the Self: The Making of the Modern Identity*. Cambridge: Cambridge University Press.

Theory, Culture and Society (1991) 8:3 (special issue on Georg Simmel).

Thompson, John B. (1981) *Critical Hermeneutics: A Study in the Thought of Paul Ricoeur and Jürgen Habermas*. Cambridge: Cambridge University Press.

Thompson, John B. (1990) *Ideology and Modern Culture: Critical Social Theory in the Era of Mass Communication*. Cambridge: Polity Press.

Thompson, John B. (1993) 'The Theory of the Public Sphere', *Theory, Culture and Society*, 10:3.

Thompson, John B. and David Held (eds) (1982) *Habermas: Critical Debates*. London: Macmillan.

Thompson, Kenneth (1992) 'Religion, Values and Ideology', in Bocock and Thompson 1992.

Thörn, Håkan (1991) 'Rörelser i det senmoderna samhället', in Jan Carle and Hans-Erik Hermansson (eds), *Ungdom i rörelse: en antologi om ungdomars levnadsvillkor*. Gothenburg: Daidalos.

Thurston, Carol (1987) *The Romance Revolution: Erotic Novels for Women and the Quest for a New Sexual Identity*. Urbana/Chicago: University of Illinois Press.

Thyssen, Ole (1991) *Penge, magt og kærlighed: teorien om symbolsk generaliserede medier hos Parsons, Luhmann og Habermas*. Copenhagen: Rosinante.

Todorov, Tzvetan (1970/1973) *The Fantastic: A Structural Approach to a Literary Genre*. Cleveland, OH/London: Press of Case Western Reserve University.

Todorov, Tzvetan (1978/1983) *Symbolism and Interpretation*. London: Routledge and Kegan Paul.

Todorov, Tzvetan (1978/1990) *Genres in Discourse*. Cambridge: Cambridge University Press.

Turner, Graeme (1990/1992) *British Cultural Studies: An Introduction*. New York/London: Routledge.

Ullestad, Neal (1987) 'Rock and Rebellion: Subversive Effects of Live Aid and "Sun City" ', *Popular Music*, 6:1.

Vigsø, Orla (1993) *Interpretationsbegrebet i hermeneutikken og semiotikken: Paul Ricoeur and A.J. Greimas*. Aalborg: Nordisk Sommeruniversitet.

Vološinov, V.N. (1929/1986) *Marxism and the Philosophy of Language*. Cambridge, MA: Harvard University Press.

Wagner, Peter (1994) *A Sociology of Modernity: Liberty and Discipline*. London: Routledge.

Waites, Bernard, Tony Bennett and Graham Martin (eds) (1982) *Popular Culture: Past and Present*. London: Croom Helm/Open University Press.

Wallerstein, Immanuel (1974) *The Modern World-System*. New York: Academic Press.

Wallerstein, Immanuel (1990) 'Culture as the Ideological Battleground of the Modern World-System', in Featherstone 1990.

Watzlawick, Paul, Janet Helmick Beavin and Don D. Jackson (1967) *Pragmatics of Human Communication: A Study of Interactional Patterns, Pathologies, and Paradoxes*. New York: Norton.

Weber, Max (1921/1958) *The Rational and Social Foundations of Music*. Carbondale: Southern Illinois University Press.

Wellmer, Albrecht (1984/1985) 'Truth, Semblance and Reconciliation', *Telos*, 62.

White, Stephen K. (1988) *The Recent Work of Jürgen Habermas: Reason, Justice and Modernity*. Cambridge: Cambridge University Press.

Widdicombe, Sue and Robin Wooffitt (1995) *The Language of Youth Subcultures: Social Identity in Action*. New York/Hemel Hempstead: Harvester Wheatsheaf.

Widerberg, Karin (1990) 'Abjektion: könets och samhällets drivkraft', *Kvinnovetenskaplig tidskrift*, 11:4.

Wilden, Anthony (1987) *The Rules are No Game: The Strategy of Communication*. London: Routledge and Kegan Paul.

Williams, Raymond (1958/1966) *Culture and Society 1780–1950*. London: Penguin.

Williams, Raymond (1974) *Television: Technology and Cultural Form*. London: Fontana/Collins.

Williams, Raymond (1976/1988) *Keywords*. 2nd edition. London: Fontana.

Williams, Raymond (1977) *Marxism and Literature*. Oxford: Oxford University Press.

Williams, Raymond (1981) *Culture*. London: Fontana.

Willis, Paul (1977) *Learning to Labour*. Aldershot: Gower.

Willis, Paul (1978) *Profane Culture*. London: Routledge and Kegan Paul.

Willis, Paul (1990) *Common Culture: Symbolic Work at Play in the Everyday Cultures of the Young*. Milton Keynes: Open University Press.

Winnicott, D.W. (1971) *Playing and Reality*. London: Tavistock.

Wirth, Hans-Jürgen (1984) *Die Schärfung der Sinne: Jugendprotest als personliche und kulturelle Chance*. Frankfurt am Main: Syndikat.

Wistrand, Magnus (1992) *Entertainment and Violence in Ancient Rome: The Attitudes of Roman Writers of the First Century AD*. Gothenburg: Acta Universitatis Gothoburgensis (Studia graeca et latina gothoburgensia LVI).

Witt-Brattström, Ebba (1984) 'Den främmande kvinnan: Presentation av Julia Kristeva', *Kvinnovetenskaplig tidskrift*, 5:2–3.

Wittgenstein, Ludwig (1945/1976) *Philosophical Investigations*. Oxford: Basil Blackwell.

Wolff, Janet (1983) *Aesthetics and the Sociology of Art*. London: George Allen and Unwin.

Wolff, Janet (1990) *Feminine Sentences: Essays on Women and Culture*. Cambridge: Polity Press.

Wulff, Helena (1988) *Twenty Girls: Growing Up, Ethnicity and Excitement in a South London Microculture*. Stockholm: Socialantropologiska institutionen.

Young, Iris Marion (1990) *Justice and the Politics of Difference*. Princeton, NJ: Princeton University Press.

Ziehe, Thomas (1975) *Pubertät und Narzißmus: Sind Jugendliche entpolitisiert?* Frankfurt am Main: EVA.

Ziehe, Thomas (1991) *Zeitvergleiche: Jugend in kulturellen Modernisierungen*. Weinheim/ Munich: Juventa.

Ziehe, Thomas (1993) 'Självrefererandet kan inte undvikas: Några effekter av under-visningens rationaliseringar', in Johan Fornäs, Ulf Boëthius and Bo Reimer (eds), *Ungdomar i skilda sfärer: FUS-rapport 5*. Stockholm/Stehag: Symposion.

Ziehe, Thomas (1994) 'From Living Standard to Life Style', *Young: Nordic Journal of Youth Research*, 2:2.

Ziehe, Thomas and Herbert Stubenrauch (1982) *Plädoyer für ungewöhnliches Lernen: Ideen zur Jugendsituation*. Reinbek bei Hamburg: Rowohlt.

Zinnecker, Jürgen (1985) 'Jugend der Gegenwart: Beginn oder Ende einer historischen Epoche?', in Dieter Baacke and Wilhelm Heitmeyer (eds), *Neue Widersprüche: Jugend-liche in den achtziger Jahren*. Weinheim/Munich: Juventa.

Zoonen, Liesbet van (1994) *Feminist Media Studies*. London: Sage.

Index

Compiled by Meg Davies (Society of Indexers)

Compiled by Meg Davies (Society of Indexers)